Into all the World

75 Years of The Peoples Church, Toronto

THE Peoples CHURCH

CHARLES PRICE · MINISTER   DR. OSWALD J. SMITH · FOUNDER

by

Diane Roblin Lee

Foreword by

Dr. Billy Graham

His word in my heart is like

fire that burns in my bones and

I cannot hold it any longer.

Jeremiah 20:9

The Living Bible

ISBN 1-896213-36-7
© 2003 The Peoples Church

PROOFREADING: Hilary Price
PHOTOGRAPHY: Wilbur Caddell
PROJECT COORDINATOR: Terry Bridle
RESEARCH ASSISTANCE: Clara Caddell
PRINTED IN CANADA: Altona Graphics Ltd.
COVER, BOOK DESIGN AND LAYOUT: Diane Roblin Lee
PUBLISHED IN CANADA: Praise Productions, Woodville, Ontario, 2003.

ALL SCRIPTURE REFERENCES are taken from the King James Version of the Bible unless otherwise indicated.

Contents

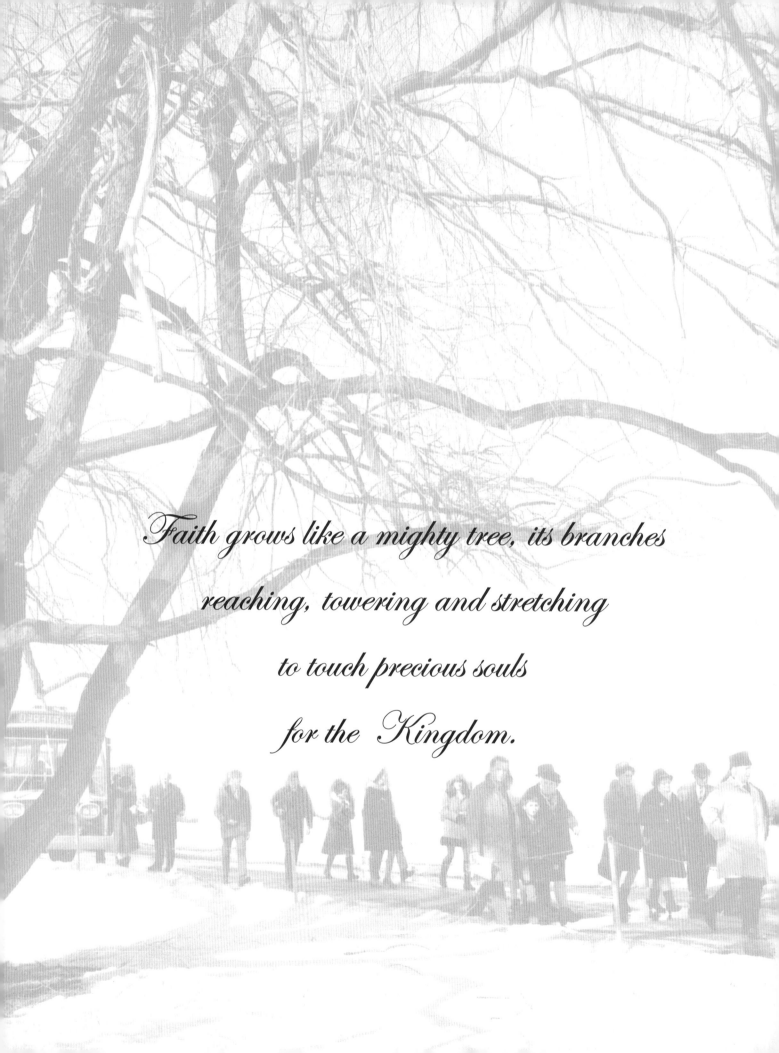

Faith grows like a mighty tree, its branches

reaching, towering and stretching

to touch precious souls

for the Kingdom.

*H*ere and there throughout the centuries, God finds one of His children looking up, yearning hungrily for His heart; and meets him or her, face to face. The faith of such a one may be small, no bigger than a mustard seed, but as he or she walks, unwavering in response to God's leading, listening – listening always for His voice – faith grows like a mighty tree, its branches reaching and towering and stretching, to touch precious souls for the Kingdom.

Such a man was Oswald Smith, founder of The Peoples Church in Toronto, Canada. This is the story of that church, and how it grew from Dr. Smith's seed of prayer, into the mighty vehicle for the worldwide outpouring of God's love it is today.

Dr. Oswald Jeffrey Smith.

Foreword

June 7, 2003

Congratulations to The Peoples Church, Toronto, on this special 75th Anniversary commemorating its founding by Dr. Oswald J. Smith in 1928.

I have been privileged to preach in The Peoples Church and to know both Dr. Oswald Smith and his son, Dr. Paul B. Smith, who succeeded his father in 1959 as Senior Pastor. God richly blessed and used The Peoples Church down through the many years of their pastorates and has continued to do so under the pastoral care of Dr. John Hull and now Charles Price.

This commemorative coffee table book will be a blessing to you as it recounts some of the things that God has accomplished through the ministry of The Peoples Church in years past. But, with the continued blessing of God, the best days of this great church may still lie ahead.

Billy Graham

One

Who was Dr. Oswald J. Smith
and
Why did God use Him?

No. 5, West Zorra School; Oxford County, Ontario.
Cody's Corners, where Dr. Smith attended school as a boy.
Miss Winters, teacher.

Four-year-old Oswald with his brother,
who became Rev. Ernest Smith.

Fourteen-year-old Oswald with
his six brothers and sisters.

Oswald Jeffrey Smith with five brothers, four sisters and parents.
L – R Top Row: Gordon, Norman, Kenneth, Father, Oswald, Wallace, Gilmour.
L – R Front: Alice, Ruth, Dorothy, Mother. (Sister Hazel deceased at age 10.)

At the train station.

Oswald Smith, age four months,
on bearskin rug.

Birthplace – farmhouse near
Odessa, Ontario; Nov. 8, 1889.

The young Oswald with his
mother, Maud Laidley Smith.

Founder of The Peoples Church

Dr. Oswald J. Smith

At the turn of the twentieth century a sickly eleven-year-old boy hiked along the rough hewn ties of the Embro Station (now Zorra) train depot, near Woodstock, Ontario. It was the young Oswald's responsibility to light the semaphore signal lamps half a mile east and half a mile west of the train station. His father, like his father before him, was a telegrapher and station agent for the railway.

No idle onlooker could have dreamt that this tall, thin, frail boy would one day take the light of the Gospel all the way around the globe as a respected missionary statesman. Watching him trudge along, swinging his coal oil lamp, who could have guessed that he would author 35 books, compose over a thousand hymns and poems, speak in 70 countries, be received by the Queen and found the greatest missionary church in the world?

But God looks on the heart, not on human strength or outward appearances. In young Oswald, He found a soul that responded eagerly to the vision He gave him for his life and a heart that would pulse with a passion for souls.

Oswald Smith was raised in an ordinary home. There appeared to be nothing particularly outstanding about either him or his family. Although his mother was a Christian, Oswald knew little about salvation. He vaguely assumed it to be a by-product of good behaviour, but nevertheless, he had a heart for God as far back as he could remember. He seldom neglected prayer at night, and he prayed daily for his father for 47 years, before the senior Mr. Smith trusted Christ.

One day, something happened in the Smith's community, which radically impacted Oswald's life. An old ditch-digger, an inveterate drunkard with a large red nose, full of holes from his heavy drinking, was saved. Filled with gratitude for his salvation, the man immediately began to hold meetings in the homes of the farmers around the train station. Something in Oswald's heart cried out for these gatherings. When they began to be held in the train station, Oswald would sit spellbound as the old ditch-digger led the singing of Gospel hymns and proclaimed the story of redemption; yet Oswald was not converted.

Oswald and his brother playing at home, the Embro (Zorra) Station.

Dr. Smith and wife, Daisy, visiting his childhood home.

Dr. Smith remembering how he used to light the semaphore lamps.

Dr. Smith beside monument erected to honour him in Embro/Zorra.

The first stirring to ministry.

One morning, the Sunday School teacher turned to the boys and said, "Any one of you boys might be a minister."

Oswald responded immediately, saying, "I will be that boy." From that day onward, despite the fact that he had not yet been saved, he never had any desire to do anything else.

In 1906, at the age of 16, Oswald read of a great evangelistic campaign being conducted in Toronto by Dr. R.A. Torrey and Mr. Chas. M. Alexander. Day after day, reports came in of the great stirring in Toronto, of people travelling over 200 miles to get there, of attendances upwards of 3,500 people, of multiplied thousands unable to gain admission. The complete texts of Dr. Torrey's addresses were published daily, word for word. Moved, Oswald and his brother asked permission to go, despite the 94 mile trip.

Salvation.

While the glitter of the concert hall overwhelmed the senses of the country boys, it did not compare with the rapture felt in Oswald's heart as Charles Alexander led in the great chorus,"When by His grace I shall look on His face, that will be glory, be glory for me." When Torrey read Isaiah 53:5, "But He was wounded for *my* transgression; he was bruised for *my* iniquity, the chastisement of *my* peace was upon Him, and with his stripes *I* am healed," Oswald joined others at the front, signifying his desire for salvation.

Though he saw no great light and felt as though nothing was any different following his prayer, something happened very suddenly: as he bowed his head and put his face between his hands, tears began to gush through his fingers and the realization broke upon him that a great change had taken place. Christ had entered and he was a new creature; without a doubt, life would be forever different.

Oswald Smith.

Dr. R.A. Torrey, under whose ministry O.J. Smith was saved.

Salvation card signed by Oswald Smith, age 16, Jan. 28th, 1906.

I believe God's Testimony

Concerning Jesus Christ, that my iniquity was laid upon Him (Isaiah 53:6), that He bore my sins in His body on the Cross (1 Peter 2:24), and that He hath redeemed me from the curse of the law of God (which I had broken) by becoming a curse for me (Gal. 3:13.)

I do now accept Jesus

as my Sin-bearer and Savior, and believe what God tells me in His word, that all my sins are forgiven, because Jesus died in my place Acts 13:38, 39.

I also believe God's Testimony

concerning Jesus Christ, that He is both Lord and Christ (annointed King); and I do now receive Him to be my Lord and King (Acts 2:36).

I yield to Him

the control of all I am and all I have—my thoughts, my words, my actions. Lord Jesus, Thou art my Lord ; I belong to Thee. I surrender all to Thee.

I purpose to confess my Lord Jesus

before the world, as I shall have opportunity (Rom 10:9-10), and to live to please Him in all that I do each day (Gal. 1:10).

I will take no man

for my example but Jesus only (1 John 2:6; Matthew 17:5-8).

Having thus received Jesus Christ

I know on the authority of God's sure word of promise that I am a child of God (John 1:12), and that I have everlasting life (John 3:36).

"THANKS BE UNTO GOD FOR HIS UNSPEAKABLE GIFT."

Date *Jan 28 4 1906*   Signed *Oswald Smith*

"Lord, what wilt Thou have me to do?"

Once home again, Oswald's one petition was, "Lord, what wilt Thou have me to do?" He could not understand a man being saved and not wanting to do something for the Lord. Day after day, he poured over the Scriptures and cried out to God to make him an evangelist.

So filled with the wonder of the Gospel was he, that he reached out, right where he was, and started a Sunday School for the neighboring children in the waiting room of the train station. As he walked the tracks before dusk, to light the semaphore lamps, Oswald sang and preached to the birds and trees in his joy. As he lay in bed at night, he made up sermons in his head and imagined he was preaching them to great crowds of people.

Oswald prairie-chicken hunting in Hollywood, Manitoba, age 20.

With his desire to preach growing ever stronger, Oswald grew restless and dropped out of high school at the age of 17, taking an office-boy job in Toronto. No one told him how much schooling was required to become a preacher and he imagined that one day he would simply walk into a village church and ask a minister to allow him to take over his services!

St. Mark's Presbyterian.

In the meantime, Oswald became captivated by the powerful ministry of J.D. Morrow, who was packing St. Mark's Presbyterian Church to capacity. Having found a man he could follow, he poured himself into helping Morrow build up St. Mark's. When he discovered that he could take lectures at the Toronto Bible Training School (now Ontario Bible College), he saturated himself in knowledge and Christian fellowship. Singing and ministering in jails and hospitals, with the other young people, was a tremendous joy to him.

St. Mark's Presbyterian, Toronto.

Turned down for missions.

At the same time, Oswald's heart began to turn towards the foreign mission field and he applied to the Presbyterian Church for an overseas posting. Despite Oswald's growing passion for missions, the Presbyterian Church saw only a scrawny, frail, unqualified 18-year-old, and turned him down.

Selling Bibles in the Muskokas.

Turning a deaf ear to disappointment, Oswald persuaded the Upper Canada Bible Society to let him sell Bibles in the Muskokas, about a hundred miles north of Toronto. It was during that time, though repeatedly refused food and shelter and becoming accustomed to having doors slammed in his face, the opportunity for which

Oswald.

Oswald had prayed so long, presented itself. The Rev. Elijah Brown (under whose ministry Grace Irwin Roblin, the mother of the author of this book, was saved in 1919) asked him to preach in his church in Severn, not once, but for three services that Sunday – in Severn, Washago and Wesley. To Oswald's amazement, Elijah Brown introduced the third service with the words, "I have received great blessing from the preaching of our young brother today." Now he was sure that God had truly called him to preach. The next morning, he purchased a notebook and titled it, *Record of Sermons Preached*, and carefully noted the date, place and topics. It was the first of over 12,000 eventual entries. He marked 1908, his 18th year, as the beginning of his full-time ministry.

The church at Severn, Ont., where, in 1908, at the age of 18, Dr. Smith preached his first sermon.

Oswald in front of church with the Indians* of Newtown, B.C.

Presbyterian Church in Prince Rupert, 1908.

Prince Rupert, 1908.

Oswald with Indians* of Hartley Bay, British Columbia.

Bibles to British Columbia.

So successful had Oswald been with his work in the Muskokas, that the Canadian Bible Society asked him to launch the work on the Pacific Coast. Travelling by train to Vancouver, he cooked his own meals enroute. Alternating between loneliness and excitement, the six-day journey filled him with wonder and awe. Voyaging up the coast to Prince Rupert, his senses were assaulted by the conditions of various nationalities travelling steerage. Applying for missions work had been one thing, but to be suddenly surrounded by a ragtag lot of foreigners was a culture shock. Once in Prince Rupert, the travellers found nothing more than a community of tents. Even the Presbyterian Church where Oswald preached, was canvas-covered. Up and down the coast, he preached and sold Bibles in the native communities and found the people so eager for them that he had to go back and get more.

Albert Bay totem poles.
Photo by Oswald Smith, 1908.

* Note: While the term "Indian" is considered by some to be politically incorrect today, it was commonly used in Oswald's day with no disrespect ever imagined. It has been used herein in the spirit of his day.

Into all the World

Hiking deep into the bush, Oswald visited the logging camps, where he preached in the dining halls at night. Often finding himself lost in the dark on the way back, unarmed, in grizzly country, he learned to pray continuously, about everything. God was surely with him.

Thoroughly relishing the rough-and-ready life, he would sing at the top of his lungs and pray aloud for hours as he made his way along corduroy roads and pathways etched in the forest. He loved preaching to the unsaved, which was the condition of most of the men in the logging camps.

With his heart connecting at a deep level with the Indians, Oswald accepted an invitation from Mr. G.H. Raley, the Methodist missionary in Port Simpson, to become a missionary to the natives of Hartley Bay. He soon found he would rather work among them than the whites any day; they were faithful at church, were natural orators, and great singers.

In *The Story of My Life*, Oswald writes:

> "Night after night I shivered in my cold, scanty bed. During the day I was kept busy trying to get the wet wood to burn, but instead I filled the house with smoke and got but little heat. Often I came home dripping wet from head to foot, to a house that was bitter cold, and had to build a fire, change my clothes and wait for sufficient heat to dry me. Sometimes my feet were so wet and cold they felt like lumps of ice, nor could I get warm at all until the stove was hot. But so great was the joy of the Lord in my soul, that I sometimes ran up and down the room until almost out of breath, singing, 'Praise God from Whom all Blessings Flow,' in spite of my wet condition and my ice-cold feet, before taking time to light the fire."

The voice of God.

> "Night after night I prayed, kneeling before a chair in the dim light of a coal oil lamp, all around me the mighty forest, dark and wild, in my ears the roar of the ocean, and on every side the homes of the Indians. My little stove burned but poorly as I shoved in green cedar. ...As I prayed there came the oft-repeated request: 'Lord, what wilt Thou have me to do?' How long I prayed one night, I do not know. But at last I undressed, replenished the fire, put out the light and crawled into my poor, hand-made bed. Suddenly God spoke. The answer came: 'Go to the Toronto Bible Training School.' I heard no sound, and yet the command was so clearly given that I could not mistake it."

Washday for 18-year-old Oswald in Vancouver.

The way west.

Indian* canoe bringing Oswald from a lumber camp in 1919.

British Columbia lumber camp.

*See note at bottom of page at left.

Billy Sunday preaching.

John Wesley.

The bitter fruit of disobedience. Despite the unmistakable direction of God, Oswald did not go to the Toronto Bible Training School. Incredibly, at the suggestion of a godly Presbyterian minister, he went instead to Manitoba College in Winnipeg. Within just a few days, he knew he had made a dreadful mistake. Not only was he not admitted to the five-year course assured by the minister, but he was told he would have to take nine years, and those away from his family in Mount Albert where he had been offered an apprentice-type pastorate which he could have filled, had he gone to the Toronto Bible Training School. Confused, he struggled for days, wondering what to do, until God gave him peace to carry on.

Martin Luther.

Inspiration.

During Oswald's first year in Manitoba, he was deeply inspired by the ministry of Jonathan Goforth, who held services at the college on the Holy Spirit and prayer. His discovery of the autobiography of Charles Finney awakened him further to God's call to prayer.

> "This is the most helpful and inspiring book outside of the Bible. It has been wonderfully used of God to awaken me and has taught me to lay the very greatest stress upon prayer and the Holy Spirit to convert men. Oh, how feeble and weak I am of myself! I believe the greatest thing I need is the baptism of the Holy Spirit. If only I had that, I know God would use me."

David Brainerd.

Hungrily, Oswald devoured more biographies.

> "These accounts of the lives of good men give me the most inspiration and help, stirring me to fresh zeal and self-sacrificing love."

Gypsy Smith.

Charles Finney.

Jonathan Goforth.

Ira Sankey.

Charles Spurgeon.

"Oh God, strip me of all that hinders the filling of Thy Holy Spirit." OJS

"I believe the greatest thing I need is the baptism of the Holy Spirit. If only I had that, I know God would use me." OJS

The filling of the Holy Spirit.

"God has laid on me a burden for revival, and in order to accomplish this, I must have His blessed Spirit. 'Oh God, strip me of all that hinders the filling of Thy Holy Spirit.' I prayed till I was too weak and weary to do so any longer, then knelt at my bedside for support until I was nearly asleep. Then I lay down on the bed and prayed still, but weariness overtook me and I could only half pray and half sleep.

"God revealed plainly the one thing that has been cursing my life and which for weeks I have been struggling to give up – the reading of the detective stories in the *Glasgow Weekly News*. I could not see how it was doing me any harm, but at last I solemnly promised God I would read no more. When the paper came, I found myself wishing I had not promised, but nevertheless, I threw it in the stove, and surrendered all to the will of God. Then with my Bible open at Luke 11:13, I read, 'If any of you then being evil knows how to give good gifts to your children, how much more shall the Heavenly Father give the Holy Spirit to those who ask Him?'

"I claimed His promise of the Holy Spirit for the purpose of winning souls for His glory. I claimed Him by faith; I believe He has filled me, although there were no manifestations such as Finney had. But the Word does not promise it. I believe He has filled me and that I will see manifestations in my words taking effect and souls being redeemed here.

"My life is changed since receiving the Holy Spirit – I cannot explain it but from that day I seem to have something extra, or rather, He has more of me. My mind has been at rest; a deep peace has stayed with me."

Back on track.

Having struggled to make his choice of Manitoba work, both in the liberal college where fellow theology students jeeringly called him, "Parson" and in his summer pastorate, west of Winnipeg, where blizzards, runaway horses and long distances between lonely prairie homes frustrated his desire for evangelistic work, Oswald sought God for direction – sought Him in agony of soul – so desirous was he to share the Gospel with the world. His vision of one day preaching the message of Christ to great crowds had been seared into his soul, and burned hotter with every passing day.

Once again, God directed him to go back to Toronto, to the Toronto Bible Training School. He returned only to find that his old friend, J.D. Morrow, the pastor of St. Mark's Presbyterian Church, had sold St. Mark's and was building a new church: Dale Presbyterian.

Manitoba College,
Winnipeg, Manitoba.

Preparation for ministry.

Following his year of theological studies in Manitoba, Oswald spent two years in Toronto Bible College, where he was chosen to give the valedictory address. He expressed his gratitude for the atmosphere in which he and his fellow students were "brought face to face with God" and his knowledge that his whole life was "utterly changed."

While studying, Oswald spent winter Sunday mornings in a prison, teaching classes. Surrendering his life to God for foreign service, he wrote, "Unless God prevents, I will go to the foreign field." He then eagerly took every opportunity to gain skills that would make him most useful on the mission field. Finding a retired Christian dentist, willing to teach dentistry to mission students, he learned about filling and extracting teeth among the Jewish community in Toronto. With the home nursing program, he accompanied a clinic doctor into the homes of the poor, learning invaluable skills, such as birthing babies and treating injuries.

Toronto Bible College – 1912.

Preparing for the
mission field.

Graduation from Toronto Bible
College – 1912 Valedictorian.

Toronto Bible College – Class of 1912.

Into all the World

First evangelistic campaign.

Like a runner waiting for the whistle at the starting line, 21-year-old Oswald found it almost unbearable to hold himself back from running into full-time service. So eager was he, that in January 1911, he had the audacity to call Rev. A.W. Roffe, the pastor of the Missionary Tabernacle on Bathurst Street, to ask if he might hold a one week evangelistic campaign. Impossible though it might have seemed, the minister agreed – despite the fact that Oswald was a stranger to him. Enlisting the aid of 17 boys from a Sunday school class, who had accepted Christ under his ministry, Oswald distributed 3,000 pamphlets. He engaged a friend to sing and persuaded his friend, Rev. J.D. Morrow, to help. He preached every night that week, and several people were saved. Oswald noted their names carefully and added them to his growing prayer list.

Sharing the good news.

While still a student, Oswald took every possible opportunity to serve God. He ushered and did personal ministry in the Chapman-Alexander Crusade in Massey Hall and helped serve meals at the Yonge Street Mission, the King's Mission, the Sackville Mission, and other centers. He became Canada's first travelling secretary for the Pocket Testament League, presenting the work from place to place in south-western Ontario, challenging all he met to carry a Testament wherever they went and to read at least a chapter a day. Earning $7.00 per week from pastoring the Congregational Church at Belwood, Ontario, he accumulated enough to cover his expenses – the registration at Toronto Bible College being just $4.00 per year.

Oswald and friend on a Belwood, Ontario farm.

Oswald had a great heart for children and it gave him deep satisfaction, during his year at Belwood, to take 35 children from the slums of Toronto and place them on farms of his church members for a vacation.

Children of the 1911 Toronto slums.

ONE SHORT WEEK

EVANGELISTIC SERVICES

To be Conducted by

OSWALD J. SMITH

in the

MISSIONARY TABERNACLE

274 Bathurst Street

EVERY NIGHT at 8 p.m.

Personal Workers' Prayer Meeting at 7.30

From Jan. 2nd to Jan. 7th, 1911

You are Cordially Invited to Attend.

Flier for first evangelistic services.

The driving focus of Oswald's life.

No activity took precedence over the driving focus of Oswald's life – sharing the Gospel with everyone he met – whether having his hair cut, riding a street car or eating in a restaurant. To him, it was as necessary as breathing. The more opportunity he got to preach, the better he got. His boisterous, rapid delivery gave way to a quieter manner, with more concentration on expression. Hungry to communicate the message of Christ with the greatest results, he studied the sermons of Charles Spurgeon and DeWitt Talmage. His journal reads:

> "Christ said, 'Launch out into the deep; go into the highways and byways.' But the modern churches are not doing this. We must discard our beautiful buildings, remove the pipe organ, and make the church a place where the common people will be at home."

DeWitt Talmage.

First hymn.

It was during the Toronto Bible College days, when Oswald's passion for Christ sometimes almost overwhelmed him, that his creative talents began to awaken and he penned the first verse and music of his first, and one of his greatest, hymns, "Deeper and Deeper".

Charles Spurgeon, friend and co-labourer with Dwight L. Moody.

> *Into the heart of Jesus deeper and deeper I go,*
> *Seeking to know the reason why He should love me so:*
> *Why He should stoop to lift me, up from the miry clay;*
> *Saving my soul, making me whole, though I had wandered away.*

McCormick Theological Seminary in Chicago.

Believing that God wanted him to secure his full standing as a Presbyterian minister, Oswald continued his studies, going to the McCormick Theological Seminary in Chicago. He worshiped under the ministry of Paul Rader in the world-famous Moody Church, never imagining that he would one day preach from that famous pulpit. There his passion for missions deepened through the study of the life of David Brainerd, and contact with the flow of dedicated missionaries passing through the church.

Paul Rader, pastor of the Moody Church in Chicago. Inscription reads: To the dear Smiths, Paul Rader, January 25-29.

Despite Oswald's love for Chicago, the surging oppression of the great metropolis branded the pain of the people, who did not know Christ, on his heart. In his journal, he wrote:

> "This last month I have felt the burden of a city. Its great sorrow has pressed in on my

Oswald with his first car, a Velie, in Chicago, 1914.

soul. Its vice and sin have bowed me upon my knees in tears.
I cried and cried to God to have mercy on the poor fallen
girls; and the burden is crushing."

Although deeply troubled by so many lost young women, Oswald
believed that genders should not be mixed in personal ministry. Thus,
he went to work sharing the love of Jesus with young boys entangled
in street gangs, and with the working men of downtown Chicago.

As his savings from his summer's work dwindled to 95 cents, and
he was turned down for a job as a waiter, Oswald again saw God's
faithfulness when he discovered he had been recommended to be
Acting Pastor in the large Millard Avenue Presbyterian Church in
southwest Chicago. There he served for four months in the spring
of 1913.

During Oswald's time at Millard, God allowed him to experience a
depth of heartbreak that would make him forever deeply sensitive to
the emotional pain of others. He received a "goodbye" letter from
Jennie, the girl from Toronto Bible College to whom he had been
engaged for two years. Because he had not told her, nor anyone else,
about his financial straits, she had not understood his long periods
away and his single-hearted focus on preparation for his life's work.
When her engagement ring tumbled out of a letter, into his hand,
Oswald was plunged into agony of soul.

Deep into the vortex of this whirlpool of despair, God poured His
healing ointment. He ministered to him by giving him hymns, the
depth of which Oswald could not have written, had he not experienced
the circumstances God allowed. Greatly comforted with the knowledge
that there was One who would never leave him, he wrote:

His Love
Loved ones may go and all I prize most dear,
Life lose its charm and sorrow linger near;
Yet there is One whose love will still abide
Through cloud or sunshine, whatso'er betide.

Sorrow but drives me closer to His side,
His love remains, His heart is open wide;
Sadly I bow and tell Him all my grief,
For only He has power to give relief.

Dear God the way is dark, I cannot see,
But still I feel that Thou art leading me;
'Mid deepest gloom as in the morning light,
Trusting in Thee I know 'twill all be right.

Into all the World

Thus, Lord, I turn my bleeding heart to Thee,
Asking that Thou woulds't shed Thy love on me;
Praying for grace to rise on angel wings
Far, far above the love of earthly things.

OJS

Among the mountaineers.

After reading the unforgettable novels of John Fox, Oswald was drawn to spend a summer preaching the Gospel to the mountaineers of Kentucky. Arriving in Cawood, he was "weak, ill, cast down, and full of grief," over the greatest loss of his life. Living alone in the little Presbyterian manse, he had never experienced such destitute solitude, and cried out to God, "Lonely! lonely! lonely! Dear God in Heaven, have mercy and send a friend to me soon." Little did he know that his life's faithful partner, a girl he had not yet met, had ministered the previous summer among the mountaineers just a few miles from where he was stationed.

As Oswald journeyed muleback over the mountains and through the valleys to preach among the poor mountain people, God filled him so full of the glory of His presence, that hymns would burst forth from his broken heart.

I have walked alone with Jesus in a fellowship divine,
Nevermore can earth allure me, I am His, and He is mine.
In my failure, sin and sorrow, broken-hearted, crushed and torn,
I have felt His presence near me, He has all my burdens borne.

On the mountain I have seen Him, Christ my comforter and friend,
And the glory of that vision will be with me 'till the end.
In the darkness, in the valley, with my Saviour I have trod,
Sweet indeed have been the lessons that I've learned alone with God.

I have seen Him! I have known Him! for He deigns to walk with me;
And the glory of His presence will be mine eternally.
Oh, the glory of His presence; oh, the beauty of His face!
– I am His, and His forever; He has won me by His grace.

In June, 1913, Oswald sat alone on his verandah, drinking in the solemn majesty of the blue hills and wrote in his journal:

"I never dreamed that such joy could be mine. But, praise God, it is. And He is now my portion, for He has satisfied me with Himself. Glory to His Name! ... I will never be able to tell what a blessing *The Threefold Secret of the Holy Spirit*, by Jas. H. McConkey, has been to me. Oh, how I long to know the secret of power for service. I am now 23 years of age. I have preached over 400 sermons."

22

Crisp, mountain watermelon.

Inside Cawood manse where Oswald lived alone.

Kentucky mountain friends.

Oswald and Kentucky friend.

Despite close calls with moonshiners, gun shots and runaway mules, Oswald slogged on amid the general indifference of the people. He was tremendously saddened with the few results of his labours, and ached for the people to know the love and beauty of his Jesus. By August 10, he had become terribly discouraged. Just ten days later, the tone of his journal was replaced with jubilation:

> "We have just had a revival in a place called Turtle Creek. Over two weeks ago Mr. Burkhart and I started a series of evangelistic meetings at this needy place, preaching the Gospel every night, visiting in the homes, praying with the people, and doing personal work through the day. Almost immediately, God began to work. The building was filled, many of the men having to stand around the walls. Night after night they came forward, until, at last, no less than 41 had accepted Christ. Immediately, they began to testify and to lead others to the Saviour.

> "As for me, God has shown me that He can and will use me. And now, more than ever, I feel the call to evangelistic work, a call that has throbbed in my heart for seven long years. But, regardless of what the future may bring, I am determined that God shall have all there is of Oswald J. Smith."

Back in Chicago.

Back in Chicago, Oswald was eager to begin his second year of studies at the seminary. On October 5, 1913, he rededicated his life to God with a three-fold commitment:
1. I will think no thought, speak no word and do no deed unworthy of a follower of Jesus Christ.
2. I will give my life for service in any part of the world, and in any capacity God wills that I should labour.
3. I will endeavour to do God's will from moment to moment, as He reveals it to me.

Just a few days later, in a direct answer to prayer, Oswald was appointed pastor of South Chicago's First Presbyterian Church, at the princely salary of 60 dollars per month.

His goals for the church were:
1. To reach the unsaved for Christ.
2. To turn Christians from worldliness to spirituality.
3. To make the prayer meeting a live service.
4. To build a large, enthusiastic Sunday School.
5. To develop a strong missionary church.
6. To increase church attendance.
7. To put spiritual men in every office.

First Presbyterian Church
South Chicago, Illinois

Oswald J. Smith, Pastor

Those goals remained the focus of his ministry throughout his life. Preaching four times each Sunday as well as at the midweek prayer meeting, wasn't enough; he yearned for more opportunities. He wrote,

" I wish there were more Sundays in the year that I might preach all the sermons and messages God gives me."

His greatest thrill came from seeing lives transformed by the power and grace of God. In an effort to multiply results, he trained 20 keen young people in personal evangelism and sent them out on street corners as fishers of men. He challenged his congregation:

"If you do not win a soul for Christ this summer, you have missed one of the greatest opportunities of your life. The warrior said, 'England expects every man to do his duty!' But listen, this summer Jesus Christ expects every Christian to do his duty! Let us cast ease aside; let us go out and win men and women for Jesus Christ."

While he was pleased to see 25 new converts that summer, the parish setting was not without its struggles. Early on, Oswald expressed frustration with home visits, feeling them so often to be a poor use of time. With most of the membership older than he, it was not surprising that they did not appreciate his reading from the pulpit the names of elders who did not attend prayer meetings! And then there was the day he addressed 300 clergymen and, for some reason, became so nervous that he couldn't remember a thing he had planned to say. For years, he smarted at the memory. All these things, he lifted up to God, saying,

"Why, God? Is this the way you choose to conquer my pride?"

"I am 25 today. A quarter of a century of life. For seven years I have had the privilege of preaching the Gospel. I am praying that God will make me:

1. A victorious man.
2. A Spirit-filled man.
3. A man of prayer.
4. A man of the Word.
5. A surrendered man.
6. A man of one purpose.

OJS – November 8, 1914.

Oswald Smith, age 25.

George Whitefield, age 24.
Below, preaching at Islington. Painting
destroyed in WWII London bombing.

Multiplying the ministry.

There was never a time of darkness in Oswald's life not given to God that it might bring forth glory for the Kingdom. Poems and melodies born of heartbreak, loneliness and soul-searching during these times always ended with a lift for the reader, encouragement that no matter what one might have to endure on earth, Jesus is with us, and will take us lovingly through.

When Oswald shared some of his writings with his music teacher, Dr. W. B. Towner, the Director of Music for the Moody Church, Towner encouraged him in arranging, polishing and collaboration. Sometimes hymns flashed into Oswald's mind, while others were the result of arduous struggles over long months.

Besides his hymns, Oswald began to publish some of his simple messages. Frustrated by his inability to find a tract that would grip people's attention and set forth the steps to salvation clearly, Oswald asked Moody Bible Institute to print 10,000 copies of *The Question of Questions*. This was his first foray into the publishing realm; he went on to write and publish 35 books, as well as countless articles and messages.

Social struggles.

With all of his intensity of heart, one might wonder about the balance in Oswald's life. Where was the fun for such a young man? What about the social ease generally developed throughout youth? Admittedly, Oswald was painfully shy in a group of strangers. While warm and affectionate with those he knew well, he struggled in social situations that focused on individuals, rather than on Christ, his passion. His social drive and joy in relationships was drawn more from seeing others draw close to Christ than to himself.

"My greatest joy is in the transformed lives around me."

"I have been reading the life of George Whitefield and it has set my soul aflame. His zeal, his prayer life, his preaching – how he inspires me! I now rise at 6:30 each morning and spend an hour in prayer and Bible study, and again an hour at night. And yet how ashamed I feel as I read of the fervor of Whitefield."
OJS – November 3, 1914.

Picnic with Chicago friends.

Missions – the burning ember.

As much as Oswald loved sitting under the dynamic preaching of Paul Rader at the Moody Church, and the flamboyant ministry of the visiting Billy Sunday, the call to missions burned in the core of his being like a hot coal waiting to be fanned into flame. He gobbled up missionary biographies like a starving man at a banquet. Of particular focus was the cry of the great "dark continent" of Africa. Four times he applied to the Board of Foreign Missions of The Presbyterian Church of Canada for a posting to the Foreign Field, but four times was rejected.

Billy Sunday.

The first stirrings of ministry in Toronto.

By the time Oswald finished his studies in Chicago, he had three offers to consider: Dr. Hall Young, the famous missionary explorer, wanted him to go to Juneau, Alaska, at $1200 yearly salary, the Chicago Presbyterian Church was urging him to stay at about the same amount, then there was Rev. J.D. Morrow's request, that he return to Toronto as his Associate Pastor at Dale Presbyterian Church, at $600.00.

In his journal, Oswald wrote:

> "Today I prayed for a long time for guidance. My soul was in agony. Slowly the vision came to me that my work must be a world work. My own dear country seemed to call me. There must be thousands in Canada who would give their lives for missions if they could be reached. I feel with Wesley that 'the world is my parish'. Perhaps the greater opportunity is offered in the call to Dale, although I would not look upon it as a permanent location. I must reach beyond to the world. I must travel and challenge others. May I listen to the Spirit's voice and not make a mistake. It is mine to obey orders, His to give them. But no matter where I go, may a world vision be mine."

Ordination.

On the Friday evening following the preaching of his farewell sermons in the South Chicago Presbyterian Church, Oswald was ordained by the Chicago Presbytery. He wrote:

> "I have spent the whole of this day in prayer and fasting. I am now a full-fledged Presbyterian minister."

"The world is my parish; even if I live in one place, I must reach out to the whole world. I must go that I can send others."

"The supreme task of the church is the evangelization of the world."

" Missions is not to be confined to an organization within the church. It is the chief work of the whole church."

OJS

Dale Presbyterian Church, Toronto.

Going directly from seminary to the second largest Presbyterian Church in Canada, was an extraordinary thing. But Oswald Smith knew that he served an extraordinary God!

Rev. J.D. Morrow, the Senior Pastor, had become Oswald's closest friend prior to his leaving for Chicago. With an irresistible personal magnetism, he was known and loved by all of Toronto. He loved the common people and was most at home when among the poor. Each Monday morning, he sat in court, watching for an opportunity to take charge of someone who had erred, someone whom he might take home and help. A gifted evangelist and Gospel preacher, he drew children to the services by occasionally getting zoo animals, including bears, and taking them into the pulpit. People flocked to Dale in multitudes for the dynamic evangelistic services. A generous man, Rev. Morrow allotted an equal share of the great work to Oswald. They preached alternately every Sunday, always to a packed house of over a thousand people.

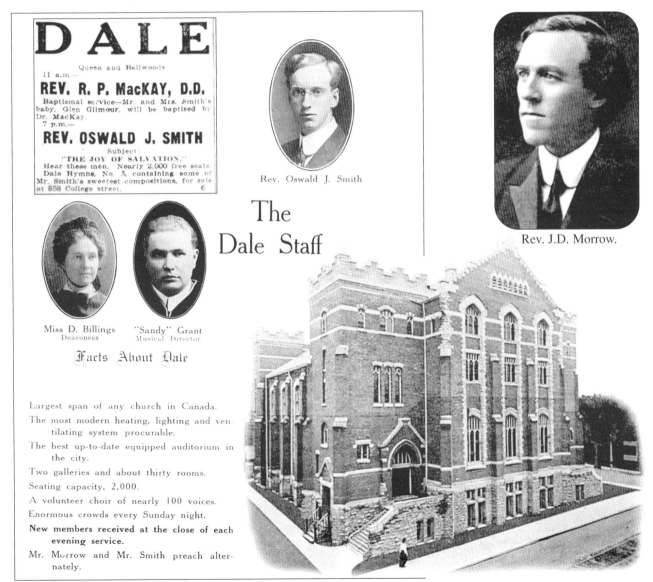

DALE

Queen and Bellwoods.
11 a.m.—
REV. R. P. MacKAY, D.D.
Baptismal service—Mr. and Mrs. Smith's baby, Glen Gilmour, will be baptised by Dr. MacKay.
7 p.m.—
REV. OSWALD J. SMITH
Subject:
"THE JOY OF SALVATION."
Hear these men. Nearly 2,000 free seats. Dale Hymns, No. 3, containing some of Mr. Smith's sweetest compositions, for sale at 858 College street. 6

Rev. Oswald J. Smith

The Dale Staff

Miss D. Billings
Deaconess

"Sandy" Grant
Musical Director

Rev. J.D. Morrow.

Facts About Dale

Largest span of any church in Canada.

The most modern heating, lighting and ventilating system procurable.

The best up-to-date equipped auditorium in the city.

Two galleries and about thirty rooms.

Seating capacity, 2,000.

A volunteer choir of nearly 100 voices.

Enormous crowds every Sunday night.

New members received at the close of each evening service.

Mr. Morrow and Mr. Smith preach alternately.

The deaconess and the pastor.
Soon after his arrival at Dale, Oswald met Rev. Morrow's deaconess, Daisy Billings. Though unimpressed with her severe, drab uniform, which Morrow commented would "look best hanging on the wall", Oswald's eye was caught by her manner and efficiency. It was obvious that she was not only loved by the people, but was a "crackerjack" preacher, preaching once a month. Once she began leaving her uniform at home and dressing more like the attractive 22-year-old girl she was, the two began finding themselves more and more thrown together on church business!

With the enormity of his church responsibilities, Oswald knew he should be pacing himself, but ignored the physical warning signs as long as he could. The result was a diagnosis of total exhaustion and an order from his doctor to go to a noted health clinic in New York for a month of treatment in mineral baths. With time to reflect and pray about the direction of his life, Oswald began to realize that Daisy, if she would have him, was the perfect helpmate that God had been preparing for him all along.

On his return, he took her for a walk along the shores of Lake Ontario and asked her to share his life. His heart thrilled at the discovery that she had loved him from the start, and at her words, "Oh, Oswald, I'll go with you anywhere in the Lord's work no matter what suffering it costs." The following week, they paddled a canoe up the Humber River to the Old Mill, where Oswald placed a ring on her finger. They were married on September 16, 1916, and enjoyed 56 years together. On June 22, 1917, they were blessed with their first son, Glen Gilmour.

Daisy Billings.

Oswald and Daisy.

Honeymoon.

Into all the World

Finney's writings became like a textbook to him, inspiring him to pray, often all through the night, with his loyal prayer partners.

Charles Finney.

Right: The famous Torrey-Alexander Choir, Massey Hall, 1906. The choir that sang the night Oswald Smith was converted.

Full charge of Dale.
Oswald was given full charge of Dale when Rev. (Captain) Morrow assumed an overseas chaplaincy in 1916. Already beleaguered by warring factions, who referred to him and his prayer warriors as "Mr. Smith and his soul-saving gang", Oswald knew it wouldn't be easy.

Many weren't pleased with his missions emphasis. He proclaimed that, "The supreme task of the church is the evangelization of the world. Missions is not to be confined to an organization within the church. It is the chief work of the whole church." When Oswald raised $600 for foreign work, the Missionary Society revolted. "Fancy sending $600 out of the church when we need it so badly right here!"

Despite the fact that the crowds multiplied under his leadership, resistance to things like the biG "GET RIGHT WITH GOD" banner Oswald strung right across the front of the sanctuary, the song sheets with energetic new Gospel songs replacing evening hymn books, and his requiring the choir to share time with special music he imported, became untenable. Oswald was deeply grieved and agonized in prayer over the knowledge that some of the people in the church actually hated one another, valuing the church mainly as a social club. He derived great solace from Finney's writings, which inspired him to pray, often all through the night with his loyal prayer partners.

Mason Lodge loyalty and affiliation determined many appointments and administrative decisions. When constant irritation was expressed over his revival meetings and prayer meetings, he succumbed to a moment of discouragement and resigned, leaving the church once again in the hands of the now-returned Morrow. Oswald's three and a half years of ministry at Dale Church were over.

Little did Oswald understand that his struggles were all preparation for recognizing and avoiding pitfalls in the great work God had ahead for him in and through The Peoples Church.

Humbled but called.

Somewhat at loose ends, Oswald attended Paul Rader's great soul-winning campaign in Massey Hall. At first he tried to help usher, but was soon set aside. When he tried to do personal work, he was ignored. Finally, he sold hymn books in the aisles while the speaker and some of his former colleagues graced the platform – the place to which Oswald had become accustomed. When the song leader announced that he would teach the crowd a new hymn , "Saved!" and announced the author as, "Oswald J. Smith, the man you see selling hymn books," Oswald was beyond mortification. Nevertheless, mortification gave way to gratification as he heard his favourite testimony hymn sung for the first time by 3,400 voices.

Utterly crushed by what he felt to be his uselessness to God, Oswald suffered greatly, crying in despair,

"Oh God, have you no more use for me? Has my ministry come to an end? Are you putting me on the shelf?"

That night, as Oswald gradually became grateful for the breaking he knew to be necessary in his heart, God spoke to him, reassuring him that he was not going to be put on the shelf.

Lumberjack preacher.

As Oswald continued to seek God for direction, an invitation from the Superintendent of the Shantymen's Christian Association, to open up the work in British Columbia, kept coming to his mind. Thus it was that he became a lumberjack preacher. In March of 1919, 11 years after he worked with the natives of Hartley Bay, British Columbia, Oswald, Daisy and little Glen boarded the train for the far west.

Oswald Smith and first son, Glen, in British Columbia, 1919.

Oswald Smith and fellow lumberjack preachers, 1919.

Oswald Smith sleeping under mattresses on the Coast of British Columbia as he endeavoured to take the Gospel to the lumberjacks.

Into all the World

Oswald's diary contains many descriptions of thrilling experiences and narrow escapes as he sought to take the Gospel to those who, for the most part, did not want it and only persecuted him for his efforts: tales of nerve-wracking rides through the mountains on logging trains, of jumping logs across a boom to get to shore, of being rescued by natives, of axes and sledgehammers being used to drown out the preaching of the Gospel, of bitter opposition from the Bolsheviks and of rejoicing that he had been "counted worthy to suffer shame for His Name".

> "July 28th: We had a long weary trudge to the boat 12 miles away. Arriving at the beach, we found all the beds full, and it was now after midnight. However, we discovered a pile of mattresses, and dragging four of them out to the edge of the Ocean, we laid one on the ground, placed two across and bound these two together by another, then crawled under the third,and, in no time at all, lost consciousness. It was one of the most delightful rests we had had."

Thus it was that, as Daisy and little Glen held the ropes in Vancouver, the work of the Shantymen's Christian Association was launched in British Columbia.

One afternoon, as Oswald made his way along the coast, he came upon a large tree which had fallen across a gully; at that tree, he knelt to wrestle with God. There, in the primeval glory of the glory of God's handiwork, with mountains rising in magnificent splendour around him and the ocean swells breaking on the lonely shore, God came very near. That night, Oswald's journal read:

> "The impression came to me with much joy and exultation of spirit that I was to return to Toronto. I saw in a vision the needy souls, and my heart went out to them. Perhaps it is to start an independent work on faith lines. I cannot say, but I am willing for whatever He wants. It was an unmistakable Call. The whole work seemed to open up before me. I saw myself as the shepherd of the people, and I felt certain that God had a work for me there."

With this impression confirmed through more prayer, the Smiths returned to Toronto in the fall of 1919.

The remainder of this book is the story of the fruit of God's Call on the life of Oswald Smith, received deep in the forests of British Columbia.

Why did God use Oswald Jeffrey Smith?

Oswald Smith would have been the first to confess his imperfections. He was human, challenged by obstacles faced by us all and yet God used him in a spectacular way. What was it that caught God's eye and set Oswald apart for a special work?

Early in his life, Dr. Smith wanted, more than anything else, to be used by God. No matter what he might be doing, whether riding his mule in the mountains of Kentucky, or pacing back and forth in his lonely little cabin, he would cry out to God in agony of soul, "*Lord, use* me. Send me out as an evangelist. Let me see revival. I have only one life to live and I want to invest it for Thee. Let me live for others. Enable me to win lost men and women for the Lord Jesus Christ. Let Thy blessing rest upon my ministry."

Then he would ask, "Lord, what are the qualifications for evangelistic work? Help me to meet the conditions, whatever they may be, so that I may not waste my life. I must not fail."

As he studied God's Word, Dr. Smith found the qualifications, and faced them – one by one – as God revealed them to him. With such overwhelming evidence of the fruit of his ministry, revealed in the following pages, we must conclude that these prerequisites were fulfilled in his life, enabling God to use him in a miraculous way.

To encourage and help prepare others who yearn to be used of God, Dr. Smith set forth the principles he learned in, *The Man God Uses*. The following points contain only brief excerpts from the book.

According to Dr. Smith, the man God uses must have:

1) a vision of the utter bankruptcy of the human race.

"As long as we think there is a spark of divine life in the heart of man, we will not accomplish much in our evangelistic work. If man already has life, then he does not have to receive life. No, my friend, there is no spark of divine life in any man; therefore, there is nothing to fan into a flame. Men are dead, lost, undone, utterly depraved, with no hope of life apart from a new birth. ... only God can meet his need."

The Man God Uses: Oswald J. Smith, Marshall, Morgan & Scott, London, 1932.

Into all the World

2) a realization of the adequacy of God's salvation.

"God has a remedy. Unless you really believe that man is utterly depraved, that he is dead in trespasses and sins, and that you have the one and only remedy, the Gospel of the Lord Jesus Christ, you will have little success as you seek to evangelize."

3) a life given over to one great purpose.

"The man who is going to be successful in evangelistic and soul-winning work is the man who has set everything else aside, who has become a man of one thing, one purpose, one aim in life. Any man with divided interests, any man with many schemes, plans and programs, any man who is interested in other things, is not going to be successful as an evangelist. Paul said, 'This *one* thing I do.'"

4) a life from which every hindrance has been removed.

"Do you remember that statement in Psalm 66:18: 'If I regard iniquity in my heart, the Lord will not hear me' ? Perhaps you are burdened by a weight of some kind, or a habit you are unwilling to give up. You may not even recognize it as sin, but it comes between you and God, and makes it impossible for God to use you. Day by day you try to go forward, but something drags you back, a weight of some kind holds you down and makes it impossible for you to run the race that God wants you to run. It may be that with all your talents and your gifts, all your accomplishments, all your education, you will be a complete and miserable failure in your evangelistic work, simply because there is something in your life, something in your heart, that grieves the spirit of God and makes it impossible for Jesus Christ to use you as He wants to, for His honour and His glory. Let Him search you. Then confess it, put it away, and come clean with God, that He may bless and own your ministry."

5) a life placed absolutely at God's disposal.

"God's great purpose is that our lives should be placed completely and absolutely at His disposal. No potter can do anything whatever with clay that continually resists the potter's attempt to shape it. If the potter cannot make the kind of vessel he wants to make, the reason is that there is something in the clay that resists his touch. Just as soon as that hindrance is removed and the clay yields itself absolutely to Him, the potter can make any kind of vessel he desires to make. So it is with your life and mine. If God is going to use us for His honour and glory, if His power is going to rest on us, if He is going to bless our evangelistic and soul-winning ministry, then our lives must be placed absolutely at His disposal."

Into all the World

6) a ministry of prevailing prayer.

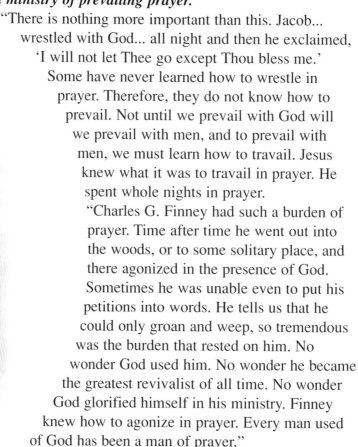

"There is nothing more important than this. Jacob... wrestled with God... all night and then he exclaimed, 'I will not let Thee go except Thou bless me.' Some have never learned how to wrestle in prayer. Therefore, they do not know how to prevail. Not until we prevail with God will we prevail with men, and to prevail with men, we must learn how to travail. Jesus knew what it was to travail in prayer. He spent whole nights in prayer.

"Charles G. Finney had such a burden of prayer. Time after time he went out into the woods, or to some solitary place, and there agonized in the presence of God. Sometimes he was unable even to put his petitions into words. He tells us that he could only groan and weep, so tremendous was the burden that rested on him. No wonder God used him. No wonder he became the greatest revivalist of all time. No wonder God glorified himself in his ministry. Finney knew how to agonize in prayer. Every man used of God has been a man of prayer."

7) a life saturated with the Word of God.

"I know ministers who never turn to the Word of God except to get sermons. Any man who does that will never get far in evangelistic work. You and I need to turn to the Word of God for the sake of our spiritual welfare. We ought to know the Book from cover to cover, and there is only one way to know it and that is to read it. Read it again and again. Meditate on it, mark it, study it, become saturated with it. Read it until it becomes a very part of you. Only then will God be able to use you as he wants to. God's Word must be on our tongues and in our hearts. As we lie awake at night, let us quote it again and again until we are saturated with it. It is not our word, remember, that God uses; it is His Word."

8) a vital message for a lost world.

"What is your purpose in preaching the Gospel of the Lord Jesus Christ? Do you want to entertain? Are you interested in the money you can make? Are you doing it because it is the respectable thing to do and because it will give you prestige and influence? If so, the ministry is no place for you.

"... a man in London, England... visited two churches. In the morning he went to the City Temple. He listened to one of the most eloquent sermons to which he had ever listened, and as he came out he was heard to exclaim, 'What a wonderful sermon.' At night, he went to Spurgeon's Tabernacle, that world-famous pulpit, that great auditorium with its two huge galleries made famous by Charles H. Spurgeon, the prince of preachers, and as he came out, he was heard to exclaim, 'What a wonderful Christ!'

"The world does not need sermons, it needs a message, and there is all the difference in the world between a sermon and a message. You can go to seminary and learn how to preach sermons, but you have to go to God to get messages. We must go out to present Christ, the living Saviour."

9) the anointing of the Holy Spirit.

"There are those today who are almost afraid to talk about the Holy Spirit. There has been so much cold conservatism and so much fanaticism regarding the Holy Spirit that they scarcely mention Him. Yet He is the third Person of the Trinity, the Executor of the Godhead, the One who takes the leading place in the Book of Acts. It was the Holy Spirit who actually did the work. He it was who guided and directed the apostles. He it was who led. The Holy Spirit convicted of sin and started revivals. He – God, the Holy Ghost – was the One who founded the Early Church.

"Today, to a large extent, He is ignored. We have an idea that we can get along without Him, that education and training will take His place and somehow become a substitute for His power, and we have endeavoured to carry on our ministry in the energy of the flesh, apart from the Holy Spirit altogether.

"Down through the years of my ministry, I have studied the lives of those whom God has used, and I have discovered that every one was an anointed man. Anointed men are not satisfied with education and training. They know that God cannot use them until they have experienced the anointing. So they wait in the presence of God until they have been endued with power from on high. If you want to see God use you, if you want souls to be convicted and saved, you will tarry until you have been endued with power from on high."

Oswald Smith could not understand
a man being saved and not wanting
to do something for the Lord.

10) the expectancy of faith.
"If you do not expect results, you will not get them. I cannot understand how any minister can be satisfied to preach the Gospel,
pronounce the benediction and then go home without having seen
anything happen. It seems to me that after I have spread the food on
the table, I ought to give the people a chance to come forward and
partake of it, and if I do not, I am leaving something vital out of
my ministry.
"Does not a lawyer expect a verdict? He does not speak to entertain.
He talks to the jury to get a conviction; and unless he gets a verdict,
his appeal has failed. So, too, should it be with the Gospel preacher,
with the evangelist. He should expect a verdict. He should get results.
His ministry should be characterized by the expectancy of faith."

11) total devotion to the glory of God.
"Your ministry must be for God's glory. If that is not your purpose,
then , if I were you, I would get down before God and humble myself
until all of self had been eliminated. I would ask God to break me so
that I might glorify Him. For unless you put the glory of God first,
you will be a dismal failure. You will never accomplish anything
really worthwhile. You must be broken if He is to use you. Otherwise,
sooner or later, there will be disaster."

"Arise and go into the city

and it shall be told thee

what thou must do."

Acts 9:6

When Oswald prayed for direction regarding what he should do
after establishing the Shantymen's ministry in British Columbia,
this was the answer God gave him.

Two

Establishing the Roots
of
The Peoples Church

Assistant Pastor at Dale Presbyterian Church,
Oswald J. Smith, age 25.

"Great success is always
followed by great conflict
and testing."

"Those who have been used of
God have had to pay
a terrific price."

"Much of my prayer life has
been characterized by
humiliation and confession."

"Though I have often failed
Him, He has never failed
me, nor have I ever been
tempted to turn back."

"God – make me
a conquering man, and enable
me to conquer myself.
I have seen the vision
and for self
I cannot live."

OJS

Into all the World

Establishing the Roots of the Church

Back in Toronto.

Despite his certainty that God had clearly called him back to Toronto to begin a work, another year and a half passed before Oswald received direction for his next step from God. With his good friend, Dr. Hooper, he gave himself increasingly to prayer and God's Word, studying an entire epistle each morning. It was a very difficult time. Once the pastor of busy, fashionable churches, ministering to multitudes, he was now virtually isolated, shut in with God. Spending a portion of his time assisting with the editing of *The Evangelical Christian*, he brought in $15.00 a week. Other than that, he floundered about, trying this door and that, in an effort to secure another pastorate, but with no success. Every door seemed to slam shut before him, little consolation for Daisy, soon to give birth to their only daughter, Hope Evangeline. These were the days of the dreaded influenza that killed so many thousands around the world. Both Oswald and little Glen became dangerously ill, but were spared. In January of 1920, Oswald wrote:

> "There has come into my heart a desire to have a spiritual work where souls will be saved and sent out as missionaries and the people trained to give to missions."

The old West End Y.M.C.A.
Towards the close of the winter, as he prayed and paced the floor, he received a definite impression of a hall at Queen and Dovercourt streets. Immediately going to investigate, he found the very hall he had envisioned; it was the old West End Y.M.C.A. Making enquiries, he found that it would seat 750 and the rent was $25.00 per night.

On the way home, the word came to him, "Behold, I have set before thee an open door and no man can shut it." (Revelation 3:8)

Waiting on God.
Having been taught in God's school of patience to "wait only upon God", Oswald did not jump into the situation, knowing God would release him into the ministry in His appointed time. Meanwhile, along with Dr. Hooper, he busied himself on a month-long trip back to Kentucky to establish a chapter of the Shantymen's Christian Association. On his return, he set up another chapter in northern Ontario, where he took the Gospel to the loggers. On his return, his heart was filled with "unutterable peace" as he prayed about the new venture he knew lay before him.

Dr. Ralph Hooper preaching to the lumberjacks of British Columbia, 1919.

"Somehow I feel that all the past has been nothing more than a preparation for the future."

OJS

Taking the Shantymen's ministry to the loggers in the Muskokas.

Devouring the 545 pages of *The Life of Trust* by George Mueller, he prayed that God would supply money to rent the Y.M.C.A. Miraculously, a total of $60.00 began to pour in from unexpected sources, one saying, "I awoke sometime during the night and a message – no doubt from God – came to me: 'Send Oswald Smith some money.'"

The day of miracles had not passed. God had set his seal on the work ahead. Three weeks earlier, Oswald had written the Constitution:

> ORIGIN – Born of God on the 1st Sunday of October, 1920, after almost fifteen months of continuous waiting upon Him in definite believing prayer, in response to an unmistakable Call.

> PURPOSE – *First* – A testimony to the faithfulness of God and the reliability of His promises, that He may be glorified. *Second* – The salvation of souls, the edification of believers, and world-wide evangelism.

> METHODS – *First*-A work of faith, wholly dependent upon God. Its needs are brought to Him in prayer, and to Him alone.
> *Second* – No collections are taken up and no solicitations for funds authorized.
> *Third* – No debts are incurred, the work being enlarged only as the Lord indicates His will by sending in the means.
> *Fourth* – One-tenth of all income is set aside for Missions.

The Gospel Auditorium.
Oswald decided to call the work "The Gospel Auditorium" and planned the first service for the first Sunday of October, 1920. When the day finally came, he arrived at the Y.M.C. A. at 6:00 p.m. and there wasn't a soul in sight. With a sinking heart, he viewed the 750 empty seats, knelt behind a door and prayed. As he prayed, he watched through the crack to see if anyone was coming: two men arrived, then a few more. When 65 had gathered, Oswald entered the pulpit.

Week after week, the rent was provided, either by way of the free-will offering boxes provided by Mr. B.L. Mullen, or through

More and more, Oswald gave himself to prayer and the study of God's Word, reading and studying an entire epistle each morning.

"I have always looked upon the Gospel Auditorium as the beginning of The Peoples Church."

(First service, October, 1920 – *OJS*)

A.B. Simpson.
Founder of The Christian
and Missionary Alliance.

Into all the World

Parkdale Tabernacle.

Massey Hall.

The great tent on College Street near Spadina Road, Toronto.

individual donations. Oswald made a covenant with God that no matter how lean the pickings in the Smith household, he would take nothing for himself until all expenses were met.

Within three months, the work became more and more established, but Oswald knew it was just the beginning of the vision. He always regarded The Gospel Auditorium as the beginning of The Peoples Church. In December of 1920, a copy of The Alliance Weekly arrived in the mail, with a picture of Dr. A.B. Simpson, founder of the Christian and Missionary Alliance on the front page. As Oswald stood looking at it, God seemed to say to him, "This is your work."

Parkdale Tabernacle.

With his leading confirmed through constant prayer, Oswald conferred with the Alliance, which led to the amalgamation of the new YMCA work with a struggling Alliance church, Parkdale Tabernacle, 1239 Queen St. West, in January of 1921. Prior to Oswald's query, the Alliance had decided to close Parkdale, as there were less than two dozen attending. God was still humbling Oswald's heart.

Three months after the merging of the two groups, Oswald advertised special meetings with the Bosworth Brothers. The audiences were so large that the doors had to be closed and many turned away the first week. The work had already outgrown the Parkdale Tabernacle!

Massey Hall.

At the beginning of the second week, Oswald transferred the services to Massey Hall, which seated 3,400, but even there, people often had to be turned away. So great was the interest, that after the Bosworth Brothers left, Oswald continued the meetings, often with special speakers, every night of the week for six months.

The 1921 College Street tent meetings.

The College Street tent.

To accommodate the growing crowds, Oswald erected a 90-foot-square tent on the south side of College Street near Spadina, at a cost of $2,000. The problem of seating was solved with a "chair shower" and 1,500 chairs poured in! It was dedicated by Paul Rader in July, 1921. People came in multitudes and scores were compelled to stand. Oswald Smith was 31 years old.

Oswald Smith's first baptismal service in Parkdale Tabernacle –
baptizing his secretary, Miss Alice Porter, with ex-Rabbi Bregman.

By the end of that initial evangelistic campaign, 61 converts requested baptism by immersion. While Oswald was accustomed to baptizing babies in the Presbyterian Church, he had never seen the need for believers' baptism. Nevertheless, by the time the last of the 61 had gone under, he understood and was, himself, baptized. From then on, he dedicated, rather than baptized, babies; leaving baptism as a step requested by a believer.

"Faith Promise" offerings for missions.

One of the determining factors that had led to merging with the Christian and Missionary Alliance, was the emphasis on missions. Like Oswald, A.B. Simpson had a passion for the souls "lost in heathen darkness". The Alliance had, by this time, sent out 500 missionaries and only six percent of the funds it took in were kept at home. That emphasis resonated in Oswald's heart.

Almost immediately after the merge, he found himself swept into the church's annual missionary convention. When handed one of the pledge envelopes, he turned it over and read, "In dependence upon God, I will endeavour to give to the missionary work of the church $___ during the coming year."

"Woe is me if I preach not the Gospel."

OJS

O.J. Smith and his Alliance
Board of Managers.

"That lets me out," was Oswald's initial thought as he reflected on his scant income. Just as he scrunched up the envelope, however, the Lord spoke to him.

> "I'm not asking you to give out of what you have. Will you trust Me to put extra money into your hands so that you may give it to foreign missions?"

With his heart almost thumping out of his chest, Oswald asked the Lord how much He wanted him to promise to give.

> "Fifty dollars," came the immediate reply.

Fifty dollars was more than half a month's salary. Just as Oswald was thinking he must have heard wrong, the Lord said"

"This is the way. Walk in it."

Thus began a deeper experience in trusting God for finances. Every month, Oswald prayed the extra in, and every month it was miraculously supplied.

Paul Rader preaching.

The Christie Street Tabernacle. Faced with the challenge of finding a new building to replace the outgrown Parkdale Church, the decision was made to build. Oswald wanted "a great spiritual center where thousands will find bread enough and to spare." He did not want to waste God's money in a beautiful building at the expense of Missions.

Land was chosen on Christie Street and a great, steel structure built, 80 feet by 130 feet; a cement block auditorium without pillars or posts to obstruct the view, seating 1,500 people. When funds ran out part way through, Oswald called a halt to construction, refusing to saddle his people with debt. When the necessary miracle happened, following a half day of prayer, the building was completed and opened May 14, 1922 by Paul Rader of the Moody Church in Chicago. Within six months, room for 500 more seats had to be built.

"The Lord did not tell us to build beautiful churches, but to evangelize the world." OJS

The great Moody Church in Chicago.

The Alliance Tabernacle, 85 Christie Street, Toronto.

Into all the World

Dedication and Opening

of

The Alliance Tabernacle
Willowvale Park

TORONTO - - - - CANADA

2,000 FREE SEATS

"Everything in Jesus and Jesus Everything"

Committee

Chairman
Chas. H. Grobb

Secretaries
J. Martin Gardner
Joseph G. Loose

Treasurers
Fred L. Syme
Chas. H. Grobb

Building Committee
W. C. Willis
W. W. Sneath

Song Leader
Fred L. Syme

Sunday School Supt.
E. W. Simmons

Geo. R. Gregg
C. L. Carden
G. P. Duffield
John Souster

The Christian
and Missionary
Alliance

Founder
Rev. A. B. Simpson, DD

President
Rev. Paul Rader

Canadian Supt.
Rev. A. W. Roffe
33 Richmond St. W.
Phone Main 1370

Pastor
Rev. Oswald J. Smith
716 Palmerston Ave.
Phone Coll. 8058-w

Deaconess
Miss Alice Porter
91 Beatice St.
Phone Coll. 4528

1922
Sunday, May 14th
11 a.m., 3, and 7 p.m.

Dedication Services

Rev. Paul Rader
President of the Christian and Missionary Alliance

Paul Rader.

O.J. Smith

May 21st to 28th

Dominion Convention

Crowds routinely overflowed the capacity and many were compelled to stand, even outside, where they jostled to catch a view through the windows.

Bringing in special speakers like the Welsh revivalists, Fred Clarke and George Bell, and lively singing groups such as the Cleveland Quintet, The Alliance Tabernacle was fast earning the reputation of being Toronto's most effective ministry. Newspapers dubbed it, "Toronto's great center of evangelism."

Outreach from the Alliance Tabernacle.

To Oswald Smith, the church was never to be a destination; it was a stop-over. His vision was to gather the unsaved, get them saved and then send them out to do the ministry of Jesus through a variety of programs he developed:

> The Wayside Mission – sent men into the wilds of northern Ontario with the Gospel.
>
> Seekers After Truth Mission – a ministry to the Jews of Toronto, led by a converted rabbi, Rabbi Bregman.
>
> The King's Messengers and Evangelistic Band – held open-air services and passed out tracts.
>
> *The Prophet* – (later *The Peoples Magazine*) a monthly magazine by the "Tabernacle Publishers."
>
> The Tabernacle Bookstore – through which tracts, pamphlets, books and Gospel Victrola records were sold.
>
> Canadian Bible Institute – with the district, a program to train young people for home or foreign missions. First President, Dr. E. Ralph Hooper.
>
> Church plants – the Alliance mothered two new churches, one in Toronto's east-end and another in Forest Hill.

> *"The Gospel is the dynamite, the power of God unto salvation, and I want to leave it wherever I go, so that every now and again there will be an explosion and someone will be saved."*
>
> OJS

Oswald watching his book being translated into Russian.

First outreach to Russia.

Birthing a worldwide ministry – 1923.

As word of the success of the church spread, Dr. Smith was invited to hold evangelistic meetings all over North America. He was a frequent guest in the 5,000-seat Chicago Tabernacle. In 1924, he took his first missionary campaign to Europe, where there was tremendous response from the Russian-speaking people of northern Europe. He returned with renewed zeal to raise support for new missionaries and funds to open Bible schools in Latvia and Spain. (See *Chapter Six*.)

Into all the World

Russia, Dark Russia.

Rev. Oswald J. Smith.   Tune: Juanita.

1. Rus - sia, dark Rus - sia, Land of sor - row, sin and night; No Christ, no
2. Hark! they are call - ing— I can hear them night and day, Moaning and
3. Mil - lions are dy - ing— I can hear their bit - ter wail; How dare I
4. No one to tell them Of a dy - ing Sav-iour's love; No one to

Sav - iour, And no Gos - pel Light. I have seen the vi - sion
dy - ing— Let me haste a - way. Wea - ry, tired and hope-less,
face them If to help I fail? Can I let them per - ish,
point them To a life a - bove. Then fare - well, dear home-land,

And for self I can - not live; Life is less than worth-less
Grop - ing still in dark - est night; To my sad, lost Rus - sia
Souls for whom the Sav - iour died, Live in ease and com - fort
I must break each ten - der tie, And to Rus - sia has - ten,

rit. . . .   CHORUS.

Till my all I give.
I must take the Light. Rus - sia, dark Rus - sia, I am go - ing
While they are de - nied?
There to live or die.

now to thee; Rus - sia, lost Rus - sia, Tak - ing Christ with me.

William Fetler,
Founder of the Russian
Missionary Society.

Oswald's first trip to Russia transformed his life.

There he experienced real Holy Ghost revival, with hundreds falling on their faces, weeping before the Lord.

Strong men, with tears running down their cheeks, begged God to forgive them.

While Oswald had always yearned to go to foreign fields, after actually seeing town after town without even one witness for the Gospel, he returned to Toronto with a fiery passion for Missions.

First missionary
hymn for
Russia
by
Oswald Smith,
written in 1924.

Miss Alice Porter,
Oswald's deaconess & secretary.

California pastorate, 1928.

Riding the crest of a revival wave.

The Alliance Tabernacle seemed to ride the crest of a revival wave in campaign after campaign; souls were being saved continually. Miss Alice Porter left Dale Presbyterian where she had worked with Oswald and began to labour with him as the crowds thronged the Alliance auditorium. Some services saw over a thousand turned away, despite the building of two additions.

Evangelism in Toronto, where meetings were held night after night, year in and year out, was an entirely new thing. Energetic Gospel songs were introduced and souls were saved and sent out to win others.

The winning formula.

Evangelism was balanced with Bible teaching and Missions. While outstanding evangelists were invited to preach, outstanding Bible teachers filled the pulpit and held Bible Conferences. Still, the major emphasis was evangelism, because Oswald knew that the church that does not evangelize will fossilize.

"The church that does not evangelize will fossilize." OJS

Interlude, 1926 – 1928.

Despite his tremendous work at Christie Street, Oswald ran into trouble with his Board of Managers, when he took on some men who did not have his vision for evangelism and missions. To end the conflict, he resigned and began to travel in eastern Canada as Area Superintendent of the Christian and Missionary Alliance. Desperately missing his pastorate, he accepted a Call to pastor The Gospel Tabernacle in Los Angeles. In less than a week, he knew he was not to stay, and so set a one-year limit on his ministry there. Although his heart was still in Toronto, huge crowds attended, necessitating the placing of chairs all down the aisles.

California transportation, 1928.

Oswald, his mother, Hope, Glen, Paul, Daisy and Oswald's father.

Oswald driving back from L.A.

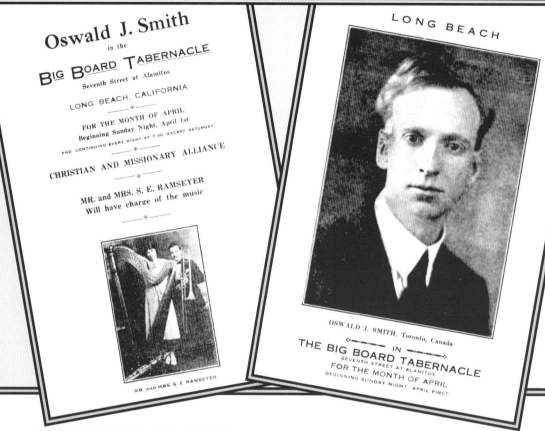

Oswald J. Smith
in the
BIG BOARD TABERNACLE
Seventh Street at Alamitos
LONG BEACH, CALIFORNIA

FOR THE MONTH OF APRIL
Beginning Sunday Night, April 1st
AND CONTINUING EVERY NIGHT AT 7:30 EXCEPT SATURDAY

CHRISTIAN AND MISSIONARY ALLIANCE

MR. and MRS. S. E. RAMSEYER
Will have charge of the music

MR. AND MRS. S. E. RAMSEYER

LONG BEACH

OSWALD J. SMITH, Toronto, Canada
IN
THE BIG BOARD TABERNACLE
SEVENTH STREET AT ALAMITOS
FOR THE MONTH OF APRIL
BEGINNING SUNDAY NIGHT APRIL FIRST

INTRODUCING MR. SMITH

• • •

For four years Rev. Oswald J. Smith had charge of a large Tabernacle in Toronto with a seating capacity of 2,300, where he preached to thousands of souls, the vast audiences at times overflowing into the annex. The Tabernacle which was built under his leadership and twice enlarged, soon became the city's great centre of evangelism and spiritual inspiration.

Mr. Smith's earlier work after five years of theological studies, and ordination, was in Dale Presbyterian Church, Toronto, where for three and a half years he ministered to large congregations, the church accomodating 1,800 people.

In evangelistic work he has travelled extensively through Canada, Europe and the United States, holding meetings in many of the leading cities and proclaiming the Gospel to multitudes of hungry souls.

For several Sundays he occupied Paul Rader's pulpit, Chicago, where his messages were broadcast to multiplied thousands... In Los Angeles he carried on a great downtown work for many months in the well-known Trinity Auditorium.

Mr. Smith is an accomplished author, editor and writer of hymns. His books breathe a spirit of revival, and contain a wholesome exposition of the fundamental teachings of Scripture. Each one has a distinctive, vital message. Thus far almost 100,000 copies have been issued.

Mr. Smith's masterly messages on prophecy have stirred multiplied thousands. Speaking on the subject "Is the Antichrist at Hand?" he answers such questions as the following: "Is the Roman Empire to be revived and will Mussolini be the seventh Emperor? Are we approaching the End of the Age and is the antichrist soon to appear? Will there be another world war, or did the last titanic struggle end all war? Who are the two beasts of Revelation 13? Are the astounding predictions from the demon world of an international catastrophy to be fulfilled? To what extent does Revelation 17 identify the antichrist? Will he be a reincarnation from the dead or an ordinary man? How are we to interpret Christ's story of the End-Time as set forth in Matthew 24? Has Satan always been a devil?

Mr. Smith is bringing with him his song-leader, Mr. S. E. Ramseyer, and also Mrs. Ramseyer who is a gifted harpist and pianist. Mr. and Mrs. Ramseyer are unusually talented. They sing and play together most effectively. In addition to the piano, Mr. Ramseyer plays a trombone and several other instruments. Their work is deeply spiritual. Mr. Ramseyer has a baritone voice of unusual quality. His solos are greatly appreciated everywhere. Their programs of sacred song and music are unique.

———◆———

GERALD B. WINROD, OF WICHITA, KAS.

IS COMING SUNDAY, APRIL 22ND

PROGRAM

Rev. C. H. Chrisman, Presiding
(District Superintendent of the Christian and Missionary Alliance)

11:00 A. M.
Orchestra Prelude
Hymn
Scripture and Prayer
Offering and Offertory
Anthem—"Praise the Lord"..Choir
Introduction of Mr. Smith..Rev. George W. Davis
SERMON—Rev. Oswald J. Smith—"The Victorious Life"
Benediction
Piano Postlude..Miss Esther Ender

2:30 P. M.
Xylophone Solo..Mr. Clifford Carpenter
Song Service
Offering
Solo
Prayer—Rev. E. O. Jago
Words of Welcome..Dr. Frederic W. Farr
SERMON—Rev. Oswald J. Smith—"Is the Anti-Christ at Hand?"
Benediction

7:30 P. M.
Song Service
Offering
Special Music
Invocation...Rev. W. E. Shepard
SERMON—Rev. Oswald J. Smith—"The Most Important Truth in the Bible."
Benediction.
6:30 P. M.—Young People's Meeting.

The Annual Convention of the Christian and Missionary Alliance will be held in this Church, from Sunday, April 17th to Sunday, April 24th, inclusive. Rev. Oswald J. Smith and others will speak daily.

OSWALD J. SMITH

Mr. Smith was for five years pastor of the Toronto Gospel Tabernacle with a seating capacity of two thousand three hundred, which was often filled to overflowing. During his ministry the missionary offering increased from Four Thousand Dollars to Forty Thousand Dollars a year.

He has labored among the Indians of Alaska—the Settlers on the Western prairies, the lumbermen of the Northwest, the mountaineers of Kentucky and the Russians of Central Europe.

Mr. Smith is an author of rare gifts, an editor of a successful religious paper and a writer of many hymns. His books have been circulated by the thousands and his volume on "The Revival We Need" is said by Jonathan Goforth to be of great value.

He is much in demand as an evangelist and has recently awakened large communities in the South by his clear Gospel preaching.

His startling messages on Prophecy have stirred the hearts of the people East and West and his book, "Is the Anti-Christ at Hand" has been printed in several editions.

Mr. Smith is not a faddist nor a controversalist. He avoids the doctrinal differences that divide. The central theme of his preaching is "Jesus Only." A spirit of revival pervades all of his ministry.

Additional information regarding Mr. Smith's life and work can be obtained from the book "Working with God," on sale at the Book Stand. Other titles also can be had at the same place.

It gives us great pleasure to present Mrs. Oswald J. Smith, and the three children, Glen Gilmour, 9; Hope Evangeline, 7; and Paul Brainerd, 5.

Mr. Smith will speak at the Glendale Gospel Tabernacle, Easter Sunday afternoon, April 17th at 2:30 o'clock.

OSWALD J. SMITH

PASTOR - ELECT

OF THE

GOSPEL TABERNACLE CHURCH

AND THE

CHRISTIAN AND MISSIONARY
ALLIANCE OF LOS ANGELES

* * *

INSTALLATION SERVICES

SUNDAY APRIL 10, 1927

11:00 A. M. - 2:30 P. M. - 7:30 P. M.

CHURCH AT CORNER OF
EIGHTEENTH AND GEORGIA STS.

A great center for winning souls.

In 1928, at the age of 38, Oswald sensed God was saying to him:

> "It's time to settle down and build a great center for winning souls and sending out missionaries and funds to the foreign field. It will be a church that will put missions first!"

The Smiths were offered every inducement to stay in Los Angeles, including wonderful gifts and the offer to build a huge new Tabernacle, but Oswald knew he was to go back to Toronto. Thus the family, with beloved helper Chrissie French, motored 3,000 miles home over gravel roads, with serious engine and tire problems.

Mr. & Mrs. Ramseyer, music leaders.

W.C. Willis, Treasurer.

Mr. H.H. Phinnemore, first Head Usher.

Two Keys to the Growth of The Peoples Church

With multitudes of seekers coming forward almost nightly, personal altar workers had to be trained to be effective. Oswald gave special instructions.

"First, you take your place beside them at the altar, and then make your way with them into the inquiry room. There you kneel with them." (Oswald never forgot how he wanted to get down on his knees when he was saved at sixteen.)
"Then deal with them individually from the Bible, taking them through the main Scriptures that show first that all have sinned; then that all our sins have been laid on Christ."

Isaiah 53:5-6, was to be followed up with John 1:12 and John 3:16 (KJV):

"But He was wounded for our transgressions, He was bruised for our iniquities: the chastisement of our peace was upon Him; and with His stripes we are healed. All we like sheep have gone astray; we have turned every one to his own way; and the Lord hath laid on him the iniquity of us all."
"But as many as received him, to them gave he power to become the sons of God...."
"For God so loved the world, that he gave his only begotten Son, that whosoever believeth in him should not perish, but have everlasting life."

"That's about all they can master at first hearing," Oswald warned. New converts went away with booklets to study at home to assure them of their salvation and encourage them onward.

"Make sure they have a Bible," he would say. There were always New Testaments to give out to those without. "And be sure you record their name and address; visit them in their home before next Sunday and offer to sit with them in the service."

Oswald knew that a strong core of knowledgeable, spiritual personal workers, always ready to join the first seeker who stepped into the aisle, were critical to work that lasts.

Another key was the group of people who loved God and knelt for prayer in the pastor's office before each service.

Massey Hall, home of The Cosmopolitan Tabernacle.
Once back in Toronto, Oswald was appointed the Canadian Director of the Worldwide Christian Couriers by its President, Paul Rader. Paul then encouraged Oswald to organize a soul-winning missionary work in Toronto, which he happily set about doing, calling it "The Cosmopolitan Tabernacle," another building block in the foundation of what would eventually be known as "The Peoples Church". Knowing that if he were to launch the work in a small building, it would take years to get it going, he chose Toronto's largest auditorium, Massey Hall. On September 9, 1928, Oswald walked to the pulpit to face almost 2000 people. A dozen went forward to accept Christ. While many claim this to be the birth of The Peoples Church, to Oswald, it began with "The Gospel Auditorium."

Many loyal supporters from the Alliance followed Oswald: his secretary, Alice Porter; his faithful friend and treasurer, W.C. Willis; and H.H. Phinnemore, who became the head usher. Mr. and Mrs Ramseyer, who had gone to California with Oswald, took charge of the music and Donald Billings was the first pianist.

Massey Hall, home of
The Cosmopolitan Tabernacle.

St. James Square Church, home of The Toronto Gospel Tabernacle, later renamed "The Peoples Church".
In 1930, the congregation rented St. James Square Church on Gerrard Street East. First calling it "The Toronto Gospel Tabernacle", the Elders changed the name to "The Peoples Church", on October 1, 1933, having found that the name "Gospel Tabernacle" had already been incorporated.

St. James Square Church, home of
The Toronto Gospel Tabernacle.

The Peoples Church

"Recalling my vision in British Columbia and the vivid picture of preaching to all the people of Toronto, I decided this was what I would call my church... "The Peoples Church."
OJS

Some of the people of The Toronto Gospel Tabernacle,
later "The Peoples Church".

Into all the World

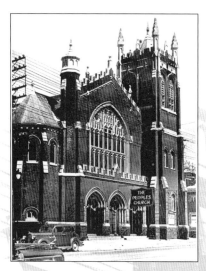

The Peoples Church, 100 Bloor Street East.

On July 1, 1934, The Peoples Church moved to the 2000-seat Central Methodist Church at 100 Bloor Street East, which had been left vacant with the union of several major denominations. It was a magnificent structure, with lovely cushioned pews, beautiful Italian architecture, and the most central location in the city. The men of the board urged Oswald to buy it. "Not until we have $10,000 of the $65,000. purchase price," he insisted. He didn't want his congregation to carry a debt, nor did he believe in paying interest when money could better be spent on Missions.

"I have no right to incur debts and then expect God to come to my aid; He can just as easily give me the money beforehand. 'Owe no man anything' applies to the church too. In my mind, debt is sin."

Thus, while Oswald prayed and awaited a miracle, the congregation rented the facility.

Anointed preaching.

Meanwhile, the services at The Peoples Church were filled to capacity. Ever since two particularly special times with God in Florida and in Truro, N.S., there seemed to be a special anointing on Oswald's preaching. He described the experiences in *Fire in His Bones.*

"My heart was filled with an unutterable love; it seemed as though my whole body was bathed in the Holy Ghost. Somehow I finished my preaching and called for a season of prayer at the altar. I was melted, broken, awed, and as my soul rose to meet Him, the tears began to come. I could do nothing but weep and praise my precious, precious Lord. The world and all its troubles faded from my sight. My trials appeared oh, so insignificant as God, God Himself filled my whole vision. Oh, it was glorious. I began to pray, but only exclamations of praise and adoration poured from my lips. I saw no one save Jesus only.

"I slipped home to the pastor's house where I was staying, and there I continued to walk back and forth, my face uplifted, my heart thrilled, praising and blessing God.

"I left the house and wandered I know not where. It seemed as though I wanted to love everybody. Every now and again as I walked along the street praising God, the tears would start to

"I simply endeavoured to do the job to which God called me and He did the rest."

OJS

Like Dwight L. Moody, Oswald had three godly women who he could trust to constantly lift him up in prayer: his wife, Daisy; his secretary, Alice Porter; and Chrissie French, a convert from the Alliance Tabernacle who felt the Lord lead her to give herself to the Smith family as a companion and helper for Daisy, with Oswald so often away.

Alice Porter, Daisy, Chrissie French and children.

Bloor Street sanctuary.

Into all the World

fill my eyes; and time after time I was choked with unutterable outbursts of worship and love that seemed almost to overwhelm me. I sang deep in my own soul my own chorus:

"Alone, dear Lord, ah, yes, alone with Thee!
My aching heart at rest, my spirit free;
My sorrow gone, my burdens all forgotten
When far away I soar alone with Thee.

"Finally I came back to my room and quieted down somewhat. I did not speak in tongues, but there was a sweet, settled peace in my heart and a light that never shone on land or sea in my soul. The glow passed, but the fragrance remained."

And then in Truro:

"The battle had been unusually severe, the assaults of the enemy terrible. I could not drive him away. My heart was lonely. I was fearfully homesick and longed to get back with my family.
"I was alone in my room reading a Sunday school paper about the fullness of the Spirit, and this stirred me tremendously. And then *He* revealed Himself. I felt the Spirit flood over me. At once my heart was filled to overflowing. I walked the floor praising the Lord in the fullness of joy of the Holy Ghost. Peace like a river flowed over my soul.
"Regarding the future, my heart was at rest. All murmuring and complaining ceased. Oh, what a Comforter He is! It was a real anointing of the Holy Spirit."

Purchasing the Bloor Street Church, 1936.
On November 16, 1936, the publisher of Toronto's Globe and Mail gave $20,000 towards the purchase of the Bloor Street Church. The whole city was moved, and the purchase of the church became a common topic of discussion. Once the deal was done, Oswald sold the elegant pipe organ to a Roman Catholic Church for $40,000, removed the pipes from the rear of the gallery and set up another 150 seats. Still the crowds overflowed beyond capacity. On radio broadcasts, he would beg listeners:
> "The fire marshall has warned that we're dangerously over crowded, so please stay home!"
Long-time member, Bruce Fogarty, recalls,
> "Then he'd announce the evening service, and it sounded so exciting you just couldn't stay away!"
Within five years, the church was entirely paid for, the missionary offerings increased all through those years.

Exciting services.

With the 100-voice choir and 40-piece orchestra leading rousing new hymns and choruses, The Peoples Church became an exciting place to be. Big-name guest speakers and musical artists were routinely invited to share the platform. While other churches geared down for the summer, Oswald geared up, bringing in "greats" like Vance Havener, John R. Rice and Harry Ironside. When Gipsy Smith arrived, it seemed that all Toronto was planning to attend. Oswald had to move the Sunday services to Massey Hall. When Jackie Burris arrived, the meetings had to be moved to Maple Leaf Gardens to accommodate the estimated eleven thousand people.

Evangelistic services at the Gardens.

Thrilling adventures.

Whenever Dr. Smith returned home from his overseas travels, people would sit spellbound, listening to stories of thrilling adventures in far-away places. His photography of the exotic lands was so good that the Royal Geographical Society of London, England, made him a life member. In those pre-television days, people came to see the breathtaking wonders of Ethiopia and Sumatra, the colorful citizens of the Solomon Islands and the head-hunters of Borneo; no dull slide show. The highpoint of each year was the month-long Missionary Convention.

Bloor Street was decked out in banners, leaving no confusion as to the level of enthusiasm, both inside and outside the church. Python skins from the Amazon, African drums and witch doctors' masks were exhibited. Music groups in their colourful native attire, sang and played their way through the crowds. Refreshment booths were set up, and the children bragged, "At our church we have hot dogs and Indians!*"

The Peoples Choir and Orchestra.
Eldon B. Lehman, Director (a remarkable man).

(* See note on page 14.) Surrounded by the realities of far-away lands, Dr. Smith pled his case for the desperate plight of those who had never heard of Jesus. Speaking of Christ's feeding of the 5,000, he asked,

> "Why should we keep on passing the bread of life to those in the front row when the back rows still have nothing to eat?"

Then would come a stirring challenge to young people to give their lives to carry the Gospel to those in heathen darkness. Every time, young people responded in droves, streaming down the aisles.

Evangelist Jackie Burris at Maple Leaf Gardens.

On the road for missions support.

Along with raising funds for missions through the annual Missions Conferences, The Peoples Church became accustomed to bidding farewell to Dr. Smith as he went on the road, time after time, presenting the needs of the mission fields to packed out crowds throughout the United States and Canada. Having seen God supply the funds, even after the crash of the stock market in 1929, Oswald pressed on, and the money came in regardless of the Depression that had paralyzed the economy. Often accompanied by his good friend, Dr. Hooper, who assisted in the ministry, he raised enough to keep the missionaries spreading the Gospel.

Rather than suffer during Oswald's absences, the church continued to grow. He always made sure that the pulpit would be filled with the very best preachers and singers available. His prescription for church growth was simple: "Go away for two or three months of the year and turn the pulpit over to preachers who are better than you are!"

11,000 packed Maple Leaf Gardens for services with Jackie Burris.

"We can't paint the auditorium; they need Bibles in the Philippines!"

OJS

When Oswald received the stunning news that the Chicago bank, which held all Worldwide Christian Courier funds, had folded, he determined to pick up the slack for all of the missionaries who would be affected, and plunged into a campaign to raise even more funds for missions.

The place to be.

The Peoples Church soon came to be a favourite for the young people of Toronto, who congregated by the hundreds. While there, they were blessed and challenged to make their lives count for God. The singing of new hymns was lively and The Peoples Church always had the best guest speakers and musicians.

The Missionary Medical Institute.

In 1936, with the assistance of Dr. Hooper and nurse Louise Kirby, Dr. Smith established the Missionary Medical Institute (now the Missionary Health Institute – International Medical Service of Toronto's North York General Hospital), to give prospective missionaries a year's instruction in tropical medicine.

The place to be on Sunday nights.

Into all the World

Organization of The Peoples Church

"The Peoples Church is an independent work, standing pre-eminently for the conversion of souls, the edification of believers, and worldwide evangelism; emphasizing especially the four great essentials: Salvation, Deeper Life, Foreign Missions, and our Lord's Return; endeavouring by every means to get the Message to the Christless masses, both at home and abroad, in the shortest possible time.

"We believe in an unmutilated Bible; salvation through the blood of Christ; entire separation from the world; victory over all known sin through the indwelling Spirit; rugged consecration to sacrificial service; practical faith in the sufficiency of Christ for spiritual, temporal and physical needs; purifying hope of the Lord's return; and a burning missionary zeal for the bringing back of the King through world evangelization.

"The Peoples Church has a Board of Managers to look after the business end of the work, a Board of Elders to take care of the spiritual work of the church, and a Board of Deacons to handle the loose plate offerings.

Men of The Peoples Church – on the move to 100 Bloor Street East.

"A paid office staff is responsible for the envelopes. At present there are 13 managers, over 240 elders and 14 deacons, all men of missionary vision, and all teetotalers and non-smokers. On February 21 1936, in order to avoid any possibility of private ownership or personal profit, we had the work incorporated under a Board of Directors, as a non-profit organization, and obtained a government charter. Our funds and property holdings therefore are thus completely safeguarded, for we can do only what our charter allows.

"Those who have been born again and are interested enough to contribute regularly to our foreign missionary work, are considered adherents of the church. At the present time we have over 4,000 on our roll. We dedicate children, baptize believers, and observe the Lord's Supper, but we do not make baptism a door to communion and church membership.

"The Peoples Church, I feel, has been the fulfillment of the vision on the log of July 11, 1919, on the Pacific Coast. To God be the glory."

OJS

Sunday night at 100 Bloor Street East. The auditorium held about 2,000. Mr. Lehman and Oswald Smith center front.

A tight ship.

In many ways, The Peoples Church could be characterized as a reflection of the character of its leader, Oswald Smith. He ran a tight ship. For every three dollars spent at the church, seven were sent to missions. Redecorating more often meant scrubbing, rather than painting the walls. Oswald would say, "Forget about painting the church. They need 10,000 Bibles in Borneo." Every expenditure had to pass under Oswald's eagle eye. Incoming elastics, string and wrapping paper were saved to use for outgoing mail. Long distance calls were made only as a last resort. Not one penny was spent that could possibly be saved and sent to missions.

"The church books are always open to anyone, and it's certain that the money goes where it's supposed to. These guys do a good job."

Concession by Gordon Sinclair, radio commentator and Canada's most caustic religion critic.

No oak-paneled refuge, Oswald's office was a desk in the corner of the general office. Privacy was at a minimum. One day when a dentist who had been stirred by listening to the radio broadcast, arrived to speak privately with Oswald, he was taken into the office washroom, the only place they could be alone. There they knelt as Oswald led the man into salvation.

Certain things, like slander and tardiness, were not tolerated. Oswald would sternly admonish the culprit: "Slander is the devil's work; don't you do it for him." Meetings began and concluded precisely on time, to the minute. Like money, time was not wasted. Platform chairs were placed close to the pulpit so that the next person to speak would take the microphone as soon as the previous person finished.

The staff was minimal: Eldon Lehman, the songleader, doubled as the bookkeeper, and two secretaries struggled on ancient typewriters to keep up with Oswald's expectations for immediacy. Everything had to be completed by the end of the week so that Mondays could begin with a clean slate. Mail was handled and dealt with only once. Despite his intolerance for slackness, Oswald was very sensitive to the needs of his workers. He always noticed if they appeared overly tired and would suggest they get some rest and start fresh in the morning. The staff were unquestionably loyal to him. They knew he prayed daily for them and was concerned with the circumstances of their lives, as demonstrated by his timely letters and gifts.

On May 31, 1936, Oswald received his first honorary Doctor of Divinity degree from Asbury College in Wilmore, Kentucky. Deeply humbled by the experience, the next week he sailed on the Queen Mary to London, to fill the pulpit in Spurgeon's London Tabernacle until the end of June. From there, he returned to the Russian mission fields – a large life for the once small frail boy from Embro.

"As He called the great apostle, so He chooses men today; I am one whom He has chosen and I dare not disobey."

OJS

Spiritual leaders.

Oswald required all of his elders, as far as possible, to be on their knees with him at the 10:15 a.m. Sunday prayer meeting, the 6:00 p.m. Personal Workers' prayer meeting Sunday evenings and at the "Half-Night of Prayer" the first Friday of every month. There was some overlapping in the organization, in that the ushers were always elders first, to ensure that the people meeting the public were mature, spiritual people. Having experienced the heartache involved from overlooking this prerequisite, Oswald developed a formula for determining who could be considered for leadership in The Peoples Church.

Oswald Smith's Requirements for Leadership

"As well as the Scriptural requirements for elders and deacons, I look for men who:
- put the spiritual work of the church first
- are men of prayer in every sense of the word
- never miss a prayer meeting
- are anxious to see souls saved.

"I watch them for months; I look for men who:
- have no use for the world or worldly pleasures *(Oswald never preached against movies, dances, or other common pleasures.)*
- back up this concern with constant giving. I know a man's heart goes where his money goes. If they have a true heart for God's work, they will see that a good portion of their money goes to God's work.

"By this and this alone we must judge all spirituality, because if a man is truly spiritual, if he is a real Bible student, if his doctrines are Scriptural,
- he will want to carry out our Lord's last orders: 'Go ye into all the world and preach the Gospel to every creature.'

"A truly spiritual man will put world evangelism first; and he will give liberally to missions. Otherwise, all our Bible knowledge, all our doctrinal standards are nothing but make-believe. Thus I discovered that if a man attended the services faithfully, including the prayer services, and gave regularly; if he showed a keen interest in souls and missions, I could generally count on him to back our purposes; he was a pretty safe man to put in office."

"Not I, but Christ."

"So much to do and so little time."

"Life is less than worthless till my all I give."

OJS

Dr. Ralph Hooper,
Associate Pastor.

Rev. P.W. Philpott,
Associate Pastor.

Dr. Robert Watt,
Visitation Pastor.

Donald Newman,
Associate Pastor.

Dr. Peter Wiseman,
Associate Pastor.

Eldon B. Lehman, Director of
Music and Administration.

Rev. F. Dickie,
Associate Pastor.

Rev. A. Sims,
Associate Pastor.

Pastoral staff.

Although Dr. Ralph Hooper, Dr. Peter Wiseman, Rev. F. Dickie, and Rev. A. Sims (an associate from Christie Street) were recognized as Associate Pastors in the early days, they did not share the pulpit in the manner of regular assistants. They were paid only when they preached and had no administrative duties. Eldon B. Lehman served as Director of Music and Business Manager from 1930 to 1941. In 1943, Rev. P.W. Philpott, an outstanding preacher from the great Moody Church in Chicago, became Oswald's Associate Pastor, and was with him for nearly ten years. Donald Newman served as Director of Music and Business Manager from 1952 to 1959. These men provided a stabilizing presence during Oswald's travels. George Stenton, Oswald's faithful prayer partner, served as a "Visiting Minister" from 1942 to 1956, upon retirement from his regular work. Dr. Robert Watt, who previously served as President of the Livingstone Press, served in the same capacity from 1954 until 1974. Oswald, however, continued to visit the very ill and the elders.

"For me to live is Christ."

Throughout all the years of birthing The Peoples Church, the Smiths took nothing for themselves beyond necessity, and only that which was absolutely designated for personal use. Once the church was properly established, they were able to live in relative comfort. Although the salary from the church was always modest, they did receive remuneration for related expenses and love offerings from other churches where Oswald preached. These were quite apart from the many thousands of dollars he raised for overseas aid and deposited with The Peoples Missionary Society. From the home base of The Peoples Church, Oswald continued to be a world-watcher. The church was never designed as an end unto itself, a traditional family church, but rather as a vehicle to channel God's love and His salvation to hearts around the world.

"The greatest need of Christians,
the greatest need of the Church, has
not changed. More than ever today
we need the unction of the Holy
Spirit. When the Holy Spirit
first came on the apostles, there was
boldness, power, conviction and
conversion. The people came gladly;
they continued steadfastly; they
praised God, suffered persecution,
and they prayed. When the Holy
Spirit takes control in a church,
there will be blessing and unity and
power. Souls will be saved. The
Gospel will go out. There will be a
spiritual work. Perennial revival is
only possible where there is continuous
brokenness of heart." O.J.S.

Into all the World

"So he departed thence, and found Elisha the son of Shephat, who was plowing with twelve yolk of oxen before him, and he with the twelfth; and Elijah passed by him, and cast his mantle upon him."

1 Kings 19:19

Into all the World

Three

The Son:

Dr. Paul Brainerd Smith

The Peoples Church
Senior Pastor
1959 – 1983

Dr. Oswald J. Smith.

Passing the Mantle

From Father...

Early years.
Paul Brainerd Smith, like his father, entered the world as a frail, delicate boy, but was destined to preach the Gospel to multitudes around the world. Born in 1921, just as the roots of The Peoples Church were beginning to be established in Massey Hall, he grew up with the church.

Paul's ministry really began at the age of five, when he began to sing in his father's meetings. He was written up in newspaper accounts as "The Golden-voiced Soloist". Though not physically strong, Paul had no trouble projecting his deep, full voice to over two thousand people. That same year, he walked down the aisle after his father had preached, and took his place at the altar with the others seeking salvation.

At the age of ten, he was the featured soloist whenever "The College Girl Evangelist", Mary Agnes Wagner, brought her old-time revival preaching to the church. He was hailed as the "local songbird" and popularized Oswald's hymn, "There is Nothing too Hard for Jesus." Paul never missed a meeting, and tagged along wherever his father went.

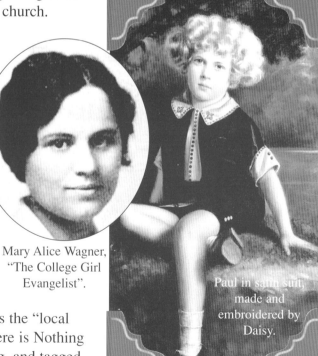

Mary Alice Wagner, "The College Girl Evangelist".

Paul in satin suit, made and embroidered by Daisy.

Paul B. Smith, "The Golden-voiced Soloist."

To Son.

Paul B. Smith

"Father didn't leave; he simply moved over."
PBS

Dr. Paul B. Smith.

Fulfilling his "faith promises."
During his high school years, Paul became fascinated with a humbug recipe and began to make humbugs in huge quantities. Rewiring the basement, so he could have adequate light, he used the heating elements from the furnace to make his candy, and then packaged it in cellophane bags to sell in the Missionary Conference; thus enabling himself to fulfill the small "faith promises" he made as a teenager.

Oswald with Hope, Paul and Glen.

Higher education.

Paul enrolled in Bob Jones University in Cleveland, Tennessee, at the age of 18. Like his father, he knew that he was born to preach, and so began to spend weekends reaching out and ministering to the hill people in the moonshine territory of the Tennessee hills.

Because of the war, Paul's American education was cut short, necessitating registration in a Canadian university where he could receive military training. At Union College, on the west coast, he was able to combine this requirement with seminary studies and receive recognition for his American credits.

Losing his faith.

However, the benefits evolved into tragedy as Paul grew increasingly cynical, thanks to the teaching of theology by liberal professors. Gradually, he lost his faith completely. Turning entirely from the knowledge Oswald and Daisy had instilled in him from birth, Paul drifted aimlessly for awhile.

These were enormous times of testing for Oswald and Daisy. Neither night nor day offered respite from the agony of losing their son to a faithless existence. Week after week, they cried out to God to return Paul to the heart of God and set him on fire to preach the full Gospel. Many nights, they prayed all through the night, asking God to forgive them for sending Paul to the wrong school.

Gradually, they began to see their son turning back to truth. Before long, he discarded the emptiness of liberality and began once again to preach with passion and blessing. He took a student pastorate in the Hillsburg Baptist Church, where he was ordained in 1945.

Graduation.

PAUL B. SMITH
BOB JONES COLLEGE
CLEVELAND, TENNESSEE

March 10, 1940

Dears —

It is 10.00 p. m. Sunday night March 10, 1940 and I have preached my first sermon — at the age of eighteen years and nine months at Conasauga Tennessee in the Baptist church.

I've been looking forward to this for a long time and now its come and gone. I preached on the text "and they all with one consent began to make excuse" I had enough material for a sermon that would have

lasted for an hour and a half, but I talked so fast that I crowded it all into twenty-five minutes. There were about sixty-five people there, mountaineers and farmers. I gave an invitation and one boy about sixteen raised his hand, but did not come forward.

The surface seems to be broken now, however, because, whereas at the start we were just seeming to hit them on the outside now we have gotten to know them and are much encouraged. After the service three of the real christian women talked to us outside the church about the work

Paul B. Smith

They want us to come out early next week and have a prayer meeting in one of their homes to pray for the service. One of the women has a husband that has drifted back into sin and she wants us to come and talk to him. They thanked us ever so much for coming out to preach and they urged us to keep on coming.

One of the women said that she loved to see young fellows preaching and that if only her son would ever get up in the pulpit she would "really take

wings and "fly".

Praise God! I believe he is going to answer our prayers and that we will soon have a break.

They even took up an offering to pay for our gas tonight ($1.08) Now there is no expense whereas it used to cost us about 40¢ each every time.

I hope you are all remembering me and our work in prayer. I'm seeing more & more that nothing can be done aside from prayer. I wish you would tell Mrs Scott about my work and let her have the women pray for me. I have more faith in the prayers of those women than

Portion of a letter from Paul to his family at home.

A young Billy Graham, guest speaker for The Peoples Church youth. Paul Smith in the front row.

Paul and Anita.

Anita Lawson moved to Canada with her family, from their native Ireland, in 1929. She was blessed with a beautiful voice and was singing in a Toronto church when she and Paul met. Married on June 8, 1946, they travelled together in his evangelistic work until the first of their three children arrived.

Paul was 25 years old when he and Anita took their first overseas trip together, an evangelistic crusade to the British Isles with Oswald, in 1946. Anita sang at every service and did secretarial work for her father-in-law.

A heart for missions.

Paul's first taste of the foreign fields was just the beginning of satisfying his voracious appetite for missions – whetted with every missions conference since the beginning of the church, and his father's wondrous tales of far off lands. Hearing the missionaries and foreign nationals who visited in his home, tell stories of how God directed the lives of missionaries,

Paul B. Smith

Rev. Paul B. Smith, B.A., and Anita Lawson, signing the register. They were married in The Peoples Church on June 8, 1946, by Dr. O.J. Smith, before an audience that overflowed the aisles and the vestibules.

Paul during his first overseas crusade to the British Isles. Here seen beside the noted well in St. Andrews, Scotland, down which the bodies of the martyred Covenanters were thrown by the Catholics.

gave Paul a great hunger to serve. He had always known he would preach. In 1949, he went to Haiti under the auspices of World Team Mission, and preached to audiences of over six thousand people several times a day.

In 1951, he attended a leaders' conference at Winona Lake, Indiana, organized by Youth for Christ. By this time, he was well known as a youth evangelist. The plea for workers to go to Formosa and Japan went straight to Paul's heart, and he responded, offering his life for service in the Far East. When he was unable to raise the necessary support, despite having been accepted to go, Paul searched his heart and cried out to God for understanding.

As so often happens, the immediacy of the devastation clouded his ability to see the greater magnitude of God's plan for his life.

Paul Smith ministering in Glasgow – 1946.

Johnny Ambrose

SECOND GREAT WEEK
with
PAUL SMITH and JOHNNY AMBROSE
in
Trinity United Church, Madoc

1958

FRIDAY, 7.45 P.M.
LOVE, COURTSHIP, MARRIAGE AND THE CHRISTIAN HOME — Family Night, a prize for the Largest Family.
I SAW EUROPE IN 1958 — Coloured Motion Pictures of Intriguing Paris, Romantic Venice, Sunny Nice and Imperial Rome.

SUNDAY, 7.15 P.M.
WHAT WILL HAPPEN TO THE PEOPLE OF MADOC WHO STAY OUT AFTER MIDNIGHT?

MONDAY, 7.45 P.M.
THE CHRISTIAN YOUNG PERSON IN THIS MODERN WORLD — How to know where to go and what to do.
WHEN VOODOOISM MEETS GOD—Colored Motion Pictures

TUESDAY, 7.45 P.M.

Second Great Week
WITH
SMITH and HENDERSON
ST. JOHN MENNONITE CHURCH
Mile East of Pandora, Ohio

Paul Smith

Ministering from sea to sea.

On the foreign field – Jamaica, 1948.

Christ for SOUTHEASTERN SASKATCHEWAN
UNION REVIVAL CAMPAIGN

Paul and Anita
Children: Jann, Glen and Jill.

Jennifer Jann Smith.

Jann's son, Chris Avalos.

Andrea Jill Smith.

Jill's children;
Hope, Connor and Jane Murdoch.

Grandchildren: Christopher, Hope, Connor, and Jane.

Oswald Glen Smith.

Jann Avalos, Glen Smith and Jill Murdoch.

Anita and Paul.

Into all the World

Joining the staff of The Peoples Church.

In 1952, the Board of Managers invited Paul to join the staff as Assistant Pastor. It was a deeply gratifying day for Oswald, who had always hoped Paul would one day succeed him at the church, so that he could be free to enjoy ministry overseas and help other congregations to increase their giving to missions.

In 1958, on his return from another South American campaign, Oswald was pleased to find everything in excellent order, and suggested to Paul that they make it official and give him the title of Senior Pastor, with Oswald retaining the position of Missionary Pastor to oversee the giving and the Missions Convention.

Initially, Paul agreed, but then submitted his resignation, saying:

"Father, it will never work. Don't give in your resignation; give them mine instead. To leave you with the missionary convention is to leave you with the heart of the church. So long as you are connected in any way with the church, you will always he regarded as the senior pastor. I would just be holding the ropes until the "real pastor" returns. I'm just "young Paul" to most of the elders, and that is what I will always be. So I'm leaving to go into full-time evangelism. You have done a fabulous job of founding and running The Peoples Church, and I agree with Billy Graham that you are undoubtedly the most remarkable man I have ever known. I stand back and watch in abject and

A global view – Dr. Paul B. Smith, Virgil Zappatta, Dr. O.J. Smith, Charles Blair and Dr. Watt.

The Induction of Paul Brainerd Smith into The Peoples Church, 1959.

mute amazement. I will never be the man you have been. It's hard to express what a son feels for a great father. You've done so much for me that to begin to enumerate would he impossible, and any kind of thank-you would be almost sacrilegious. I want you to know that I am very proud of you as a great man, and I love you very much as a father."

Reflecting on the words of the letter, Oswald understood the struggles of Paul's heart. Nevertheless, remembering the letters of resignation he would have given anything to retrieve in his own years of ministry, he simply slid the letter into a drawer and did not mention it to anyone.

When he realized the letter had not been given to the board, Paul simply continued his usual duties until one day when Oswald again broached the subject.

"Paul, I see what you mean about the crowds beginning to slack off. All that you have been saying is true: there are no empty pews yet, but the people are no longer parked in tight. They rarely are standing around the back or sitting in the aisles any more. So many have moved to the suburbs, as you have pointed out. If they drive back downtown, there is no place to park here. It's not like the old days when everyone used to come by streetcar. I've decided you are right – the time has come to relocate. But that is a task I feel too old to undertake, whereas you are just coming into your prime. You are the one who must head it up, choose the new location, design and build the new complex, bring in the people. Will you do it?"

Realizing that such a move would signal a "new day", Paul agreed, and was inducted as Senior Pastor of The Peoples Church on the first Sunday of 1959. Immediately following his Induction, Paul assembled the board and proposed finding a building site.

"I have only one piece of advice, Paul: don't let your people get bored. A pastor should never overexpose himself. Your people should hear other voices, better voices than your own. And remember, it takes all kinds of bait to catch all kinds of fish."
OJS

Four

Moving the Church

Bloor St.
to
Sheppard Ave.

Facts About the Work...

PEOPLES CHURCH

FOUNDER AND PASTOR EMERITUS
REV. OSWALD J. SMITH, D.D., Litt.D., LL.D.,
F.R.G.S., M.R.S.L., M.S.C.A.

PASTOR
REV. PAUL B. SMITH, B.A., F.R.G.S.

ASSISTANT PASTOR
REV. ROBERT WATT

ELDERS

Abbott, Gordon	Leigh, O. A.
Alm, Olaf	Lenaghan, Jas.
Anderson, J. C.	Lennox, R. C.
Ashley, Ray	Linton, John
Atkinson, Kenneth	Lutey, T. C.
Bakewell, W.	MacQueen, Douglas
Baldock, A.	McCartney, Mel
Barrington, F. N.	Mackintosh, K. M.
Baxter, Robert	Malcolm, J. D.
Bell, Alex.	Manthorpe, Ross
Bender, G. C.	Marek, Joseph
Betsworth, William	McClure, A.
Black, W. H.	McDowell, Melvin
Botsford, H. N.	McIsaac, Thos.
Bowman, Karl	McKibbon, Billy
Brown, A. G.	McLeod, J. F.
Bignell, H. H.	McQueen, Geo. H.
Billings, C. S.	Merenick, James
Billings, D. G.	Neal, Geo. J.
Boyd, Glover	Nelson, Oscar
Buchanan, D. W.	Niles, L.
Budgell, John	Orr, A. N.
Bugden, Torrey	Owen, H.
Caddell, Wilbur	Parker, Lloyd
Chadwick, F. R.	Paul, Cornelius
Champion, A. B.	Pelman, H. Ross
Chote, J.	Petch, Glenn
Clark, Leonard	Phinnemore, H. H.
Courtney, J. W.	Pike, Jesse
Crouch, Harvey	Pratt, Edward
Dade, John	Ralston, Clare
Dick, Russell	Redner, Bernard
Dickey, R. W.	Reed, Walter
Eakin, S.	Reid, D. G.
Ellis, E. H.	Reid, Robert
Fearn, Alfred	Roberts, E. G.
Ferguson, Dr. W. N.	Roberts, Watkin R.
Fleck, Wm.	Robinson, A. H.
Fogarty, Bruce	Rochester, W. M.
Ford, A. F.	Russell, Herbert
Gibb, Douglass	Scott, James
Gillespie, Wm.	Sharratt, A. H.
Graham, Lloyd	Shock, P.
Greenwood, G. W.	Small, W. L.
Hadlow, Ernie	Smith, Dr. Glen
Hall, T. G.	Smith, G. Carl
Hamilton, Wm.	Soule, Henry
Handy, Elmer	Squirrell, H.
Hammond, T. R.	Spencer, David F.
Hill, J. D.	Stedlebauer, Elliott
Hoag, E. S.	Sweeny, Desmond
Hoyler, Thomas	Topping, A. R.
Huffman, F.	Trenchard, Frank
Hunt, E. L.	Turner, H. Earl
Hunt, Stan	Turner, K. B.
Huntley, Walter	Turvill, W. N.
Irving, Harold	Veitch, M. L.
Jackson, Chas.	Wanless, H. P.
Jones, E. P.	Ward, Thos.
Kennedy, Lloyd	Warner, A. F.
Kennedy, Stanley	Webb, Thomas
Kerr, Frank	Webber, Gus
King, Gerald	West, D. G.
King, L. Y.	West, J. H.
Klemm, E. L.	Wickware, Ralph
Laksmanis, A.	Wilton, Joseph
Leck, Roy	Williams, Robt.
	Wright, W. F.

THE PEOPLES CHURCH

The Peoples Church is an independent work, standing pre-eminently for the conversion of souls, the edification of believers, and world-wide evangelism, emphasizing especially the four great essentials: Salvation, the Deeper Life, Foreign Missions, and our Lord's Return; endeavouring by every means to get the Message to the Christless masses, both at home and abroad, in the shortest possible time.

We believe in an unmutilated Bible; salvation through the blood of Christ; entire separation from the world; victory over all known sin through the indwelling Spirit, rugged consecration to sacrificial service; practical faith in the sufficiency of Christ for spiritual, temporal and physical needs; purifying hope of the Lord's return; and a burning missionary zeal for the bringing back of the King through world evangelization.

We dedicate children, baptize believers, and observe the Lord's Supper.

THE PEOPLES MISSIONARY SOCIETY

President .... Dr. Oswald J. Smith
Vice-President .... Rev. Paul B. Smith

The Peoples Missionary Society contributes over a quarter of a million dollars a year toward the "personal" support of over 350 missionaries in some 40 Fields under 35 Faith Missionary Societies. Ask for particulars.

Send your gift for the support of this great work, and you will receive an official receipt, and "The Peoples Magazine", which contains spiritual articles and up-to-date reports direct from the Fields.

Make cheques payable and address all communications to The Peoples Missionary Society, 100 Bloor East, Toronto, Canada.

THE PEOPLES MAGAZINE

The Peoples Magazine is the official organ of The Peoples Church and the Peoples Missionary Society, Dr. Oswald J. Smith, Editor, Rev. Paul B. Smith, Assistant Editor.

Those who contribute $2.00 or more, which is the subscription price, will receive The Peoples Magazine for two years, free.

Advertising Rates: $50.00 a page; $60.00 for outside back cover. No smaller Ads accepted.

Entered as 2nd class matter, P.O. Dept., Ottawa.

GOVERNMENT

The Peoples Church has a Board of Managers to look after the business end of the work, a Board of Elders to take care of the spiritual work of the church, and a Board of Deacons to handle the loose plate offerings. A paid office staff is responsible for the envelopes. Only men who are backing our great world-wide program are chosen as Elders, and if at any time they are unable to support the policies of the Church, they are automatically dropped. At present there are 14 managers, 130 elders and 11 deacons, all men of missionary vision, evangelism and spirituality.

On Feb. 21st, 1936, in order to avoid any possibility of private ownership or personal profit, we had the work incorporated under a Board of Directors, as a non-profit organization, and obtained a government charter. Our funds and property holdings therefore are thus completely safeguarded, for we can do only what our charter allows.

Those who have been born again and are interested enough to contribute regularly to our foreign missionary work, are considered adherents of the church. They do not join, but they are closer to us as they attend, give and serve, than they could possibly be had they been enrolled as members. If they have not given for three years they are automatically dropped, so that our list is always up-to-date. At the present time we have approximately 3,000 on our roll.

OUR CHURCH POLICY

No conflicting meetings are ever held during evangelistic campaigns, Bible conferences, or missionary conventions, either inside or outside the church, or on the nights when regular services are held. Everyone co-operates in the work of the whole church.

OUR AMERICAN OFFICE

Refugee Evangelistic Association (Rev. M. Billester, Pres.), Box 152 El Monte, Calif.

AUDITORS

The Auditors of The Peoples Church are the well-known firm, Gunn, Roberts & Co., chartered accountants. Their Financial Statement, showing receipts and expenditures, is published each year.

MANAGERS

President .... Paul B. Smith
First Vice-President .... Oswald J. Smith
Second Vice-President ...... John E. T. Dade
Secretary .... Clare Ralston
Treasurer .... Bruce Fogarty
W. Bakewell, C. S. Billings, Harold Botsford, Wm. Hamilton, Walt Huntley, E. L. Klemm, H. H. Phinnemore, Carl G. Smith, M. L. Veitch.

DEACONS

Chairman — Chas. Jackson
W. H. Black, D. W. Buchanan, H. Irving, Frank Kerr, L. Y. King, T. C. Lutey, W. L. Small, H. E. Turner, Art Orr, W. F. Wright.

The new Senior Pastor

New beginnings for the "Old Time Religion".

Paul Smith knew that the power of the Gospel lay in the Gospel itself, rather than on any flashy spins he might conceive. For that reason, The Peoples Church family was able to relax with Paul, secure in the knowledge that the fundamentals would remain solidly intact.

While he recognized the importance of staying slightly ahead of the times, Paul never fell into the trap of reflecting popular trends. His father's "old-time religion" was good enough for him.

Paul's style differed somewhat from that of his father. While Oswald had a wonderful sense of humour, it was cast within a restless intensity of purpose. Paul, on the other hand, had a more relaxed, though forthright, joviality.

Other things did not change. Like his father, Paul was very much in tune with the importance of maintaining an underlying sense of excitement, and continued to generate enthusiasm for the work of the Lord. Both father and son spoke to the hurts of individuals, connecting them to the Source of all healing, reconciliation and power. Neither used flashy rhetoric nor strutted for the cameras. Their focus was to give glory to God and hope to the hopeless.

The same focus... expanded. A strong family church.
While assuring the people that the missionary zeal of his father would not be diminished under his leadership, and that there would be no less passion for the salvation of souls, Paul encouraged the congregation to look at the changing face of society.

Post-war Toronto was moving towards the suburbs. This meant that evening services were thinning, because, rather than arriving by streetcar, many were driving their cars long distances into the heart of the city, and then paying to park once they got there. More mothers were working, meaning that they were tired, and less willing to attend campaigns night after night. The once sedate "Toronto the Good" was increasingly encouraging sporting events and shopping on Sundays. With the advent of television and the variety of entertainment now available in the city, The Peoples Church was no longer regarded as "the best entertainment in town".

In order to remain a strong missionary church, it was time for The Peoples Church to become a strong family church. It needed to be equipped with programs and facilities to capture children and families for Christ before they got lost in the midst of a Christian environment. It needed to become, *"The family church that puts World Missions first."*

Into all the World

The importance of music.

With his background in music, Paul understood the tremendous importance of music, not only to the church in general, but to young people in particular. Thus, one of the first things he did, was to hire a full-time Minister of Music.

David E. Williams, a brilliant composer and musician who attended the church in his student days, earned his music credentials at Bob Jones University and the University of Toronto. His job description, as outlined by Paul, involved the development of the "finest music program any church could have, one that can involve every age group and every member of the family."

Music in The Peoples Church
By David E. Williams, B.A.

Listen: all music has ceased. The woods are silent, for the birds refuse to sing. The choirs stand silently in the choir loft; they refuse to sing. The orchestra sits in place, but there are no enchanting melodies because they will not play. The band waits in silence. No stirring, thrilling music breaks the monotony. "We will not play."

What has caused this tragedy? How is it that these makers of beauty in sound will not play or sing? I will tell you: It is because the indifferent soul has voted "NO MUSIC". "When did I vote?" you ask. When you refused to open your hymnal to sing God's praises with the congregation, you voted NO CONGREGATIONAL SINGING. When you refused to use the voice God has given you to join in the choir ministry, you voted NO ADULT CHOIR. When you refused to bring your child to junior choir, you voted NO CHILDREN'S CHOIRS. Yes, when you would not use the talent God gave to you to play with the band, you voted NO BAND. So this is the result: NO MUSIC.

There is no music in the woods either. The birds refuse to sing because they are not all trained. They cannot read music. They never sang in a choir before, and so they will not venture out to fill the air with their golden sounds.

Now you and I both know that the birds do not refuse to sing. Instead of excuses and reasons, from hearts filled with praise for the God who made them, their tiny throbbing throats pour out a myriad of magic melodies.

What a shame that we owe God the most, seem to love Him the least. When so great salvation is ours, we should be the most thankful; every voice and talent raised in glorious praise to a glorious Saviour. "O sing unto the Lord a new song: sing unto the Lord, all the earth" (Psalm 96:1).

"Make a joyful noise unto the Lord, all ye lands. Serve the Lord with gladness: come before his presence with singing" (Psalm 100:1, 2). "Praise ye the Lord. Praise God in his sanctuary: praise him in the firmament of his power . . . Praise him with the sound of

David E. Williams

the trumpet: praise him with the psaltery and harp . . . Praise him with stringed instruments and organs" (Psalm 150:1, 3, 4b).

Throughout the ages of time, music has played a most important part in the religions of all peoples. It has varied from the restricted simple rhythms of the aboriginal peoples, to complex melodies and harmonies of modern civilization.

Here at The Peoples Church, music plays just as important a role in the church programme as it does anywhere today. In accordance with this importance, in cooperation with the Pastor, and with the total church programme taken into consideration, I have set out some goals that will have to be achieved. Reaching these goals will enable us to come much closer to the spiritual effectiveness that the music ministry should have.

A ministry as important as the ministry of music cannot be allowed to go along in a slip-shod manner. It must be as effective and efficient as we can make it. Therefore, our first need is for a comprehensive and efficient organization.

Also in the future we are looking to the time when we will not only be able to sing evangelistic songs in a true evangelistic manner, but be just as competent in presenting Handel's "Messiah" or Haydn's "Creation" with a choir of over one hundred voices. This means a sound training programme starting with little children. Therefore, a completely graded choral and instrumental programme is a must. This is a vast opportunity for spiritual training for these youngsters as well as musical instruction, and we intend to make every use of it.

Finally, we could have the best music in the world and it would mean nothing unless used and directed in a spiritual manner. Remember, we use music for the sake of Christ, not for the sake of music itself. Therefore, incorporated along with the organization, the children's choirs, the ensembles, the instrumental work, and the musical aid given to all phases of the church programme, there will be a strong emphasis on not just spiritual music but consecrated musicians as well.

Sunday School.
Oswald never took his own children to Sunday School; he paid close attention to their Bible teaching at home, but did not want to weary them with too much church. While the Bloor Street Sunday School attendance occasionally tipped the four hundred mark, it was never a focus for Oswald, who believed the 10:30 a.m. prayer meeting to be of greater importance.

The Peoples Church – an early Sunday School group.
Oswald Smith far left.

All that was about to change. Paul surprised the elders with his announcement that he would be teaching a Sunday School class for them at the regular Sunday School time.

> "We'll pray and I'll teach a lesson. I am deeply concerned about our own boys and girls who look saved and act saved, lost in the midst of a Christian environment. We must do everything we can to capture them for Christ. We must do all we can to help fathers and mothers bring their children to a full commitment with Jesus Christ. And it starts right here with us – we must set an example of attendance at all the services of the church."

While Paul's foresight was critical to the life of The Peoples Church, the development of a strong family program, in the cramped Bloor Street facilities, was next to impossible.

A time of important decisions.

The search for a building site.
With all of these factors in mind, the church began to search in earnest for a suitable building site. Following consultation with a city planner, it was determined that the intersection of the 401 Highway and Yonge Street would mark the center of the urban sprawl within 15 or 20 years. Thus it was that Paul directed the real estate agents to find a plot of land within a one-and one-half mile radius of the intersection. Before long, they returned with a five-acre property almost right on target, on Sheppard Avenue. It was purchased for $151,250.

The

PEOPLES
MAGAZINE

OSWALD J. SMITH, Litt.D., Editor

Volume 40   TORONTO, CANADA, SECOND QUARTER, 1961   Number 4 - 6

THE TABERNACLE ERA

By Paul B. Smith

My father ministered through the Tabernacle Era in America. He founded and pastored a huge work in Toronto, Canada. However, this was just one of a great network of similar places that stretch from Canada to Florida and from the Atlantic to the Pacific coasts in North America.

I was reared in those days and remember them quite vividly. The Alliance Tabernacle in Toronto, which my father built and where I spent my early boyhood days, was typical. It grew out of a great evangelistic campaign that drew unprecedented crowds in the city and stirred up a great deal of newspaper publicity.

My father, Dr. Oswald J. Smith, had been one of the organizing directors of the campaign and pastor of a struggling little local Christian and Missionary Alliance Church.

He capitalized on the momentum of the crusade by immediately erecting a tent, larger than Toronto had ever seen, for religious meetings. For six months without a break — Sunday through Sunday — he promoted a daily series of evangelistic campaigns.

The crowds continued to come. There was so much interest that when the first newspaper advertisement indicated that the tent was erected but there were no seats, the people brought their own kitchen chairs and literally furnished an entire "Canvas Cathedral" without spending a cent. This was typical throughout the country.

Sensationalism, originality, and unflagging zeal were combined with an unusually deep spiritual program to set in motion an evangelistic movement that held aloft the Christian flag when it was in danger of being smeared hopelessly in the mud of modernism.

My father often reminisces about those days and has admitted that sometimes the evangelists were quite mediocre and the music, in the beginning, was completely unprofessional.

Paul Smith

None of the musicians received any honorarium. The pianists and song leaders were usually business men who considered this an outlet for their Christian service.

When the famous Cleveland Colored Quintette came to Toronto the first time, they were all still in business in Cleveland and simply took leave of absence long enough for the Toronto Campaign. They worked for twenty-five dollars a week and slept on cots erected in the meeting place. But the crowds came and many souls were saved.

PERMANENT STRUCTURES

The next step was from the tent to some kind of permanent structure. A regular church edifice would never have sufficed. There were already hundreds of church buildings in Toronto — most of them empty and dead, caught in the strangle hold of a form of modernism that is seldom seen today.

There was no thought of Sunday School space for educational facilities. The main thing was to produce the cheapest kind of building that would accommodate the most people. A steel barn constructed of hollow tile served this purpose.

There was no real design to the Alliance Tabernacle in Toronto. It looked like an indoor skating rink or stadium with benches packed as closely together as possible.

The Peoples Magazine — Second Quarter, 1961   3

In many cities the sawdust floor of the tents was brought right into the new religious barn and, in some cases, it was years before a proper floor was laid.

The building in Toronto seated over 2,500 people and cost only $40,000. I can still remember the crowds that used to come.

Those were the days when people would pour off the street car like sheep out of a truck. By six o'clock every Sunday night they would run all the way from the street car line to the Tabernacle — two full city blocks—to assure having a seat.

This was true on week nights as well. Sometimes there would be as many as a thousand people on the outside looking through the open windows and hoping in vain to get in.

The choir, ushers and personal workers came every evening without fail. I do not know how they managed it, but they came. The unpaid song leader never missed a service.

The book stand was always open week days and thousands of volumes were sold, carrying a steady flow of Gospel literature and Bible teaching into multitudes of homes.

The same thing happened in other big cities. My father did a considerable amount of evangelistic work in those days, as he does today, but most of the places where he ministered were tabernacles similar to his own in Toronto— great sprawling, growing centres of evangelism that had caught the ear of a public that had been lulled to sleep by a lifeless form of denominationalism and churchianity.

SOLDIERS OF THE CROSS

I remember some of the places and names. W. T. Watson had one in St. Petersburg, Florida. His was so big that he was able to attract such men as Gypsy Smith, Billy Sunday, W. B. Riley, Gerald B. Winrod, Paul Rood, and countless other great Soldiers of the Cross.

George Ziemer spearheaded an aggressive work in Milwaukee, Wisconsin. There was John Minder in Tampa, Tingley in Birmingham, Churchill in Buffalo, Cadel in Indianapolis, Rediger in Fort Wayne, Williams in Minneapolis, David in

What is His Worth?

"Oh, what is his worth, sweet maiden?"
    I asked in an anxious tone,
"This one whom you love so dearly,
    Come, tell me, for what is he known?"

The maiden turned in the twilight
    As with radiant face she said,
"The one whom I love so dearly
    And whom I some day shall wed,

"Can buy me the things that I long for
    And give me a home of my own;
He is able to keep me in comfort,
    His wealth is entirely unknown.

"His figure is manly and handsome
    And dearly he loves me, I know;
Oh, I'm sure that with him I'll be happy
    Wherever he wants me to go."

She paused and I waited a moment,
    Then slowly and sadly replied,
"And is there no more you can tell me
    Of the one who would make you his bride?

"Have you ever thought of the question
    Regarding his standard of life?
Is it clean, is it noble and manly,
    Is he worthy to call you his wife?

"He demands that you shall be faithful
    For his standard of woman is high,
But unless he's as pure as you are
    'Twere better that you should die.

"Have you thought of his daily habits,
    Does he take of the fatal glass?
Oh, beware lest the bride of the present
    Be the wife of the drunkard, alas!

"Does he love to study his Bible,
    To frequent the house of pray'r?
You need not fear the future
    If his life is centred there.

"It may be that he loves you at present
    But a day will be coming when
The glow on your cheek will vanish,
    Are you sure he will love you then?

"Oh, tell me, sweet maiden, I pray you,
    Come, tell me his worth ere you go."
She sobbed thro' the fading twilight,
    "I can't for I do not know."
                    —OSWALD J. SMITH
Chicago,
Feb., 1913.

Atlanta, Berg in Miami, Richey in Houston, Fitch in Ottawa, Swain in Nashville, Springer in Englewood . . . and scores of others.

All of them drew huge crowds, ran a continual series of evangelistic campaigns, and saw hundreds of souls saved. Perhaps an aggregate of the spiritual decisions made from coast to coast in the tabernacles would leave modern evangelism far in the background.

Such a list could never be completed without the name of Paul

Rader and the Chicago Gospel Tabernacle. Rader built a barn in the roaring centre of the Gateway to the West that could accommodate five thousand people.

He invited evangelists from all over the world to share his pulpit, but always drew larger crowds when he preached himself than his guests could ever attract. My father was a speaker in nearly all of the great tabernacles, and probably more often in Chicago than any of the others.

A few of the tabernacle works were of the type described by Sinclair Lewis in "Elmer Gantry". Unfortunately, every time the secular press or the critical novelist describes a church that is not associated with one of the major denominations, they delight in choosing these lurid examples of an extremely fleshly form of tabernacle work.

There were (and still are) some of these, and we all regret it, but most of the places I remember were no different from the denominations as far as creed and doctrine were concerned. They differed in that they preached their doctrine instead of leaving it buried in a book.

They were well established works, standing for the conversion of souls, the edification of believers and world-wide evangelism, emphasizing the four great essentials — salvation, the deeper life, foreign missions, and the Lord's return.

WAR ON MODERNISM

This era lasted from the end of World War I until the beginning of World War II, and there was a reason for it. The older generation can remember it well.

Modernism — an extreme deity-denying form of modernism and higher criticism had come over Europe and had a spiritual strangle hold on most of the seminaries and hence the churches. Social reform and universal brotherhood had driven the spiritual message of regeneration out of the pulpit and classrooms.

The fires of evangelism were little more than embers compared to the Moody days. The people in these churches who had a hunger for

The Peoples Magazine — Second Quarter, 1961

spiritual things were being starved, and when an advertisement appeared in any city newspaper announcing an evangelistic effort in a tent or a theatre or a tabernacle, there was a group of spiritually minded people in every church who flocked to the colors.

Many of them would maintain their own church membership, probably with the hope that all was not lost and eventually the Gospel would be preached again in their church, but in many instances they would pull out and throw in their lot with the tabernacles.

Today the Tabernacle Era is over. There has been a transition from Tabernacle Evangelism to Church Evangelism.

Some of the Tabernacle men have been able to make the transition, but many have fallen by the wayside, defeated remnants of a new order.

It would be a form of family pride for me to say that my own father had some sort of religious genius. On the other hand, it would be a false humility to disparage his ability.

Any man who founds, builds and maintains a world-renowned church certainly possesses some Divine gift that the rank and file do not have. In father's case, I have always thought that one of his greatest gifts has been the ability to weather the storm of change.

Almost without losing a step in the march, the Gospel Tabernacle became The Peoples Church.

The tent is gone, the Tabernacle is now a factory, the sawdust has been swept up, and the musicians receive small honorariums, but the main spiritual thrust of the work has continued unabated in the form of a consolidated, well-organized, evangelistic church program.

THE NEW ORDER

Some of the tabernacles never managed to make the transition. Very often they disintegrated when their founders passed off the scene and in other cases they struggled on, a mere ghost of their former magnitude.

There are a few left standing today, but they seldom are filled.

More often they minister to a handful of people huddled in the front rows of a huge barnlike structure.

They have been reduced in seating capacity by the addition of partitions, Sunday School rooms, office space, and spread out opera seats that require equal floor space but seat only a fraction as many people as the old benches.

I have often asked my father why he was so fortunate, and without any trace of doubt, he always declares that the missionary vision of the church saved the day.

Early in the history of the work in Toronto, in addition to the continual stream of local campaigns, the people were trained to send their money to the foreign mission field. The task of world evangelization grew until it became the dominating factor, the brilliant beacon light, the vision without which any work — church or tabernacle — is doomed.

• •

God First

I've heard it said, if you will put
    God first in all you do,
That He will send both wealth and fame,
    And all these things to you;
I doubt that statement very much,
    And yet I could be wrong,
But I believe you'll find these things
    Held by the worldly throng.

God never pays in dollar bills
    For anything we do:
He does reward one here and there,
    But they are very few;
I know it says, "I will repay
    A thousand fold or more",
But those I know who put Him first
    Are far from rich, they're poor.

Let's face the facts and then we'll see
    The ones who put Him first,
If it be those with wealth and fame,
    And yet for more still thirst;
Or those who heard the Master's Call,
    And went at His command
To do His will what'er the cost,
    Out in a foreign land.

No comforts there, no wealth and fame,
    No television shows;
No fancy cars, no luxuries,
    But burdens, trials and foes.
These are the ones who put Him first,
    I'm sure you will agree;
And tho' their treasure here is small,
    They'll reap eternally.

—WALT HUNTLEY
Cooksville, Ontario
Canada.

• •

The reason for the tabernacle-church transition is c o m p l e x. Modernism today is not what it was a generation ago. Every theological student knows that the last ten years have seen a marked swing of the theological pendulum toward a more conservative evangelical direction. The swing is not as complete as we might wish, but it is a real thing, which has changed the entire picture.

We are seeing evangelistic efforts in the most unexpected places coming from sources that are surprising, to say the least.

Very few large denominations do not have an aggressive department of evangelism today. Instead of one central tabernacle being the only evangelical light, churches of all kinds are sponsoring their own campaigns.

I can remember when my father led the only really aggressive evangelistic program in Toronto. Today I can open my newspaper to the church page and see five or ten crusades in different churches.

Despite the tremendous crowds that used to run for seats in the Toronto Tabernacle days, undoubtedly there are more people hearing the Gospel in this city today than ever before.

COOPERATIVE EVANGELISM

This is the situation that Billy Graham has taken advantage of. Fifteen years ago he would have held a city-wide campaign in many metropolitan areas, but it would have been sponsored by one large evangelistic centre, not representing the church life of those cities.

These are the sort of meetings that most of the evangelists — my father included—of those days conducted.

It was so easy for them to work only with fundamentalists because the churches did not want evangelism. They were trying a Social Gospel approach. The campaigns were not really Union in any sense of the word. They were city-wide, and there is a vast difference.

Since the war we have lived to see the unprecedented opportunity presented by a church that has tried the New Gospel and has been dis-

The Peoples Magazine — Second Quarter, 1961

appointed, and by a group of scholars who are confronted with archaeological discoveries that have proved many of their pet theories about the Bible to be erroneous.

The churches are far from having all of their problems solved, but at least they are willing to give a man such as Graham an opportunity to preach the Gospel of the Bible. This is a miraculous move in the right direction and God's answer to the prayers of men like my father, who fought their way in the tabernacles through an era when the organized Christian church wanted nothing to do with evangelism.

Thank God for the great, glorious, enthusiastic, bench-packed, sawdust strewn, soul-saving Tabernacle Era, and thank God for this church-centred, well-organized, denominationally-backed, soul-saving period of Church Evangelism.

June 5, 1961.

THE PEOPLES CHURCH   TORONTO

PEOPLES CHURCH SOLD

On June 5, 1961, The Peoples Church in Toronto, Canada, was sold for $650,000.00, enough to pay for the construction of a new building legally seating more than two thousand people with adequate educational facilities.

Central Methodist Church was erected over one hundred years ago. It was one of many churches left vacant in Canada at the time of Church Union in 1925. It was purchased by The Peoples Church in 1935, under the leadership of Dr. Oswald J. Smith, for $75,000, and from the beginning was called upon to accommodate crowds far beyond its sixteen hundred-seat legal capacity.

The interest and enthusiasm has continued under the ministry of Dr. Paul B. Smith, who succeeded his father as Pastor in 1959. Throughout the past year extra chairs have had to be brought in almost every Sunday night and many have had to stand. The Financial Report of 1960 indicates the second largest year in the history of the work. The new move will take The Peoples Church from the business center of the city to the heart of the residential district.

During the last thirty years The Peoples Church has spent four and

My Motto:

No Attack!
No Defence!

—*Oswald J. Smith*

Rom. 12:18.

a half million dollars on Foreign Missions and practically nothing on the maintenance of the home base. Visitors have always been amazed at the lack of paint, old-fashioned equipment, and inadequate facilities that are apparent in every part of the century-old building. While the people have sent this vast sum overseas, God has increased the value of the property to such an extent that a completely new and modern plant in an ideal location will be paid for with no lessening of the missionary effort. The only funds that will have to be raised will be whatever is necessary for interior furnishings.

It is expected that the congregation will move in September of 1962. In the intervening months the church will be allowed to continue in the old building.

Farewell, Bloor Street.

Memories of the last service.

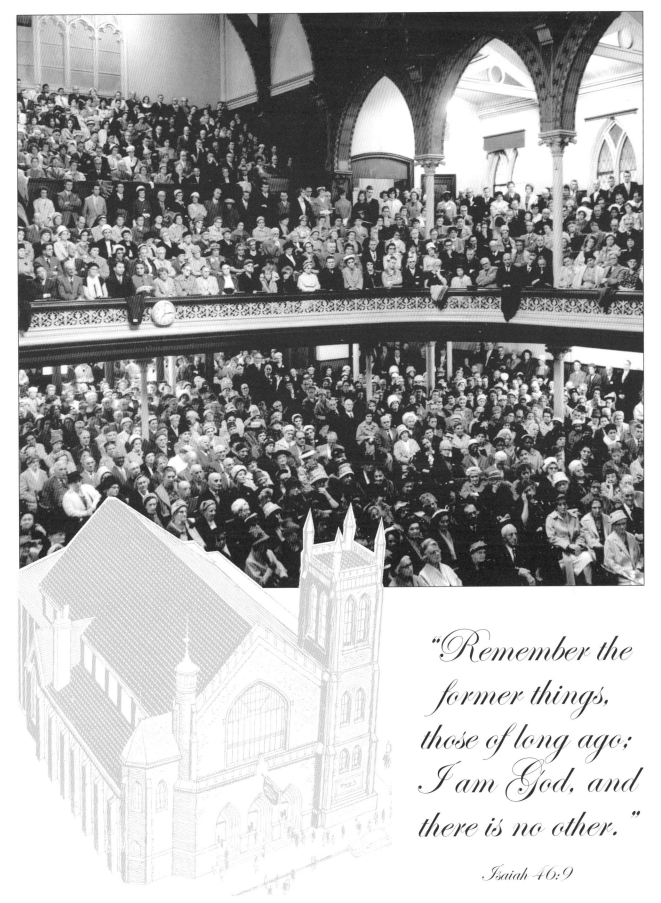

"Remember the
former things,
those of long ago;
I am God, and
there is no other."

Isaiah 46:9

Into all the World

The

PEOPLES MAGAZINE

OSWALD J. SMITH, Litt.D., Editor

| Volume 41 | TORONTO, CANADA, FIRST QUARTER, 1962 | Number 1-3 |

New Home for The Peoples Church

By Paul B. Smith

In September of 1962 The Peoples Church family will move into a magnificent new building worth upwards of $750,000 and the whole undertaking will cost the congregation less than $100,000.

This story could be the missionary miracle of the twentieth century. Most Evangelical Christian people around the world are aware of the fact that for the past 30 years this large Canadian Church under the leadership of its Founder and Missionary Pastor, Dr. Oswald J. Smith, has given more than $4½ millions toward foreign missionary work. During most of these years the Church has been able to send $7 overseas for every $1 that was spent on the budget of the home base. In order to do this the local congregation had to sacrifice a great many conveniences and comforts that are taken for granted in the average modern church.

The big C e n t r a l Methodist Church which was bought by "Peoples" in 1934 is now well over 100 years old. Very little repair work has been done on it except those things that were necessary to prevent it from falling down or being condemned by the city. The floor of the main auditorium is still the rough lumber, and the only finishing material that has ever been put on it has been the carpets that run down the main aisles. The

building is badly in need of paint and the brick-work on the outside is in desperate condition. Only a few weeks ago the Fire Department had to be called because part of the steeple was beginning to fall away.

Now God has rewarded the congregation for their faithfulness to the cause of foreign missions and made it possible for them to move to a brand new location and put up a modern building with all of the facilities that are necessary for the work that has developed during these three decades.

Realizing their desperate need of a larger auditorium to accommodate the Sunday evening crowds, which always over-tax its capacity, and

Dr. Paul B. Smith

adequate educational facilities to take care of the growing needs of a modern Sunday School, the Board of Managers on September 7, 1954, decided to sell part of the lot and try to build a new structure on the front. The property was listed with the Snelgrove Real Estate Company on March 31, 1955, for $150,000.

At that time there were no buyers, but a big business concern in the city offered to enter into a combined project which would result in a large office building that incorporated a church. After the plans had been completely drawn this company declared bankruptcy.

In 1959 Dr. Paul B. Smith became Pastor of the Church and during the first two years of his pastorate a total of six similar business propositions were presented and processed by the Board. One involved an office building. Another suggested an apartment block. Still another had a magnificent plan for a combination apartment block, office building and church. In every case, however, the propositions fell through, either because the firms concerned did not have adequate resources or the facilities they offered the church were too limited.

It was a momentous night when on November 28, 1960, for the first time, the Board of Managers considered selling the entire property

The architect's drawing of the new Peoples Church. After giving practically everything (4½ million dollars) to Missions for 30 years, God is giving us a brand new church free of charge. We bought the old church for $75,000 and we sold it for $650,000. For more than a quarter of a century now, The Peoples Church has had the largest Sunday evening audience of any church in Canada.

and building of the old Church and moving its location to another section of the city. Six months later the deal was completed with a construction company for $650,000.

Thus in a period of 30 years of concentration on Foreign Missions God turned the original $75,000 investment in the old Methodist Church into a sum more than eight times as large—$650,000. The only money that will have to be raised by the congregation is approximately $75,000 for the furnishings and equipment in the new building. The land has already been purchased, the new building is paid for, and the move will be made without any retreat in the missionary work of the Church.

The new location will still be in the centre of the City of Toronto, eight miles north, and will draw from the entire Metropolitan area, but instead of being down town where there has been no local constituency for many years, the Church will be in the centre of the residential section. This means that in addition to having a city-wide influence the new Peoples Church will also have a local constituency consisting of thousands of families who will now be within walking or short driving distance.

The new property will provide adequate parking facilities for the congregation. This has become an increasingly difficult problem in the down-town location and many of the adherents have been forced to park three, four and five blocks away from the Church and walk from their cars, very often through inclement weather. Now they will be able to drive across the main throughways of the City of Toronto, enter the lot from three different directions and be assured of a parking place within a stone's throw of the building. There will be parking for 300 cars.

The auditorium is built in the shape of a huge fan with a balcony that goes around three sides. With extra chairs brought in it will easily accommodate over 2,500 people. The choir loft alone will seat 120.

For the first time in its history The Peoples Church will have adequate educational facilities so that the Sunday School can be completely departmentalized and will be able to more than double its present enrolment.

Two items that are of the greatest importance to the local congregation are (1) the fact that they will be moving into the centre of an entirely new constituency that will give them an evangelistic ministry among hundreds of families that have never been inside a gospel preaching church and, (2) the increased congregation will enable the Church to expand its missionary program so that in the years that lie ahead, instead of contributing towards the support of some 350 missionaries, our objective will now be 400 missionaries on the field, and rather than being limited to a foreign missionary budget of around $300,000, our new annual goal will be in the vicinity of $400,000.

The Bible promise upon which the congregation is standing during these days is found in the book of Haggai where God said, "The glory of this latter house shall be greater than of the former."

> *"The glory of this latter house shall be greater than of the former, saith the Lord of hosts: and in this place will I give peace, saith the Lord of hosts."*
>
> *Haggai 2:9*

4

Turning the sod – November 12, 1961
374 Sheppard Avenue East.

Rev. R. Watt and
W. Huntley.

Once the architects' plans were approved, it was time to turn the sod in preparation for building. On Sunday afternoon, November 12, nearly three thousand people marched silently around the land, praying and claiming the promise, "Every place that the sole of your foot shall tread upon, that have I given you." Joshua 1:3

It was a verse Oswald had often stood upon when claiming new property for God. Only the hundreds of people who were on the scene that day, can appreciate the sense of electricity that pervaded the atmosphere. Scores of cameras recorded the historic occasion, as all gave glory to God.

Mr. Thos. Webb
and W. Huntley.

Mrs. D. Mason
and W. Huntley.

Reeve N.C. Goodhead, Daisy Smith,
Dr. Paul and Anita Smith.

The land –
374 Sheppard Avenue East.

Mr. John Dade
and W. Huntley.

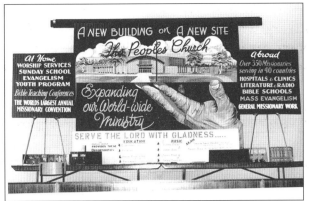

Into all the World

THE LAYING OF THE CORNERSTONE
June 3rd, 1962

History was made on Sunday afternoon at three o'clock, June 3, 1962, when a crowd of between three and four thousand people assembled in front of the New Home of The Peoples Church to witness the Laying of the Cornerstone.

The building was about half finished for the service and God gave us a day with brilliant sunshine, very little wind, and ideal conditions for pictures.

The service was conducted by the Pastor, Dr. Paul B. Smith, and the actual Laying of the Cornerstone was done by the Founder, Dr. Oswald J. Smith.

The outside atmosphere and the confusion of construction materials on all sides did not detract from the dignity and solemnity of the occasion.

To remind future generations that The Peoples Church believes and preaches the entire Bible, Dr. Paul Smith placed in the Cornerstone Box a copy of the Word of God. He then added the church page from each of the three Toronto daily papers, each of which contained a full story of the work, with pictures, of The Peoples Church.

Rev. Robert Watt, the Assistant Pastor, placed in the box a copy of the book, "The Peoples Church and Its Founder", giving the history of the work. Mr. John E. T. Dade, on behalf of the Board of Managers, added a letter signed by the Members of the Board which read as follows.

"The Peoples Church was founded by Dr. Oswald J. Smith on September 9, 1928, in Massey Hall, and Dr. Paul B. Smith became the Pastor on January 1, 1959. We have always emphasized the four great essentials: Salvation, the Deeper Life, Foreign Missions, and the Lord's Return.

"In this new venture of faith we are fully determined that by the grace of God we will continue this fourfold emphasis in this new building and new location. The Peoples Church has no excuse for existence apart from a consistent attempt to evangelize the unreached people of the Metropolitan Toronto area and an intense effort to take the message of the Gospel to the whole world through our foreign missionary programme.

"We believe that 'The Supreme Task of the Church is the Evangelization of the World' and therefore endeavour to send more money to the Regions Beyond than we ever spend on our local budget. During the last thirty-four years we have contributed more than two-thirds of our income to Foreign Missions— a total of some five million dollars.

"To this end the Directors and Members of The Peoples Church have drafted this letter and placed it in this Date Stone and herewith sign our names and place the seal of The Peoples Church."

Finally, the Missionary Pastor added two copies of The Peoples Magazine, which he has edited for over forty years. As he did so he read the Biblical account of God's command to Moses to put the Law in an ark and seal it for posterity.

After these items had been placed in the Cornerstone Box, Dr. Oswald J. Smith went down to the Cornerstone where the General Contractor, Mr. W. Malaniuk, presented him with a silver trowel on which was inscribed these words: "This Stone was Laid to the Glory of God by Dr. Oswald J. Smith on June 3, 1962". Then Dr. Smith placed the Cornerstone and it was sealed in its position, perhaps to be opened by some future generation, should the Lord tarry.

The Peoples Church Brass Band, with Frank Trenchard at the Hammond Organ provided a fitting musical background for an impressive service that will be remembered for many years to come.

—Photo Wilbur J. Caddell

Dr. Paul B. Smith and Dr. Oswald J. Smith filling the Box for the Cornerstone

Remembering the day.

Into all the World

MINISTERS

The blending of the 120 joyful voices of one of the largest choirs in the land will musically mark the opening tomorrow of a new era for the remarkable Peoples Church.

At least 3,000 persons are expected to cram the spaciousness of the church's new $750,000 building at 374 Sheppard Avenue East for the first service there.

Going from strength to strength, Peoples, which gives more money to overseas missions than any other congregation in Canada, will open a suburban ministry.

The shift may not be as traumatic as it sounds, Pastor Dr. Paul Smith explained this week. "We've always had a city-wide congregation and we expect to maintain that city-wide ministry. But we expect to attact a local constituency as well."

The old church (where the choir-loft accommodated only 66) at Bloor Street East and Park Road, was sold for $650,000. This sum plus the $100,000 contributed for the new house of worship means a debt-free opening.

More important than this fact is Dr. Smith's expectation that Peoples Church Sunday school will grow from its present 500 to more than 2,000 and thus become the largest in the Dominion—the objective of the enthusiastic pastor.

Records have been broken without difficulty by Peoples. Founded 34 years ago, it has consistently—even in its increasingly cramped downtown location—attracted 2,000 worshippers to its evening services.

Last year it raised $325,000 for mission work and thereby supported 350 missionaries in 40 countries. Its missionary givings were seven times as much as the church spent for itself.

The founder and spark of the church is bouncing 72-year-old Dr Oswald J. Smith, the Pastor's father. "Dr. Oswald" is a missionary, evangelist, author (more than 1,000,000 copies of his 25 books have been published in 35 languages), writer of 1,200 hymns, pastor, poet and world traveller.

He was ordained a Presbyterian minister. In 1958 he celebrated the 50th year of his ministry.

Billy Graham has called him "the most remarkable man I ever met" His work is continuing to prosper in a world where Christianity is often on the defensive.

Gus Ambrose. The man who did the magnificent publicity work for the opening of the new Peoples Church in the Toronto newspapers and also on his Night-watch broadcast for which we thank him.

Rev. Paul B. Smith, B.A., D.D.

is the Minister and President of the Board of Managers. He succeeded his father, Dr. Oswald J. Smith, on January 1, 1959, and it is under his administration that the move from the Bloor Street location has taken place.

Rev. Oswald J. Smith, D.D., Litt.D.

is the Founder and Minister of Missions. He built the work under the hand of God from the ground up and on the human level is responsible for a church in the City of Toronto that is known throughout the Christian world.

Rev. Robert Watt

is the Minister of Evangelism and Teacher of the Homebuilders' Bible Class. He was ordained to the Baptist ministry many years ago and has served with The Peoples Church for the past eight years.

Mr. David E. Williams, B.A.

is the Minister of Music. He commenced his activity in The Peoples Church on Sunday, October 9, 1960 and leads a choral and instrumental programme that has in it an outlet for almost every age bracket and Christian musical interest.

Rev. Daniel L. Edmundson, Ph.D.

is the Minister of Christian Education. He holds his doctorate degree in the field and correlates the entire Christian Education programme of the church.

•••••••••••••••••••••••••••••

—Photo by The Evening Telegram

*The first audience to ever meet in the new Peoples Church. There were nearly
2,500 present and 120 in the choir.*

THE OPENING DAY

How can we describe the opening day in the new Peoples Church? Words fail us when we try to convey the tremendous enthusiasm of the vast congregations. God has indeed done the exceeding abundant above.

Three services were held, morning, afternoon, and evening. The auditorium was packed to its utmost capacity for each service. Nearly 2,500 people were present at each service, 7,000 in all for the day. For the afternoon, in spite of the rain, we were crowded out and at the evening service large numbers were compelled to stand or were seated in the aisles. It was a never-to-be-forgotten experience.

We did not leave God's blessing at Bloor Street. He was with us on Sheppard Avenue. Some eight or ten walked out to accept Jesus Christ as Saviour at the evening service and were dealt with by our counsellors in the chapel.

Dr. Paul B. Smith, the Pastor, preached in the morning. Dr. Charles E. Blair of Denver, Colorado, in the afternoon and evening. Mayor Nathan Phillips and his wife were present at the afternoon service. His Worship brought words of greeting. The Reeve of North York, Mr. Norman C. Goodhead, was also present and he too spoke. Dr. Oswald J. Smith took part in all the services.

In the afternoon there was a processional by the choir, singing as they marched, "O God Our Help In Ages Past." It made a deep impression. Dr. Oswald Smith was dressed in his gown and hood for the occasion. Mr. Zalhout and his family played the violin and sang at all three services.

The Sunday School which met in the morning saw an increase of over 250—the largest attendance in the history of the church. There is parking space for 270 cars but there were 430 cars at the morning service.

The band and the choir occupied the platform, approximately 140 all told. Everyone remarked about the singing. The choir stretches from one side of the platform to the other, three deep, and presents a marvelous picture. The voices can be heard from anywhere in the auditorium.

Every pew faces the pulpit so that no matter where one is sitting, he does not have to even turn his head in order to see the platform and he can hear distinctly in every part of the building. Moreover, there is not a pillar or a post anywhere to obstruct the view. There are no windows. Fresh air is pumped in continuously and there is no dust coming in through open windows and no drafts of any kind. The acoustics are perfect.

Everyone admired the beautiful little chapel where small weddings will be performed. The chapel will also be used as an inquiry room and for special prayer meetings. The young people will find it most convenient for many of their meetings.

The Peoples Magazine — First Quarter, 1963

"Evangelism, I have proven,
will pack any church.
The converts generally remain
and will pack any church." OJS

About the Building
By Hanks, Irwin and Pearson, Architects

The basic plan of The Peoples Church is fan shaped and was so determined in order to bring the speaker as close as possible to each listener, to create a feeling of intimacy which could not be achieved by the traditional nave type church, and to give the speaker the feeling that he was 'in the midst' even when addressing an audience of over two thousand. In addition the auditorium floor is ramped to give the best visual aid to the listeners.

In an auditorium of this size there were many structural problems of which the carrying of the clear span roof over a distance of 170 feet was one. This necessitated erection of huge steel girders 110 feet long and 5½ feet deep and the transmitting of the resultant huge loads to adequate foundations. Another was the construction of a large gallery which had to be cantilevered from the walls in order to maintain the uninterrupted clear main floor area. The gallery was necessary in order to keep all seating as close to the speaker as possible.

The auditorium is built of very simple concrete units in order that there might be few distracting influences. The only adornment is some simple mahogany panelling behind the choir.

The auditorium is enclosed by a Christian Education complex, comprising nursery, beginners, primary, junior and intermediate departments, a small panelled chapel, administration department, board room, book room, radio room and a minor auditorium seating four hundred which is provided with a functional kitchen for social activities.

The main entrance is through a series of six wide doors into a spacious foyer or narthex with curved precast concrete roof and flying stairways on each side. The foyer is lighted from the front by tinted glass behind pierced masonry screen which lends a cathedral air to the impressive entrance.

The materials were chosen with the idea of permanence and minimum cost in upkeep and this is reflected in the aluminum windows, simple block walls and tiled floors. Even the acoustic treatment has added a quiet richness in addition to its utilitarian function.

On the outside the walls are brick in a contemporary beige shade and the passer-by is arrested by the tall free standing cross which in sunlight puts its seal on the building.

Building again.

By Christmas 1963, any empty spaces in the pews were filled. The church was becoming part of its new community, and was even being used by groups such as The Toronto Symphony Orchestra for concerts and special events. Both children and parents were finding their way to the various services and programs. A "Kids Krusade", with Dr. Frank Wellington, attracted over a thousand children every night for a week.

The following spring, less than a year and a half after the move, the church won The National Sunday School contest. First out of 1,000 competing churches from all over North America, attendance continued to climb over the one thousand mark every Sunday.

Soon, the church was crowded to crisis proportions and the decision was made to add an Education Wing. On Sunday, December 6, 1964, sod was broken yet again. Since the original construction in 1962, there have been five additions of space. The Education Wing was built in three phases: the first in 1965 at a cost of $89,000; the second in 1967 (the Centennial Wing) at a cost of $110,000; and the third (the third floor of the school) in 1971 at a cost of $103.000. In 1968, the balcony was extended to accommodate 150 more people at a cost of $18,000. The final construction involved the erection of the Paul B. Smith Academy and church facilities, in 1976, at a cost just over $900,000.

Into all the World

Into

Above – The Board of Elders of The Peoples Church. Below – The Board of Managers.

Organization of The Peoples Church

"The Peoples Church has a Board of Managers to look after the business end of the work,
a Board of Elders to take care of the spiritual work of the church,
and a Board of Deacons to handle the loose plate offerings." *OJS*

The Peoples Church Family

Praying

Growing

Breaking Bread

Together

Leading

Into all the

... *Burning the Mortgage!!!*

1985

Into all the World

Dr. Oswald J. Smith.

Dr. Paul B. Smith.

Dr. John Hull.

Charles Price.

Five

Passing the Baton:

John Hull
Charles Price

Passing the Baton.

Preparation for the next step.

In September of 1985, the highly regarded Charles Price, Principal of Capernwray Bible School in England, was in Toronto speaking at the Ontario Bible College and Seminary (now Tyndale College and Seminary).

Having never met Dr. Paul Smith, he was surprised and pleased to receive an invitation to meet him for coffee. Charles had known of Paul for many years and had read a number of his books.

The meeting of Paul Smith and Charles Price.

Upon their meeting, Dr. Smith said that he had been listening to tapes of Charles' messages and he wanted him to spend some time ministering at The Peoples Church. Continuing, he invited him for a month in June, 1987, to preach at each Sunday service and each Tuesday night at the summer Bible conference. In addition, he suggested a preparatory weekend visit in October, 1986, to give people the opportunity to get to know Charles before the month long visit.

On the last Sunday morning of Charles' visit in June, he was quite taken aback when Paul announced publicly from the platform that Charles should continue doing what he was doing at Capernwray for five more years, and then replace him at The Peoples Church.

Dr. Paul B. Smith and Charles Price.

Although Charles and his wife Hilary had developed a deep love for The Peoples Church, they had a nagging uncertainty about the timing and were somewhat relieved when the invitation wasn't formally issued to them. In the following years, although Dr. Smith occasionally repeated his hope that Charles might one day pastor the church, he suddenly cooled. In retrospect, Dr. Smith was right on two counts. Firstly, he accurately discerned that one day God would have Charles Price pastor The Peoples Church, and secondly that the timing was not right. The immediate successor would be Dr. John Hull.

Dr. John Hull.

In early 1993, Dr. John Hull, the Senior Pastor and Founder of the Mountain View Church of Atlanta, Georgia, asked Dr. Paul Smith to speak at his Missions Conference. They had become friends in 1989, when Paul spoke at Mountain View's second annual missions conference.

Throughout the intervening years, the two men had corresponded from time to time. John's concerns with regard to Paul's health increased as the conversations and brief visits confirmed that he was faltering. John feared that the 1993 missions conference could be the last opportunity his church would have to be blessed with the ministry of Dr. Paul.

Dr. Paul B. Smith and Dr. John Hull.

Dr. Paul B. Smith.

Paul ministered at Mountain View for five days, struggling to get through every message. When John picked him up at his hotel before the final service, Paul complimented him on the way the church had grown since he had been there four years earlier – and on how well he thought the missions conference was run. He was clearly gratified in seeing the success John had had with the development of the conference, after using the pattern of The Peoples Church.

As the two friends drove closer to the church that evening, Paul told John that his health was poor and that he was wanting to wind down his ministry. He then gave voice to the thoughts God had so graciously given him. It was a historic moment in the life of The Peoples Church. Ever since its founding, the church had been led by the Smith family. Thoughtfully, yet with the surety of one who has gleaned the details carefully from God, Paul asked John if he would consider moving to Toronto and succeeding him.

Further discussions ensued later that evening, which led to a week-long visit to Toronto a few months later, where Paul had asked John to oversee the final week of services for the missions conference. While there, Paul arranged for a meeting with the Church board for an interview. An offer came days later. In August, 1993, Dr. John Hull moved to Toronto and began his new work. His installation service was held on May 15, 1994.

Preservice Music
The Trinidad Steel Drum Band

A Welcome and Invocation

We Sing Together
"The Song of the Soul Set Free" #82

The Faith Promise Offering

The Ministry of Music
"The Lord Is My Light"
Diane Susek, Guest Soloist

Introduction of Guest Speaker

The Evening Message
Dr. John Wesley White

The Service of Installation
Scripture Reading
Prayer

A Response
Rev. John D. Hull

A Reading
Dr. Richard Schmelzle, narrator

The Ministry of Music
"Thank You"
Cloyd Knight, Guest Soloist
Dr. David Williams, Guest Director

Dr. Glen Smith and Hope Smith Lowry with a family response.

Dr. Paul Smith,
Sharon and Dr. John Hull.

Presentations
Various Presenters

A Family Response
Glen Smith and Hope Lowry

The Ministry of Music
"Ten Thousand Joys"
Diane Susek and Cloyd Knight, duet
The Peoples Church Choir and Orchestra
Dr. David Williams, directing

A Media Presentation
of the Ministry of Dr. Smith
Concept by John Hull • Created by Hal Warren
Music: "Revelations Theme"
Written by Jeff Boze and Danny Daniels

A Musical Response
"By-and-By"
Everyone Singing

By-and-by, when the morning comes,
All the saints of God are gathered home.
We will tell the story how we've overcome.
We will understand it better by-and-by.

A Prayer of Blessing

Dismissed to Reception
Everyone is cordially invited to attend the reception
honouring Dr. Smith in the Peoples Academy Gymnasium
immediately following the service.

The
Hull
Family.

John and Sharon,
Mary Alice and Andy.

J. Hull
C. Price

Dr. John Hull – Background.

A preacher's kid, John Hull became a Christian at the ripe old age of eight. Following high school, he headed to the University of Georgia in Athens, Georgia, and graduated in 1980 with a degree in journalism and telecommunications. In 1983, he received his Master of Divinity degree from Liberty Baptist Theological Seminary in Lynchburg, Virginia. The Southern California Theological Seminary conferred a Doctor of Divinity degree on him in 1993, and he received his Doctorate in Ministry in 1996 from the Gordon-Conwell Theological Seminary in Boston.

Early ministry years.

Upon graduation from seminary in Virginia in 1983, John returned to the community where he was raised in suburban Atlanta, with the goal of planting Mountain View Church. He and Sharon, who he had met at the University of Georgia in 1978, were married on June 18 that same year. Three years later, they were blessed with a son, Andy, and then a daughter, Mary Alice.

In the third year of developing Mountain View Church, a seminary classmate, who had since become a missionary to Indonesia, stopped by to visit while home on furlough. As John proudly showed him the burgeoning facilities and expressed to him God's faithfulness since the church's inception; the missionary was impressed. He asked a question which became a defining moment in John's ministry, "This is great John, but tell me, what are you doing for missions?"

Initially, the question frustrated John. Did the fellow not have any appreciation for the enormity of what was being accomplished at Mountain View? But as the question simmered, John began to understand what was at the heart of the inquiry. Truly, God had blessed the growing work, but what *were* he and the congregation doing – intentionally and strategically – to get the Gospel to the nations?

From that point, John began to search out leaders and churches which were making a difference in global missions. Before long, he was introduced to the ministry of The Peoples Church. In 1988, Mountain View hosted its very first annual World Missions Conference and received its first faith promise offering. The following year, in 1989, Dr. Paul Smith was the main speaker.

In 1990, Dr. Paul asked John to speak in Toronto at the church's historic world missions conference. The subject was to be "faith promise giving". John was terrified, and claims that he preached a most forgettable sermon that day. From the time he arrived, it was "just one of those days". Even when he pulled up to the crowded parking lot at the church on that Sunday morning and tried to park where an associate pastor had told him to go, he was scolded by one of the parking lot attendants who said, "You can't park there!" Fortunately, he did manage to get parked, and the rest is history – as they say.

Into all the World

107

*Dr. Paul Smith
on passing the baton
to the third generation.*

(Abridged from The Peoples Magazine, December, 1993.)

My first contact with John D. Hull was in Jackson, Mississippi. He was the minister of the Mountain View Church in Atlanta, Georgia and in February, 1989 he invited me to speak at his missionary conference. During that conference there was a bonding of our spirits that was very significant. He invited me to return again in 1993.

I was very much impressed by his ability to manage the platform, introduce the speakers, and in general his unusual ability to conduct a service.

When he helped me conduct the services at our missionary conference of 1993, his last activity in the conference was to take up the faith promise offering and conduct the breakfast/lunch meeting we hold annually for the adults in our congregation. As soon as he was finished he had to leave to catch his flight. *As he was walking through the brunch crowd, they gave him a standing ovation. This was almost unprecedented in the history of The Peoples Church.*

During the past two years there has been a considerable amount of unrest in our church. Almost five years ago I had decided to step aside as Senior Minister and two of my very closest friends urged me to stay and convinced me that my work in The Peoples Church was not as yet completed.

Although I knew that the next Senior Minister of The Peoples Church must be a great preacher, I was very much aware of the fact that he would have to have a very special ability on the platform. We have a great many guest preachers. Some of our most faithful members are people who came to our church the first time to hear some guest preacher in whom they were interested. The Senior Minister of The Peoples Church must have the ability, not only to preach himself, but to introduce and promote the guest preachers who fill our pulpit so often.

During these last two years I have been looking for this kind of person who would have the ability to carry on the unique ministry of The Peoples Church.

During the last six years as I have been in contact with Rev. John D. Hull the Spirit of God seemed to be telling me that he was the man who could carry on the ministry of our church for another generation. He was only thirty-five years of age but I was convinced that at last we had found God's man. When I first suggested his name to the Board of Managers there was some resistance, primarily because of his age. However, they agreed that we should invite him and we did so. Rev. John D. Hull accepted our invitation and commenced his ministry on August 1, 1993.

At the end of our World Missions Conference in 1994 I will be stepping aside. John Hull will become the Senior Minister of The Peoples Church and I will become the Minister of Missions.

The Third Generation is now well in place and ready to go into what I believe will be a more extensive ministry both at home and overseas than anything we have ever seen before.

J. Hull
C. Price

THE PASSING OF
THE MANTLE

by John Wesley White, D.Phil. (Oxon)

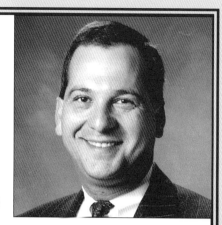

"Perhaps one of the greatest honours I have had in my life is to stand here this evening and express my thanks to Dr. Paul B. Smith for his selfless and indefatigable labours as the Senior Minister of this congregation for which we as a family have belonged for many years.

Let me allude to the marvelous ministry we've had the luxury of enjoying for nearly a generation in this, Canada's largest congregation for virtually all of that period. Dr. Paul B. Smith started 68 years ago on the platform when his father introduced him as a four-year-old singer, and he had a big voice for a four-year-old! He preached his first sermon in a little Tennessee mountain church while a student at Bob Jones University. (Paul says he ate a lot of grits there, and it's given him the grit and grace to be great in this church!)

Paul became an international Youth For Christ evangelist, shoulder to shoulder with Billy Graham. The first time I heard him was at Winona Lake in 1950; there were thousands of people swirling around him in Billy Sunday Tabernacle and I couldn't get near him.

He continued conducting evangelistic crusades in 84 countries, great city-wide gatherings, until Dr. Paul's earthly father conferred with the Heavenly Father and they agreed he should become the senior minister of this congregation. That began in 1959 and by 1962 Dr. Paul had led this congregation in the building of this very utilitarian church, — utilitarian because it was dedicated to world missions.

The church wasn't here long until the Sunday School, which was compartmentalized and the records computerized by Dr. Paul, had exploded from 400 to 1600 with gusts up to 1828 to win the National Sunday School Contest in which a thousand churches on this continent were participants.

Many other things happened back in the 60s which Paul initiated, for instance he called together 150 pastors from 30 denominations and here at Peoples the Evangelical Fellowship of Canada began.

I remember my late brother-in-law Elmer McVety and Tom McCormack bringing together a shoe-horn crowd for a once-a-month Men's Fellowship — we were so packed into Founder's Hall that we had to sit sideways. An internationally known athlete or entertainer who had been born again would give his testimony, then Dr. Paul would preach the gospel and many were brought in by that means.

John Wesley White, D.Phil. (Oxon)

It was then that the Singles Ministry began, another first in Canada. Then a vital ministry to Seniors was started — there are more over-60s in this country than there are teenagers.

By 1971, Dr. Paul, who when planning each of the six additional educational expansions, had in mind the opening of a Christian Day School and it has gone to 500–600 in the Oswald J. Smith Elementary School and the Paul B. Smith Academy for high-schoolers.

And then Dr. Paul brought in that genius, Dr. David Williams as Music Director and many times we've come into this auditorium to see a four-story set of spruce-boughs and human beings right up to the top, and 30,000 twinkling lights in The Living Christmas Tree, another first for Canada, and that brought in tens of thousands of people who never went to any church at any other occasion.

In 1972 this congregation was expanded to half-a-million per week when Dr. Paul did a first by putting the Sunday morning service on television, on six stations across Ontario and then coast-to-coast across Canada. For this he engaged two geniuses, Hal Warren, a CBC-TV audio-engineer and editor, and Lloyd Knight who had a set of larynx like John McCormack and looked as if he walked out of Hollywood; Lloyd was the featured personality with Dr. Paul preaching. Nielson ratings indicated that half of the viewers were men — that's incredible for a Christian television program.

The Peoples Magazine, August 1994

And many of the liberals around wondered: Do they ever do anything for the bodies, for poverty stricken people? And Dr. Paul went on world relief telethons and raised $350,000 for the Ethiopian starving, and $205,000 for the famine famished in Mali, and $169,000 for the flood victims in Bangladesh. And it was shown that this church had a heart for the whole person.

I think Paul could always see into the future, he had good future vision: his father had had evangelistic campaigns almost year round, every night. But with the advent of television, that didn't work, so he would bring in the best speakers for one service — Billy Graham has been twice in this pulpit which is very rare for any church congregation in the world. I'd like to call Dr. Paul the greatest preacher of this generation but I might be out of a job tomorrow. But he is certainly the greatest announcer! Foster Hewitt or Gerry Howarth might have come close.

We would gather here in this congregation and we'd hear Malcolm Muggeridge, and Paul Harvey, Francis Schaeffer, and Tony Campolo, Alan Redpath, Billy Kim, Bill Bright, Corrie TenBoom, Dale Evans, David Mainse, E.V. Hill, John Hagee, Franklin Graham, George Sweeting, Harold Ockenga, Harold Lindsell — these were all giants of the faith. And Ken Moon, Luis Palau, Leighton Ford, people like Ollie North and Paul Kaufman, Pat Robertson, Rex Humbard, Richard Wurmbrand, Richard Roberts. I remember the packouts for Tom Skinner and Torrey Johnson, and Warren Wiersbe. Will we ever forget the night Ken Campbell brought Anita Bryant, and Dr. Paul Smith has never had egg on his face but he had a pie on his face that night delivered by a dissident who had other ideas about what should be proclaimed from this platform. And then there were those who would tell us how soon the Lord was coming, Hal Lindsay has been here regularly, and Jack Van Impe, and John Walvoord. — We've just had a wealth of proclamation from this pulpit.

But I suppose the greatest feature has been these World Mission conferences, and can you believe it, $37 million dollars raised during the incumbency of Dr. Paul Smith. But that's only a fraction of what's been raised by Dr. Smith in the 84 countries around the world where he's triggered and proliferated these missionary conferences which were initiated by his father but Paul was the improviser.

Tonight he passes the baton to Dr. John Hull.

Let's dream together, and together let's watch what God will do as this church continues to say:
THE SUPREME TASK OF THE CHURCH IS THE EVANGELIZATION OF THE WORLD.
Thank you and God bless you.

And now I am called to deliver a charge on behalf of this congregation and the retiring senior minister; and to welcome to this pulpit and to this authority Dr. John Hull. I refer you to the passage read tonight, II Timothy 4: 1-8: "I charge thee therefore before God, and the Lord Jesus Christ . . . Preach the word . . . reprove, rebuke, exhort with all longsuffering."

J. Hull
C. Price

And I charge you, Dr. John D. Hull, to do three things:
1. Evangelicalize
2. Evangelize
3. Eventualize

Paul is an old man writing to the young man Timothy and he says: 'I CHARGE THEE therefore.' And he has three points that I'm sure Dr. Paul Smith would want to stress to Dr. John Hull.

Number One: Evangelicalize: Preach the Word.

With regard to what and how we are to preach, Dr. John Hull, there are three words:
The first is REPROVE, or prove it, convince us from the Word of God.

And then, not only REPROVE, but REBUKE, and the better word here is CORRECT. We have some lifestyles around here that don't square with the Word of God, and Dr. John Hull, we need you to correct us from this pulpit.

But don't hammer us too hard because the third word after REPROVE and REBUKE is EXHORT, and it

means ENCOURAGE. We get down on ourselves sometimes, so far down that we have to look up to see bottom; we could play pingpong against the curb. We need you to lift us up and encourage us.

Secondly, EVANGELIZE. There are two slogans around here:
THE LIGHT THAT SHINES FARTHEST AROUND THE WORLD SHINES BRIGHTEST HERE AT HOME, and also:
WHY SHOULD ANYONE HEAR THE GOSPEL TWICE BEFORE EVERYONE HAS HEARD IT ONCE?
So we need evangelism here. We need that message crystal clear,

Finally, don't ever neglect, Dr. John Hull, to EVENTUALIZE us. Because as Carlisle said, 'He who has no vision of eternity will never get a true hold of time.' And Paul writes to the young man

There's been no church in this generation that has put its arms around the whole world like this congregation has, led by Dr. Paul Smith. And I'm sure there'll be a continuity.

And that's what I'd like to conclude with regarding Paul Smith and John Hull: it's my prayer that pivoting from Peoples Church both of you, as the Lord grants his strength, will take the gospel from your hearts to the whole world.

In the Name of the Father and of the Son and of the Holy Ghost, Amen.'

Chairman of the Board, Jack Allen, then led in the dedication: "To you, our congregation, today we celebrate a partnership in ministry

This partnership to make disciples must include the whole church in REACHING THE BACK ROWS AND STRENGTHENING THE BELIEVER. You are charged by God to take your place as the spiritual leader of The Peoples Church according to gifts bestowed by the Spirit of God. Be careful to balance your ministry and service with renewal, recreation, and careful attendance to the needs of your family.

Finally, your most important charge is to love — unconditionally, consistently and simply — after the example of our Lord.

Paul Smith then invited Sharon Hull to join her husband on the platform. Turning to John he said: "I am wearing tonight my father's robe. In 1959 when I became the senior pastor of The Peoples Church he gave me this robe and I've worn it for a generation. And now at last it's time to pass it on." And with a dramatic flourish, Paul lifted the heavy robe from off his slight shoulders and placed it around the younger man. "I'm glad to get rid of that, it's getting hot," Paul quipped with his typical quiet humour.

Dr. John Hull,

looking back

on his six wonderful

years of ministry at

The Peoples

Church.

Looking back.

Following his six years of tremendously fruitful ministry at the Peoples Church, Dr. John Hull was asked to summarize the impact his ministry had on the life of the church from his viewpoint.

"God used me to be someone to stabilize the ministry. Initially, I felt great responsibility to lead the transition from Dr. Smith with a great amount of care and dignity. The late 1980's and early 1990's were the most turbulent in the church's history. Dr. Smith's failing health, an aborted relocation plan, and a terrible economy took it's toll on the congregation. People were uneasy, impatient, and anxious about the future. So, I set out to try to instill a culture of stability in the midst of an unstable period. Dr. Smith passed away on April 30, 1995. In the two years we worked together, he was supportive of my efforts to take The Peoples Church into a new era of ministry. I will forever be indebted to him for his confidence in me.

"I also sensed that the world mission image of the church had lost some of the luster and needed some new energy. So, I lengthened the conference from three Sundays to four (some thing Oswald Smith had done in previous years). We worked very hard to get the church to once again focus on what Oswald called "the back rows" of the world, away from our problems at home. I also formed a more traditional style "missions committee" made up of lay people, to oversee the management of mission funds and to review our mission policy. That was very healthy for us and was one of those behind the scenes strategies that eventually brought greater public confidence to the "faith promise giving" plan.

"The church, due to economic issues and uncertainties about who would succeed Dr. Smith, had experienced a drastic drop in donations. In fact, during my first few months on site we struggled just to make the payroll. Some drastic measures had to be taken. So, with the help of some bright board members, we publicly went to the congregation and disclosed where we were and what we needed to do to correct our indebtedness. We were creative, bold and transparent – and the people got behind us wanting to correct our course.

I also wanted the church to experience great worship once again. The music ministry had never gotten back the momentum that had been present after David Williams had retired. So, I hired Danny Daniels to become our Minister of

Danny Daniels and family.

Dr. John Hull,
filming missions conference.

Dr. Timothy Starr.

Music and Worship Arts. Danny was with us for four years. He got The Peoples Church singing again. I was convinced that when our worship once again became powerful, our leadership credible, and our missions emphasis re-energized, The Peoples Church would recover. By God's grace, I was right. I believe my main contribution was in helping the church to regain confidence and rediscover its vision.

"As the church got healthier, we experienced better health in the other arenas of the organization. The Christian school excelled, the missions ministry expanded, and the television ministry became more technologically current. The Peoples Magazine was given new luster under the unmatched leader ship of Dr. Timothy Starr. We added a second morning service. We completely remodeled the auditorium as well as other areas of the building. We attempted a contemporary Saturday night service, which admittedly struggled, but it was a radical and faith-filled effort. Wonderful board members and a great ministry are the reasons that Peoples experienced the comeback that it did in the nineties. It was hard work, painful at times, but it was worth every sacrifice. Today, the church is thriving and surpasses in influence far beyond what Oswald Smith would have ever thought possible. In short, in 1993 we were mourning. By 2000, we were dancing!"

John Hull – taking the next step.
In 2000, Dr. Hull received a request from the Injoy Group, based in Atlanta, Georgia, to become its senior vice-president. The opportunity to challenge over 100,000 churches worldwide to put missions first, offered great scope for furtherance of the Kingdom. Thus it was that The Peoples Church said its sad goodbyes, grateful for Dr. Hull's wonderful ministry.

In January, 2003, EQUIP International launched the "Million Leaders Mandate" under Dr. Hull's leadership. They are committed to training and resourcing one million church leaders by 2008. Over 290,000 leaders are participating in this initiative. John and his team travel all over the world speaking and motivating pastors to better their leadership skills so that they will more effectively fulfill the Great Commission of Jesus Christ. As a frequent speaker at pastors' conferences and global outreach events, John frequently speaks at many well-known Christian organizations, including Ravi Zacharias' International Ministries, Campus Crusade, Focus on the Family, Moody Bible Institute and Billy Graham School of Evangelism. He recently co-authored, *Pivotal Praying,* with Tim Elmor.

Louise Cartagenise,
Dr. Hull's personal assistant.

A Tribute to the Hull Family

We give of our best for missions...

By William F. White   *(Abridged.)*

William F. White
Chairman, Board of
Directors and Managers.

Little did The Peoples Church know the enormous impact God had in mind when He brought Rev. John D. Hull to serve as pastor in 1993. Pastor Hull was 36 years of age when the Hull family arrived in Toronto. God called them to Canada from Atlanta, Georgia to follow Dr. Paul B. Smith, son of Oswald J. Smith who founded the church in 1928. It was a moving service, when on May 15, 1994 Dr. Paul Smith took off his ministerial robe, the one his father gave him 34 years earlier, and placed it on the shoulders of this young, energetic pastor.

As with most successful leaders, John Hull immediately began the job of building an effective leadership team, reinforcing and affirming our gifted pastors and leaders in the field of administration, pastoral care, seniors, youth and children's ministry. This team would operate the daily activities of the total organization, enabling our pastor to spend 50% of his time on global missions. Our staff embraced growth for God's kingdom, and with God's blessing this growth has resulted in a broader financial base, enhancing stability and long term potential for ministry.

We believe it is the plan of God to reach the uttermost parts of the earth with the gospel by working through His own people. The Faith Promise Offering is made in dependence upon God and is a promise in faith to give a certain amount over a one-year period in support of missions. In the Bible Paul illustrates this faith in II Corinthians 9 by a farmer who reaped what he sowed in faith, believing the sun and rain that God provided would prosper the amount of seed he had sown. God honours this faith commitment of Christians.

In order for godly men and women to be more fruitful, they must be ready to be transplanted when God so wills. On March 5, 2000 the Hulls announced their leaving for Atlanta, where John will become senior vice-president of the Injoy Group, a Christian leadership development ministry. Pastor Hull's relocation is a most significant hire for John C. Maxwell, the founder of Injoy, and an enormous loss for The Peoples Church. Dr. Hull's new role with Injoy will be to develop and present seminars, curricula and programming on the Faith Promise Offering. He will be working with more than 100,000 churches worldwide, enabling them to use the Faith Promise Offering and challenging these churches to put missions first. Dr. Hull is gifted and equipped and called by God in this area of responsibility. We give of our best for missions, and Pastor John Hull and his family are our very best.

We have been blessed with Pastor Hull's God-given ability to preach the scriptures with relevance to everyday living without compromise. Pastor John's wife of 17 years, Sharon, has been a blessing to all who have come to know her. She is a kind and gracious woman reflecting God's own heart. The Hull's elder child, Andy, is 13 years old and will be going into grade 9 this September. Andy is known for his smile and warm personality. Mary Alice is 10 years old and will be going into grade 6. She is a model of good behaviour and a real joy. After their move, the Hull family will be living twelve minutes away from both sets of parents and grandparents where they will be available to them during their senior years. God cares for families and it is time, John and Sharon know, for them to be where they are most needed and called by God.

For I know the plans that I have for you, says the Lord, plans to help you and not to hurt you, plans to give you hope and a future. (Jeremiah 29:11).

God cares for families and it is time, John and Sharon know, for them to be where they are most needed and called by God.

Please join us on Sunday, June 18th at 6:30 pm
for an evening of dedication of the Hull family to their new ministry,
and celebration of what God has done through them
at The Peoples Church over the last seven years.

Dr. John D. Hull

The impact he has had and will continue to have...

Dr. Vern Heidebrecht

"The storyline John shaped at The Peoples Church drew people like a magnet. The impact he has had and will continue to have in my life and many other lives, is treasured. You are the man, John! John and Sharon, we bless you as you transition to your new area of ministry. You are a wonderful couple with a great family, As Brennan Manning puts it, 'May your life continue to have The Signature of Jesus.'"

Dr. Vern Heidebrecht, Senior Pastor
Northview Community Church
Abbotsford, B.C.

"From our vantage point today the evidence is overwhelming – this has been an 'Esther - moment', a divine appointment. How thrilling it has been to see what God has done through your gracious servanthood, visionary leadership and solid biblical preaching. Our love and prayers are with you as you begin a new chapter in your walk with God."

Dr. William McRae
Tyndale College & Seminary
Toronto, Ontario

"Many outstanding American pastors have served with distinction in Canada over the years, but none have more effectively identified with Canada and done it as rapidly than John Hull. Although facing many significant challenges in his large church, he was always available to help other churches and organizations. Thank you, John, for modeling servant leadership! Thank you for leading, not only The Peoples Church in missions but the whole city of Toronto and beyond through your nation wide TV program."

Dr. Arnold L. Cook, President
The Christian and Missionary Alliance
in Canada

"For the time I've served as President of Focus on the Family, Canada, I've counted it an honour to know and work with the [Hull's] on behalf of families across the country. John, Sharon, Andy and Mary Alice – thank you for being faithful to God's call in coming to Canada. You've made a real difference here for the Kingdom. And I know our Father has even greater work for you in the years to come!

Darrel Reid, Ph.D.
President, Focus on the Family Canada

"I'll not forget my first meeting with John. He quickly established himself as one who understood the issues at hand and had both the fortitude and vision to move ahead. His public ministry and reaching out to the marginalized have given us all better standing as ministers of the Gospel and evangelicals in particular. I recall an aunt of mine in Winnipeg, now unable to get to church, telling me that she doesn't feel so disadvantaged now as she has another pastor. I asked her who. She responded, "Pastor Hull".

Brian C. Stiller, President
Tyndale College & Seminary
Toronto, Ontario

"John Hull, an excellent ambassador for Christ, has blessed Canada greatly by his clear and forceful proclamation of God's Word on television. Dr. Hull, in a wise and compassionate way, kept the high mission of The Peoples Church alive in the minds and hearts of all Canadians. Because of his leadership, Peoples continues to be #1 in missions."

David Mainse, President
Crossroads Christian
Communications Inc.

Dr. William McRae

Dr. Arnold L. Cook

Darrel Reid, Ph.D.

Brian C. Stiller

David Mainse

J. Hull
C. Price

The Peoples Magazine

When the Church Prays

God's purpose and plans

By Reg Andrews

(Abridged.)

Never is pastoral leadership so challenged as when a decision is made to undertake a prayer initiative. Personnel shortfall and facility roadblocks seem to suddenly appear. Programming conflicts which are normally quite easily resolved become huge obstacles. The will and determination of church leadership to continue a prayer emphasis are seriously tested. The notion of spiritual warfare shifts from objective fact to subjective reality.

The value of prayer is well established both in the Word of God and in the history of the church.

The role of prayer in the ministry of the apostles is evident from the reading of such scriptures as Colossians 4:12 and Romans 12:12. The role of prayer in bringing revival to the church and renewal in society is on record. The Laymen's Revival of 19th century America and the great Welsh Revival at the turn of the last century are among the many historical attestations to the power of corporate prayer. The great prayer warrior of a bygone era, E. M. Bounds wrote:

> Prayer concerns God, whose purposes and plans are conditioned on prayer. His will and His glory are bound up in praying. The days of God's splendour and renown have always been the great days of prayer. God's great movements in this world have been conditioned on, continued and fashioned by prayer. God has put Himself in these great movements just as men have prayed.[1]

Here's a compelling invitation to the 21st century church "LET US PRAY"!

[1] E. M. Bounds *The Weapon of Prayer* Grand Rapids: Baker Book House, 1978 p. 10

Interim leadership.

Perhaps one of the greatest tributes to the ministry of John Hull came over the span of the 15 months between his leaving and the arrival of his successor. So solidly had he restructured the foundations of the church, that it not only survived, but grew and prospered under the leadership of the existing support staff.

Although it was a time when many pitched in with prayer, abilities and energies, the history of The Peoples Church would not be complete without noting the outstanding leadership of three men: Rev. Reg Andrews, the Senior Associate Pastor; Rev. Don McNiven, Headmaster of The Peoples Church Academy and Minister of Music; and Brian Dawkins, the Business Manager.

In the Interim...

Rev. Reg Andrews.

New Beginnings

Let us seize this new day

By Reg Andrews *(Abridged.)*

The Peoples Church is set to begin a new era of ministry. The ministry of Charles Price will bring with it a fresh approach, a new emphasis and every reason for renewed optimism. His teaching gifts will challenge us in new ways and provide us with inspiration and promise.

Essentially, though, The Peoples Church will continue to be The Peoples Church. It will be held by the same doctrinal moorings and will be guided by the same core values to which it has cleaved historically. World evangelization and Christian maturity among believers will continue to be the goals that we seek to achieve. Our foundation as a church will allow us to face new beginnings with the greatest optimism.

What an exciting future we have before us! At this present time, we can be confident in the future because of what God has done and said in the past! Let us seize this new day and, at the same time, adhere faithfully to the foundational truths which have made us who we are.

As for God, his way is perfect; the word of the Lord is flawless. He is a shield for all those who take refuge in him. (Psalm 18:30)

The Peoples Magazine

We Celebrate What Jesus Has Done

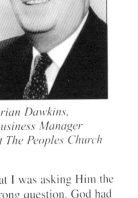

*Brian Dawkins,
Business Manager
at The Peoples Church*

As I sat with my children, Scott and Stephanie, in a Scarborough public school gymnasium, on Mothers' Day, 1980, God spoke to my heart, at a Sunday service of The Anglican Church of the Nativity. At a child-sized balance beam that served as the alter rail for the church, Jesus Christ entered my life in a very profound way. The series of events leading to this day were filled with turmoil, and the days that followed continued to challenge my new found relationship with Jesus Christ.

In 1978 after 9 years of marriage and two children, we discovered that my wife, Brenda, had a brain tumor that required surgery. The operation was successful, but in 1979 Brenda had to return to London when her condition seemed to worsen. During the night a Christian nurse came and read Scripture and prayed with Brenda. This ignited her search for the meaning of life which culminated in her acceptance of Jesus as Saviour and Lord. The change in her was so dramatic that it was not long until my search began, culminating on that Sunday in May, 1980.

The next 10 years were filled with more surgery, many epileptic seizures and ultimately Brenda's death at age 41, but we were never without hope. How fitting that Brenda should pass into Jesus' presence on the Saturday between Good Friday and Easter Sunday, 1989. I so clearly remember being with my church family on that Easter Sunday as we celebrated what Jesus had done for each of us. How real it was to realize that He had already prepared a place for Brenda.

If I thought the days leading to Brenda's death were tough, I had much to learn. I threw myself into work to mask the pain with busyness. Our company had been sold to another major oil company, and the work of putting the two companies together had begun in earnest. It was easy to get busy because there was so much to do. No matter what time I arrived home from work, the same despair and self pity greeted me at the door. I attended church and prayer meetings every week, but was there in body, not in spirit. In early June at a prayer meeting, I asked for prayer, and for the first time in more than a year, I was open to God's intervention.

I arrived home to a written message marked 'urgent'. I was to call my wife's friend, Sharon, who told me she had met a woman at her office who would be 'perfect' or me. Liz and I met at a Strawberry Social at Bayview Glen Church later that month, and it was evident that God had been keeping her single just for me. I proposed in November, 1990, and we were married in May, 1991. My trials were over... Or were they?

What followed the joy of our wedding day and honeymoon was to stretch us and deepen our faith. Rebellious teens, long periods of unemployment and financial difficulties left me asking God "Why me?" Hadn't I endured enough? What I learned through these trials was that I was asking Him the wrong question. God had wanted me to ask Him "Lord, what are You trying to teach me through this?" In 1994 He impressed on me that I simply had to trust Him in all things. When I submitted to His will, He presented me an opportunity to work at The Peoples Church.

Today finds me happily married to Liz for nearly ten years, fulfilled in my call to serve my Lord as the Business Manager at Peoples, and proud to be the father of 2 beautiful, responsible, independent, tax paying young adults.

In Jeremiah 29:11 God's Word says, "For I know the thoughts that I think toward you, saith the Lord thoughts of peace, and not of evil, to give you an expected end." KJV.

His plans for us are perfect! All we have to do is surrender to Him and listen carefully for His instructions.

J. Hull
C. Price

Tribute to the McNiven Family

Fun loving, caring, serving...

By William F. White

*William F. White
Chairman, Board of
Directors and Managers.*

Little did we know the impact God had in mind when He brought you to us.

One of the most exciting aspects of any ministry is seeing God at work in the lives of leaders such as Don and Sue McNiven. Don and Sue have attended The Peoples Church since 1980, except for a period from 1983 to 1990 when Don was called to be President at Niagara Christian College. In 1990 Don was asked to return to Peoples Christian Academy. These were difficult years financially for The Peoples Church, due to the failed relocation of the church, and Don proved to be God's chosen vehicle for getting the school back on track. As an effective leader, he

managed to build a capable team, reinforcing and affirming the gifts of the principals, teachers and all those involved in the education process.

The past seven years at the academy represent a time of significant growth and substantial change. From our success in attracting top quality staff to the impact of our teachers on the lives of the young people God has placed in our charge, we see the evidence of God's hand at work. In 1993 the student enrollment was approximately 450 which has expanded to 750 in 2000. Demand for our school has increased yearly and Don and his team have worked creatively to meet that demand on this campus. Our financial results have been positive each year under Don's leadership and much work has been done to improve our school facilities. The Peoples Christian Academy revenue now exceeds $3,500,000 per year. More importantly, approximately 80% of our graduating classes achieve Ontario Scholars status, demonstrating the academic excellence that prepares them for further education and development. We are grateful to God for Don and Sue, all teachers, staff and volunteers who work so well together to accomplish our goal of delivering quality education in the context of a Christian day school with emphasis on preparing the next generation for the Lord's service.

Having fulfilled a God-given determination to turn Peoples Christian Academy around and return it to its

The Peoples Magazine

glory, Don is retiring from the position of Headmaster on September 1, 2000. Recently ordained, he has now taken on the full time position of Minister of Music and Worship Arts for The Peoples Church. A gifted musician, he has for years been serving in this capacity whenever called upon.

In addition to being the Minister of Music and Worship Arts, Don continues as a senior staff member of the Board of Directors and Managers of The Peoples Church. As such he works in close consultation with Reg Andrews, Brian Dawkins and the Search and Selection Committee for finding our new Senior Pastor.

Don and Sue are a fun loving, caring and serving family. Their son, Christopher and his wife, Jennifer are presently living in Chicago where Chris is pursuing his Masters Degree at Trinity Divinity School. Their daughter, Michelle, and her husband, Brad, (both teachers) are living in Toronto and have two children, Daniel and Caitlin.

Thank you Don and Sue for your pursuit of excellence in the work of God. Little did we know the impact God had in mind when He brought you to us: *For I know the plans that I have for you, says the Lord, plans to help you and not to hurt you, plans to give you hope and a future* (Jer. 29:11)

Don McNiven in 1980.

J. Hull
C. Price

We are grateful to God for Don and Sue, all teachers, staff and volunteers who work so well together to accomplish our goal of delivering quality education...

1990

Enjoying his grandchildren

The Peoples Magazine

The Price Family

Welcoming the Price family:
Left to right: Charles, Hannah, Matthew, Laura and Hilary.

A new era.
Having been skillfully transitioned from the world-changing Smith era, and repositioned on a solid foundation by Dr. John Hull, the church was prepared for meeting the demands of the twenty-first century.

Passing the baton to Charles Price.
In 2000, Charles Price was the guest speaker at the Toronto Spiritual Life Conference, planned by an inter-church committee, but held at The Peoples Church for four nights in January. On one of those evenings, as Charles sat on the platform during the first part of the service, he had a strange, but very strong, sensation. As he looked around the auditorium, he felt that God whispered in his ear, "This is where you belong."

Though vivid and unmistakable, it seemed unrealistic and impossible. John Hull was obviously riding the crest of a wave, seeing significant growth, was greatly loved by the people and likely to be the Senior Pastor for the long haul.

Upon his return home to England, Charles told Hilary about his strange impression. She replied, "I knew you would come home and say something like this." Tucking the experience into the back of their minds, Charles and Hilary believed that if this was of God, it would come to pass in His timing. Conversely, if not of God, it would die a natural death.

About six weeks later, an e-mail from Toronto arrived with a casual comment that John Hull was resigning from the church and moving back to Atlanta. Turning to Hilary, Charles said, 'This will change our lives – but we will tell no one, and do nothing to indicate any interest on our part. If this is from God he will work it out."

Some weeks later, Reg Andrews, Senior Associate Pastor of The Peoples Church, called Charles inviting him to Toronto for a weekend to assist in filling the pulpit soon to be vacated by John Hull. Despite initial difficulties in coordinating dates, Charles was confident that if God wanted him at The Peoples Church, it would be without any manipulation on his part.

Charles met with the Board of Directors on the Saturday morning of his visit, and the subsequent developments led to his induction on September 9, 2001.

J. Hull
C. Price

Ordination and Installation of
Charles Price
New Senior Pastor
of The Peoples Church
Sunday, September 9th, 2001
6:30 p.m.

Guest Preacher: Dr. Gary Walsh
President of Evangelical
Fellowship of Canada

Special Guest: Dr. Don Jost
Former Senior Associate Pastor

Guest Musician: Pat Russell

You are invited to greet our
New Pastor and His Family
during the Fellowship Hour.

Charles Price – the early years.

Charles Price grew up in a Christian home in the rural county of Herefordshire in the West of England. Despite the fact that he recited the language of "asking Jesus into his heart," he had no assurance that he was a Christian. The mechanics were in place, but without any sense of reality.

When he was 12 years old, the local "Youth For Christ" committee was holding monthly Saturday night evangelistic rallies in the city of Hereford. One month, they advertised the showing of a Billy Graham film, "Shadow Of The Boomerang," which had been filmed against the backdrop of a Billy Graham crusade in Australia. Charles' family hardly ever saw movies, and with no television in their home, he and his older brother were very excited about going to see it.

The two arrived at the Town Hall venue and found the building jam-packed. With no seats left, they stood against the side wall as the story unfolded for 90 minutes. The leading character became caught up in a series of dramatic and tense events which led to his listening to Billy Graham in a landline relay to his community. As the invitation to receive Christ was given thousands of miles away in the city of Melbourne, this man walked to the front of the small outback building, to stand with a few others before a huge wooden speaker, and gave himself to Jesus Christ. As the film drew to its close, Charles felt a surge of desire to know Christ himself. He knew God was speaking to him.

At the conclusion of the film, a man got up at the front, reiterated the main points of the Gospel and invited people to "come forward" as an indication of their desire to receive Christ. People began to move to the front. Although Charles longed to become a Christian, he stayed where he was, too embarrassed to do anything so public – but, standing against the wall, he prayed, telling God about his lack of assurance and that, more than anything else, he wanted to be a Christian. He asked for forgiveness and invited Him to live within. This time, although there was no defining sensation, Charles planted a firm intent in his heart that Jesus Christ should be Lord of his life. Nevertheless, if someone had asked him later that night if he had become a Christian, he still wouldn't have known for sure.

The next day being Sunday, Charles went to the small village Brethren Assembly, as was the family custom. For the first time he could

Billy Graham.

Mr. and Mrs. Price, Sr. Charles' parents.

Charles (left – with "walnut whip hairstyle!"), John and Stephen.

Charles, far right, and siblings.

Charles Price.

Into all the World

remember, the service was interesting. When he returned that evening, he was pleasantly surprised that the preacher made sense. It *amazed* him that the people had changed overnight; the meetings, once dull and boring, were interesting! It suddenly dawned on him that it was not "they" who had changed, but that something had happened to him, the evidence of his salvation being a new appetite – a hunger and thirst for righteousness. He was excited – certain – and knew life would not be the same again!

Very quickly, Charles sensed that God would one day lead him into some kind of Christian ministry, probably as an evangelist. Eager to get on with his calling, he began to organize meetings where he could preach to kids his age – in barns during the summer with hay bales for pews, and in the Price living room on wintery Sunday afternoons.

The fact that he had no idea how to preach didn't stop young Charles. Getting hold of some *Hour of Decision* booklets containing Billy Graham's sermons, he used them to pattern his own simple messages. Not overly fussy about his audience, he would preach his heart out to the livestock when alone in the barn. Other days, he would walk over the hills and through the woods, preaching to an imaginary crowd. At least one person saved in one of those barn meetings continues to live for Christ, almost forty years later. About the cattle, we're not so sure!

At the age of 16, Charles made the transforming discovery that the Christian life was not about him doing his best to live for Christ, but about Christ living *His* life in Charles and doing *His* work *through* him. While working during his summer vacation at Capernwray Hall (a young people's conference center and Bible School in the North of England), he was exposed to the ministry of

men like Major Ian Thomas, Stuart Briscoe and Billy Strachan. Under such teaching, he began to understand the meaning and significance of Christ's indwelling in his life as his only source of strength and power.

That same summer, Charles, with a few friends, began to get together on Saturday nights to try and reach young people in the area with the Gospel. First going to popular hangouts for teenagers, they soon began to preach on the streets of Hereford on Saturday afternoons. Before long, they were being invited to take Sunday evening evangelistic services in small churches around the county of Herefordshire and up into the bordering Welsh hills. By the time Charles was 17, he and his friends were taking services almost every Sunday night.

Discipled.

With his background in farming, at the age of 18, in 1968, Charles secured a job managing the livestock section of a large farm in Zimbabwe in Southern Africa. He wanted to see the world before settling down to fulfill God's call on his life. However, before the plane had even gotten as far as Paris, he was filled with a terrible fear that he was out of God's will. Thankfully, the doubts disappeared upon meeting Martin and Jill Tracey (for whom he worked and with whom he lived for the following two years). They quickly became like friends, family and mentors. Farming to the Traceys was a means for God to use their lives and possessions to accomplish His will. They exhibited uncommon commitment and practical godliness in every area of their lives. Thus, Charles found himself in a discipleship school, learning to incorporate God into every detail of his life. Quickly finding opportunities to preach, he ran a Saturday afternoon Bible class for teenage boys and a youth group.

With enough money earned to pay his school fees, Charles returned to Britain to attend the one year Capernwray Bible School and then, for three years, the Bible Training Institute (now the International Christian College) in Glasgow, Scotland. During vacation periods, he engaged in Christian service, preaching most weekends, conducting evangelistic missions in village halls and churches around Britain, and for two summers, smuggled forbidden Bibles into Eastern Europe.

At Capernwray, Charles met Hilary, a high-spirited, beautiful young woman who definitely caught his attention. They married in 1980, and over the next 10 years, God blessed them with three children: Hannah, Laura and Matthew.

I had working for me many (mostly Christian) managers over the fifty years of my farming. I never had any occasion for anything but praise for Charles and his consistent witness to the Lord Jesus Christ.

When he was on the farm and when I had to be away, he took over and led, with the help of an interpreter, the Bible studies which I used to take weekly for the people of the workforce. He also took over the conduct of services in a small chapel where my wife and I ministered to a very small congregation.

A very close relationship swiftly developed between us which has lasted all the years. He called in on us in Adelaide last month. The five hours we had together were so wonderful that it was hard to tear ourselves apart.

Martin Tracey.

Into all the World

Capernwray Missionary Fellowship of Torchbearers.

On completing his studies in Glasgow, Charles was invited by Major Ian Thomas, the founder and director of the Capernwray Missionary Fellowship of Torchbearers, to join his staff at Capernwray Hall. It was the headquarters of the movement that had spread across the world with more than twenty conference centers and Bible schools. Charles' job description was very simple: "Preach Christ!" Although he was to direct the summer conference program and teach in the year-long Bible School, for more than six months of the year he was to travel and preach wherever God opened doors.

Over the next quarter of a century, until 2001, Charles' feet hardly touched the ground as he traveled and preached in every part of the British Isles and into most European countries. He made exactly one hundred visits to the North American Continent; twenty-seven to Australia and New Zealand; and numerous others to the Caribbean, Far East, India and Middle East; and to Southern, Western and Eastern Africa. In 1993, he became Principal of Capernwray Bible School.

Major Ian Thomas,
founder and director of
the Capernwray Missionary
Fellowship of Torchbearers.

J. Hull
C. Price

Uniting hearts for missions.

With the uniting of the two hearts, that of The Peoples Church with that of Charles Price, the major emphasis of The Peoples Church on world missions is being carried forth into the twenty-first century. Oswald Smith's pattern of sacrificial giving, which has enabled the church to send many millions of dollars across the world, and in particular to invest in unreached parts of the world, goes on. The church remains effective when it puts the spreading of the Gospel first. Charles says,

> "I live every day with a sense of privilege at being part of what I consider to be one of the most strategic churches in the world, serving a wonderfully kind and loving congregation, with a superb staff team in one of the great cities of the world. And underscoring all of that is the confidence that despite all my limitations, inabilities and fumblings, God put our family here, and in that we are secure. If I have a life verse, it is,
>> 'The One who calls you is faithful, and He will do it.' *(I Thessalonians 5:24)*
> God has undertaken the responsibility to accomplish what He has called us to. Our job is to be available, obedient and dependent, and to leave the consequences with Him."

Into all the World

Welcome, Charles, Hilary, Hannah, Laura & Matthew

From the Chairman, William F. White

*William F. White
Chairman, Board of
Directors and Managers.*

Charles and his family have been associated with The Peoples Church over the past 15 years.

As Chairman of the Board of Directors and Managers, it is a great privilege and honour to introduce to you our new Senior Pastor, Charles Price and his lovely family, who will be joining us in a few weeks.

He has written six books which are currently in print: *Christ For Real* and *Alive In Christ* (both published in the USA by Kregal, and in Britain by Kingsway Publications under the titles *Stop Trying To Live For Jesus*, and *Christ In You*), *Commentaries on Joshua* (published by Crossway in the UK), and *Matthew* (Christian Focus Publications). *Paul: Moulded By His Message* (Kingsway) was published in January this year, and a history of the famous Keswick Convention, *Transforming Keswick*, was jointly written with Ian Randall and published in July 2000. He also contributes a monthly column to *Evangelism Today* (in the UK), and has written for a number of periodicals in the UK, America and Australia, including *Decision* magazine, published by the Billy Graham Evangelistic Association. He has spoken at some of the major Christian gatherings in the UK, such as the Keswick Convention, and Spring Harvest, and was recently appointed to the Council of the Keswick Convention. Hilary has been editing books, speaking at women's conferences, teaching Sunday School (as does Hannah), attending court for witness support, and doing freelance instructing at the local education centre.

Charles and his family have been associated with The Peoples Church over the past 15 years. An internationally known Bible teacher and evangelist, he has preached many times in our pulpit, and has never been far from our hearts. When he suffered a serious heart attack, while speaking at the staff training week at Muskoka Sports Resort in the summer of 1998, we prayed and helped bring his family over to him, and then praised God for his recovery. Charles has been very dear to us as a church over the years, even called by us several years ago, the fulfillment of that call we are now seeing in God's perfect timing.

God willing, we look forward to the arrival in September of Charles, Hilary, Hannah, Laura, and Matthew, who have each been called to be with us. We welcome them with open arms and pray for a smooth transition from their responsibilities back home to their happy establishment in our city and in our church.

The Peoples Magazine

The ministry of Charles Price in Australia has been incredibly used of God to bring many into a living relationship with the living Saviour. Charles' tapes have gone out to the length and breadth of the country. Hence, even when he is not with us we are still hearing his teaching and being blessed. Charles, by his life as well as his talented ability with words and expression to convey truth in a meaningful way, declares palpably to all who know him, "For me, to live is Christ."
Richard and Glenys Drew.
Richard Drew – Professor of Etymology, University of Queensland; Leader of Capernwray, Queensland.

I've known Charles Price for many years and taught Mission at Capernwray Bible School where he was the Principal.

Charles was enthusiastic about the place of world missions in the teaching program at Capernwray and took every opportunity to ensure that Mission had a high priority.

I also knew Charles through his contributions to the Keswick Convention and will never forget one night when he preached the missionary message of the Convention and gave the appeal which followed. His passion for the Gospel to be known throughout the world came through so clearly in that ministry.

I'm delighted that Charles is now with you at the Peoples Church. I believe his Biblical ministry and his continuing emphasis on Mission will be extremely fruitful in the work there.

Peter Maiden.
International Director of Operation Mobilization and Chairman of the English Keswick Convention.

My introduction to Charles and Hilary Price came in 1980, when they came to speak at the small conference center we ran in the southern mountains of New Zealand. They were in their first year of marriage and we had no idea we we would be entertaining "angels unawares".

Charles and Hilary have impacted our lives along with thousands of other New Zealanders (kiwis). Charles has unlocked inspirational energy wherever he has gone in New Zealand. To use his term, "the penny drops" as he explains, with in-depth analysis, scriptures that used to be in the "too hard" basket.

Peter Yarrell,
Christchurch, New Zealand.

Canadians sometimes get caught in a squeeze: from the US dynamic and flamboyant preachers and from the UK laid back and stodgy. This time we are remarkably blessed. Charles Price brings to our world powerful insights from the Word in a challenging and winsome way. He models for us all an understanding of preaching which is not only rooted in the Word but presented with a rich Holy Spirit anointing. My prayer is that his ministry will help raise up a new generation who both love to, and know how to, preach in this post-modern age.

Dr Brian C Stiller,
President, Tyndale University College & Seminary.

J. Hull
C. Price

So extensive has been the thrust of The Peoples Church into foreign missions, that these pages can touch only briefly upon selections, like skipping stones across an ocean, seeking to send ripples of inspiration to those who will cry, "Here am I, send me."

Six

Into all the World

Missionary Travels

Missions come first at The Peoples Church. Everything else is viewed in light of that focus.

Sympathy for the lost is not preached so much as giving, in order to carry out God's program, which is to evangelize the unevangelized tribes of the earth and thus bring back the King, according to

Revelation 5:9
Acts 1:8
Matthew 24:1

Into all the World

The passion of Oswald Smith's life was, "to bring back the King through world evangelization." He reasoned with his people from the platform:

"'Why must we continue to reach out?' you ask. 'Souls are being saved here by the scores. Why not concentrate here, and evangelize our own country?'

"I ask you why did David Livingstone leave for Africa before everyone in Scotland had become a Christian? Why did William Carey go to India and leave so many of his own countrymen in darkness? Why did Judson go to Burma before winning the last American to Christ? Why did the Apostle Paul leave Palestine and journey to Europe before he had evangelized his own country?

"Because it was God's plan. Every tribe and tongue must hear. The field is the world, not one section of it, but all of it. 'God so loved the world.' Not a part of it, but all of it. When God thinks, He thinks in terms of a world. You and I must get a world vision if we are to have God's vision.

"Do you remember when the Lord Jesus fed the 5,000, He had them sit down row on row? Then do you remember how He took the loaves and fishes and blessed them and broke them and gave them to His disciples? And do you remember how the disciples started at one end of the front row and went right along that front row giving everyone a helping? Then do you recall how they turned right around and started back along that front row again, asking everyone to take a second helping? No – a thousand times – no! Had they done that, the people in the back rows would have been rising up and protesting, 'Come back here. Give us a helping. We are starving. It isn't right; it isn't fair. Why should those people in the front row have a second helping before we have had a first?'

" I want to see more of the distant fields. I must go; I cannot stay here. Lord, send me out with heart aflame!"
OJS

"There are countless millions in those back rows famishing for the Bread of Life. We must train those in the front rows to share what they have with the back rows, to reach them with the Gospel. 'Unto the uttermost part of the earth,' was His final command. How dare we disobey?

"The front rows, the home work, will never lack. Let those of us who have seen God's vision and heard His call, send out the Gospel to all the world for this is the one and only task that Jesus left for His church to do. If we withhold the Gospel, 'his blood will I require at thine hand,' will apply to us.

"If the King is to reign, we must finish the task. He is counting on us. How long are we going to keep Him waiting? Let us lay everything else aside and concentrate on this one great objective, the completion of the evangelization of the world in our own generation. This, and this alone is the most important work of the hour."

"Just when I get nicely settled, and look forward to years of home life with my family, suddenly I am arrested by the Spirit of God. I hear His Call, and I have to go. I am restless. My soul is stirred within me. A vision of earth's perishing multitudes grips me and sends me forth."

OJS

Opposition to missions.

Secularists today insist that people native to particular cultures should be left alone to live according to their own beliefs. They claim that native traditions need to be not only respected, but encouraged. What they don't understand, is that the true mandate of Christian missions is not to take our brand of civilization to the uncivilized, but to take Christ to people who do not know Him. The goal is to help nationals who become Christians, to deveop their own variety of Christian civilization and build churches that are supported and manned by their own people.

Experience with the brutal situations encountered by Christian missionaries, contrasted with the quality of life enjoyed by the nationals after accepting the Gospel, would give the secularists pause. They would do well to study the cruelty practiced, prior to the introduction of the Jesus factor, in many of the lands through which they travel so comfortably today. Only Jesus can heal the pain in hearts and cleanse people of the anger that makes them lash out against others. Only He can replace depression with bubbling joy. Only He can give solid hope of eternal life.

"The light that shines the farthest shines the brightest nearest home."

"The supreme task of the Church is the evangelization of the world."

OJS

Cannibals.

After retuning from a trip to the Solomon Islands, Oswald wrote about the ministry of a local missionary, Miss Young, in The Peoples Magazine. The story is a clear example of individual and community transformation through the sharing of the Gospel.

"Away up on the hills inland, the fierce, wild bush-men of Malaita are practically inaccessible. They live in the dense forest in fear and dread of one another, for murder stalks abroad, and enemies are on every side. There is no open warfare – men, women, aye, and little children too, are shot, or speared, or clubbed by hidden, treacherous foes, who have no personal grudge against them, but are hired by others to do the dark deed, and rewarded with pigs or strings of native shell money.

"The chief incentive to murder is the belief that all deaths are caused by witchcraft. When a man dies his friends consult a witch-doctor. 'Who has caused this death?' they ask. The witch-doctor goes through some incantations and fixes the guilt upon some unfortunate man, who of course is quite innocent.

"The relatives either kill this man or offer a reward for his murder. If the accused man cannot be found, any man of the same line may be killed in his stead. If they cannot kill a man, a woman will do, if not a woman, then a child. The consequence is, that for almost every death, someone is murdered. The people are often afraid to sleep in their houses at night but hide somewhere in the dense scrub and sleep by day.

"A certain chief in the Uhu Lagoon died. As usual a witch-doctor was consulted as to the cause of his death, and he fixed on a couple named Piri and Polly who had lately returned from Queensland, and Piri's old father. They were living with a little company of Christians at the southern end of the lagoon.

"A big canoe load of heathen warriors came down the lagoon. They lit fires on the mainland for the cannibal feast to follow, and crossed to the small island opposite demanding their victims. Poor Barnabas, the Christian teacher, had no means of defending his flock except by urgent prayer to God. While he was praying, a labour vessel entered the lagoon and anchored. Barnabas took the three frightened victims on board and they sailed away.

"The natives were furious. They threatened to destroy the whole village, and the chief (himself still heathen) in an agony of fear threw out his young daughter, a girl of fourteen or fifteen, to pacify the murderers, and she was killed and eaten that night!"

"In another incident, there came one day to Taravania a hideous old man, dirty in the extreme, for he had never washed. His hair hung in long, filthy strings. He was a witch doctor, and prided himself on its length, and also that he lived in the men's area and never ate food cooked by women. He was reckoned a big fighting man in the bush, and had earned his wealth and his evil reputation by innumerable murders. Years before, he killed and ate his own wife. He even sent his son for water to use in cooking her! When the lad objected, the wicked old father threatened to kill and eat him with his mother!

"The son ran away and found a ship going to Queensland. There he heard the Gospel for the first time and became a bright Christian. He thought about his old father away up in the bush – but surely he was a hopeless case – old and hardened, sunk in degradation and sin, ignorant, superstitious, wicked. By and by, however, he went to see his father and took him down to Taravania to the missionaries.

"There the father heard of Jesus Christ, and within a fortnight God did the impossible thing. That dreadful old man was converted – re-created – changed into a new man within and without. He had his first bath! cut off his long hair, and lived with the Christians, eating the common food cooked by the women. His whole appearance changed.

"He would not go back into the bush, and the people came again and again for him. They brought money and said he must return. He was their witch-doctor. They could not do without him. But the old man told them he was never going back to serve the devil; he had served him all his life. Now he was going to serve the Lord Jesus. In the old days he had gained large sums of native money for murders he had committed, which he had buried somewhere, but he refused to let anyone know where the treasure was hidden, because he said it was the devil's money, and he did not want any one to use it.

"He had a very intelligent grip of what the Lord had done for him, and spoke to every one about Him. At the open-air meetings for the market people he would tell his testimony."

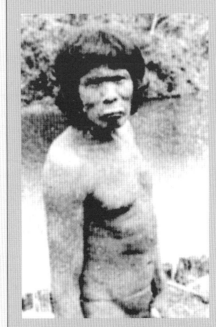

Into all the World

The darkness of secularism.

If those in pagan cultures believe their lives to be improved through accepting the Gospel message, how dare the secularists attempt to impose their beliefs upon them, insisting that they be left in ignorance, just to preserve destructive traditions?

It is one thing to convince secularists of the blatant evil of cannibalism, but quite another to convince them that they and people who look and act the same way they do, need the salvation offered by Jesus Christ. It is not much wonder that secularists oppose proselytizing. The very word "missions" challenges their own hearts. Evil pervades the whole earth, not just the jungles of the Solomon Islands.

Penetrating the darkness of secular Europe with the light of Jesus.

On his return from the Russian fields in 1936, Oswald wrote of the spiritual darkness of Europe in *The Peoples Magazine*.

> "From time to time I have been conscious of demon influence. Evil spirits are real here in Europe. Satan is indeed the god of this world. In certain countries I have been oppressed by forces invisible and yet real. Hosts of wicked spirits have surrounded me, and fought for my life. Again and again in sheer desperation I have had to plead the merits of the Blood, and the power of the Name, to overcome them. Sometimes for days I have been conscious of their presence. Experiences that I have never known in America have been mine in these foreign countries. How easy it would be to allow these demon powers of darkness to swallow me up! Just to let down and give way to them would be the end. I have had to walk the floor and pray through again and again. Yes, demons are real, as every missionary can testify. And only God is able to deliver. Millions in Europe are under their control all the time."

Reaching out with the love of God.

The Spirit of God within Oswald's heart sheltered him from the complacency of human comfort, and thrust him into the battle for the souls of precious men and women. In recounting his experiences in Czechoslovakia during his 1936 trip, he compared the living conditions of Europe to those of North America, and left little doubt concerning the reason for the stark contrast.

> "I saw the ancient castle of the kings, and the revolting prison where men were cruelly tortured and left to die. In the center of a small room, there was a hole large enough for a man to fall through.Below the hole, a smaller room with no windows, no air except from the hole above, and no light. It was a drop of some

Into all the World

John Huss, 1369-1415.
A Bohemian religious reformer
whose teachings were forerunners
of those of the Protestant
Reformation. Burned at the stake
on a charge of heresy.

twenty feet. Through this hole, prisoners were deliberately dropped, the fall generally breaking legs, arms or ribs. Around them, putrefying flesh; the corpses of other victims. These they were commanded to gather up with their hands in the pitch darkness and thrust down a second hole. And then for days they had to lay there bruised and ill in their own filth, until they died. Such is the heart of the natural man – brutal beyond expression.

"I saw the room on the city square where the twenty-seven noblemen spent their last night. The Roman Catholics were then in power. Through the upper windows they were led out and beheaded. One was nailed to a beam through his tongue. Another had his tongue cut out and was then quartered. All had their heads placed on spikes on the bridge tower from where they gazed down on the people for ten long years.

"Most famous of all men in this old Czechoslovakian city is John Huss, the martyred priest. A hundred years before Martin Luther, he saw the Light, and what he read in the Bible he boldly preached. Awakened to the truth by the Word of God, regenerated and enlightened by the Holy Spirit in an age when darkness covered the earth, this man lived, preached and died, a monument of God's grace. The Roman Catholics burned him at the stake. But before his death, the truth prevailed. The memory of John Huss will never fade. The darkness of the middle ages had begun to disappear. Bohemia awoke.

Darkest Europe
A Magazine with a Vision. Edited by Oswald J. Smith
and
Published occasionally in the interest of Russian
and Spanish Missions
by the
World Wide Christian Couriers, 22 Kendal Ave.,
Toronto, Canada
Paul Rader, President; Oswald J. Smith, Director for Canada;
A. G. Malcolm, Secretary; W. C. Willis, Treasurer.
Rev. M. Billester, Western Director.

TEN CENTS   TEN CENTS

"That was a cruel age, the age in which Huss lived. And men have an idea that such scenes can never be witnessed again. Civilization and modern education, they tell us, has changed men's hearts. Is that so? Then what about Russia? And what of Spain? A few days ago I travelled through Spain. All was peaceful. It was hard to think that the courteous soldiers to whom I spoke could ever act like brute beasts. But now look at Spain. A country deluged in blood. Atrocities of all kinds being committed. Civil war. Bolshevism at its worst. Women and children fighting. Priests and nuns buried alive. Cities and towns in ruins. More than 35,000 killed already. And all in this enlightened twentieth century.

"No, my friend, the unregenerate heart of man has known no change. Man without God is still a beast. Civilization, education and culture may hold him in check; but give him his liberty, remove restraint, and his passions will drive him on to the same or even worse deeds of desperation and cruelty than his forefathers ever knew. Only the Gospel can change the hearts of men.

"Europe, my friends, is darker today than Africa, by far. Here in Prague there is a church for 30,000 of the population, and a saloon and a dance hall for every 500. Gospel halls and preaching places are for the most part on back streets, or behind houses, out of sight, and but few in number. Immorality is rampant. Prostitutes abound and solicit openly on the streets. Moral standards in Europe are far below those in America, even including Hollywood. I prophecy that a great revival or a great war will break out in Europe in the not distant future, for Europe is ripe for judgment.

"What, you ask, is the remedy? The Gospel. Millions of salvation tracts should be distributed in every country. The cities should be deluged with Gospel messages. A Million Pocket Testament Campaign would be a God-send. Denominations should be forgotten, and Gospel, soul-winning, evangelistic meetings held in tents and halls everywhere.

"What is it that has saved the Anglo-Saxon nations from the sins of Europe? The Gospel. For even America, with all her crime and divorce, is ablaze with the light of the Gospel. Hundreds of thousands of churches adorn her streets and country highways. Sunday schools care for her children. Open-air services are held from coast to coast. Evangelistic campaigns are conducted in almost every city and town. Multitudes of Christian workers are engaged in spreading the Gospel. Countless millions of Gospel tracts are being distributed. The Bible is a well-known Book. Christian homes abound. Revivals have swept through many sections of the country. America has given the world by far the largest number of Gospel hymns. I find them, translated, wherever Christians meet. Finney, Moody, Sunday, and a host of evangelists have been God's gifts to America. Christian periodicals and books in thousands are published and circulated. There is perfect freedom for the worship of God and the preaching of the Gospel.

"Oh, privileged America! God-blessed America! Little did I appreciate her liberties and advantages until I saw other less-favoured countries. Not for all the world would I want my children to grow up in Europe. Give me a country where the Bible is revered and the Gospel proclaimed, where I can see the children going to Sunday School and the people attending church – where I can listen to the singing of Gospel hymns and associate with God's children. How dark are the countries where there is but little Gospel light! Again and again I have thanked God for Canada and the United States."

Capturing the Cities for God

"We must capture the cities for God!"

"So much to do and so little time!"

"God help us to do more than we have ever done before to get out the message and bring back the King!"

"For years we've been sending missionaries to the jungle when we should have been sending evangelists to the cities. You seldom hear what is happening in the country; but what happens in the city is known everywhere."

"The Apostle Paul always headed for the great cities, the centers of population, knowing that if he could reach them, the country also would be reached."

"He generally had an uproar. It is seldom that anything is accomplished until there is an uproar."

"People must start talking about the Gospel. That was what happened in our campaigns."

OJS

With eyes fixed on the Calling.

Although the Europe of which Oswald wrote predated the Second World War, the unregenerate heart of man still has known no change – even with the turning of the twenty-first century. Neither has the understanding of The Peoples Church changed with regard to spiritual realities. Ever since the hearts of Oswald's people were kindled and set ablaze through his passion for souls, the church has been fuelled by its dedication to taking the Gospel to those who have never heard. Led by Oswald and his three successors – Dr. Paul Smith, Dr. John Hull and Charles Price – tremendous efforts have been undertaken in foreign evangelism and fundraising for the work.

To the ends of the earth.

Oswald Smith spoke in 70 countries. Beginning at the age of 18 with his ministry in British Columbia, he went to Europe 14 times, as well as to Africa, Asia, Australia and South America – always with one all absorbing passion – to preach Christ. Although the loneliness of missing his family was sometimes almost unbearable, he knew he had to obey God rather than man.

The Missionary Travels of Oswald Smith.

1924 – England, Holland, France, Switzerland, Germany, Russia, Lithuania, Latvia, Poland and Luxemburg.

1929 – England, France, Belgium, Monaco, Italy, Austria, Germany, Latvia, Estonia, Lithuania, Spain, Poland, Switzerland, Russia and Belgium.

1932 – England, France, Spain, Egypt, Palestine, India, Ceylon, the Malay Peninsula, the Dutch East Indies, French Somaliland and Ethiopia.

1935 – Cuba.

1936 – England, France, Spain, Germany, Poland, Latvia, Sweden, Denmark, Czechoslovakia, Rumania, Bulgaria, Turkey, Greece, Yugoslavia, Hungary, Austria, Belgium and Scotland.

1938 – Hawaii, Samoa, Fiji, Australia, the Solomon Islands and New Zealand.

1940 – Cuba.

1941 – Jamaica.

1946 – England, Ireland, Scotland, Wales and Eire.

1948 – Eire, England, Switzerland, Holland, Belgium, France, Italy, Germany and Iceland.

1949 – Scotland. Ireland, England and Iceland.

1950 – England, Belgium, Norway, Scotland, Germany and Denmark.

1955 – The Azores, Portugal, Senegal, Liberia, the Gold Coast, Congo, North and South Rhodesia, South Africa, Sudan, Egypt, Italy, France, England, Scotland and Newfoundland.

1957 – Brazil, Argentina, Chile, Peru, Uruguay, Ecuador, Colombia and Panama.

1959 – Iceland, Norway. Sweden, Finland, England, Ireland, Eire and Scotland – Japan, Hong Kong, and Honolulu.

1960 – Alaska and Japan.

1961 – Hawaii, Fiji and Australia – England, Germany, Italy, Kenya, Rhodesia, South Africa and Sudan.

1962 – Reykjavik, Iceland.

1963 – Ireland, England and Wales.

1965 – Trinidad& Barbados

1968 – Honolulu, the Fiji Islands and Australia.

1969 – Scotland, Norway, Sweden and Denmark.

1970 – England, Sweden and Liberia.

OSWALD J. SMITH

Loneliness and illness.

Along with loneliness, illness dogged Oswald as a great trial. He was very sick in Spain, desperately ill in Africa, and almost at death's door in the Solomon Islands and Australia with malaria. However, as the children got older, Daisy was able to accompany Oswald, a great comfort to both. Oswald most often paid for their own transportation. When accommodated in the homes of Christians, Oswald found tremendous enjoyment in inspiring the children of the home. Otherwise, he always sought out the cheapest hotel accommodations.

Each tour a story in itself.

Each tour was a story in itself – stories of thrilling and dangerous experiences in distant places where death lurked far too often, of trials and tribulations as Oswald followed new trails through great Russian forests and pioneer outposts; of the kind of revival known by Charles G. Finney. Huge crowds gathered wherever Oswald spoke. Men and women by the hundreds, weeping over their sins, thronged aisles and enquiry rooms. Many, many thousands of people were gloriously saved. Most often, it was difficult to find buildings large enough to take care of the crowds. But it was to God that Oswald gave all the glory.

Year after year, Oswald travelled from the Atlantic to the Pacific, and from the Gulf to Northern Canada, holding evangelistic campaigns and missionary conventions in the larger cities, but for every invitation he accepted, a dozen had to be refused.

Because of the magnitude of the effect The Peoples Church had on the world through the ministry of Dr. Smith, it is possible in this brief history to give only small glimpses into his missionary travels. Deeper insight can be found in his book, *My Worldwide Ministry**.

* *My Worldwide Ministry:* O.J. Smith, Marshall, Morgan & Scott, London, 1965.

Oswald Smith (center) in Russian crowd following a meeting.

WORLD TOURS IN PICTURES

Rev. Oswald J. Smith will review his three World Tours, with hundreds of beautifully colored slides, in the Toronto Gospel Tabernacle, 42 Gerrard St. E., near Yonge, on the following nights:—

March 21st
"Switzerland, France and Italy"

March 29th
"Egypt and Palestine"

April 5th
"Ethiopia, India, Ceylon and Singapore"

April 12th
"The Dutch East Indies"

April 19th
"The Isle of Bali"

April 26th
"Spain, the Land of the Inquisition"

May 3rd
"The Russian Mission Fields of Europe"

So great were the crowds when these pictures were first shown that many hundreds were turned away; hence, Mr. Smith has been asked to repeat the lectures. Time 7.45 p.m. Come early.

A conference of
Russian missionaries.

Travelling into the interior of
Russia, 1924.

Oswald Smith (left) visiting
a Russian home.

Taking the Gospel to Russia in 1924.

Oswald's first trip overseas came in response to a 1924 invitation from Pastor William Fetler (founder of the Russian Missionary Society) to work with him in Latvia. The great Russian mission fields, which had taken root among the 2.5 million Russian prisoners-of-war held by Germany during the First World War, were suddenly opened up under Oswald's ministry, and revival broke out among the Russian-speaking people of northern Europe. There, he preached to vast congregations of Russians, Latvians and Poles. Returning home, he raised support for 60 new missionaries and funds to open Bible schools in Latvia and Spain.

1929 – to Russia again.

In 1929, Paul Rader asked Oswald to visit the Russian fields again, this time under the auspices of The Couriers. His travels to the province of Latgalia, on the Russian border, shook him. Full of witch-craft and paganism, it was the spiritually darkest place he had ever visited. Most in the population of 550,000 had had no contact with the Gospel. Although people attended his meetings, they were wild and noisy. The girls took turns standing up, laughing and mocking throughout the entire service. Oswald continued the meetings for nine days, having been prepared for the reception by the loggers who had heckled him back in the forests of British Columbia. Although the cir-cumstances of his visit were uncomfortable (to the degree that vermin swarmed everywhere, even where he slept), Oswald wrote:

> "But oh, these teeming multitudes – how they have won me! My heart has been stirred, my soul burdened by this virgin mission field that I have now seen with my own eyes. How

A great audience of Russians and Jews, many of whom had never heard the Gospel, to whom Mr. Smith preached in Europe in 1924. He can be seen standing in the middle of the group.

Into all the World

A Russian drosky with
Pastor Kurcit and Dr. Smith
driving over the cobblestone
road to a meeting.

The farm home in which the
missionary lived.
The lower door of the house
opens into a pig pen.

Missionaries to Russia supported by
The Peoples Church.

great is the harvest! How few the labourers! Would to God I could spend months touring through Latgalia, telling the story to the tens of thousands who have never heard of God's salvation!"

Taking his cue from John Wesley, Oswald immediately organized "The Russian Border Mission," and appointed the pastor of the largest Baptist Church in Latvia as superintendent. Giving him funding to open a Bible school, Oswald promised to send books, tracts, Bibles and bicycles for the evangelists who would be trained there. The first 50 graduates were sent all over Latgalia and Spain, evangelizing. From the first outreach, thousands heard the Gospel and over 3,000 were converted.

Riga.

Moving on to Riga, it was only four days until people were standing in the aisles. Oswald recorded:

"And then the power of God fell on the audience. Men and women knelt everywhere, and oh, such prayers! Such tears! Such testimonies! How they sang! Again and again choruses of gladness, victory, and triumph were joyfully sung. 'Hallelujah," they cried aloud. "Glory be to God!" It was heaven on earth. The Holy Spirit Himself came and made His abode with them, praise be to God. At the four o'clock service they were back. Once more the power of God was present. Tears flowed freely. Joy unspeakable and full of glory was seen on many a face.

"At 6:30 I preached again, and at 8:00 o'clock, four times in one day. Soon after I returned to my room there was a knock at my door. One of the students entered and told me how God had spoken to him. He described his great hunger of heart – 'I have determined to pray all night for I will not cease until I know the power of the Holy Ghost in my life.' As we prayed together, he sobbed aloud.

"Then came another knock on the door – would I meet with some in an adjoining room? There I found the office staff on their faces; to them also God had spoken. Again, there was agonizing prayer; sin was dealt with and put away, and a full surrender made, for again the Holy Spirit had His way. "Presently in trooped all the students in a body, and kneeling down, in Russian, German, Latvian and English they poured out their hearts to God. Oh, what a melting time! How they wept before the Lord! What joy it was to be in such an atmosphere of revival and to see the Holy Spirit Himself at work!

Finally they left, to continue in prayer in their own rooms; how late I do not know. At twelve o'clock I returned to my room and with joy and gratitude in my soul, went to bed. What a blessed day it had been."

The next morning, the altar was full. Many days, Oswald preached four times a day, some of the services lasting three and four hours, keeping him from getting to bed until after midnight.

The Spanish Gospel Mission.
Responding to an urgent invitation from the Spanish Gospel Mission, Oswald travelled through the night to get there. Finding great hunger in the hearts of the people, he wrote:

> "The greatest need is a Bible School, where Spanish workers may be quickly trained and sent out. They alone can evangelize their own country; foreigners can never hope to do it. I feel I must undertake the responsibility of this great work. Think of 23 million souls without Christ, with only a handful of missionaries and 45 national workers!"

Poland.
Leaving Madrid and journeying on to Poland, where he was scheduled to hold a workers' conference, Oswald found that half of the audience was Jewish. Listening eagerly to the Scriptures, 75 responded in the first meeting. Over 100 missionaries, many having walked 25 to 50 miles to attend the meetings, had gathered. All of them, including Oswald, slept together on straw in the barns.

Desperate sacrifices.
Oswald was deeply moved by the desperate sacrifices of the missionaries he encountered. One pair with a tiny baby had practically nothing; another couple was trying to exist on eight cents' worth of food a day. Oswald gave them what he could, but determined in his heart to do what he could to increase their support when he got home.

Returning home.
On that first missionary journey organized by Paul Rader's Worldwide Christian Couriers, Oswald visited 14 European countries, and preached 143 times in 114 days. On his return, the crowds, unaccustomed to worldwide travel, jammed Massey Hall to see his 150 breathtaking, coloured stereopticon slides. He poured out his heart to them:

> "I have found mission fields worthy of every effort we can make for their evangelization. The waiting multitudes in Europe, I can never forget."

Oft heard sayings of Oswald Smith.

"The Church that ceases to be evangelistic will soon cease to be evangelical."

"If God wills the evangelization of the world, and you refuse to support missions, then you are opposed to the will of God."

"Give according to your income, lest God make your income according to your giving."

"Let me burn out for Christ"

"This generation can only reach this generation."

"Not how much of my money will I give to God, but, how much of God's money will I keep for myself."

OJS

Oswald went on to present clear recommendations, not in a clinical summary of detached observations, but with a vibrant urgency that communicated the reality of the need to his listeners. Connecting them personally to the mission fields, with direction for realistically effecting change, he was greatly encouraged when all of his recommendations were accepted. A Bible school was established in Riga. Missionaries sent to evangelize Latgalia. Work was undertaken among the refugees of France and Belgium. A Bible school was established in Spain and a dean, Rev. F. David Sholin was sent out.

Rev. F. David Sholin.

Organizing The Peoples Missionary Society.

Remembering the plight of many of the missionaries he had met, and being made aware that many others did not receive regular income, Oswald determined to do what he could to relieve missionaries of financial anxieties so that they could do their best work. He organized what is now known as, "The Peoples Missionary Society." Its mandate was to stimulate missionary interest and raise funds wherever possible for the support of missions work and missionaries throughout the world – but not to employ missionaries of its own. Initially, the Society supported 50 Russian and Spanish nationals in Europe. It then set sights on French Indo-China and the Dutch East Indies. There, through the Christian and Missionary Alliance, 43 national evangelists who reached thousands for Christ, were supported.

Mrs. F. Sholin.

Involving the Faith Missionary Societies.

By 1934, various "Faith Missionary Societies" were already organized and functioning in response to the vision to evangelize the unreached millions. They relied on God rather than on any particular churches for their support, practicing self-denial and sacrifice in their efforts to reach the world with the Gospel.

Oswald could see that duplication of their efforts was unnecessary and resources would go further if used in support of their established routes. In response to the Lord's injunction to pray that labourers would go into the plentiful harvest, he began to ask God to burden these Societies to send out more missionaries. To encourage them to do so, he led The Peoples Church to offer personal support, if needed, to all those who would go from Canada. It was a tremendous boon to a number of the Faith Missions. Nothing was deducted for administration from whatever funds were raised. The church looked after the full overhead.

Movies of missionary travels.

A highlight of Oswald's return home to the people of The Peoples Church, was always the showing of the photos and films of his travels.

Several of the leaders travelled close to 1000 miles to hear Oswald speak. He challenged them to a deeper walk with Christ, saying:

"You can produce only what you yourself are.

"A carnal pastor produces carnal people. A missionary-minded pastor produces a missionary-minded congregation."

Into all the World

Rev. Peter Deyneka.

The movies he took of the natives of the Solomon Islands were so sensational, that they were shown each week to audiences that would begin to arrive at 5:00 p.m. in order to get a seat for the 8:00 p.m. service. The church across the street had to be rented to accommodate the crowds. Oswald would show the films to more than two thousand people in The Peoples Church, then trade churches with Eldon Lehman, who would keep the crowd across the street singing while they waited patiently.

Russian Bible Institute.

In 1943, in cooperation with Rev. Peter Deyneka and the Russian Gospel Association, the church launched a Russian Bible Institute for the training of Russian students.

Below: The students and teachers of the
Russian Bible Institute, 14 Park Road, Toronto – Fall, 1944.
L – R seated: Rev. Moses Gitlin, Teacher; Rev. H.H. Janzen, Principal;
Rev. Charles Porter, D.D., Board Member and Associate Pastor, Moody Church;
Dr. O.J. Smith, President; Rev. Peter Deyneka, General Director; Rev. John Huk,
Teacher. Standing: student body.

Brands from the Burning

By Judge George Urban

DURING the past eleven months we have published 129,000 copies of gospel booklets and tracts in Russian, and these have been distributed, not only in France and Belgium, but by mail to distant fields. The third edition of "From Death to Life" in Russian, by Oswald J. Smith, has been printed. In addition many thousands of tracts published by other Societies have been distributed. Over 1,000 New Testaments have been given out besides many more Gospels.

We have opened a new hall for our meetings in the very heart of Paris, and thus we will be able to reach the entire population with the Gospel. The work in the centres among the Russians, such as Geneva and Lausanne in Switzerland and six centres in France, have been visited and meetings held.

Our magazine, "The Call", is sent to every country in the world except Australia. We publish 15,000 copies each month. Letters have been received telling of untold blessing and many souls have been won to Jesus Christ. Many Russians thirsting for God have found Him through reading "The Call". Our magazine goes into Soviet Russia and most touching are the letters received. "You can't imagine," writes one, "how difficult life has become here. There is no bread. We have nothing but soup made out of grass. Yet the greater our trouble, the more real our Saviour's help. Many are facing death by starvation."

Through reading "From Death to Life" a Russian lady was recently wonderfully saved. A few weeks ago a Russian Jewess accepted Christ. More recently still a young woman who used to laugh at everything serious, turned to God. The other day a Russian lady surrendered herself to Christ. One man stated that he had been seeking release from his awful sins for thirty years and upon being handed a copy of "The Call" he found deliverance through Christ and is to-day rejoicing in Him.

At one of our Stations 52 children are enrolled in the Sunday School as a result of the work of Brother and Sister Koulakoff. Every child has a copy of the New Testament and reads it. Their parents openly acknowledge that their children know more about Christ than they do. Several have yielded to Christ and have already been baptized. Many others are reading the Word of God and "The Call". There are a large number of secret believers in every part of France.

We held a meeting in a distant city among the Russians and the room was crowded. People came from long distances. Some twelve souls responded to the invitation to accept Christ. Our literature was distributed in a few moments. All were eager to get it. It was the first time the Gospel had been preached in that community. Many homes were visited where we preached Christ.

We have been working among the Russian miners in Belgium. The miners are most dangerous. The men live reckless lives. Their free time is spent in drinking and card playing. On Sunday afternoons practically everyone is drunk and penniless. However, they eagerly read the New Testament and our books and then ask for more. Thus God is working mightily in the hearts of the Russian Refugees everywhere. Many thousands are hearing the Gospel and scores upon scores have already been soundly converted. Eternity alone will reveal the results.

During 1933 we published and distributed 144,000 copies of gospel literature.

Just recently a magazine published by the Greek Orthodox Church gave several pages to a criticism of your article, "Three Solemn Facts", which appeared in the first number of our publication, "The Call". The criticism is very superficial, however, and reveals modernistic tendencies. Nevertheless, this proves most conclusively that our work is telling. Opposition meetings have been held by the Greek Church and many slanderous reports circulated regarding our work. Thus Satan is busy. However, God is working, for just recently we baptized four new converts, and several others are ready and waiting.

Let me appeal to my American and Canadian supporters to stand back of us in this great enterprise, both by their gifts and their prayers. The work is hard, the problems many, but our God is able. There are still thousands to be reached with the Gospel. Let us not fail them. We will do our part if you will hold the ropes.

Send all gifts for Russian work to The Peoples Church, 22 Kendal Ave., Toronto, Canada.

Is the World Going Mad?

EIGHTEEN million men are under arms today. Led by the United States of America, the major nations of the world are engaged in building a vast naval tonnage. There are armed conflicts or revolutions in progress on four continents. There are at least eleven international boundaries where shock troops stand against feared imminent invasions. Governments have broken international covenants, defaulted debts, withdrawn from international relationships they could not intimidate or bend to their national will, and some have repudiated pledges to their own people. The threat of war is graver this year than at any time since Germany moved against Belgium.

Is the world going mad?

Whatever the so-called "Great War" was, this next conflict, if it ever comes, in world proportions, will be immeasurably greater and it will be a war inevitably

Judge Urban and his family.

against civilization, a war against women and children, a war whose battle cry, "We will not sheathe the sword" can have only one translation into reality—*"We will not stop killing babies"*.

Read Beverly Nichols' "Cry Havoc". Read the cold—no, the white-hot, horrible details of the experts. Three drops of one liquid on any part of the skin causes death, and one plane carrying two tons of the stuff could cover an area seven miles long and one hundred yards wide, killing every living thing within the area. In a city the fatal area would be several times as great—this is from the statement of General Bradner, Chief Research Officer of the Chemical Warfare Service of the American Army. And from another expert I read, "The most energetic production of gas is to be found in America".

With one poison gas one hundred planes could cover Paris with a cloud twenty metres thick—and do it within an hour! On any still day or night Paris would be annihilated within sixty minutes.

Physically, organized society as we know it now could not survive the next world war. Morally? It would be a lie against the dead of the last war, which we vowed was to end war. Spiritually? It would destroy Christianity and be the rape of religion.—*The Christian Herald.*

What a Visitor Saw

OH that I had words with which to describe what I saw and heard in Europe, as I travelled from station to station, covering many thousands of miles, preaching day after day, accompanied by the missionaries who are making such heroic sacrifices in order to win their fellow-countrymen to Christ!

No greater opportunity has ever been given to God's stewards than that presented by the work of The Peoples Church in France under the able leadership of Judge George Urban, who is in charge. This devoted man of God, formerly a Russian judge, has gathered about him a group of the most consecrated missionaries I have ever met. Their activities never cease. On trains, in street cars, at the doors of Russian churches and in political meetings—anywhere, everywhere, they are at it, giving out gospels and tracts, talking to people about their souls, pleading with them to accept Christ. Meetings are held regularly all over France and Belgium and the Gospel faithfully proclaimed. Many have already been won to Christ.

How can I forget them! Oh, how my heart was stirred! I can see them now—Captains, Generals, Counts and Nobles, the aristocracy of old Russia—today discouraged, homesick and broken-hearted. Hope has died. The future holds nothing for them. Driven from their homes, they must exist as best they can in a foreign land.

Ah, but therein lies our opportunity, and God help us if we neglect it! Now is the hour to give them the Gospel. And they are ready for it. To see them as I have, Russia's former nobility, men and women who never would have darkened a church door in their days of prosperity, now gladly, with tears filling their eyes, listening to the Gospel Message, is a sight never to be forgotten. And then to watch them kneel and with hearts broken and contrite, confess their sins and receive Jesus Christ as their Saviour, is an experience vouchsafed to but few. But such scenes I have witnessed, not only once, but again and again. Nor can I ever forget them.

Some day Russia will be open again, and then these intellectuals, in thousands, will go back. And remember, every Russian is a missionary. So that when they go back, if they have been saved, they will take the Gospel with them. We cannot cross the Border into the land of the Soviets ourselves, but God has sent out a congregation of a million souls for us to evangelize. There will come a day when they will no longer be accessible, but meanwhile we are responsible. Oh, my friends, what are we going to do about it? Dare we ignore such an opportunity?

With all my heart and soul, after much personal observation, I recommend this glorious work. The work of The Peoples Church in France is certainly worthy of our support. Each worker is sacrificing to the limit. No money is wasted. Every cent counts. Why should a Mission be handicapped for funds? Already a great work is

Let Me Forget

Let me forget, O God, let me forget,
  The past I cannot change, then let it
    die;
But let me claim the present, and rely
  Upon the future, and I'll conquer yet.

Let me forget the scenes of other days,
  The hallowed dreams that never can
    come true;
But let me live this day my life anew,
  And for the future build with joy and
    praise.

Let me forget the visions of the past,
  The wreck of blighted hopes, the
    years of pain;
Let me forget the pledges made in vain,
  The promises to which I anchored
    fast.

Let me forget, O God, the sin, the stain,
  Forget my love of self, forget my
    pride;
But let me keep my eyes, whate'er be-
    tide,
  Upon the future, Lord, and live
    again.

Let me forget the heart-wounds of
    regret,
  Nor open them afresh in this new
    day;
To bury what is dead and turn away,
  Is best; so then, dear Lord, let me
    forget.
             —Oswald J. Smith.

being accomplished, but gifts are urgently needed with which to advance. Here is an opportunity for investment, and God alone knows what the results will be. Halls must be rented, tracts printed and distributed, Gospels and New Testaments purchased, allowances increased, new workers immediately taken on, and many other dire and urgent needs met and met this year. What is to be our share in this great enterprise? God help us to do something and to do it now. Time is passing. Soon it will be too late. Now is the hour, *now!*

But now when I come to speak of the work on the Soviet Border of Russia, words fail me altogether. For right in the former geographical Russia, there is a work being done that beggars description. A group of missionaries under the superintendency of Pastor J. Kurcit, are preaching the Gospel to thronging multitudes in one of the darkest sections I have ever visited. The province of Latgalia is as dark as Africa, India or China. Horrible superstitions still hold the people in bondage. Crime of every description abounds. Immorality and drink dominate the people.

Yet into this dense darkness the missionaries of The Peoples Church have plunged. Everywhere the people throng to hear them. Scenes that I never can forget flash before me as I write. Hungry multitudes. Halls packed to suffocation. Meetings lasting for three and a half hours. Eager listeners. Heart-broken sobs. Murderers, thieves, adulterers crying to God for mercy. Lives utterly changed by the power of the Gospel. People clamoring for more. No rest. No leisure. Day or night, hard at it. Travelling from place to place. Preaching until exhausted. Hundreds accepting Christ. Thousands reached by the Gospel.

Yes, my friends, God is working and working mightily among the Russian people of Latvia, as well as among the Letts. The spirit of Revival is everywhere in evidence, and old-fashioned conviction is the order of the day. Within one week I saw over 600 turn to Christ. Oh, what a harvest! It seems as though God is specially working among the peoples of Russia today. And where God is working, there you and I ought to be busy.

And these missionaries are only receiving from $20.00 to $30.00 a month, an allowance that, in cases where there are several children, must be increased at once. Others are waiting to be engaged, splendid sacrificial workers. Meetings in many places are held in hot, suffocating kitchens because there is no money for the rent of halls. Hundreds of outlying villages could be visited and meetings held every night, if only funds were available for travelling expenses. A constant demand is heard from all the missionaries for Gospel tracts, New Testaments and Bibles to scatter among the people. Able Evangelists are waiting and ready to go as flaming Revivalists from village to village, but there are no funds for this purpose. The need is appalling. But oh, what an investment! And remember, no one will ever appeal for help in the life to come. Then it will be too late to give. Now is our one and only opportunity.

Send all gifts for Russian Work to *The Peoples Church*, 22 Kendal Ave., Toronto, Canada.

France and Spain

The Second Section of the Story of My Fourth Trip to the Mission Fields of Europe---By Oswald J. Smith

MR. and MRS. HERBERT WHEALY, our new missionaries, who left for Cuba on October 15th, under the auspices of The Peoples Church. A great farewell service was held on Wednesday, the 14th.

UPON arrival in France, we were met at the station by Judge George Urban and his faithful workers. What a thrill it was to see Paris once again!

Never have I been so deeply impressed by the work among the Russian refugees. It simply beggars description. What a heroic band of missionaries! Talk about sacrifice, they put me to shame! How they have ever managed to live and accomplish so much on their meagre allowances, I do not know. I doubt if there is a more spiritual church anywhere in the world. It is New Testament, not only in doctrine but also in practice.

The condition of the Russian exiles in France is worse than ever before. They are absolutely poverty-stricken. Vast numbers of them can get no work, and of course, they receive no help from the government. They are not allowed to travel from place to place to look for work without permission. The French come first. Hence starvation stares them in the face. They are both helpless and hopeless—a people without a country.

The believers try to help each other as much as possible. Their small salaries are divided with the destitute and starving. Many of them cannot attend the services because they do not have the carfare. We must have a "Saints in Need" fund for these sick and hungry souls. The missionaries cannot help them all out of the little they get, and no one seems to care whether they live or die. Yet they struggle on as best they can—God's children, waiting for help. Those of us who have always had three meals a day know nothing about it. Judge Urban can use a lot of relief money for the believers alone, better than any man I know. And it will be a God-send to them.

I have listened to the stories told me about the sacrifices of the missionaries, and it brings the tears to my eyes. At one time when they were hard pressed, one of them—a woman—sold the small inheritance left her for the future and gave the money in full to the work. When they face special needs, they meet for prayer, and in one way or another God works. But their testings are many. They live in a godless country, for France is utterly godless, a nation without an anchor, slowly but surely drifting to revolution and war.

Our workers are untiring in their efforts. They get the lists of all the Russians who are ill in the hospitals, and visit each one, giving them tracts, books and Bibles, always dealing with them about their soul's salvation. Sometimes there are a hundred on the list. Thus many are won to Christ.

Literature

Our Russian magazine, "The Call", goes to scores of countries and is in great demand. There is nothing like it. It always makes plain the plan of God's salvation, and many are saved through reading it. But it is impossible to respond to all the demands. Many who ask for it have to be refused for lack of postage. We have been publishing 15,000 copies per month. It is now our hope to be able to issue 25,000, and to provide more for postage so as to send it to thousands who are still in darkness. Our Russian books, "From Death to Life", "The Salvation of God", and "What will You do with Jesus?" are also in great demand. And many have found Christ through their messages. Thus our literature is a very important factor in the evangelization of the Russian refugees.

I have spent hours in conference with Judge Urban, and have decided that we simply must increase the allowances for France and Belgium. If our missionaries are to do their best work, they must have more. If the poor, destitute, broken-hearted Russian refugees are to hear the Gospel, a larger investment will have to be made. Somehow, God will supply our need. I have seen the work. I know whereof I speak. There is no waste. If the Christians of America could live with these heroic missionaries as I have and see them at their work, if they could look into the faces of those who have found Christ and see some of the results, if they could hear the story of the thousands, scattered as sheep without a shepherd, and then get the vision of the possibility of reaching them for Christ, they would pray and give to their utmost, and multitudes would be saved. I know of no work more worthy of support.

As for me, I have re-dedicated my life to the task of Russian evangelization. To settle down at home and take it easy is out of the question. I must be true to the vision. God has called me to do what little I can for those who need Christ, and He will provide the means. May He help me to be faithful. More than half a million Russian refugees in France alone are still without Christ. God help us! What a task!

Spain

Leaving France, Mr. Billester and I boarded the train for Spain. I almost dreaded the journey, and well I might, for I had taken it twice before, and knew what I would have to face. But this time was the hardest of all. Through France it isn't so bad. Much of the road is electrified. The trains are fast, very fast. But in Spain it was terrible. We changed at Bordeau, then Irun, going through the customs, getting our money changed, showing our passports, etc., as usual. Our next change was Madrid, then Baesa.

We left Tuesday morning, June 30th, travelled all day and all night, getting what sleep we could. It was far too expensive to take a pullman, so we sat up. Spanish food is terrible, so we had but little to eat. It is cooked in oil. Whenever possible we ordered boiled eggs.

I am simply amazed at the cost of living. A meal on the train is always twenty francs, about $1.40. An additional 10 per cent is added for service.

Coffee is extra. In Spain it is eight pesetas. The dollar has lost its value; hence travelling in France and Spain is very expensive. It used to be cheap. We did not go into the diner, except to order some things a la carte. It was too dear. And besides we could not digest the food.

We had been travelling for a day and a night. Next day we changed to a very poor, rough and slow train, and at 10.25 p.m. expected to arrive at Granada to be welcomed by the Sholins. But 10.25 came and went and there was no Granada. Presently we became concerned. What had happened? We turned to the passengers, all Spanish. They could not understand us. We showed them our tickets, and they threw their hands up in amazement. Finally they made us to understand that we were on the wrong train. We should have changed at a station away back. But in Spain the conductor takes no responsibility.

We were tired, oh so tired! For dinner we had only had boiled eggs. Expecting an American supper at the Sholins, we had taken nothing else. It was now 11 p.m. What should we do?

Finally the train stopped. We found that we were at Almiria on the Mediterranean. We had gone right across Spain. Taking a taxi, we went to a Spanish hotel, and sent a telegram to Granada. In a few minutes Mr. Sholin telephoned us long-distance. Oh, what a joy it was to hear his voice! And how disappointed he had been in not meeting us! He would come for us tomorrow, so he said. What a relief!

We went to bed, and sure enough next morning he was there with his car, and we had a delightful drive around the coast of the sea, to Granada, where we were welcomed by Mrs. Sholin and the two boys. We found them all well.

Granada is beautifully situated. It is a great tourist centre, this city of 120,000 inhabitants, for it is the city of the Alhambra. Here Washington Irving wrote. Here Queen Isabel reigned. I was in the very room in which Columbus asked permission of Queen Isabel to go on his voyage of discovery, which resulted in the discovery of America. What marvellous architecture! What beautiful gardens! Fountains everywhere. Cypress trees, flowers and running water. Steam baths. All the work of the Moors. Had the Moors continued to dominate, Spain would not now be the degraded, hopeless, uninviting country it is. But the Spaniards followed and they ruined everything.

Wherever Roman Catholicism has gone, the people are ignorant, dirty, superstitious and degraded. Rome never

uplifts. It is the same in Mexico and throughout South America. Most of the priests of Spain are fathers of children. True, churches have been burned, nuns liberated, and the Jesuits crushed, but the results are still in evidence. The blight remains.

Spain is a most nerve-racking country. There is a terrible restlessness. Everywhere there are soldiers. The country swarms with them. All have rifles and

MRS. ALAN REED,

who left for Ecuador, South America, on Oct. 13th. Mrs. Reed, who was formerly Miss Marjory Malcolm, was the first leader of the Young Peoples' Work of The Peoples Church. She spoke over the air on Sunday, October 11th.

revolvers. They go in groups from place to place. There is a feeling of insecurity in the very air. The Government trembles for its life.

Our missionaries have been stoned again and again. They have been shot at. Rotten eggs have been thrown at them, and all kinds of abuse heaped on them. Their stories sound like the days of the Early Church. Persecution has been the order of the day. Yet, in spite of all they have suffered, they have gone back again and again, no matter how often they were driven out. Few of us know anything about physical suffering for the cause of Christ as they do.

At the first meeting I heard their testimonies. I refer now to the young men trained by Mr. Sholin in the Bible School —the Heralds—miracles of grace, every one of them. They gave their reports, one by one, and I was thrilled and fascinated as I listened. Their sufferings they

scarcely mentioned, and when they did, they spoke about them in such an incidental way that it sounded as though it was the usual, ordinary, expected thing.

"I went to such and such a town to preach the Gospel and they stoned me so that I barely escaped with my life," one would say. "And then when I went back they fired at me with revolvers, but God preserved me."

"When I went back," I said to myself. "Would I have gone back?"

Why, if I were to be shot at in Canada, it would be in all the newspapers. Here it is merely a part of the programme.

We found it hard to rest in Spain. The noise on the streets is terrific, and it lasts all night long. The people always holler at one another. How the Sholins stand it, I do not know. And then the smells. Well, enough said. In the natural I could not love the Spanish people. And nothing could induce me to visit Spain as a tourist. Only for the cause of Christ would I go. But when they are saved, they are like all others. One cannot help but love them.

We left Granada after I had preached, Sunday night, and sat up to Madrid. From Madrid to Irun all next day we had a trip that tried us to the limit. There was only one second-class coach attached, and four first-class. Into this dirty second-class we squeezed. Every seat was taken and many were standing. Tourists cursed. Even the natives found fault. Baggage was piled in the aisle, and a hen lay on the floor. The heat was awful. And dirt—my face and hands were black, my hair matted. Our clothes were filthy. We were weak and sore. Our heads ached. Then to make matters worse, we missed our train at the border and had to spend the night in a French hotel, going on to Paris next morning.

The delay was caused by the necessity of counting all the passengers' money. No one is allowed to take more than 500 pesetas out of the country, a very foolish regulation, and yet strictly enforced in Spain, Germany, Poland and other European countries. There is no liberty such as we know in America at all.

I am leaving Spain with a greater realization of the need of evangelism than ever before, and a deeper appreciation of the work of Mr. and Mrs. Sholin and our Spanish Heralds. Spain is today a wide-open door, but any moment it may close, and our workers have to flee for their lives. Let us give them the Gospel while we have an opportunity. "The night cometh when no man can work."

Poland and Latvia

The fourth instalment of my fourth trip to the Mission Fields of Europe

By Oswald J. Smith

Missionaries of The Peoples Church in Latgalia.

ON July 11th, very reluctantly, we left Germany for Poland, arriving in Warsaw in the evening. On the morning of the 12th we reached Luck, and attended a missionary conference. The Sunday meetings were crowded, with many standing, a spirit of revival permeating the atmosphere, and a number professed conversion. It was a great joy to meet the Russian brethren again, and to preach in the large central hall made memorable by my meetings in 1929.

Poland, except where settled by Germans, is a backward country. The beautiful gardens seen in France and Germany are conspicuous by their absence. In Germany every little plot of land is under cultivation, while in Poland vast stretches lie waste. The people are poverty-stricken; poor beyond expression. Women and men, clad in rags, sit huddled in the doorways, utterly destitute. The streets are rough and dirty, the sidewalks broken and the houses dilapidated. Droskys take the place of taxis. The serving women go about barefooted even in the hotels. If the people are happy it is because they have never known anything better.

Among the educated classes there are many very beautiful Polish women, while the men are most courteous and polite. When they meet or separate the lady holds out her hand and the gentleman bends over it and kisses it. The men wear gloves. As for the Russians, the men kiss the men and the women the women, always twice and on both cheeks. The Jews kiss a dozen or more times, anywhere.

There are large farming areas with splendid, crops. Both men and women labour in the fields. The grain is cut by hand. Vast forests cover the land.

The food is hard on a foreigner. Tea is served in a glass, generally with lemon, Russian style. Again and again, during this trip, I have thanked God for hens. For when I could eat nothing else I have been able to live on eggs, either boiled or fried. And they are the same in Poland as in America. Thank God, I say again, for hens. I take off my hat to them.

Poland is about one thousand miles across and has a population of thirty million. It is made up of Poles, Russians and Jews. The Poles are Roman Catholics, and the Russians, Greek Orthodox. The Jews have their own religion. There are thousands of evangelical believers of all sects, and a dozen or more Societies are at work.

The spiritual outlook is not any too bright. In some provinces there is opposition from the local officials. But the most serious difficulty lies in the fact that the various movements and societies are at war with one another. This lack of co-operation the government officials cannot understand, and they want it ended. The greatest need of Poland is a united, autonomous Church, with thoroughly-trained pastors and evangelists. This would necessitate a strong, well-manned Bible School in the country itself, with capable leadership. Foreign missionaries are not needed,

apart from a few carefully chosen leaders to train national workers. If the Pauline methods were adopted in Poland it would become one of the most fruitful missionary fields in the world. The work throughout the country, so far as American Societies are concerned, requires a Pauline administration.

Latgalia

Leaving Luck at five o'clock Wednesday morning, we travelled by a very slow train all day, spent the night at Wilno, and arrived the next day, July 16th, at Daugavpils, Latvia, where we were welcomed by our Superintendent, Pastor John Kurcit, and our faithful Latgalian missionaries. How good it was to see them all again after seven years' absence! And how glad they were to greet us!

After a most helpful conference with them, I preached that same night in Pastor Eglit's church, and three young men responded to the invitation.

Next morning we set out in a taxi to visit the Latgalian Mission field. What a ride! Never will we forget it. There were seven of us in a five-passenger car, with all our baggage besides. Most of the road was rough and it was not long before our bones were aching and our muscles sore. Yet on and on we went.

Presently we came to the field of Miss

Pastor Kurcit beside train and missionaries accompanying Dr. Smith to the interior.

Alvine Lielmezs. She took us to the house where she began her work, and introduced us to a woman of ninety who had been saved. We were warmly welcomed by the entire household, a typical Russian family. And then, mile after mile we pushed on through village after village, and past hundreds of farmhouses, where our heroic missionary, both in the heat of the summer and throughout the cold winter months, had spread the Gospel.

Stopping at her meagre lodging at noon, she refreshed us with milk and bread. We saw the little bed in which she slept, and the barren rooms where she lived all alone. We heard the story of how she pulled on her long, leather boots and waded through the deep snow, and our hearts went out to her. For here was a heroine indeed, a woman sent by God. Oh, what sacrifice! What an amazing piece of work! And what a reward will be hers at last!

Finally we drove out of her field and entered the territory of just as faithful a worker—Miss L. Silin. And again we drove for miles past houses in which she had visited. Miss Silin lives in the home of a humble Russian peasant in the country, built, of course, of logs. Every time a meal is cooked the room is filled with smoke, for the large Russian fireplace is badly in need of repair.

She told a thrilling story. We heard of how she had been turned away from every house she visited. Of how it was at first impossible for her to secure shelter, simply because she came with the Gospel, so that she was compelled to tramp on and on through the storm and cold until she could scarcely stand. That was in the early years.

But oh, what a change! One by one converts were won and churches formed. Now there are many believers and Miss Silin is a welcome guest in scores of homes. Drunkards have been converted. Wife-beaters have found Christ. And in hundreds of homes the Bible is known and read.

And so we went on. The night found us at Zilupe, right on the border of Soviet Russia. I could see buildings on the other side. Here stands the Gate of Paradise through which the train passes to Moscow. How well I remember my last visit! It was in 1929. What thoughts were mine at that time! Will I ever forget them?

That night I preached in Zilupe, and next morning we took the train for Ludza, where again I proclaimed the Gospel. Leaving Ludza we proceeded to Rezekne and Balvi, and had good meetings in both places. At Ludza our missionary is Brother P. Sinjachevsky, and at Balvi, Brother J. Bucholc.

It was most thrilling to hear the story of how a man who had committed murder, rushed upon Brother Bucholc as he was conducting the service, with a long knife, threatening to kill him and of how God miraculously delivered him.

No words of mine can describe the amazing changes that have taken place since we commenced our missionary work in Latgalia seven years ago. The whole population has undergone a transformation as a result of the preaching of the Gospel.

For instance, when I first visited Latgalia seven years ago, the people did not know how to act. They were wild and noisy in the meetings. Many of them kept their hats on. They were restless and curious. Nor had they any understanding of what was going on. When I held my hand over my eyes in prayer, they demanded to know why the foreigner would not look at them. And when I gave the invitation they laughed in my face.

But today all is changed, thanks to the power of the Gospel. Everywhere I was listened to with respect and attention, and the people acted as we would at home. They sang their hymns with us and united in prayer. Oh, what a change! Does missionary work pay? Has it been worth while? Who can doubt it?

Countless thousands have now heard the Gospel in dark, benighted Latgalia, and large numbers have been saved. Congregations are meeting regularly. In one place where there was great opposition and not a single believer, there is now a church of seventy members. And thus God is working through our faithful band of missionaries. Pastor John Kurcit, our Superintendent, is untiring in his efforts, and in spite of his years, he is ever on the go, travelling from station to station as the father of the work.

Latgalia is a very beautiful part of ancient Russia. It is the country of a thousand lakes. Every now and again we passed by picturesque bodies of fresh water, both large and small. If it were not for the dilapidated houses and the cobble-stone streets, I would think I was in parts of America. I enjoyed the scenery everywhere.

I did not enjoy the company I had at night. By the time I left Latgalia I was bitten from head to foot. But that is all a part of the day's work.

After surveying the entire field very carefully, we decided to engage one new worker, a Brother Lambert, to supply all with bicycles, and to increase the allowances, since the dollar has lost so much of its former value.

A house in which services were regularly held.

The house in which the missionary (sitting on the logs) held her first meeting.

Mission Travels

Among the Savage Kayapo Indians of the Amazon

By Evangelist J. L. Burris, *Field Director of The Peoples Missionary Society*

I AM writing these pages in the jungle forests of the interior of the great country of Brazil. I have travelled a thousand miles inland, up the mighty Amazon River, shooting the rapids of the raging Xingu River, and then by small canoe up the Rio Fresco to the last outpost of civilization, a quaint little village of grass and mud huts, named Nova Olinda. After having the joy of witnessing for Christ to the Brazilian people all along our journey, we have come up the Riozinho into the very heart of the hunting ground of the Kayapo Indians, the most savage, murderous tribe of Indians yet known to mankind. Hardly a week goes by but more Brazilian rubber gatherers are murdered in these forests. This is probably due to the fact that civilized (?) business men, with their lust for money, have invaded these forests, that for centuries have been the happy hunting grounds of these Indians, in search of rubber, nuts, and other valuable products of the tropics. They treated the Indians as though they were beasts, killing them off by the thousands. This, of course, has left an inherited hatred within the "Redman" for the "White-man".

One can readily see how these conditions have created an almost impassable barrier before the missionary who has caught the vision of carrying the Gospel message to *every tribe* and *every tongue* who have not yet heard. Christ died for Kayapo Indians; it is our commission from our God to tell them the story, regardless of the hazards that are involved.

In 1935 three of our missionaries, known as "The Three Freds" (Fred Roberts and Fred Dawson from Australia, and Fred Wright from Ireland), had the vision of carrying the blessed Gospel of Christ to these "Wild Indians of Amazonia", who had never yet heard the story. They travelled the same waterways and trails that I have travelled in the last few weeks; in fact they rode on the same launch from Altamira to San Felis that I have made my home up the Xingu River for over a week, the "Dois de Julio", meaning in Portuguese

Jackie Burris with dinner – a roasted monkey.

the "Second of July". The "Three Fred's" were after lost souls, eager to tell them of the Saviour's love. Mr. Dawson, in his last letter to friends, wrote—"My great desire is that the Christ of Calvary may be taken to the Indians whatever the cost may be"; and Fred Wright expressed his deep joy that the Lord had "honoured" him to be one of the party.

The wild Kayapos are among those who kill at sight, and look upon all white men as "invaders" and consider them as their prey. The "Three Freds" realized this, and in their last letter, written from "the last outpost of civilization", one of them said: *"Brethren, stand by us as one man—Continue to pray for us, and should the result be that which we least want, pray and send others out to continue what the Lord has commenced. Remember, He died for the Indians of South America".* They did not rush "blindly" into this danger, but after counting the cost, they went forward with flaming hearts in love with the Lord Jesus Christ and with a passion for perishing souls, making every precaution possible, without turning back. They wrote from

Nova Olinda: "We are taking every precaution, that neither foolhardiness nor negligence may be laid to our charge. . . Brethren, stand by us as one man. Do not criticize; we are beyond criticism as we go forward in the Name of the Lord and at His command, having first fully counted the cost."

As they travelled through narrow forest trails, not far from the spot where I am now writing, they must have been conscious that they were being watched by hundreds of piercing eyes of wild, savage men whose hearts burned with hatred, but on they went. They had gathered enough of the Kayapo language to make themselves understood, at least after a fashion. They were well supplied with "gifts" to present to these wild men upon meeting them, as tokens of their friendship. They were thinking and praying for wisdom as to how best to impress upon the Indians that they were not there to harm them, to plunder or cheat, but rather to bring to them the most precious thing in all the universe— Salvation through faith in the Lord Jesus Christ.

But they never had that chance. They were clubbed to death and left to be devoured by the buzzards and vultures which are very numerous in this part of the world. Six months later the search party, composed of Horace Banner, who had been working among the Indians for seven years, and William Johnstone, a young missionary from Scotland, as well as nine Brazilians from Nova Olinda who were hired for the journey, started out. Of course they were heavily armed, and even then "scared to death".

At "Smoke Falls", which was the headquarters of the Kayapos, they found the boat and the smashed motor of the "three Freds", as well as some of their clothing and belongings, swarming with white ants. It was impossible to keep the hired Brazilians in this territory—as soon as they saw this sight there was no holding them. We have since talked to some of the eye-witnesses of their murder. Some of the Kayapos on the station now established have re-enacted the death of the

The Three Freds who were clubbed to death by Kayapos Indians

Fred Wright.

Fred Roberts.

Fred Dawson.

Rev. Jackie Burris and three converted witch doctors in Haiti, 1940. Rev. Burris raised hundreds of dollars in his campaigns for the Peoples Missionary Society. His help was a great encouragement.

"three Freds", and to say the least, "it was horrible". They were clubbed to death and thrust through with huge wooden spears. The very sight of these naked savages in a jungle forest, and to hear their "war whoop" and their blood-curdling screams is enough to make your heart stop beating.

The "three Freds" became martyrs of the cause so dear to their own hearts. The cause of spreading the Gospel message to the ends of the earth. Their last message was—"Should the result be that which we least want, pray and send others out to continue what the Lord has commenced.

God has burned this vision into my heart, to *follow up on the trail of the "three Freds".* I have left the comforts of home in the United States to experience the hardships one must endure in this primitive land. I have known loneliness for my wife and baby at home, spending sleepless nights in a hammock stretched between trees in the forest, thinking about those at home, with my heart longing and aching to be with them. Leaving behind good food and living on rice, farinha and beans, and many times the water not safe to drink and yet your tongue hanging out with thirst. The sting of the "Pium" (insect) in the daytime, and the mosquito at night is almost unbearable, also the danger of "shooting" through rapids that have been the doom of many others who have travelled this way before you. Walking many hours through thick forests, serenaded by screaming monkeys and screeching birds, and wondering if you will reach the next point of contact with civilization safely. I have received my "degrees" now as a full-fledged missionary, in the form of a baptism of suffering from malaria fever and dysentery, which is a form of diarrhoea in its worst form. I have ridden on the back of a donkey or mule all day through the burning sun, and then had a service at night when you feel more like dropping into your hammock and resting your weary body. I have walked five miles through difficult trails, up and down hills, to a little colony, preached three times, walked back again, and then had another service before retiring to my hammock.

Some may ask the question: "Why have you left your evangelistic work at home, where you have had nightly audiences numbering into the thousands? Why have you left your comfortable car, to walk. ride on the back of a donkey, or in a tiny canoe through dangerous rapids? What is your purpose in coming to the wilds of the interior of Brazil?

To these and similar questions my answer is this:

As a sinner, saved by the grace of our Lord Jesus Christ, I have become a member of The Church, the Body of Christ, to which Christ has given a great commission: viz., to "Go into *all the world* and preach the gospel to *every creature*". To "Go into *all nations*", till "every nation and tongue and tribe has heard".

After two thousand years this command has never yet been carried out. In fact, we in America are so busy about our own programmes of men that we have almost completely lost the vision of the *one great, supreme task of the Church,* of preaching this Gospel as a witness unto *all* nations. God has shown me most clearly that even evangelical, evangelistic work as it is carried on in America today, has been, and is *localized and selfish in its vision.* When we get God's vision we get a *world-wide vision.*

Why is it that evangelists do not plead the cause of *world-wide evangelism?* Why is it that we never hear appeals for the regions beyond from the evangelist? Why is it that they never take an offering for missions? It is a known thing that the church with no missionary vision will *die out.* But my contention is, what about the evangelist? Has he no responsibility before God? I say, and I am sure that every honest person will agree with me, that he has. The facts of the case are, *we are selfish. We have lost the vision. Hence our own work is suffering as a result.* Everyone knows that evangelism is dying out in America. We have many excuses—we place the blame on others, but we are to blame ourselves. *If we are honest with ourselves we will confess before God, with a broken heart that we have not been pleading the cause of missions and world evangelism, because we have never caught the vision! or we have backslidden and lost the vision that God had given us; or we are so downright selfish and idolatrous of money that we are afraid we will lose something ourselves.* May God forgive us, and may we have a heaven-born revival based upon *a world-wide vision.*

I have come to Brazil to see the work that I am pleading for at home, so that I am positive that I am asking Christians to give their support to something that I am absolutely sure is worthy of support to the point of real sacrifice. So that I may touch the lives of the missionaries, live as they live, suffer as they suffer, and have a better understanding.

(Abridged.)

Mission Station.

Two young warriors demonstrating how the "3 Freds" were clubbed and speared to death.

Horace Banner and Indians.

Jackie Burris and Indians.

Woman going to hunt in forest.

Indians of the Amazon

The Outpouring in Jamaica

By REV. STANLEY HARRIS, Kingston, Pastor

The visit of Dr. Oswald J. Smith of Toronto to Jamaica will long be remembered as a "red-letter" period in the annals of evangelism in this Island.

After a few meetings in the Memorial Tabernacle, he conducted a week's evangelistic campaign in the Ward Theatre, the largest auditorium in Kingston, which has seating accommodation for about twelve hundred, but which, night after night, was packed to capacity. People stood against the walls and in the aisles, besides overflowing to the stage which was also packed till there was no more room. It is estimated that fully 2,000 people were in the theatre on the last night of the campaign.

The most notable feature of the meetings was the deep conviction of the Holy Spirit on the people which resulted in a remarkably prompt response to the invitation to confess Christ by going forward into the inquiry rooms which were the dressing rooms of the theatre behind and above the stage. Night after night, with a minimum of pleading, people all over the building rose from their seats in the top gallery, first gallery and the ground floor, or left their standing positions and wended their way down and forward, often with great difficulty on account of the crowds that stood in the aisles, up the ladder to the stage and through the wings upstairs to the inquiry rooms where willing workers pointed them to Christ. During the week of meetings 811 sought and professed Christ, not including many backsliders who were restored.

The writer has had 37 years' experience of evangelistic meetings in Jamaica, the United States of America and Canada, and had never, before the meetings under review, seen such prompt and large responses to the Gospel message. He personally dealt with many of the seekers, and can testify to a genuine work of the Holy Spirit in conviction resulting in penitence with tears, followed by an easy readiness to trust Jesus Christ for forgiveness and salvation. To God be all the praise, honour and glory.

This review would not be complete without giving my impression of the dear man of God who was the chief instrument in the blessing which Jamaica received during the meetings. I can find no better way of doing so than by quoting from an unknown author:—

"I saw a human life ablaze with God,
I felt a power divine
As thro' an empty vessel of frail clay
I saw God's glory shine.
Then woke I from a dream, and cried aloud:
'My Father give to me
The blessing of a life consumed by God
That I may live for Thee'."

Dr. Smith, as far as the physical is concerned, appears to be a "vessel of frail clay". As he would take his seat for a short time after delivering God's message and appeal, it seemed to me as though the eager soul of the man had almost worn through the body in his burning desire to get the message across, and I would pray: "Oh Father, quicken thy servant's mortal body by Thy Spirit that dwelleth so richly in him." No studied oratory characterized his messages, no high-flown language going over the heads of the majority of his audience, but an earnest unchecked flow of terse, simple words that seemed to pour forth from a bursting heart directly to parched and longing souls. It is evident that he knows His Master intimately and has learned the secret of being "a channel only" for His use.

During his week of ministry to the ministers at the Marlboro Conference at Mandeville which followed the evangelistic campaign in Kingston, he introduced us to some of the secrets of his successful evangelism, which he had learned at the Master's feet. Many of the ministers went back to their churches with a fresh vision of Christ, and already reports have come to hand of blessing and revival in several of the churches.

May God abundantly bless, strengthen and continue to use him in His blessed service until He calls him to his reward.

The Kingston Campaign

By Rev. James Carnegie, (Retired Moravian Minister)

Dr. Oswald J. Smith of Toronto, arrived at the Island by plane on the 13th February, 1941, and held his first meeting the same evening in the Memorial Tabernacle, 58 East St., and afterwards at the Ward Theatre also.

I attended the second of these meetings on the 14th. The Memorial Tabernacle was filled to capacity. The Doctor made a very favourable impression on his audience and at the very start awakened the interest and enlisted the sympathy of all, and these were sustained to an increasing extent throughout the campaign.

Now how did the people manifest this deep impression made on them?

(1) In the large and ever increasing attendances at the meetings. After the first meetings the people seemed to have been so satisfied that they wanted others also to enjoy them, so they went out as advertisers, speaking up the meetings wherever they could, the result being that every next meeting was more crowded than the preceding. Even the Ward Theatre, the largest auditorium in the city, was packed beyond capacity and hundreds had to be refused admission.

(2) In their behaviour. The order in these meetings was commendable. There was no sign of listlessness or restlessness, no talking. All seemed to have had one aim viz., to obtain a blessing.

Now we may ask what there was in Dr. Smith to create this favourable impression on his audience. Was it his scholastic attainments? Indeed, these are admirable helps and enhance one's usefulness tremendously, but they do not draw crowds around a preacher, neither can he satisfy the people with mere scholastic knowledge. People want to hear the voice of God. Herein lies the secret of Dr. Smith's success:

(1) He is fully charged with the Spirit of God, and He, the Holy Spirit, works in him and speaks through him to the people. As soon as he begins to speak one hears the ring of his voice and at once one recognizes that a man of God is speaking, or to put it the other way round, one hears God speaking through the man. That is the power by which Dr. Smith was able to impress the people of Kingston so favourably and to hold the vast crowds throughout the campaign.

(2) He uses other means, but they are all suggested by the Holy Spirit, e.g.—he uses the simplest language, thus enabling the people to "hear in their own tongue the wonderful works of God," and to understand all he says.

(3) He sets forth the truth in Jesus Christ so plainly that each individual may know clearly whether he is saved or not.

(4) By his earnestness and sincerity he impresses one that he is an Ambassador of Christ and about His Master's business.

(5) He expects men to be saved and he looks for results.

(6) At the close of each address he invariably makes an appeal to those who are willing to receive Jesus as their personal Saviour, to intimate their willingness by holding up their hand or by standing up. These are invited into the enquiry room to accept Jesus.

We thank God for the help Dr. Smith has been to Kingston and Jamaica. May God long spare him and his wife who accompanies him on his missions, and bless him abundantly in his evangelistic campaigns as well as in his other activities.

Dr. and Mrs. Smith left Toronto on Monday, Feb. 3rd, with $25.00, all that the Canadian Government would let them have. But meetings were held almost every night and offerings taken, so that all their needs were supplied.

The great Ward Theatre in Kingston, Jamaica, where Dr. Smith preached for nine days. There were 835 decisions for Christ.

A Christmas and New Year Campaign under the auspices of the Presbyterian Churches of West Belfast has been in progress since Sunday, December 22nd, conducted by the Rev. Oswald J. Smith, D.D., Litt.D., F.R.G.S., famous pastor of The Peoples Church, Toronto. The large Albert Hall has been filled almost to capacity by interested and responsive congregations.

Since the opening, night after night, increasing attendances testify to the growing interest, especially amongst young people. The purpose of the campaign is three-fold — evangelistic, missionary, and the deepening of the spiritual life; and the response to all three challenges has been notable.

Dr. Smith is a gripping, forceful preacher. He has had a wide experience of Gospel ministry as a pastor and evangelist, and as a missionary traveller in many lands. His opening address of the campaign on "The Revival We Need and How to Get It" deeply impressed the vast congregation and moved many to acknowledge their need and acceptance of spiritual renewal. On Christmas morning Dr. Smith spoke on "The Virgin Birth of Christ," and in the evening, to a packed house, he delivered a stirring appeal to defeated Christians on "The Victorious Life;" and at the close, almost fifty testified to their acceptance of Christ as Saviour, Victor, and Lord.

The showing of technicolour films illustrated the work of the Gospel amongst the Eskimos of Alaska, the Indians of Mexico, and the Solomon Islanders.

Dr. Smith is ably supported in the campaign by his son, Rev. Paul B. Smith, B.A., as song leader and trombone player, and Mrs. Paul Smith as soloist, and a large Gospel choir.

No one who was present in the Albert Hall on Monday night, December 30th, will ever forget the scene witnessed at the conclusion of the service conducted by Dr. Smith. When the service opened at 7:45 the Hall was packed to capacity, with dozens of people standing within the doors of the auditorium.

The subject of the evening was "The Supreme Task of the Church — The Evangelization of the World", introduced

The great crowd in Dr. Smith's campaign in Albert Rev. W.P. Hall, Minister, with Dr.

12 Great Days with Dr.

with a technicolour film illustrating Christians and cannibals in the Solomon Islands; after which Dr. Smith delivered a powerful address in which he reviewed the condition of the world for which Christ died, and the moribund condition of the Church. What the Church needed in every land, he declared, was to be delivered from the purely local conception of its program and catch the world view which is God's view — "God so loved the world" — and Christ's view — "Go ye into all the world and preach the Gospel."

From the results obtained in the experience of his own ministry, the preacher showed how even the local problems of church finance resolved themselves when the missionary interest and outreach to the regions beyond gripped the people,

and released their powers to give of their prayers and service and substance. During the entire address in which he pleaded the cause of the Christless millions, the vast audience was held spellbound; every eye and ear and heart was fixed upon the preacher and his message. He spoke as he was moved by the Spirit of God—none could doubt it. His marshalling of facts and statistics and cogent arguments were amazingly clear and convincing, and his appeal for personal decision and dedication was electric.

The immediate response resulted in the crowding of the aisles and passages as, from all parts of the building, young men and women under thirty years of age, rose and made their way to stand in solid ranks in front of the platform

Hall when hundreds were turned away.
Smith and his party by the pulpit.

Oswald Smith in Belfast

and register their names as willing to accept the call to Service. It was a never-to-be-forgotten scene. It demonstrated to all the power of the Gospel to call forth the spirit of youth to adventure into the noblest self-sacrificing service for the redemption of mankind.

Many ministers and Christian workers were present and assisted in tabulating the names; and arrangements were made to follow up and conserve the movement initiated.

During the campaign, Dr. Smith gave two special addresses on Prophecy, the first entitled, "Why I Believe, after Several World Tours, that the Only Hope of the Nations is the Return of Christ;" and the second, "Signs of the End-Time, or Prophecy Fulfilled To-

day." These were listened to with rapt attention by large congregations and unquestionably many have been moved to study the prophetic Scriptures concerning the glorious hope of our Lord's return.

The Watch-Night Service was another memorable occasion when, in answer to the appeal, a number of young people went to the enquiry room to accept Christ and begin the New Year in the joy of His salvation.

On Thursday evening, January 2nd, Dr. Smith delivered to a full house an impressive message on "Four Essentials of the New Life." It was a message specially addressed to young converts but it gripped the hearts of all Christians by its practical counsel, illustrated

out of the preacher's own experience, emphasizing the essentials of Bible-reading, prayer, fellowship in worship, and witness-bearing in active Christian service. The campaign reached its climax on Friday evening when half an hour before the announced hour of commencement, the Hall was packed to overflowing and some hundreds were unable to gain even standing room. The usual song-service conducted by the Rev. Paul Smith was abbreviated, and Mrs. Oswald Smith came to the platform and addressed a few words of greeting to the vast congregation, expressing her appreciation of the wonderful reception which had been given to her husband and his messages. Mrs. Paul Smith, who had been ill for some days, was also present again and sang a duet with her husband and also charmed the audience with one of her Gospel solos.

Dr. Smith's subject was the story of his boyhood, of how a newspaper was the means of his conversion, and of his early attempts at preaching. It was a thrilling story which held his audience spell-bound, sometimes provoking laughter and sometimes moving to breathless intensity of feeling and tears—the story of how a Canadian country boy was won for Christ and called out into a Gospel ministry which has borne the rich fruit of missionary and evangelistic labours in many lands.

The campaign closed on Saturday night with a praise and consecration meeting in which many testified to blessing received; and prayers were offered for the campaign, to be opened on the following day at the Metropolitan Hall, Dublin.

The writer was Chairman for the Campaign, which was enthusiastically supported by the ministers of eight local Presbyterian Churches. All gratefully testified to the strengthening of the Gospel witness in the district, and to the large numbers, especially of young people, who have been called out into decision for Christ and dedication to His Service. Throughout the whole campaign, much prayer was offered by devoted groups which met daily and the more consistently as they saw the windows of Heaven opening and the pouring out of blessing so abundantly.

by Rev. W. Patterson Hall, M.A.

Mission

Father & Son Preach to 150,000

10,000 attend nightly, 15,000 to 20,000 on the last night and 2,000 accept Christ. Largest crowd Jamaica has ever seen

Dr. Oswald J. Smith has just held a great campaign in Jamaica, a campaign that almost became a revival. Night after night crowds gathered beginning with 4,000 and rapidly increasing until during the last week, according to the caretaker of the Race Course and many others, there were 10,000 present each night.

A conservative estimate for the last night would be 15,000. Most said 20,000. Over 475 decisions were counted that one night. The Grandstand was jammed over an hour before the service commenced. Thousands stood throughout. Jamaica had seen nothing like it for any kind of meeting in its history. It was a crime to stop. The campaign should have continued for weeks.

It was a common thing to see 150 to 400 push through the great crowd night after night to accept Christ. The personal workers were swamped and had to deal with the seekers in groups. There were at least 2,000 who made the great decision but there were many others whose names it was impossible to get.

Dr. Smith and his son, Rev. Paul B. Smith, B.A., preached by turns; one speaking in the Ward Theatre in the afternoon and the other at the Race Course at night. It made no difference which one spoke the interest was the same. Many declared the son was the better preacher of the two. His messages were serious and convincing and resulted in hundreds of decisions; his deep, penetrating voice easily reaching the vast throng.

The people packed every inch of sitting and standing space in the Grandstand so that no aisles were visible. Then the vast open space in front which had been seated was likewise filled, thousands standing on either side. Hundreds of parked cars filled with listeners covered the field outside the fence, and scores upon scores who have climbed up, sat everywhere upon the roof. Never

in all his ministry had Dr. Smith preached to such multitudes.

In order to deal with the converts the huge Grandstand had to first be cleared while the seekers waited patiently at the front after having shaken hands with the evangelist, and then surging up the steps, they were at last dealt with and led to Christ. In spite of the great crowd there was perfect order.

A conservative estimate would be an attendance of 150,000 during the two weeks of the campaign. They came in large trucks from various parts of the Island. They were there at 7 o'clock every night and most of them an hour before. They jammed the Ward Theatre and then had to stand. For two hours they stood in thousands shoulder to shoulder and scarcely moved. The newspaper compared it to the days of Wesley and Whitfield and said the Race Course had never seen the like before.

Rev. Paul B. Smith led the vast congregations with his trombone and Mrs. Verne Smith, brilliant pianist, accompanied him. He kept the huge audience together in a masterly way and every-

Paul Smith and his trombone with
John Henderson, Associate in
Evangelism at The Peoples Church.

one enjoyed the song services. Dr. Smith's own book, "Victorious Hymns", was used and 4,000 copies distributed. Mrs. Paul Smith sang her lovely solos, her clear soprano voice reaching every heart. There she stood, day after day, looking for all the world like an angel, as thousands of eyes were focused on her slim, frail figure, her blue Irish eyes glistening and her almost transparent face a picture never to be forgotten. At nearly every service she sang a duet with her husband.

Rev. Paul Smith has been urged to return next winter and conduct campaigns all over the Island. He and his song leader, John Henderson, may accept the invitation. It will be real missionary work. There are few young preachers so gifted for evangelism. Rev. John Huffman, in whose church he held a campaign in Cambridge after his meeting in Tremont Temple, Boston, said, "For his age he is the best preacher I have ever heard." It may be that God will use him mightily in Jamaica.

One night while Dr. Smith was preaching it started to rain, and in a moment the vast multitude got up, everyone lifting a chair and holding it over his head. There they stood in the downpour waiting for it to stop. Those who could crowded under the platform of the Grandstand. When it ceased there was a wild scramble and in a few seconds the thousands of chairs were placed where they had been before and the meeting went on. Leaders said it was the first time in history that they had ever known the Jamaican people to remain when it was raining, but so great was the interest that no one left.

Day after day the noted Minneapolis Girls' Quintette stirred the vast crowd with their happy, sunny faces and made a tremendous contribution. No one in Jamaica who heard them will ever forget them.

~THE~
PEOPLES MAGAZINE

OSWALD J. SMITH, Litt.D., *Editor*

| Volume 29 | TORONTO, CANADA, FOURTH QUARTER, 1950 | Numbers 10-12 |

Oswald Smith in Norway

Crowded Churches — Great Interest — Inspiring Messages — Scores of Volunteers
Pastors Stirred — Souls Saved — Revival Spirit — Overflow Meetings

By REV. CHRIS HVIDSTEEN
Acting Pastor of Bethlehem Church, Olso, Norway;
Former Missionary of the China Inland Mission, and Dr. Smith's Interpreter.

Norway expected to have a visit from Dr. Oswald J. Smith in 1948, and in fact he had bought the ticket, but in Paris his plans were altered, and he had to go to Rome. But Norway could not afford to miss his visit, so he was invited to come to Oslo after the Youth for Christ Convention in Brussels.

And in August he came.

The first meeting was held in the Bethlehem Church, which was crowded to capacity. All the free Churches in Oslo had agreed to co-operate in the campaign, and most of the meetings were held in the two largest churches of the city, Bethlehem seating 1,200, and Philadelphia seating 2,300.

Dr. Smith was already known in Norway through his writings, so that the Christians were looking forward to his coming with great expectancy. The halls were filled long before the meetings were to start. The seats were all occupied and people were standing everywhere, in the vestibule, and all the way to the front door.

There has been nothing like it in Norway since the great revival meetings of Frank Mangs fifteen years ago.

In the first meetings he gave plain Gospel messages, but he preached in such a way that he won the people's hearts from the very beginning. He called for personal workers, and very many responded, and to them he gave most helpful instructions as to how to deal with

different groups of people, and how to meet their need.

His sermons on prophecy were listened to with immense interest, and after those addresses many came forward to accept Christ as their Saviour.

In the middle of the day, at twelve o'clock, he preached to Christians about Bible Study, Prayer, the Victorious Life, etc. About one thousand people attended these noon meetings regularly, and they were highly appreciated. In a very simple way Dr. Smith spoke about the

DR. OSWALD J. SMITH

practical things of the Christian life, and what he said will be remembered for ever.

His missionary meetings were, perhaps, the strongest of all. He emphasized Missions in such a way that everyone was convinced that the greatest task of the Church is foreign missions. After his powerful appeals many young men and women came to the front and dedicated themselves to the Lord, offering to go to the mission field if God should call them. Dr. Smith dealt with these young people with fatherly sympathy. He gave them much good advice and showed them how to be sure about the Lord's will.

All the pastors co-operated heartily. They were most thankful for the meetings. Several of them said that the visit of Dr. Smith meant a turning point in their life and ministry.

Old Christians, who had seen several revivals, said: *"Dr. Smith is the Franson of our generation."* (Franson, the famous world missionary, created great interest in foreign missions and soul-winning some sixty years ago. He helped to found the Norwegian Covenant Mission, and he founded the Evangelical Alliance Mission of North America.) Others said: *"These meetings are just like Frank Mangs meetings of fifteen years ago."* (Mangs was the instrument God used to kindle revival fire in Norway.) Dr. Smith himself seemed to be at home among us.

1955 – South Africa.
Oswald was 66 years old in 1955, but far from being ready to slow down. He and Daisy embarked on a South African tour that left the country changed forever.

In Cape Town, the Weekend Supplement of, *Die Burger,* carried the story.
"Dr. Oswald J. Smith, who is regarded as the greatest Evangelist Missionary of his time, was unknown to most people in South Africa when he started his Union-wide campaign in Pretoria. But it very soon became known that a most extraordinary man had arrived in South Africa. The number of people that went to listen to his messages increased nightly. In every town the churches and halls were ultimately too small to accommodate the large numbers, and hundreds were turned away.

Dr. & Mrs. Smith on top of Table Mountain.

Home sweet home. Dr. & Mrs. Smith's hut in Africa.

A church leader commented:
"But have you heard Oswald Smith preach? Have you felt the prophetic fire, the apostolic fervour of his messages? An electric current of life runs through them; they go straight to the point. Trained by years of speaking with an interpreter, Smith uses short, pithy sentences that smash like sledge-hammer blows against the heart. There's a powerful simplicity, an incisive directness, a sincerity and unmistakable authority as he preaches the Word of God. Every child could under stand his messages, and yet no adult could hear them indifferently. You feel he is speaking to you alone."

Some time after the South African campaign, Dr. John F. Wooderson, pastor of the Durban Tabernacle, sent word of the fruit of Oswald's visit.

God's amazing creation.

"As we listened to your challenge, we realized that we are right on the edge of an enormous mission field. We set a goal for "faith promise" giving, and to the praise and glory of God's Name, we exceeded our goal by more than 100%. But the greatest achievement was that numbers of people began to prove the unfailing faithfulness of God in enabling them to keep their "faith promise" to Him and each year as they promised more to missions, their faith rose, and what followed in the spread of the Gospel was something in which they had a tangible part.

Dr. Smith with children from the Dorothea Mission.

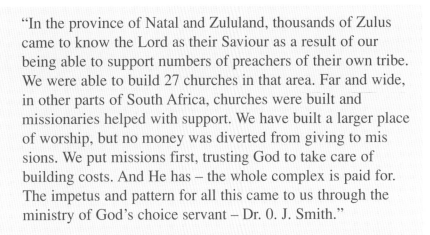

"In the province of Natal and Zululand, thousands of Zulus came to know the Lord as their Saviour as a result of our being able to support numbers of preachers of their own tribe. We were able to build 27 churches in that area. Far and wide, in other parts of South Africa, churches were built and missionaries helped with support. We have built a larger place of worship, but no money was diverted from giving to missions. We put missions first, trusting God to take care of building costs. And He has – the whole complex is paid for. The impetus and pattern for all this came to us through the ministry of God's choice servant – Dr. O. J. Smith."

Zulu chief.

On returning to Canada via Rome, Paris and London, Oswald was greatly impressed by the Pentecostal work in Rome.

"I have very high regard for the Pentecostal work in Italy. It is by far the largest denomination in the country and it is winning thousands of souls to Christ."

Raising funds to change the world.
Oswald barely had time to sort his films before setting out for the States and the Pacific coast of Canada for a round of fundraising in missions conventions. The result was $166,000. for missions.

1957 – South America.
In 1957, Mrs. E. Spitzer arranged for Oswald and Daisy to tour Brazil, Argentina, Chile, Peru, Uruguay, Ecuador, Colombia and Panama, holding eight great campaigns in three-and-a-half months. For the first time ever, 25 denominations cooperated. With crowds of 25,000 and 4,500 first-time decisions for Christ, these were the largest united evangelistic campaigns in the history of South America. With many of the meetings televised, multiplied thousands heard the message of salvation. In an attempt to explain the success of the campaigns, Dr. Martin Durksen, president of the Executive Committee for Buenos Aires, wrote,

Durban's rickshaw man.

"Perhaps the success of Dr. Smith's preaching lay in his delightful simplicity and the strong personality that backed his clear and plain words."

One of the workers noted:
"Many of us had read his books and caught some of his evangelistic zeal and missionary vision. But then to see with our own eyes what God can do through a life wholly consecrated to Him."

The 350 voice choir and part of the congregation in Curitiba, Brazil.

Into all the World

Making History in South America
by Rev. Jack McAlister, Director of World Literature Crusade

"It's never happened before"; 'It's the first time in the history of this country"; "It's a miracle—we can't believe our eyes"; "To you this may not seem especially significant—but this Crusade is *making history*."

Everywhere we went Christian leaders were saying the same thing.

For almost seven weeks I travelled with Dr. Oswald J. Smith as Associate Evangelist in his Latin American Crusades. As I sit in this aeroplane—(flying back to North America)—and analyze everything that I heard—I'll do my best to convey to you the facts which were forcibly drawn to my attention—facts which have caused evangelical leaders to make these rather startling statements.

FIRST ASPECT

The first "history-making" aspect of these Crusades was the "first-time-ever" *unity* among evangelical denominations and missionary societies. Until now, almost all denominations worked separately and alone. Consequently, the results had been relatively small—the testimony of Christ had not had the impact on major cities and nations which it could and should have had . . . because of lack of understanding, mistrust, and in too many cases, plain jealousy and denominational pride among evangelical leaders and missionaries. In many cities they said, "This is the *first* time all evangelicals have co-operated in a soul-winning Crusade." I heard this so often that I could have become wearied with the repetitious refrain—except for the glow of amazement which rang in every voice that repeated these words.

At long last—we evangelicals dealt a blow to the Roman Catholic propaganda which says, "Protestants are all divided—we are united in one powerful witness for Christ." Neither statement was completely true—*but it looked* like the truth

to the general public — which included more than 100,000,000 Latin Americans.

During these Crusades—the public saw that as Evangelicals we sang the same hymns, we prayed to the same God, we preached the same Gospel, and we invited people to come to the same Christ for salvation from sin. What a glorious triumph for our Christian testimony! This united effort made such an impact on great cities that radio, newspaper and television gave these soul-winning Crusades — *wide and favourable* coverage , , , in traditionally Roman Catholic countries. Pray that such a united witness may be given again, and again, and again.

SECOND ASPECT

The second aspect of this "history-making" series of Crusades that was evident — concerned the vast crowds which came to listen to the Gospel. In Curityba, Brazil (capital of the State of Parana) the newspaper said, "Never in the history of this city of 300,000 people has such a large crowd gathered in the arena — even for political or sporting events." This arena is the largest auditorium in the entire State of Parana.

Rev. Jack McAlister

In Montevideo, Uruguay, they said, "This is the largest Protestant gathering in the history of this nation."

Last Sunday night in Buenos Aires Dr. Smith rested in the hotel and gave me the privilege of preaching to 23,000 people, which I was told was the largest gathering for an evangelical service in the history of Argentina—from the standpoint of a united effort by all denominations.

Crowds in the first six days of the Buenos Aires Crusade exceeded 90,000. What a contrast to the 25 and 50 who attended most evangelical meetings all over South America during the last 50 years. No wonder struggling, hard-working missionaries and national pastors (who laid the foundation for these Crusades) are saying, "It's a miracle—I can't believe my eyes."

THIRD ASPECT

The third aspect of these "history-making" crusades was the number of decisions for Christ. Obviously, the first two points I mentioned were major contributing factors. What a thrill for faithful missionaries and national pastors . . . who have never seen more than a dozen souls come to Christ in one service . . . to see *hundreds* and *hundreds* almost leap out of their seats and surge forward to accept the Saviour!

I ask every Christian who reads these words—to definitely pray that these missionaries and national workers will spare no effort to carefully "follow-up" every convert.

It is reported that Billy Graham was asked, "Will your converts stand?" His reply was, "It depends on the care they get." Pray that the pastors will lovingly care for these thousands of "lambs" in cities all over South America. (The old rams can look after themselves for a few days . . . it's the lambs who *need* the care!)

The Peoples Magazine — Second Quarter, 1958

Dr. Oswald J. Smith, besieged by rejoicing Argentinians.

25,000 at Luna Park

The Gospel in the heart of Buenos Aires.

Don Newman and the King's Men.

Smiths in Australia

Don Newman

Koala friends.

Twenty-three years is a long time. Much too long for friends to be separated. Thus it was with a warm sense of anticipation, that Australian Christians awaited the return visit of Dr. Oswald J. Smith.

Although alone and very ill with Malaria in 1938, this time he was accompanied by Mrs. Smith and despite the fact of an added 23 years, he displayed great vigour and energy. This continued throughout all his meetings. Everyone was simply amazed at his vitality and youthfulness. They had been expecting an aged gentleman. Instead they were greeted each evening by a man obviously in his prime.

The ministry of Dr. and Mrs. Smith was marked by the miraculous. Everywhere they went it was the same story! What was thought to be an ample supply of Dr. Smith's books, was sold out in two nights in each place. Hundreds of additional orders had to be placed. Perhaps one of the most significant contributions to evangelism in Australia was Dr. Smith's emphasis on Christian literature. Of course, every penny realised from the sale of Dr. Smith's books will go to Foreign Missions.

Our own Association has been so challenged on this issue that we have agreed to distribute both Dr. Oswald Smith's and Dr. Paul Smith's books on an identical basis. Every penny of not only the profits, but the entire proceeds from the sale of these books will go to Foreign Missions. Half of it will be used for the printing of foreign literature. The rest will be used to reach the Australian Aborigines under the A.E.A.M.

Some of the facts and figures connected with the national campaigns will indicate to some extent the measure of blessing. The entire nation is rejoicing in the fact that nearly 1,100 young people offered themselves for full-time Christian and missionary service if God should call. This will mean much

in the days ahead for Australian Bible colleges and institutes and eventually, the foreign mission field.

Even as missionaries recruited in Dr. Smith's 1938 meetings have greeted him on mission fields around the world, even so we believe there will be many hundreds who will do likewise in the years to come. Perhaps Dr. Smith's most lasting contribution will be the dynamic challenge delivered to the youth of Australia.

In addition to the hundreds of volunteers, there were several hundred decisions for victory, as well as first-time decisions. Every service saw results. People forced their way through the crowded aisles and vestibules to record their decision for Christ. The scenes were reminiscent of the great Graham Crusades of 1959. In campaign after campaign, auditoriums were not large enough to cope with the crowds. Hundreds upon hundreds were turned away.

One service was set aside in each campaign as a missionary service. An offering for foreign missions was received and in each case, the single offerings were among the largest ever received in Australia for this purpose. Melbourne's offering totalled £1,200, Sydney's was the same. Brisbane gave £700 for the evangelization of the world and the Easter Convention at the Australian

Don Newman.

Institute of Evangelism contributed £600.

Mrs. Smith's Ladies' Meeting in the Chapter House of Sydney's St. Andrew's Cathedral, was an excellent accompaniment to her husband's evening meetings. Over 400 ladies were present and heard something of the early days of Mrs. Smith's ministry. They were challenged not only on the duties of discipleship, but the responsibilities of motherhood as well. This was the story in each campaign. Her obvious total dedication to the cause of world evangelism and her gracious and charming personality endeared her to all.

It was also a great joy to have Dr. and Mrs. Smith speak on our daily broadcast on three consecutive evenings. Dr. Smith was most warm in his words of appreciation to the team and his detailed account of up-to-date missionary activity was a source of enlightenment to the vast radio congregation reaching out over Australia and even into New Zealand.

Unfortunately, Adelaide was not able to join in the Oswald Smith Australian Crusades this time. It had been the scene of great victories in 1938, but it was not to be on this visit. When Dr. Smith stopped over to visit his friends, Dr. and Mrs. Donald Kidd, in Adelaide just before leaving for home, a hastily arranged service in the large downtown Baptist Church resulted in an overflow congregation.

Every one of Dr. Smith's books were sold in the meeting that night and scores of additional orders had to be recorded. There was a most encouraging response to the invitation and in addition to the great evening meeting, Dr. Smith was able to squeeze in a visit to the Adelaide Bible Institute as well as two other smaller meetings. The Christians of Adelaide are simply demanding that Dr. Smith return on his next visit.

The Peoples Magazine — Third Quarter, 1961

NEWS FROM ABROAD

Letters from our Missionaries

ETHEL DONER—HAITI

I thank the Lord for His faithfulness in supplying my need and I am very grateful to Peoples Church which has been the channel He has used.

I remember the farewell service in Peoples Church and being committed to the Lord and His service by the pastor and elders. I came to Haiti in 1944. The support from Peoples Church these eighteen years amounts to $9,360.00

The girls' orphanage was opened in September, 1945 and that is the work I have been engaged in most of my time here on the field. I have spent some time at the boys' orphanage too, when help was needed. I have seen girls grow up here and some are in the Lord's work now. Several are married and have christian homes. Two are nurses and are witnessing for the Lord. At least five are teaching school. We have 38 children in our care at present.

Thank you for your gifts and prayers. May the Lord bless you.

JEAN GRASLEY—HAITI

July 16, 1948, was my first day in Haiti. Since that day, my service has been greatly varied—teaching in Bible School, helping in the press, keeping the Bookstore, encouraging young people's groups in country districts and now, another new post—treasurer, choir leader and Bible teacher in our Christian High School.

The first half of this present term was spent living alone in one of the smaller cities and doing country work from there. The need in the High School necessitated my moving back to the capital, but my heart is still with those country youngsters. Many of them are mountain children, uneducated, unable to read the Word for themselves. Their knowledge of the Bible is appallingly small.

This one ordinary missionary has received $5,150 from Peoples since that church began helping with my support. As I've calculated afresh what has been done for me alone, my heart is filled with gratitude. My sincere thanks to Dr. Smith and all the friends of Peoples.

GERTRUDE HEPPNER—HAITI

I first arrived on the field on May 24th, 1955. The Peoples Church has regularly sent my full personal support totalling $3,750.00 during a period of 75 months from July, 1955 until March, 1962.

After completing language study I worked at our home for orphan boys for 2½ years until I was transferred to the press department to help at the bookstore part time and as vari-type operator at present. In spite of the high percentage of illiteracy there is a great demand for Bibles, Scripture portions, tracts and other Christian literature. I also have opportunities to serve the Lord in Sunday School, Junior Church, street meetings and visitation ministry.

I appreciate all that you have done through your prayers and financial assistance to make this ministry possible and trust that many more souls may find peace with God during these days of unrest.

AILEEN REID—MEXICO

When I first crossed the border into Mexico in 1950 it was with a feeling of deep peace and joy in being in the country to which God had called me. There have been discouragements and difficulties but always there is that awareness of the great privilege that is mine to serve the Lord on the mission field. I am thankful for those in Peoples Church who have contributed to my support during the past ten years (a total of approximately $6,000).

May the Lord continue to bless and use you in this great missionary task.

I have worked among the Totonac Indians of the State of Puebla. The Lord has enabled us to publish the Gospel of Mark in this language, to prepare a number of Bible stories and to translate in first draft a number of other Books of the Bible. We have seen something of what it means to a people to hear the Word in their own language and to worship God in their mother tongue.

Thank you for your prayers as well as your gifts. We would ask you to pray for continued guidance in translation work and for the Lord's blessing on His Word to the hearts of the Totonacs.

LEONARDO REINKE— DOMINICAN REPUBLIC

The Lord led us forth to the Dominican Republic under the Unevangelized Fields Mission in Sept., 1953.

Peoples Church promised us their support as from that date; and due to their faithfulness to God during these past eight and one-half years, their contributions total $10,200. We are humbled before the Lord of the Harvest (Mat. 9:38) for that Sacrificial giving enabling us to make known our Redeemer's Saving and Keeping Power amongst this ignorant and idolatrous people.

It has been our privilege to share in pastoral work, child evangelism, tent evangelism, children's camps, Bible Bookstore and Colportage work, and now in house-to-house visitation with "Every Home Crusade" of which we are Regional Directors here in the north of this island.

The Peoples Magazine — Third Quarter, 1962

The Bible School at Makassar, D.E.I., in connection with which
The Peoples Church supports 25 national evangelists. *(1937 photo and caption.)*

Volume 48   TORONTO, CANADA, SECOND QUARTER, 1969   Number 4-6

CAREY'S TOWN – CALCUTTA

by Paul B. Smith

Despite the fact that the British East India Company fought desperately to keep the people of India from being evangelized, William Carey and his associates were able to found the Lall Bazaar Chapel in the heart of Calcutta It was dedicated on New Year's Day, 1809. After Carey's death it was renamed The Carey Baptist Church.

Exactly 160 years later on Sunday morning January 26th, it was my privilege to stand in the pulpit of the same church. This is the church that owed its existence humanly to the man who on his death bed looked up at Alexander Duff and said, "When I am gone, Dr. Duff, speak not of Dr. Carey, but speak of the Master of Dr. Carey."

Carey Baptist Church is still going strong under the able leadership of Rev. Walter Corlett. He is a delightful man who was unusually gracious to me during my Crusade in Calcutta. His ministry for over forty years in India has been most effective and far-reaching.

Calcutta

Most Indian people will readily agree that Calcutta is their dirtiest and most explosive city It is India's largest with a population in the area of six million but condensed into a considerably smaller space than the second largest, Bombay.

To say that there are people everywhere is an understatement. The main streets and the small side streets seem to be crowded constantly. You cannot walk down the sidewalk at anything like a brisk pace. You must wend your way through dense crowds and weave around a never-ending line of sidewalk salesmen who have their wares laid out at your feet.

The crowds of Calcutta tend to be explosive. If a taxi driver should run into a rickshaw, he has to get out of his car quickly and run for his life. If the crowd were to catch him, they might beat him to death or at best set fire to his taxi.

Dr. Paul Smith
being welcomed to India.

God Calls the Church

Our Crusade was held in the large St. Andrew's Church — founded by the Church of Scotland and located at the intersection of several main streets. It is the only air conditioned church in Calcutta. We started on a Thursday night with less than half the space filled. We concluded the meetings on the following Monday with the place packed — both ground floor and balcony. Each time the invitation was given there were those who came forward and went into the counselling room.

Under the theme "God Calls the Church", the Director of Calcutta Youth for Christ gathered a widely representative group of church leaders to organize the meetings. Vijayan Pavamani is an intense man with a burden for souls and is typical of the kind of Indian leadership that is being raised up by God during these days when the missionaries are being squeezed out by a Hindu society that controls the government and is very much afraid of the evangelical zeal of the Christian Church.

The long range plan of the present government would seem to be twofold: 1) to completely eliminate the foreign missionary — perhaps within five years, 2) to cut off foreign funds from the Indian Christian Church.

The Peoples Magazine — Second Quarter, 1969

Bombay Gateway

by Paul B. Smith

It was Thursday night. An eight-piece Salvation Army band played "Onward Christian Soldiers", the choir sang "Saved, I'm Saved" and a packed church listened intently as the Gospel was preached.

As I gazed long and deep at the scene before me I realized that I was seeing a cross section of the results of 179 years of missionary effort in India. And what a brilliant success story this is! If only the early pioneers could have seen what I saw in Bombay they would have rejoiced. Undoubtedly with the eye of faith they did see it, and it was this vision that drove them from their homes in the cities of Europe to face the unbelievable heat, the drenching rains, the crippling diseases and the dominating religions that are India.

Most assuredly the man who said: "Attempt great things for God, expect great things from God", has realized all of his expectations and more. Somewhere in the glory William Carey, his associates and the hundreds who followed now know that it was indeed worth it all. Perhaps as the people sang the invitation hymn they were augmented by voices from another world — the voices of hundreds of missionaries who sacrificed some part of their lives to preach the Gospel in India.

Beyond — Bombay

Beyond the sanctuary walls lay the seething, pulsating, congested, booming city. Bombay is the largest city in India — between five and six million people, more than one quarter the population of the whole of Canada. It is a cosmopolitan city dominated by Hindus but also including some Moslems, Sikhs, Parsees, Christians and a few Jews. There are those who are extremely wealthy and those that are unbelievably poor with all the economic levels in between.

I was told that there are 65,000 registered prostitutes in Bombay and perhaps three times that many who are not registered. Five minutes away from my hotel I saw the "cage" girls — an entire area with a network of streets given over for prostitution. They stand on both street and first floor level at the doors of tiny rooms about the size of a sentry box. The doors are generally made of vertical iron bars which makes them look like cages.

A visit to this area naturally is a shock to an outsider, but perhaps it is no more of a blemish on Indian society than syndicated crime is on our society.

All Indians are not starving to death. As a matter of fact, the majority are well fed and many of them have as much of a weight problem as some of our people. On my flight from Bombay to Hyderabad I shared my seat with an Indian man who just could not get all of himself into his own. He kept bulging over on me and I found myself wishing that he had not been so well fed.

Even the beggars on the street may not be starving. As I entered a large Hindu Temple I passed a very old lady sitting in the typical Indian "Squat" position with outstretched hand and pathetic appeal, "Bucksheesh, bucksheesh." After touring the temple I passed the same pathetic figure but now it was lunch time and she was very busy with an enormous bowl of yellow rice.

Some Indian people live in the

Dr. Paul Smith
and Dr. Billy Graham.

magnificent apartments that stretch along the Marine Drive — modern, luxurious and above the squalor of the city. However, the huge majority live in extremely small rooms and generally under very crowded circumstances. One or two rooms may often house a large family.

The "Hutments"

Then there are the "hutments". These are almost impossible to describe. They may be made of corrugated siding but often seem to consist of a sort of sack cloth tied together in some mysterious manner. They may appear almost anywhere. Enroute from the Bombay airport there are whole communities of these things. But they may also be seen on the city streets. The wall of a building will serve as one wall and the sacking makes up the other three. In most cases you would have to bend over to go into them. Entire families may spend their lives in this kind of a "home."

The Streets

Finally, there is another bit of Indian society that does not bother to erect a shelter of any kind. They literally live on the streets. They build fires and cook their meals there, they transact their business there, and when evening falls, they stretch out on the pavement, pull a shawl over their heads and go to sleep there.

The Miracle

With this very scanty picture of an Indian city as a backdrop, you can not help but interpret the work of the missionaries as one of the great success stories of the past two centuries.

Our Crusade was held in the Shushanti church established by Presbyterian missionaries from Switzerland. It would accommodate about a thousand people. The crowds ranged from five or six hundred to a packed house on the final night.

The Peoples Magazine — Second Quarter, 1969

Dr. Smith In Denmark

By Dr. Karl Viktor Nielsen

Ever since I was a young man I have read the books of Dr. Oswald J. Smith and they have had a tremendous influence on my life. I have always dreamed of the day when I would meet the author, either here in Denmark or in the great Peoples Church, Toronto. Now the dream has come true.

I am Director of World Literature Crusade for Denmark and Minister of Education for Technical Examinations and I am a member of the Mission Covenant Church.

I suggested to the Evangelical Alliance of Denmark that Dr. Smith be invited to hold meetings in our country and they agreed. Thus all the Evangelical Christians were behind the campaign.

For two generations now, Dr. Smith's books have had a tremendous influence on the lives of the Christians in Denmark and for years we have felt that his messages on the Deeper Life and Missions would be of vital importance to our people. Therefore we began to pray and at long last Dr. Smith accepted our invitation and for the first time came to preach in Denmark.

My wife and three boys and our little daughter consider that we have had a great privilege in having Dr. and Mrs. Smith in our home. We have experienced wonderful blessing and we will never forget them as long as we live.

First of all, we took a trip to Oslo, Norway, by boat and there Dr. Smith spoke both afternoon and evening on a Friday. There were approximately 2,000 people present in the Filadelfia Church at the evening service and about 300 young people responded to the invitation and volunteered for full-time service. It was a wonderful sight.

Dr. Smith is young and vital in his appearance. Again and again both in Norway and Denmark, the people insisted that I had made a mistake and that Dr. Smith, with his athletic appearance and strong voice must still be in his fifties.

The first meeting in Denmark was held at Aalborg on Sunday afternoon, October 12th in the Mission Covenant Church but all the Evangelical denominations co-operated. People came as far away as 100 miles and the church was packed. They listened eagerly to his message and there was a wonderful response. About 40 young people volunteered for missionary service and as they stood at the front, the people sat in perfect silence while Dr. Smith spoke to them.

Before starting the campaign in Copenhagen, Dr. Smith met the entire committee and was welcomed to Denmark. They listened very attentively as he spoke. There were about 30 Pastors present at the Luncheon and each one received a real blessing. They went away feeling that they had met one of the greatest personalities of this generation.

Throughout the week the meetings were held in different churches, including the State Church, the Methodist, the Baptist, the Mission Covenant, the Pentecostal, and others. Thus people of all denominations had an opportunity of hearing his messages. Each night the church was packed well ahead of the time to begin the service, and scores of extra chairs had to be carried in.

Oh what messages! Those who know Dr. Smith need not be told that they were penetrating and biblical, that they were Spiritual and practical and above all, filled with challenge as well as encouragement.

Every morning, Dr. Smith spoke on the Deeper Life and many of those who attended left the wilderness and entered the Promised Land. There was a splendid attendance every morning.

On Saturday night and on Sunday night, there were two revival meetings the like of which Denmark has not seen for years. Dr. Smith delivered Gospel messages at both services. The results were evident. Many surrendered their lives to the Lord and passed from death to Life. The Saturday night meeting was held in the world famous Tivoli Concert Hall which seats 2,000. At the close of the service, I spoke to some of the officials and they said they had listened to an unique man with a unique message.

Two of Dr. Smith's books had been translated into the Danish language in preparation for the campaign and more than 1,000 copies were sold in his meetings. Thus he has left something in the homes of the people that will continue to speak long after he has gone.

A young man came all the way from Norway to attend the meetings and when it was over, he said he felt like Elisha in the presence of Elijah.

It was my privilege to be Dr. Smith's interpreter at every service in Denmark, and what a joy it was to stand beside him in the pulpit and interpret his inspiring messages.

Mrs. Smith was a great help. She is a brilliant conversationalist. Often times when Dr. Smith sat in silence to rest his voice, she took over and held the interest of all present as she spoke in her energetic way, and, of course, she won all hearts by her winsome smile. Very often she addresses mass meetings of women in Dr. Smith's campaigns around the world. We were so glad she was able to come with her husband. My wife could not help falling in love with her even though she speaks very little English.

Dr. Karl V. Nielsen

The Peoples Magazine — First Quarter 1970

The Paul B. Smith
Academy Orchestra

by Jean Austring

Why would Ethel Wright even consider such an undertaking? Taking The Paul B. Smith Academy Orchestra to Mexico was no small matter. Was her intention merely to give the sixty-six young people the time of their lives? If so, she succeeded. But the purpose reached far beyond fun and enjoyment. The trip was intended to encourage our teenagers in three areas—to use their musical ability for God, to develop appreciation for other countries and cultures, and to catch a missionary vision by being missionary helpers for the week.

It was soon evident that music was an attraction, a common language, and a remover of barriers. Eight concerts were given. It was quite a task transporting sixty-six uniformed musicians, setting up stands and chairs, and tuning instruments! The two presentations given in evangelical churches served to draw some unbelievers and to uplift fellow believers. Deep appreciation was shown by happy smiles and warm embraces. We also made our "joyful noise unto the Lord" outside the churches—twice in open "plazas", twice in schools, once in a municipal auditorium, and once in a hotel court yard. Music drew crowds and opened doors of opportunity.

This busy schedule of concerts enabled us to mingle with Mexican people and experience a cross section of their culture. Being guests for the first three nights at the Mexico Bible Institute near Mexico City, we had the opportunity to enjoy their hospitality. Also, wherever our programme was presented, social times were provided and snacks were served. Often we were entertained, in turn, by a band, a singing group, or a small instrumental group, Latin American style. We even shared in Mexican problems— water shortage, an electrical blackout at the Institute, and an earthquake. (Being in buses on a bumpy road, we were actually unaware of the earthquake until later.) We learned Mexican philosophy regarding clocks. Fortunately the phrase "subject to change" had been printed at the bottom of our schedules. "Probably" and "maybe" became common words in our vocabulary. All this cultural education was beyond the obvious absorbing of some of Mexico's history and geography.

As well as musical experience and educational gain was the spiritual impact. We saw God's Word being eagerly received and read. We observed different missionary methods for different situations. In an Indian village, Atlica, we thrilled at the exciting results of missionary effort. Thirty years ago the Whealys, under Wycliffe Bible Translators and supported by Peoples, entered this village. We heard stories of persecution and victory. Impressions were at times too deep for words. We were actually there!

There is no doubt that our three-fold purpose was achieved—and probably much more. Only the Lord knows how far-reaching the effect of this trip will be.

Our three reporters: J. D. Pipher, Mrs. Jean Austring and Denise Newson.

by J. D. Pipher

Imagine sixty-six musicians, ages twelve to nineteen, sitting on long wooden benches in a dimly lit square at night. Closely surrounding the playing group are hundreds of Indians, unable to speak English or Spanish. The younger members of the subdued audience squeeze in beside backbencher players in the Orchestra, watching every move and listening to every sound.

This is a picture of just one of the eight concerts that took place while The Paul B. Smith Academy Orchestra was in Mexico. It was the most unusual one and perhaps the most spiritually profitable. Listening to the story of how Christianity struggled through persecution in this small Indian village was enough to make anyone feel the presence of God in a very real way.

However, our spiritual endeavours were not limited just to concerts in very remote places. Giving out tracts in the streets of Acapulco and attending a Spanish Prayer Meeting in Mexico City were fantastic spiritual experiences which none of us will ever forget.

One of the most remarkable things about our trip to Mexico was the uninhibited friendliness of the Mexican Christians. Our churches could learn a vast amount about warmth and caring for others from the people of Mexico. If the Orchestra members put into practice even a small part of what was seen and experienced while we were in Mexico, we could influence and change many lives.

The Peoples Magazine, June-July-August, 1978

Our Kids on the Mission Fields

by Donald J. Jost
Associate Pastor, Ministries

This Summer an all time high number of Youth Summer Missionaries take up unusual ministries around the world! From Alaska to India, Pickle Lake, Ontario to Beho, Belgium; building mission outposts; serving on Gospel teams; radio work; installing water lines! You name it!! Our young people will be busy in missionary support teams.

When young people sign up with a mission for their short term posting, The Peoples Church, through its missionary program underwrites 60% of the travel and missions cost. We ask all young people to raise the 40% remaining through outside sources (uncles and aunts, grandparents, etc). We discourage our young missionaries from going to people within the church because they are already giving to our missions program. This gives them opportunity to pray in funds and learn to trust God, which is all part of the missionary training experience. Young people who attend the Paul B. Smith Academy but who may not necessarily attend The Peoples Church receive an encouraging amount to get them started in their support.

Keep this prayer list handy. Pray for all these people but also remember a host of our other young people who will be working in our Bible Conferences and Camps in Canada.

Please remember the following of our young people who are serving as Summer Missionaries during June, July and August.

NAME	COUNTRY	MISSION BOARD
Raye Ackerman	Pickle Lake, Canada	Teen Missions
Andrew Adkins	Caripe, Venezuela	Teen Missions
Heather Campbell	Bethlehem, Israel	Teen Missions
Greg Constable	Voitsberg, Austria	Teen Missions
Denise Cymbaluk	Bethlehem, Israel	Teen Missions
Pamela Cymbaluk	Orphanage, Egypt	Teen Missions
Ray Cymbaluk	Kentani, S. Africa	Teen Missions
Connie Fiander	Santa Marta, Col.	World Outreach
Patti Findlay	Peru	S.American Mission
Carolyn Gerber	Berg, West German	Word of Life
Monica Gerber	Berg, West Germany	Word of Life
Deldyn Grams	Secunderabad, India	Teen Missions
Todd Graves	Secunderabad, India	Teen Missions
James Inks	Secunderabad, India	Teen Missions
Brad Johnston	Bonaire, N. Antilles	Trans World Radio
Bill Portengen	Alaska	Missions Outreach
Paul Ralph	Graz, Austria	Teen Missions
Grace Sedstrem	Tent, Scotland	Teen Missions
Fred Serez	Secunderabad, India	Teen Missions
Lisa VanderVinne	Beho, Belgium	Teen Missions
Jodi Lynn Williams	Orphanage, Egypt	Teen Missions
Derek Wiseman	Secunderabad, India	Teen Missions

July – September, 1983.

Dr. Paul autographing his Father's Biography. The Chinese translation of *Fire in His Bones* had just arrived in H.K. Harbour. Esther Fan (back to camera) is one of our National Representatives in H.K. (CNEC)

Hong Kong

gathered in good time in front of the church. When they were admitted at 6:30-6:45, the hall was very quickly packed and late-comers had to go to other rooms in the church building, the small chapel, choir room, carpark, and Sunday School rooms where closed circuit television had been installed. Even these rooms in the church building were also quickly filled up and attendants who came later had to go to a high school building in the vicinity where closed circuit television had also been installed. It was estimated that the average attendance was 1,800 in the morning, and 2,600 in the evening. In the last two evenings, it went up to above 3,000. It was therefore estimated that the total attendance exceeded 50,000—really a big event in the church history of Hong Kong.

by Rev Enoch Yang

The Hong Kong Bible Conference took place on Monday August 1 to Wednesday August 10 as scheduled. The venue was Kowloon City Baptist Church in the peninsula of Kowloon.

Before the conference, a prayer meeting of all workers was held on July 31, at which the chairman, Rev. Enoch Yang, introduced the speakers of the conference: Dr. Daniel Lau for the 10:00-11:00 session, Dr. Fred T. Cheung for the 11:15-12:15 session, and Dr. Paul B. Smith for the evening session.

We saw unprecedented blessing from the Lord. It was good weather throughout the conference. This is very rare in the summer, which for Hong Kong, is the typhoon season. There were showers on occasions. But as the rain fell some time before the meetings, it only helped to cool down the air and made it more pleasant for attendants to come to the church. The attendance exceeded previous years. The great hall of the Baptist Church was all crowded to capacity in the two sessions in the morning. As to the evening sessions, many participants

"Dear Dr. Smith:

I wish to thank you for your letter of August 22. It is really a blessing from God that we could have you ministering to the Christians in Hong Kong in the recent Bible Conference. The committee wish to join me to thank you and Mrs. Smith for coming here in August. Brother Kam Nip (the interpreter) wishes to add his thanks for your nice and encouraging letter to him. Personally I am also most grateful to you for your words of commendation on my work on "Lectures on Revelation".

When you were in Hong Kong, you asked for a report on the Conference. We've got that sorted out now and I enclose herewith a copy for your consideration. If you wish to have further information, please let me know."

May the Lord bless your work for Him all the more.

Yours sincerely,

Enoch T. C. Yang
Chairman

In several evenings, Dr. Smith invited attendants to come forward to seek revival. On all of these occasions, the space in front of the platform, the space behind the pulpit on the platform and the aisles of the great hall were all fully packed—a response far exceeding what the organizing committee expected. Altogether 1,157 came forward to seek revival, 368 dedicated themseles for full-time service to the Lord. Dr. Smith also reserved one night for a gospel message.

Front row, second from left, Anita Smith, Dr. Paul Smith, Chairman Enoch Yang. Extreme right, interpreter Nip Kam-Fan.

On July 10, 1986 a group of sixteen adults led by Wilfred J. Wright boarded a plane at Pearson International Airport bound for Manila, Philippines. Twenty-eight hours later we were greeted by the heat, humidity, noise and pollution of Metro Manila and by the warm smile of our hostess, Emilie Famadico, from Action International Ministries.

After presenting each of us with a welcome lei of fragrant sampaguita, Emilie loaded us into a bus bound for our hotel. We rapidly developed an admiration for the skill of drivers in Manila. In this crowded city of ten million people, driving is both a science and an art! While we were told there are rules of the road, creativity is absolutely essential to survive. Thousands of jeepneys, tricycles, taxis, buses and cars fill the streets at all times. Short-tempered or shy drivers would not last in this city. In addition to crowds, they have to cope with the weather. With little notice during the rainy season the clouds open and heavy rain and backed up sewers flood the streets with several feet of water.

After a long flight we allowed day one for recovery from jet lag. On day two (Sunday), we were taken by Ron Carlson to an exciting service of praise at Metro Manila Bible Church. This is a new church located in an old, large movie threatre right in the heart of Manila's busiest shopping district. The service consisted of songs, skits, the spoken Word and small group prayer. Tears of shame filled our eyes as we heard of personal pain and tragedy experienced by the Filipinos who were so radiant with God's joy. This was the product of the "Good News" brought by missionaries to this busy crowded city.

On Sunday evening we met with senior representatives of CGM to be given a better understanding of the Mission and what we would be doing during our two weeks in Manila.

CGM is just one of many missions in the Philippines. One exciting difference in their work is the wide variety of ministries. We were told that we would be active participants, not onlookers, in each of these — jail, home Bible studies, camping, street kids, prostitutes, tract distribution, open air meetings and, in addition, they would show us most of their other projects which include — the Home of Joy for abandoned children; the Rescue Mission for older street kids; the Second Mile that trains converted ladies to become tailors and men to become carpenters, auto mechanics, etc.;

Jesus — the only Answer for the Phillipines.

by Charlene and Pauline Webb

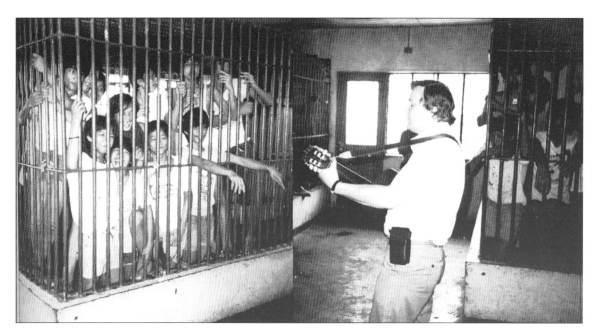

Bob Huntington ministering in one of the jail services in Manila

The Peoples Magazine. October 1986.

and World of Women that is reaching middle and upper class women with the gospel.

CGM split our total group into four working teams of four. Each team was given its assignments by day for the entire time in Manila. Every morning a CGM Filipino national leader met each of the four teams at 8:00 a.m. and left for that day's assignment, generally by local transportation. On the first Monday

— team one went to the jails where the ladies sang, others gave testimonies while one of the group gave a message
— team two went into homes in what is referred to as the swamp area and conducted Bible studies with new converts
— team three went out with camp ministry workers finding young people to attend an upcoming camp
— team four went with a group of nationals to witness to university and college students.

The Manila Swamp — "Home sweet home" for some

This continued each day, only the assignments changed every day for each team enabling us to meet and witness to a variety of people. At the end of the day of heat, humidity, often rain, we returned tired, somewhat unkept, full of exciting stories and filled with a love and concern for a people who humanly speaking had very little but who warmly received us into their humble homes with an unexpected openness to the gospel.

The thrust of each ministry is identical: presenting the gospel, then discipling the converts. The style of ministry varies with the circumstances. We were challenged to be flexible! One day we would be singing and speaking while standing in flood waters, and the next day visiting families in typhoid-infested swamp shanties. These are the everyday tasks of the CGM national worker.

It is extremely difficult to capture the essence of CGM's ministry in a few sentences. Their mission field is a large CITY, whose people are subject to extreme poverty, disease, natural disasters, political corruption and dominated by a large religious organization. Ministry under these conditions is quite unsophisticated, but very effective. Songs,

Thank you very much for coming to the Philippines. You were certainly a blessing and challenge to all of us and we praise the Lord for you!

I'm not sure if you realize this or not but you were one of the most highly thought of teams we have ever had; very appreciative, hard working, uncomplaining, you showed a real concern for the poor, for evangelism, for the masses, for discipleship, etc.

I'm enclosing a letter to you from Emilie. It would be great if you could keep in touch with her and the rest of us as you have the opportunity.

I also want to thank you for your concern for our CGM *team members*. Please continue to remember them in prayer.

II Thessalonians 3:3 is a real blessing to us these days, "But the Lord is faithful, and He will strengthen and protect you from the evil one."

Sincerely in Christ
Doug Nichols

testimonies, and personal visits are being used by God to bring many to himself.

"To the uttermost parts" in Manila surely means the garbage dump community. This is a "city" built on waste. Twenty thousand people live there because they can scavenge and earn some money — just enough to survive. As we drove up to the area, we were informed that this would be an initial visit to a new "suburb". We were given stacks of two different kinds of literature, then sent on our way through the mud to witness to the people.

When we started to talk, crowds of people gathered, eager to receive the tracts and hear the gospel. There was no room for shyness in these situations. The CGM worker would usually make the introduction in Tagalog, the local language, and then give us a chance to talk about God's relationship to man and their own relationship to God. The CGM worker would make sure the English spoken was understood. Most responded to the message! Before we left, Bible study groups were formed.

Crusade in Liberia – 1987

Dr. Paul
held
evangelistic crusades
in 84 countries
on five continents.

Bishop Augustus Marwieh Reports:

The country has never witnessed an event like the one that took place last month when a team of forty-two Canadian Christians headed by Dr. Paul B. Smith of The Peoples Church of Toronto, Canada, stormed the nation's capital with the Good News of the Gospel of our Lord. They were everywhere: prisons, hospitals, market places, street corners, government offices, army barracks – you name it. They came with a mind to work in a nation whose doors are as widely open to the Gospel as the open sky.

I shall never forget the experience of the night when Dr. Smith preached a missionary message challenging the youth of the nation for missions. That experience shall stand out in memory as a spiritual monument. When Dr. Smith gave the invitation for a call to the mission field, more than three hundred and forty young Liberians responded. Never in my life have I experienced in a meeting a personal excitement as intense and an inner satisfaction as deep as that which I experienced as I saw a huge crowd of Liberian young people coming forward to surrender their lives for the service of the Lord.

The arrival of sixteen American Christians headed by Mr. and Mrs. Daniel Denk from the Inter-Varsity Christian Fellowship five weeks before the crusade was designed by God to make the crusade preparation a stunning success. For five weeks they visited churches and pastors preparing them for the crusade. They were with us in the planning of every detail. How we thank our God for their remarkable contribution to the success of the crusade.

Our Missionary Trip to Liberia

Center: Dr. Paul Smith and Gus Marwieh.

In the afternoon our group was assigned to visit the National Police Headquarter's Jail. We thought we were going to be assigned a nice quiet area with seats and have some sort of church-like service. Imagine our bewilderment when none of this materialized and we were sent right into a caged off section with guards surrounding us in the middle of the prisoners. There was shouting and shoving and altogether a very noisy melee of agitated prisoners. The jail pastor was able to bring some harmony to the chaos by starting to sing "Jesus Loves Me." They all joined in like children, and after a few songs Al Cawfield was able to bring some of his message and the ladies sang. Then we tried some personal testimony and ministered as well as possible, which appeared to be ineffective because of the noise of 125 prisoners yelling and shouting among themselves.

Some had already been there for a number of weeks without a trial. In the meantime, neither the city nor the government feed them. They are entirely dependent on relatives or friends to bring them food.

In the juvenile section (which was separate from the main jail) were five children, the youngest two and a half years of age. He didn't know where his mother was! They apparently had no other place to keep this little boy.

On our way out, we were reprimanded by the jail pastor, who said: "You ministered to them spiritually, but you should have first ministered to them physically".

Oh – how true that was! None of us had actually realized the need of these people. But praise God, we were in a position to correct this. We collected some money among ourselves and spent the next day purchasing bread, bananas, fruit juices, boiled eggs, cheese and plastic bags.
It took us the day to accumulate sufficient food for a 125 prisoners. Miriam Radley organized it in such a way that we formed an assembly line. Within forty-five minutes we had over 130 packages ready for distribution. We then returned to the jail and went into the cells with the guards and the jail pastor. We ministered to their physical needs!
They then sang – this time again "Jesus Loves Me" with a much deep feeling of thankfulness. We praised the Lord, we prayed and we shared our faith
Who was able to stay cool and collected ed? The response was overwhelming and we were used mightily in God's Service Oh what satisfaction! This alone was worth the trip to Liberia.

by Jacob van de Stouwe

TERRY AND GINNY

Our Ambassadors To The Communist World

by Terry Bridle

For the last seven years, Ginny and I have been entering Poland in order to minister in song and word to the Christians of this country, as well as to bring the message of salvation to the unsaved. This is a country that suffers under the dual oppression of a communistic regime and a Roman Catholic heritage, both of which have contributed to undermining the real power of God to change lives.

This year we have been joined by Dan and Laurie Dzikewich, also from Peoples Church, to augment the effectiveness of our musical ministry. Dan has offered his considerable talents in both keyboard

A major Concert-Crusade Tour Into Poland

---

playing and musical arrangement, and he and Ginny together have had a measurable impact in presenting the gospel message wherever they have ministered together. Laurie has contributed to our ministry in a supportive role, as administrative and secretarial assistant. We have seen much blessing as a combined team in our various avenues of European ministry in 1987.

Our special "project" for the year, however, was the planning and carrying out of a major concert/crusade tour into Poland, which took place in September/October of this year. As a result of previous visits and contacts made, we were invited this time as a group, on behalf of a prominent children's charity organization in Poland, to present several concerts in large public theatres. The

intention was that we would donate all profits from ticket sales to these concerts to the charity if they would fill the theatres and promote the concerts. Our group involved, in total, 15 people comprising a band and supporting crew to take the gospel musically into Poland. The crusades saw many brought to a knowledge of God's love and salvation through this medium.

The team members were brought from both England and Canada, including Annie Legge from The Peoples Church, who contributed excellent back-up vocals to the group. We were also privileged and blessed to have a young Christian friend from Poland accompanying us for the 6-week tour. We ar-

ranged for him to visit England for the first time and then return with us to Poland for the duration of the tour. He was thrilled to be able to see "the West" and was a great help to us with translation in Poland and at border crossings, as well as physically helping with the equipment set-up and tear-down. It was a little sad to have to leave him after six weeks of getting to know and love him.

The tour was besot by difficulties of an unexplained nature from the beginning — which we can only attribute to spiritual warfare. Some examples were: six flat tires and a broken wheel bearing, computer breakdown (which rendered Dan's computerized keyboards inoperable, 9 out of 24 lightbulbs in

lighting rig broken, a near-road accident, multi-media slide show jammed, P.A. and lighting systems that would not work, our van vandalized outside concert hall, etc. We must add, however, that miracles occurred in all these areas. Every concert went on as planned, and people came forward at each invitation. American computers are not normally attainable in Poland, yet we located a man who had just brought an Atari computer from England — a miracle in itself — and he loaned it to us at a nominal charge. There were also evidences of Satanic influence and witchcraft in Poland and we truly believe these were the powers we were working against when we proclaimed the gospel.

Highlighting our tour were two unprecedented outreach concerts in Auschwitz, location of the infamous Nazi concentration camp during World War II. This city still holds a tangible pallour from atrocities that occurred here over 40 years ago and the local pastor (of the only evangelical church — 30 members) considered it a miracle that so many people came out to hear and respond to the gospel preached at our two successive

concerts. We were both awed and blessed to have been involved in this initial impact for Christ and we know this was a step towards furthering the Kingdom even in a place with such a history.

The tour on the whole was a success. The music style and quality were professional and entertaining, but the message was clear and uncompromising. The words to each song were translated into Polish and were posted on a back-lit 9' × 9' screen as the songs were sung, making the message unavoidable. The

audiences of Polish young people (and young at heart) received us very openly and unanimously invited us to come back again. It was hard work but a mutual blessing ministering to the Polish people, as they showed each of us overwhelming hospitality when we stayed in the homes of the local Polish Christians.

The current religious Freedom in Poland is unique in the Communist block.

Poland is a real missionfield for seed-planting and for harvesting. The current religious freedom in Poland is unique in the Communist Bloc and the Christians there are all too aware of how easily it could be taken away from them. We feel God has called us to respond to the needs of this particular country and look forward to future ministry in Poland. We value your continued prayers and support.

The Peoples Magazine. September 1988.

A Most Remarkable Experience

by Dena Persaud

This summer, I left my comfort zone. I pulled myself out of the mire of Scarborough and embarked on the most remarkable experience of my life. For two weeks, I, along with my youth group from church, learned more about myself, God, and His creation. This all transpired in Leon, Spain.

In Spain, I found myself in a pleasant countryside full of varying picturesque mountain villages. The adobe village I resided in was an idyllic magic world. Full of medieval walls, old quarters and squares, it gave the true meaning of a fairyland. The Spaniards of the village are a close-knit family. Between cups of coffee and evening strolls, I found love for their simplistic, moral-oriented society. Amazed and culture-shocked, I explored my new world. I walked the steep, narrow streets that shimmered out of an extraordinary historical heritage. I roamed the magnificent castles that enclosed the hauntings of the past. I basked in the immensity of cheeses, meat, and ham from Villamann. I skipped like a giddy child alongside the river under the pink and blue dusk. I embraced Spain with both arms wide open. My black and white vista of the world vanished. Life was now given colour as I wrapped myself up in the rich culture of Spain.

However, in the midst of this European splendour, my group had a mission. Our passion for Spain was subdued compared to our passion for the Divine. We, as Christians were led to Spain to complete God's task. Laboriously, we sweated to finish the expansion and renovation of the Toral Camp in Leon. Each drop of sweat showed our devotion for the Almighty. However, the holy needles that bore into Jesus' head, causing sweat to trickle down his forehead, paled our efforts. It humbled us to remember. "This beautiful mess", as we fondly called our camp, will some day be used year-round by churches and organizations for seminars and retreats.

Isn't it funny how a person gains so much knowledge about one's self in an environment so unfamiliar? It scared me. My aspirations changed. My view of life was altered. My endurance level increased. But most importantly, I had a pious revelation about the capacity of God. The same powerful God who made the impressive scenery of Spain is the same detailed God who took time to create each individual so unique and special. That's God!

DENA PERSAUD IS A GRADE 12 STUDENT AT WEST HILL HIGH SCHOOL AND IS ACTIVE WITH YOUTH AT THE PEOPLES CHURCH.

The Peoples Church tour to Israel with Dr. John Hull, 1999.

THE PEOPLES MAGAZINE
Spring, 1999.

Putting 'Byte' Into Missions

by Reg and Darcie Sawilla

When we left for Niger to serve in computer systems support, I had no idea what it would be like. My preconceived notions about Niger and working here were wrong as these most often are.

I thought that I would be doing the simplest of computer work here and that people would barely know how to turn their computers on. The truth was, some were even writing their own software to cope with their unique requirements.

One of the hardest things for missionaries serving abroad is enduring the difficulty in communicating with family and friends they have left behind. It has been exciting to watch the changes the advancing technologies of the Internet have brought. We are now able to e-mail regularly with loved ones around the world as well as telephone over the Internet for 5% of what a long distance call would cost. People who have left the field burnt out have returned and said how encouraged they are by the new and better ways to

communicate. However, bringing these technologies to people serving in remote villages is a challenge.

SIM has a large hospital in Galmi, a village where 400 outpatients per day are treated by a team of 30 missionary staff and 100 nationals. Currently, we use HF (High Frequency) radios to communicate with the hospital. There are no direct dial phones and Galmi is 500 km from Niamey where our main office is. Twice a day they contact us to relay any messages and let us know everything is all right. The Galmi missionaries e-mail by putting their messages onto a diskette and sending it to Niamey with a traveler. At the office, we send their messages and return any new messages received for them with the next traveler. Their two-week turn around time is faster than the post but not much!

Presently, I am working on converting the radio system so that we can e-mail over it the same way you can over the telephone line. This involves working with special equipment, software and complex operating systems that I can hardly pronounce, let alone program. Apparently it is possible though and I always welcome a challenge. There are no books entitled "Set Up Your SMTP/POP3 System On IP Over Packet" but I intend to write some clear instructions once I figure them out!

It is exciting to see how God is able to use us in a non-standard missionary role to facilitate His work here. We are excited about how this will make living in remote areas easier for people and they are excited about same day turn around on e-mail.

REG AND DARCIE SAWILLA SERVE WITH SIM IN NIGER.

Hugh and Mary Rough,
missionaries for 21 years in Zambia and England with the
Africa Evangelical Fellowship.

THE PEOPLES MAGAZINE
Spring, 1999.

Mission
Travels

Our Missionaries to West Africa

By Carol Lowes

Brian and Kim Mitton and their children Eric, Nicholas and Jonathan, are serving in Benin, West Africa.

In June, Brian and Kim Mitton will return to Canada with their three young boys, Jonathan, 9, Eric, 7, and Nicholas, 5, for an eight-month home assignment.

The Mittons have served in Benin, West Africa since 1990; their first two terms in rural settings, leading TEE (Theological Education By Extension), and since then in Cotonou, where they oversee a SIM guesthouse, teach in local SIM churches, and assist in administrating the seaport, airport, and immigration department. Dependence on God is a central theme in their lives.

For Brian, tracing God's hand leads from Guadeloupe in the French West Indies, where his parents were missionaries; to Newmarket, Ontario, where he attended high school; to Briarcrest Bible College in Saskatchewan and finally to Verdun, Quebec, where his parents had moved to run a Christian bookstore, and where he met Kim Breidon while home from college for the summer. They were married in May 1986 and together began to seek God's leading. Although they both desired to serve God as full time missionaries in Africa, they didn't know just where. When introduced to Benin, a strongly animistic country, at SIM candidate school, they soon realised it was the country of God's choosing for their lives.

Remembering God's faithfulness sustained Brian and Kim during the frustrating early days of trying to learn a new language and settle into a new culture. "We couldn't communicate to the people we loved so much," says Brian. "We had many nights when we just wanted to call it quits, pack up and go home. The fact that we could see the hand of God in our lives each step of the way before arriving in Benin was enough to see us through."

We couldn't communicate to the people we loved so much...

Unity and Oneness In Christ

Loving God and Father, we thank You for sending Your beloved son, Jesus, to the world as our Redeemer and Saviour. In Your great love for us, You have allowed Jesus to unite us, so that we would become holy and worthy to be called Your precious sons and daughters.

Jesus is the expression of Your love for us. You have given Him for us so graciously, and in large measure. Father, make us pure and deserving, to receive Him whole-heartedly into our lives. Help us to love Him, serve Him, and please Him through our brothers and sisters as we joyfully celebrate the second millennium of Jesus' birth.

Send forth the light of the Holy Spirit to touch the hearts of people all over the world. Then there will be unity and oneness in recognizing Christ as the head of all creation, both in Heaven and on earth.

Teach us to love You more each day. Walk with us as we continue to grow in our faith journey. At such time that we can bring into completion the work which You have given us, and reap the crown of glory which You have promised. In Jesus' name we pray.

Amen

Substitutes

Go ye therefore and teach all nations...

By Heather Lyon

Heather Lyon works for Pilot Insurance and is active in EE at The Peoples Church.

Jesus said, *Go ye therefore, and teach all nations, baptizing them in the name of the Father, and of the Son, and of the Holy Ghost* Matthew 28:19 (KJV).

The founder of our beloved Peoples Church, the late Oswald J. Smith, had a personal desire to obey Jesus in this great commission but was unable to do so due to poor health. It was Dr. Smith who coined the phrase *"You must go or send a substitute."*

On July 16, 1999, The Peoples Church sent the following 17 "substitutes" to the seminary of the Free Evangelical Church of Finland near Hanko for a two-week work project in partnership with Greater Europe Mission:

Bob Corrigan	Kate Kricfalusi
Rolinda Corrigan	Heather Lyon
Nancy Foster	Michelle OuWai
Don Kenney	Julie Rahn
Martha Kenney	Anna Pettigrew
Mary Goode	Ruth Pettigrew
Kris Gustafsson	Brian Mackenzie
Eric Huebner	Ron Tsang
Tom Kangasniemi	

Team members donated their vacation time and paid for their own airfare, room and board. Fundraising events were held to subsidize some of the cost. Generous supporters also helped with financial donations. The cost for project materials was underwritten by The Peoples Church. Most importantly many prayer warriors faithfully interceded for us, without which nothing of eternal value could ever be accomplished for the Kingdom of God.

This labour of love was made possible thanks to the help of all our faithful supporters.

Approximately $70,000 worth of work was completed for the seminary, a school that trains pastors and evangelists to go take the light of Jesus Christ into the dark areas of Eastern Europe and the former Soviet Union.

Most importantly, the Finnish people we worked with and met along the way were blessed immensely by our willingness to serve them. After our departure locals were inspired and mobilized to pick up where we left off.

Glory to God!

...many prayer warriors faithfully interceded for us, without which nothing of eternal value could ever be accomplished...

WELCOMING MISSIONARIES ON FURLOUGH

by Doug Nichols

Some of our missionaries have arrived home for a two- or three- month (or even a year) furlough and their home church has not recognized them publicly or given them any kind of welcome either in the main church services or in the smaller fellowships like Sunday School. Not so with what I witnessed on one occasion at The Peoples Church in Toronto, Canada, where I was speaking one Sunday evening. (This wasn't during a missions conference.)

I had already been introduced and was preparing to speak after the special music number. During the solo, an usher came in one of the rear doors, urgently made his way around the side, up onto the platform, and over to the pastor, Dr. Paul Smith. I thought this was quite unusual, especially since pastors usually do not appreciate movement or anything to interrupt a meeting. The usher urgently handed a note to Dr. Smith. The soloist was just coming to the end of her song, when Dr. Smith, after reading the note, reached over and touched my arm saying, "Wait, before you speak, I need to take care of something."

He approached the microphone and said, "Ladies and gentlemen, it is a great privilege to announce that one of our missionary families from this church has just arrived for furlough from Brazil. They arrived only an hour ago at the airport here in Toronto and were brought directly to the church. They have just now arrived at our service!"

At that time, about four ushers approached the couple and their three children who had sat at the back of the church. They were escorted to the front and up the steps onto the platform. They

were very shy and embarrassed. You could tell from their wrinkled clothes and haggard appearance they had been traveling for many hours.

Something then happened that I have not witnessed either before or since. As they reached the top step and began to make their way across the platform towards Dr. Smith, **the 2,000 people in the auditorium rose as one and gave this shy, embarrassed little family a standing ovation!** We then witnessed the look of fear and embarrassement leave

The Augustine family, (photo 1986) supportedby The Peoples Church for many years both financially and prayerfully, in missionary service in Santiago and Costa Rica. One of three generations of missionaries.

the faces of the mother, father and their three small children. It was replaced by amazement as they walked slowly across the platform to the outstretched arms of

---

"As I didn't get out Sunday, June 30th., to my own Baptist church, I turned on the T.V. to The Peoples Church and your choir, band and message gave me such a lift, and I do praise God for that. The Rev. Hull from the USA gave a message that brought tears to my eyes and I truly thank him for the message he delivered on storms in our lives."

Brantford, Ontario.

Dr. Smith. The congregation stood for several minutes as they clapped, **welcoming their missionaries** home! I (and many others) stood with tears because of the beauty and family warmth of it all! The elders of the church then came to the platform and circled the family as Dr. Smith led in prayer, praying that God would use them mightily during their furlough and return them to an effective ministry in Brazil for God's glory.

Many times, since witnessing this great event, I've wondered: **why do not all churches welcome their missionaries home in this way?**

The above article was printed in the September 1993 British Christian newspaper, "Evangelism Today." Doug Nichols is International Director of Action International Ministries. PO Box 280, Three Hills, AB TOM 2A0 Canada; PO Box 49, Bothell, WA 98041-0490; PO Box 694, Rhyl, Clwyd LL18 1JU, United Kingdom.

Our Beverley In Lebanon

In spring time in Lebanon there is still snow on the mountain tops, everything is green and the almond trees blossom. The fields are full of wildflowers and olive trees; grape vines grace houses along narrow winding streets. Beverley Timgren lives and works in Marjayoun, a rural, mountainous region in south Lebanon, where for the past fourteen years she has developed and directed a dental clinic. She doesn't like to call herself a missionary, she considers herself simply a Christian serving outside her own country. A question she hears often is "why did you leave your safe and comfortable home in Canada to come to war-torn south Lebanon?" Answering that question gives Timgren the opportunity to share her faith. Although the civil war in Lebanon is over, there is still guerilla warfare in the south and the sight of soldiers with machine guns is common. When she first arrived, the area was poor and desolate, damaged by years of war. It is a period of restoration now, although power cuts still occur and Timgren says she has learned to work with a steady hand despite the booming of artillery cannons near the clinic. "The fact that I am doing something very practical to help in difficult circumstances speaks loudly and gives more credibility to my word of testimony," she says. "It is a joy to share and touch someone's life with God's love."

Away from the security and familiar surroundings of home, Timgren has experienced God's faithfulness and care. One summer night, she heard a crash and tremendous thud. "The room filled with dust, debris, and the overpowering smell of gunpowder," she says. An hour before, she had been working in a back room. Now, the window there was broken and there was something on the floor. "I touched it and it was hot. Then I realized it was the head of a rocket," she says. If it had exploded, it would have destroyed the whole apartment. Timgren says she was shaken, but at the same time she had a sense of peace. "I knew that God had protected me and spared my life." She read from Psalm 91. "He who dwells in the shelter of the Most High will rest in the shadow of the Almighty. I will say of the Lord, 'He is my refuge and my fortress, my God, in whom I trust.' ...A thousand may fall at your side, ten thousand at your right hand, but it will not come near you."

MISS TIMGREN IS SUPPORTED BY THE PEOPLES CHURCH.

When young people leave for the field, there is always a solemn service of dedication just before they go. Elders lay hands on them and set them apart for the work to which God has called them.

PREPARED BY GISELLE CULVER, MEMBER OF THE EDITORIAL COMMITTEE.

Meditation

Do not waste time bothering whether you love your neighbour; act as if you did. As soon as we do this we find out one of the great secrets. When you are behaving as if you loved someone, you will presently come to love him."

– C.S. Lewis in *Mere Christianity*

Mission Travels

L'Arcada In Spain
Building into Lives...Making a Difference

by David and Debbie Frank

Spain, a country once steeped in religious traditions, now boasts of "freedom" from those historical chains, only to be bound by other chains: skepticism, humanism, relativism, secularism, materialism. Only about 4/10 of 1% of Spain's 40 million people profess to have a personal relationship with Jesus Christ.

How does one reach the hearts of Spaniards so bound up in themselves and so alienated from God?

Located in the NE corner of Spain are 763 acres of forests and fields, part of a small valley nestled among the foothills of the Pyrenees Mountains. God provided this location for L'Arcada , a camp and conference ministry of Greater Europe Mission, and is using L'Arcada to touch and change lives. The first camp was held in the summer of 1991 with 23 kids. Last year, over 700 excited participants attended summer programs and many more joined in the variety of programs and activities offered during the fall, winter and spring. Fifty percent of the full-time staff are Spanish nationals, as well as the over 100 summer volunteers. This is a tremendous blessing for the ministry.

L'Arcada provides a place where non-Christians can participate in a desired activity and come in contact with God's love lived out in the everyday lives of the staff. Much time and prayer is spent designing quality programs with innovative ways of sharing the gospel message. Depending on the camp, 40-80% of those attending are non-Christians.

Discipleship and leadership training are also vital components of the L'Arcada ministry. Christian youth and adults are encouraged and challenged to live effective, dynamic and godly lives, totally committed to the Lord and available for His use to impact their society.

Children and youth from 7-22 years of age enthusiastically attend the summer Basketball, Native American, and Adventure Camps. A great variety of activities, as well as beautiful surroundings and dedicated, caring staff, produce many special memories for each participant. A high percentage return each year, bringing friends and family members along. Family Camp has become quite popular since the first one held in 1997. The programming is designed to draw families together through unique experiences in fun, activities, discussion topics and fellowship and encourage them to set solid foundations for their family based on biblical principles.

Existing summer facilities are used to the maximum to carry out the above programs. Other camps, training sessions and youth activities are offered throughout the year in rented facilities off the property. At present L'Arcada is launching a new Master Plan which will give potential of reaching thousands of Spaniards through ministries held in year-round facilities.

Having observed the amazing things God has done to date, the L'Arcada staff is convinced that they have seen only a brushstroke on the canvas of God's design for the future. Sincere appreciation goes to the many individuals who have sacrificially spent time in prayer, participated on workteams, and given financial gifts to see this ministry move forward. The future is exciting and many more partners are needed to help L'Arcada *build into lives, thus making a difference in Spain!*

DAVID AND DEBBIE FRANK ARE MISSIONARIES WITH GREATER EUROPE MISSION. THEIR ADDRESS IS C/O PINTOL SOLIVES, 64 17820 BANYOLES (GIRONA), SPAIN

Camp is fun!

Brian & Carol Foutz

For us, that ministry is to teach and encourage...

By Giselle Culver

...they represent a powerful force in the future of missions...

Set amidst the exotic, tropical jungle of rural Philippines is the steamy urban jungle of Manila, home to 12 million of the nation's 60 million inhabitants. This modern, cosmopolitan city has all the conveniences of a North American city, as well as the pollution, poverty, corruption - and traffic - of any large, crowded city. Brian and Carol Foutz serve in Manila as teachers at Faith Academy, the largest school for children of missionaries in the world.

"Faith Academy ministers to nearly 600 children whose parents are missionaries in the Philippines and neighbouring Southeast Asian nations," says Brian. "Our job is rewarding in that we are helping frontline missionaries to translate the Bible, to plant churches in unreached areas, to train and equip national leaders and to provide for the basic needs of the poor. Even more rewarding is the opportunity to work with MK's. These special young people are learning important cross-cultural skills in a Christian environment. Because of this,

they represent a powerful force in the future of missions."

Brian teaches high school social studies; Carol is an elementary school teacher who taught at the Oswald J. Smith Elementary School before leaving for Manila. Both felt called to become missionaries as young teens while attending missionary meetings - Brian in Seattle, Washington and Carol while a student at the Paul B. Smith Academy. They met during their first year of teaching at Faith Academy and were married in Toronto in 1990. They have two children - Bethany, 7, and Daniel, 4.

Although their love for kids and gift for teaching is part of what led them to the Philippines, Brian says: "It is so easy to become focused on our ministry instead of our mission. For us, that ministry is to teach and encourage the missionary kids at Faith Academy. Your job is probably quite different from ours, but our mission is exactly the same - to bring glory to God. We will know when we have succeeded in this mission if others are drawn to Him".

Mission Travels

STUDENTS DISCOVER MISSIONS

By Connie Mycroft

Connie Mycroft is the Principal of Peoples Christian Academy

...everything is affected by our relationship with God through Jesus Christ, not just our spiritual life...

"Why is it that we think we are 'the people' and that we are more important than any of the other peoples of the world?"

OJS

As I sat at the back of the mercifully soft-lit Chapel of Peoples Academy watching students make their way to an open-microphone to tell what God was doing in their lives, I couldn't keep back the tears, as was happening to teachers and students all around me – leaving me, indeed, at the end of the event with one super-soggy tissue! This was "pay day" for weeks, months, even years of praying, planning and working with high school students, who don't have an easy time of it these days.

For, since Plato, the western world has lived with the notion that life is a duality: The spiritual and the natural are unrelated; daily living and religious experience have little to do with each other. The church has always taught against this notion, but the beliefs and values resulting from it have become a powerful and ingrained ideology that is confirmed daily in everything the students meet.

As Christian educators, however, we are in a unique position to teach students the Biblical worldview: That life is holistic, not dualistic; that everything is affected by our relationship with God through Jesus Christ, not just our spiritual life, and all that curricula are to be studied through the lens of Scripture so that faith and learning, and thus all of life, becomes an integrated whole.

As we work toward our students becoming serious disciples in their chosen professions, or understanding and acting upon God's call to service and missions, we have recently felt a call of our own to renew our commitment to an annual school missions trip which will become part of our senior's school program. Peoples Christian Academy has graduated many students who are currently serving in missions, worldwide. And while students have participated in the annual Peoples Church Missions Conference and gone on missions trips, our goal is to give every senior student an opportunity to catch God's vision for the world through ministering in a cross-cultural setting. So, while many are questioning the value of missions, we are going to send 13 students and 4 faculty members to the Caribbean island of St. Vincent this March break to help in a Christian school construction project, and to be involved in Bible studies, church services, open-air presentations, and one-on-one time with local students.

For the past three months, we have been teaching the students about prayer support and letters, enculturation, team building, evangelism, and trusting God with finances, fears and family, which has been particularly stressed for new believers. Now these dear students must "Go," as Jesus commanded in Matthew 28:20, "and teach all nations" the things Jesus has given them as the message of eternal life, taking with them His promise of Acts 1:8, the empowerment of the Holy Spirit to be His witnesses.

As they take this big step toward obeying God's call, we, the faculty, look forward to seeing what God will do in each of their lives, and to what next year's open-microphone chapel session will yield.

ON THE MISSION TRAIL WITH DR. JOHN HULL

Mizoram, 1999

Israel, 1998.

Indonesia, 1999.

Indonesia, 1999.

Lebanon, 1998.

Singapore 1999.

Mission Travels

Into all the World

"FATHERLAND OF DIGNITY"

Burkina Faso (formerly the Republic of Upper Volta), West Africa, means "Fatherland of Dignity". No stretch of the imagination would allow it to live up to its name. In common with other African countries that have no access to the sea, it is extremely poor. The climate is harsh, being mostly hot and dry. It has experienced many years of drought and inadequate harvests. There are almost no tall trees and the roads, for the most part, are dusty bare dirt tracks.

Burkina Faso, with its poor economy, high population density and few natural resources, relying heavily on subsistence agriculture, has an infant mortality rate of 110 per 1000. Burkina Faso is the country where Christian Blind Mission projects

Tiny, severely malnourished orphan fits easily onto a serving dish.

Village Children

assisted 510 blind people, 91 disabled and 125 people with epilepsy in 1995, and where their mobile eye clinic treated 1615 patients from January to October of the same year, an annual average of 1113 patients. In Burkina Faso, CBMI restores the eyesight of one blind person every week. It is here that The Peoples Church missionaries, Fred and Marion Horn and their daughter, Sara (who attended Peoples Christian Academy) are serving under CBMI in the village of Diebougou. Fred is in charge of developing a community-based rehabilitation program focused on integrating disabled and blind people into their families and communities.

As a guest of Art Brooker, Christian Blind Mission's Canadian Director, Senior Pastor John Hull went to Burkina Faso in November, his first trip to Africa. What a sight met his eyes!

Fred Horn took Pastor Hull and Art Brooker to many villages. They felt the intense heat, and saw the poverty-stricken people, the physical and spiritual needs.

"The responsibilities in Toronto have kept me close to the home base since I became pastor. It was good to again get out to a mission field. That's where the action is. And that's how to keep the burden for world evangelization fresh and vivid. It was obvious that Burkina Faso is in great need of medical assistance. I'm glad The Peoples Church is able to play some role in providing aid. It is a great thing to see Fred and Marion Horn 'living Christ' in that difficult country. They are sharing their faith in Christ as they help the physically blind to see. There's something very special about that".

Pastor Hull plans to visit Asia later this year to meet and encourage a number of The Peoples Church missionaries and nationals in the Orient.

Blind, epileptic boy, burned when he fell into a fire, shown with Pastor John Hull.

An eye operation in progress.

Mittendrin

Right in the middle of it

By Gale White

Jason and Sue Holm are church planters with GEM in Germany, in partnership with The Peoples Church. Their ministry is in Bergish Gladbach, a town of some 107,000 people, where they are reaching "people who are no longer interested in traditional church but are looking for meaning in their lives and open to something new." As the church Jason and Sue are planting is a downtown church, they have chosen the motto "Mittendrin" for it. Mittendrin means literally *right in the middle of it.* "That is exactly where we want the new church to be," says Jason.

"Accessible. Not just close by, but right in the thick of things. Jesus is our example. Emmanuel—God with us. Friend of sinners. He spent most of his time with sinners—not cooped up in some Synagogue somewhere [Mk 2:16, 17]. He was among the people, right in the middle of their hustle and bustle, pain and parties. He lived with them and loved them.

"How do we reach people? One of the ways we have seen God use is a technique we call "The Pastor is in." It's kind of like Lucy (from Charlie Brown) setting up her stand: "The psychiatrist is in." It is amazing how effective this has been. Traditionally street evangelism tends to be somewhat aggressive—causing people to steer clear. But when a pastor just makes himself available to people, they respond."

"Theology on Tap" is another way in which the Holms reach turned off people who are "still thirsting for meaning and truth. Informal teaching flows in the informal, comfortable setting of a traditional German Brauhaus. A theme is expanded through a led discussion: Questions are encouraged, real needs are determined, and the Bible is applied to the areas of need."

Jason and Sue met at Capernwray Bible School (Germany) in 1977. In 1980 they married, and after further education, a couple of pastorates in the U.S. and language school, they planted their first church in the Cologne suburb of Porz in 1993. They presently meet in a restaurant, free of charge. They have two handsome, bilingual sons, Sam (17) and Roy (13). Sue's father, Reuben Goertz, was Canadian Director of GEM in Oshawa from 1973 until he retired in 1993.

You can visit the Holm's website at www.Jholm.de

Jason, Sue, Sam and Roy Holm, serving Greater Europe Mission in Germany.

Questions are encouraged, real needs are determined, and the Bible is applied to the areas of need.

Mission
Travels

An Inspired Gift

Meeting physical, spiritual and emotional needs

By Doug Stiller

Doug Stiller is President of World Relief Canada.

For I know the plans I have for you, plans to prosper you and not harm you. Plans to give you a hope and a future.
(Jer. 29:11)

Joy is the key ingredient in both giving and receiving gifts – the wonder of receiving something special and the pleasure of seeing the look on the face of a loved one who opens a gift from us.

When I reflect on the partnership that exists between World Relief Canada and The Peoples Church, I'm amazed and grateful for your faithful generosity throughout the years. The Peoples Church has shared our vision for meeting the physical, spiritual and emotional needs of poor and hungry people in the name of Jesus Christ, most recently by joining with us in meeting the desperate and urgent needs of thousands of earthquake victims in India and El Salvador.

It may be easy to imagine your gifts helping dig a new well or building a new shelter. But have you ever thought of how your gifts change the lives of Christians who are inspired and enabled to move out of the pews and into the mission field?

When I visited our "Hope for Cambodia's Children" program some time ago, I met an extraordinary young woman whose life was changed in such a manner.

Joke (pronounced YO-ka) van Opstal once sat in a church in Holland and wondered how she could use her life to help others, eventually serving at a refugee camp on the Thailand-Cambodia border after finishing her nursing studies.

One day, Joke saw a little boy walk by in tattered clothes. "Hope is not children dying from (preventable) sickness," she says of that heartbreaking moment.

"God loves them individually and has a hope that is not just physical but also spiritual."

Joke remembered the words in Jeremiah 29:11: *For I know the plans I have for you, plans to prosper you and not harm you. Plans to give you a hope and a future.* It was at that moment that she gave her life to the children living in the squatter slums of Cambodia.

Today, Joke van Opstal is a mother to many poor and desperate children suffering from malnutrition, disease and hunger. She directs an effort to teach 20,000 children each week preventative health care and spiritual discipleship through puppet shows, drama and music. Through Joke and the rest of the team in Cambodia, an astonishing spiritual transformation often takes place in the lives of these children, with the result that many parents are opening their hearts to the gospel.

Your partnership with World Relief Canada makes it possible for people like Joke to change lives in the name if Jesus.

God is opening doors and opportunities everyday for service in his world. Who in The People's Church will be next to do something extraordinary like Joke? Whether your gift is financial, prayer for our ministry or even making your life available for God's service like Joke van Opstal, your gift is precious and vital to delivering God's love to poor people around the globe.

World Relief Canada is supported through the World Missions Program of the Peoples Church.

Carol Lowes is a professional writer and graduate of Carleton School of Journalism. She is also a member of our Editorial Committee.

The Peoples Church has made an effort to help refugee claimants who face homelessness.

Peoples Supports Creation of Adam House

A new shelter for refugee claimants

By Carol Lowes

W"ho is my neighbour?" a legal expert asked in reaction to the commandment "love your neighbour as yourself." Jesus responded by telling him a story about a man who was robbed and beaten as he travelled along the road between Jerusalem and Jericho. Left "half dead," the man was ignored by a passing Levite and priest. A Samaritan – one from a group despised in Israel at the time – helped him. This is the Story of the Good Samaritan.

Today most people think twice about being 'Good Samaritans.' Among the victims in many horror movies are people who show concern for strangers. There are also the real-life stories – people who pretended their cars weren't working so they could prey on those who stopped to help. And there are tales about lawsuits, such as stories of off-duty surgeons who were sued for errors made at American accident scenes. It's little wonder that people can be reluctant to 'lend a hand.'

This is the climate of "healthy skepticism" that greets refugee claimants.

News reports tell of forged passports and shiploads of economic migrants. But, they also present the political, racial and religious persecution occurring abroad. The latter coverage reflects a glimmer of the horror that engulfs the lives of refugees.

Some 23,000 people came to Canada to claim refugee status in 1999. Immigration and Refugee Board figures suggest that 65% of Canada's claimants come to the Toronto area. People who

claim to be refugees don't arrive with work visas and are not eligible for social assistance. They live with others or support themselves while waiting for a hearing before the Canada's Immigration and Refugee Board. Most wait for six months to a year for it. Some who cannot support themselves for that length of time end up among Canada's homeless. In 1998, this fact garnered Canada a scathing critique from the United Nations.

The Peoples Church has made an effort to help refugee claimants who face homelessness. Peoples gave Arab World Ministries $10,000 to help it found Adam House – a shelter for refugee claimants. It will open later this year at a location in downtown Toronto that has yet to be determined. Adam House is the third Christian-affiliated shelter in the city. Three years ago, Canadian Baptist Ministries opened the first house known as Matthew House. The second, World Vision's center was converted last year from a center serving sponsored refugees to one for claimants. The directors of both shelters say that Adam House is needed because their centers often operate at capacity.

"Every night we turn away one or two claimants seeking shelter," says Anne Woolger, director of Matthew House. "Once we had to refuse a doctor who had fled political persecution in the Middle East. He had been tortured and his overnight stay in the men's quarters of a shelter for the homeless re-traumatized him."

Spring, 2001.

TELEVISION

Ethiopia...
"Cradle of Humanity"
Land of Great Need

By Robert Wells

Robert Wells, Director, Peoples Worship Hour

Invited by our Senior Pastor, Charles Price, the Peoples TV production crew and I loaded 10 heavy cases of "portable" video equipment on February 23rd and headed off to Ethiopia. Twenty-two hours later the plane finally touched down in Addis Ababa, the capital city, for what was to become a life impacting journey. The Peoples Church, Toronto is "A Community of Believers Putting Missions First." Charles had been invited by SIM Ethiopia to be their keynote speaker for SIMCON, a bi-annual 5-day conference designed to encourage and refresh career missionaries in the field. It was a perfect opportunity for the TV crew to travel with Charles to get a first hand look, with the hope of recording several reports on the good work being undertaken by SIM personnel.

Ethiopia has suffered for years with the image of being an undesirable destination for the traveller. Unstable governments, war, famine and desolation have been synonymous with this country, one of four comprising the western "Horn of Africa." In this land of 58 million, the per capita income is $160.00 Canadian, with 80% of the population living in rural areas, most relying on subsistence farming.

After receiving permission from the Ethiopian Minister of Information to take pictures, the crew met up with Arnell Motz, senior pastor of

International Evangelical Church in Addis Ababa, which is supported by Peoples Church. This dynamic multi-cultural church with seating for nearly 1,000 conducts two Sunday morning services each week. Arnell, with his wife Terri, encourages their church to reach out to the community through various life changing programs.

For the first few days our Peoples TV crew video taped testimonies from key leaders involved with these programs. Many of these will be aired on upcoming Worship Hour programs.

Berhanu, a former soccer star, found Christ during the Communist years. He was given the choice to denounce his faith or face torture. His story is riveting, as he held fast to his faith during his trials, and now heads a soccer league of 85 teams in Addis for

Amsaleganet (below), co-ordinator of the"People in Need" program," reaches out to the poor – above with Charles Price.

Over 30,000 people sitting in a field for four days, hearing the Word of God preached in their own language...

TELEVISION

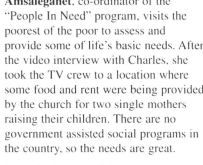

boys and girls, leading many children and parents to faith in Christ.

Amsaleganet, co-ordinator of the "People In Need" program, visits the poorest of the poor to assess and provide some of life's basic needs. After the video interview with Charles, she took the TV crew to a location where some food and rent were being provided by the church for two single mothers raising their children. There are no government assisted social programs in the country, so the needs are great.

Serawit, director of the "Women at Risk" program, described to Charles on video how she is fulfilling the desires of her heart by changing the lives of prostitutes. She and her team continually visit and befriend several women working on the streets, then attract them one by one to their rehabilitation centre, showing the love of Christ through training programs.

Radio anchor
in Addis Abada

Churches are springing up all around the country at a phenomenal rate, so this training centre is strategic.

After this exciting beginning in Addis Ababa, the TV crew along with Charles packed up and drove down country for several hours to Lake Langano, one of SIM's projects which includes a medical clinic, school and conference centre. This 96 acre compound had been seized and used as a military base during the Communist occupation, but returned back into the hands of SIM in due course, to provide medical care so desperately needed in the area.

Dan and Kim Scheel oversee this project. Kim, a registered nurse, took Charles Price on a walking tour through the medical clinic, which accommodates over a hundred patients each day. Some of these patients walk for many hours to receive treatment. Charles' heart was touched by the story of "Addis", a twin baby boy close to death, whose undernourished mother had only enough resources to nurse one. Kim was able to provide medication and nourishment to save his life, and has found a couple to care for him until healthy enough to eat solid foods, and be returned to his mother. This was the sixth baby Kim has saved in recent years.

The TV crew then left Charles and travelled several hours further down country to Sodo to videotape an amazing annual conference staged by the Woyaitta speaking churches of this area. Words are inadequate to describe this event. Over 30,000 people sitting in a field for four days, hearing the word of God preached in their own language from morning to night, was an awesome sight. The crew also commented on the awesome spirit of giving as offering time arrived and these wonderful Christian people gave out of their poverty to further the gospel in other lands.

The Peoples Magazine

Window on Missions

There is still much to do…

By Craig Shugart

I t is a narrow perspective indeed, which claims that September 11, 2001 was "the day the world changed." Possibly more correct is to acknowledge this as the day that we in North America joined the rest of the world, a world in which security and safety cannot generally be taken for granted, and where tragedy and victimization on a large scale are commonplace. What sense can we Canadian Christians make of that dark day? I would offer two suggestions to help us find our way.

First, we need to work hard to deliberately listen to the voices of the Christians of the Middle East. As we do so, we will hear their testimony resonating throughout a long history of difficulty and uncertainty. We will understand more of the splendid diversity of the Body of Christ, and of our own roots and heritage. Condolences and expressions of sympathy have come from every part of the church in the region, all the more potent because they have the credibility born out of the crucible of suffering themselves. They speak with gentle reasoning and insightful rebuke for our tendency to generalize about the character of people from the region, and our limited view of justice and truth. But they also come with a rich,

undaunted spirit of hope and vision for reconciliation to empower us to minister with integrity in a world becoming ever more dangerous.

Second, we need to work hard to deliberately engage with the voices of Muslims of the Middle East. It has been well said that we do not ordinarily meet Islam, we meet Muslims, and the truth about the cultures they represent is far better served if we are in personal touch with them. There is a profound risk of polarization within the Christian church over what to make of Islam. Is it peace loving? Or is it violent to the core? Our strong sense is that we may be on the cusp of the greatest openness to the gospel ever witnessed in the Muslim world, arising out of the most profound degree of introspection and vulnerability ever experienced by Muslims world-over.

Without doubt, one of the greatest God-given characteristics of the human race is our resilience, our ability to get back up and move on. But in our strength lies our frightful weakness, the possibility of both Christian and Muslim missing the voice of God through the events of our age and carrying on with "business as usual." May God overcome us with His perspective!

Craig Shugart
Executive Director
Interserve Canada

"*Without doubt, one of the greatest God-given characteristics of the human race is our resilience, our ability to get back up and move on.*"

The Future of Missions at The Peoples Church.

Missions *is* the future of The Peoples Church. In paying tribute to Dr. Oswald Smith, Jack McAlister, Founder of the World Literature Crusade said, "No man ever walked on this planet with more of a passion to get out the message. And his message was, 'The supreme task of the church is the evangelization of the world.'"

Continuing the vision, each of Dr. Smith's successors has echoed his passion. That is why The Peoples Church remains a unique phenomenon among churches.

As Charles Price, steering the church through the early years of the twenty-first Century, continues to speak at Bible conferences, missionary conferences and evangelistic events, the focus remains steadfastly on missions. In 2002, he represented the ministry of the church in Ethiopia, Hong Kong, Ireland, Latvia and Switzerland, Australia, Germany, England and Canada (Ontario to British Columbia). Various parts of the U.S.A. (Florida to California) are planned for 2003. Besides his North American travels in 2004, Charles will hold meetings in Thailand, England, New Zealand, Australia, Uganda and Ireland.

And the vision continues...

Into all the World

SOUTH AFRICA GENERAL MISSION

DARKNESS

The entrance of Thy words giveth light ... it giveth understanding unto the simple.

Psalm 119:130.

1928 to 2003

2003

Action International Ministries

Bringing hope to the urban poor in Asia, Latin America and Africa

Discipleship   Evangelism   Development

Wouldn't you like to be in this picture?

OPPORTUNITIES TO MINISTER

Into all the World

Seven

Mission Conferences

Inflation Calculation of The Peoples Church Missions Giving – Year by Year.

A basket of goods & services that cost "amount below" in "year to the left" would cost "amount below" in 2003.*

Year	Amount	2003	Year	Amount	2003
1928	$22,793	$259,165	1969	$423,396	$2,260,566
1929	$14,715	$165,780	1970	$442,336	$2,263,286
1930	$43,891	$485,569	1971	$506,730	$2,550,264
1931	$36,660	$445,728	1972	$682,820	$3,262,657
1932	$36,151	$487,840	1973	$728,725	$3,289,979
1933	$23,586	$340,748	1974	$702,339	$2,874,908
1934	$27,181	$383,658	1975	$958,409	$3,534,313
1935	$28,526	$407,325	1976	$1,032,000	$3,481,582
1936	$36,290	$506,410	1977	$1,129,788	$3,548,286
1937	$30,616	$417,738	1978	$1,488,912	$4,302,080
1938	$40,069	$529,083	1979	$1,421,604	$3,762,349
1939	$39,084	$527,419	1980	$1,285,011	$3,112,413
1940	$45,435	$593,555	1981	$1,284,646	$2,762,776
1941	$54,418	$681,891	1982	$1,243,798	$2,397,777
1942	$60,279	$704,977	1983	$1,262,384	$2,269,704
1943	$78,413	$917,059	1984	$1,330,062	$2,287,558
1944	$117,724	$1,338,565	1985	$1,740,447	$2,884,304
1945	$114,854	$1,305,933	1986	$1,513,291	$2,407,152
1946	$122,440	$1,379,416	1987	$1,400,756	$2,139,463
1947	$138,335	$1,451,926	1988	$2,041,998	$2,992,331
1948	$177,474	$1,602,486	1989	$2,055,370	$2,881,272
1949	$180,879	$1,542,496	1990	$2,306,492	$3,071,987
1950	$177,077	$1,489,387	1991	$2,068,985	$2,592,565
1951	$216,443	$1,661,200	1992	$1,767,552	$2,181,461
1952	$228,960	$1,663,686	1993	$1,303,554	$1,578,663
1953	$245,260	$1,825,329	1994	$1,150,329	$1,390,358
1954	$280,423	$2,062,033	1995	$1,153,722	$1,364,904
1955	$283,406	$2,071,563	1996	$1,031,723	$1,203,187
1956	$289,503	$2,116,129	1997	$1,229,701	$1,406,027
1957	$265,973	$1,877,097	1998	$1,409,727	$1,596,997
1958	$298,316	$2,035,178	1999	$1,567,953	$1,758,398
1959	$261,955	$1,777,242	2000	$1,517,438	$1,651,963
1960	$282,221	$1,893,811	2001	$1,318,411	$1,400,527
1961	$303,345	$1,992,020	2002	$1,673,471	$1,745,983
1962	$297,712	$1,995,029	2003	$1,703,942	$1,703,942
1963	$329,241	$2,127,937	TOTALS		
1964	$308,348	$1,951,811		$51,707,638	$137,177,137
1965	$301,081	$1,857,310			
1966	$292,197	$1,741,835			
1967	$321,880	$1,864,475			
1968	$353,272	$1,962,977			

* Source: Inflation Calculator, Bank of Canada website. www.bankofcanada.ca/en/inflation_calc.htm

ACCORDING TO YOUR FAITH Mat. 9:29

210⁰⁰⁰
205⁰⁰⁰
200⁰⁰⁰
190⁰⁰⁰
180⁰⁰⁰
170⁰⁰⁰
160⁰⁰⁰
150⁰⁰⁰
125⁰⁰⁰
100⁰⁰⁰
75⁰⁰⁰
50⁰⁰⁰
25⁰⁰⁰

Into all the World

Mission Conferences.

Annual Missionary Festivals.

The high point of the focus on missions at The Peoples Church is the Annual Missionary Convention, the purpose being:
- to kindle missionary fire in the hearts of all hearers.
- to challenge people to carry the Gospel overseas.
- to raise funds for missions.
- to create a sense of global responsibility in evangelism.
- to provide personal experience with distant cultures.

Oswald Smith felt these gatherings to be the defining days of his life purpose – the central vehicle for spreading the Good News to the nations. The conferences were expressions of his heart. Even after the 1959 appointment of his son, Dr. Paul Smith, to the position of Senior Pastor, Oswald carried on the work of The Peoples Missionary Society and conducted the yearly festivals. At the age of 78, in 1967, he finally passed the responsibility to Paul.

Oswald Smith and R.G. LeTourneau.

Into all the World

1930

This was one of the earliest Missionary Conventions. The main speaker, Paul Rader, can be seen in the front row below the convention sign.

At that time, the church was called "Toronto Gospel Tabernacle", and was housed in a rented facility, St. James Square Church, on Gerrard Street East.

The Mason Jubilee Singers, also in the front row, are flanked by Oswald Smith on the left and Paul Rader on the right.

The missionary work during those years was all channeled through the World Wide Christian Couriers, Paul Raders missionary organization.

Despite the depressed economy, $43,891 was raised for missions that year!

St. James Square Church, home of
The Toronto Gospel Tabernacle, renamed
"The Peoples Church" in 1933.

Into all the World

Into all the World

"We thank God for the information and inspiration that the Conference imparted, and we trust that many have been led out into a life of intercessory prayer on behalf of the Christless masses both at home and abroad."

OJS

Willing to give.

It soon became apparent that once people were made aware of the need in foreign lands, they were willing to give. As Oswald shared his experience in trusting God to meet the need of a faith promise, they opened their hearts and their wallets, as they continue to do today.

First "Faith Missions" Conference – 1934.

In the early thirties, when the church began its close association with the "Faith Missions", it sought innovative ways to attract new missionaries to go out into the field. In 1934, with that in mind, and with the cooperation of Dr. Robert H. Glover, Home Director of the China Inland Mission (now the Overseas Missionary Fellowship), 13 Faith Missions were invited to the first annual Peoples Church Faith Missions Conference – an eight-day gathering unlike anything Toronto had ever seen.

No one who attended will ever forget those eight days. Every night, three speakers held the audience transfixed with stories of far away lands and the great need for workers. Large numbers who had never before known about the work of the Faith Missions had a whole new world opened up to them. Musicians strolled through the crowd, singing and playing. Inspiring testimonies were given by new recruits, who shared the leading of God in their lives. Oswald preached as "a dying man to dying men". Every time he gave the appeal for young people to dedicate their lives to missions, dozens would stream down the aisles in response.

Morning Prayer Meeting.

Perhaps most amazing gathering of all was the morning prayer meeting. Day after day, the room was filled to capacity. Extra chairs had to be brought in. A great spirit of prayer gripped the hearts of the people as they were brought face to face with the physical and spiritual needs of the world.

> *The grand finale*
>
> *of the Missions*
>
> *Conference*
>
> *is the closing*
>
> *Sunday service.*
>
> *The excitement*
>
> *builds and builds*
>
> *until the climax,*
>
> *when the total*
>
> *of the Faith*
>
> *Promises is*
>
> *announced.*
>
> *Every increase is*
>
> *joyously*
>
> *celebrated.*

Exhibit rooms.

One of the main attractions was the exhibit rooms. Each Mission had a booth in which were displayed maps, literature and curios, some of which had never before been seen in North America. Many of those in charge were dressed in native costume. Hundreds of people thronged the exhibits between sessions – asking questions, examining the curios, securing the literature.

Missionaries talked with prospective candidates, imparting the missionary vision of The Peoples Church and communicating its central focus – the evangelization of the world.

Newspapers enthusiastically got caught up in the thrill of the goings-on. "With all the excitement of a circus ringmaster, Oswald Smith stages two shows daily, featuring colourful, native music groups and costumed missionaries."

Spending their time inspecting the curiosities of the world in the displays and attending inspirational sessions, the crowds eagerly responded to the call to support those who would go to shed the light of the Gospel into the dark corners of the world.

The final night.

By the closing night, on November 25, scores upon scores of people were compelled to stand in the aisles and vestibules after the vast congregation had occupied every bit of seating space. Many hundreds were turned away. In response to Dr. R. H. Glover's impassioned appeal, 160 young people volunteered for foreign service. Tremendous gratitude was expressed by the missionary organizations.

Thus began the tradition of united missionary conventions. From that gathering, the church began to send out and support missionaries under the Faith organizations. It was only a beginning...

From slides to Power Point.

After 75 years of ministry, The Peoples Church is giving support to 361 missionaries, 157 nationals, 72 agencies and 65 countries. 34 missionaries have been sent out from the church.

From the first Faith Missions Conference in 1934 until today, yearly conferences have come and gone. While Power Point has replaced the thermometer and a techno-saturated audience has forsaken slides for fast moving multi-media productions, the central purpose of the Missions Conferences remains. It is hoped that snapshots from along the way will kindle in readers, the passion for service and giving, first set aflame in the hearts of participants throughout the years.

REV. ROBT. H. GLOVER, M.D.
Home Director of the China Inland Mission, who will take part.

REV. R. V. BINGHAM, D.D.
Director, Sudan Interior Mission, who will be present.

REV. J. H. W. COOK
Home Director, Evangelical Union of South America, who will take part.

Canadian Conferen

1934

IN THE PEOPLES
NOV.

Inspiring Addresses and Beautifully Colored Slides

First Annual
8-Day Conference
of Faith Missions

10.30 a.m.
2.45 p.m.
7.45 p.m.

•

A cash offering will be received on the closing Sunday which will be divided among the missions represented . . . .

Speakers and missionaries present at the Conventi

Plan to Spend the Entire

ce of Faith Missions

CHURCH, TORONTO

18 to 25, INCLUSIVE

, representing more than a dozen Faith Missions.

Each Mission will have a booth displaying its maps, literature and curios

The Purpose of This Conference

•

1—To establish a Canadian Centre for Faith Missions.

2—To impart a world - wide vision.

3—To provide a missionary outlet for young people.

4—Information — Inspiration Intercession.

REV. H. N. KONKLE
Secretary of the Mission to Lepers, who will be present.

REV. A. W. ROFFE
who will have charge of the 10.30 o'clock prayer hour.

Conference in Toronto

REV. E. J. PUDNEY
Secretary, Unevangelized Fields Mission, who will be one of the speakers.

CONFERENCE
Letters of Appreciation

DR. GLOVER'S LETTER

My Dear Mr. Smith:

I was deeply impressed with the thoroughness of your preparations, notwithstanding the shortness of time available, and with the delightful smoothness which characterized the programme from beginning to end. There seemed such a happy atmosphere of unity and harmony throughout.

I have seldom seen such well-sustained attendance, and enthusiastic interest at any Conference over so long a period, and the fact reflects real credit upon your dear people. I have long been convinced that spiritual life is the only satisfactory basis for missionary appeal.

That wonderful spectacle, on the last evening, of 160 young people rising promptly to their feet to offer their lives unreservedly to Jesus Christ for His missionary service, was itself a clear evidence of preparation of heart through faithful antecedent preaching of the pure Gospel and teaching of the deeper truths of the Word of God.

Again and again during the meetings the thought came to me of what a tremendous difference it would mean to the task of world evangelization if even a bare proportion of Christian churches were to follow the example of your church. For what you and your people are contributing to the Missionary cause, by prayer and the dedication of young life and material resources, is only what might be duplicated in other churches, if only the Word of God was given its proper place and the Spirit of God His full right of way. May the Lord use the example of The Peoples Church to convict many other churches, to impart to them true missionary vision, and to stir them to consecrated action.

The Missionary Exhibits were wonderfully fine and not only interesting but of real educational value.

Last, but best of all, the morning seasons of united prayer were, I believe, the greatest single factor in making the Conference what it was and will continue to be.

Sincerely yours in Him,

ROBERT HALL GLOVER.

China Inland Mission.

LETTER FROM MR. ROBERTS

Dear Mr. Smith:

Toronto is to be congratulated for the privilege it has had of securing first-hand information of the Faith Missions. It could not have been other than a source of inspiration and blessing to all who attended.

That large number of God's people who met for daily morning prayer was perhaps the most significant feature of the Conference, and undoubtedly the stimulus for prayer for Faith Missions will have the most lasting and far-reaching effect of the gathering.

Steadfastly yours in His faithfulness,

V. D. ROBERTS.

The Bolivian Indian Mission.

REV. ARTHUR J. BOWEN'S LETTER

Dear Brother Smith:

The Conference was one of the best that it has been my privilege to take any part in. From the very commencement one was conscious of the presence and power of God.

The morning prayer hour was solemn and sweet, and to this part of the Conference I attribute the wonderful and harmonious spirit which signalized the entire Conference. I did not observe the slightest dissentment.

The large crowds attending the various services proved that it is possible to make missionary meetings attractive as well as edifying. Thousands must have been reached during the eight days, and without doubt the heathen world will be greatly enriched by many doughty warriors of the Cross, while the Home Base will be strengthened immeasurably.

Personally, I thank God for the blessing received and for the great spiritual uplift the Conference was to me.

Not only has God given you the gift of organizing a great Conference for His glory, but He enables you to preside in a most Christ-like Spirit.

Fraternally yours,

ARTHUR J. BOWEN.

South African General Mission.

IMPRESSIONS
from Missionary Leaders

THIS FROM REV. A. W. ROFFE

Dear Mr. Smith:

I am sure your heart has many times been filled with thanksgiving to God for the full measure of blessing bestowed upon your efforts in connection with the first Faith Missionary Conference in Canada. I rejoice with you for all our Lord is doing in your midst.

Praisefully and prayerfully yours,

A. W. ROFFE.

✦ ✦ ✦

REV. E. J. PUDNEY'S LETTER

Dear Mr. Smith:

The Conference was a time of real joy and help to one's own soul. To live in such a missionary atmosphere for a week, and the fellowship with God's children, will long be remembered.

It gave the Faith Missions an unprecedented opportunity for publicity and the bringing of their work before the Christian public. It has enabled God's children to get a very real idea of what is being accomplished throughout the world by such Missions, and has proved to them that God does own and bless such endeavours to the salvation of precious souls.

I trust that it has also enabled them to understand something of the task that yet remains, and has opened up before them avenues through which they may have a share in this greatest of all tasks committed to the Church.

Furthermore, it has, I am sure, been a real stimulus and encouragement to each one taking part, who under God are sharing the responsibility of these great undertakings.

Very sincerely in His service,

E. J. PUDNEY.

Unevangelized Fields Mission.

LETTER FROM REV. H. D. CAMPBELL

Dear Friend:

To my mind the Conference was the best I have attended in years. I do not write as a novice. I have been an attendant of Missionary Conferences for more than forty years, and your Conference at Toronto in its spirit took me back to the early days of my missionary experiences when we saw men and women really moved by the Spirit of Missions to give of their substance in some adequate measure, and to give of their lives unreservedly to get the Gospel to the Regions Beyond.

I was impressed with the atmosphere of prayer, not only at the crowded morning prayer meeting, but throughout the day, and for the real interest manifested on the part of the great congregations in the missionary messages given by His servants.

The last day of the feast, the Lord's Day, was a time of gracious fellowship. It was delightful to us to notice how the people crowded into the meetings and how some of them had to be turned away, not able to get in.

In praying for you and your church the rich blessing of God, we say that we are asking that this first Annual Missionary Conference may be in a very real sense the beginning of things, and may be the opening up of a gracious missionary revival in Ontario and throughout Canada.

One notable feature of the Conference was the fellowship of the brethren representing the various Missions. That was delightful, and as our beloved friend Dr. Glover put it, there was no spirit of competition, but we felt ourselves to be what we really are, colaborers with Christ.

Yours sincerely,

Africa Inland Mission.   H. D. CAMPBELL.

In a missions convention a small boy filled out a Faith Promise envelope. He printed his name and address and promised to give 25 cents per month for missions. Then across the bottom of the envelope in uneven block letters he printed: "My daddy will pay this".

That statement captures the spirit of Faith Promise giving. A Faith Promise is based not on your known resources but on faith in what your Heavenly Father will do. It is promising to give to missions what you believe God is going to supply.

What is a Faith _Promise?_

Faith Promises are usually received during a Missions Conference or a missionary service. The pastor gives each person an envelope and asks the people to fill in their name and how much they believe God would have them give to missions each month for the coming year. By totalling all the promises, the pastor can determine the church's missions goal for the year. .

There are several important truths that should be understood about Faith Promise. First, a Faith Promise is made according to your faith. You promise to give what God provides. It is not a pledge. Pledges are made on the basis of what you foresee as possible for you to do from your known income.

Second, a Faith Promise is an agreement between you and God. No one will come to collect it. Your promise represents a personal goal of what you want to attempt for God.

Third, a Faith Promise is a plan for giving in addition to your regular tithes and offerings. Traditionally a tithe is understood as one-tenth of your income that belongs to God. Offerings are your gifts above your tithes for special needs or projects. As Christians are faithful in giving their tithes and offerings, the operational needs of the church are met. Faith Promise giving is a step beyond tithes and offerings: it is believing God to supply funds that you as a steward can give toward reaching the world with the Gospel.

Fourth, Faith Promise giving enables every

Believing God to supply the funds

"I had to *trust* God for it"

You *promise* to give what God supplies

Christian to have a part in fulfilling the Great Commission. The command of Jesus, "Go ye into all the world, and preach the gospel" (Mark 16:15), is not directed just to those whom God calls as ministers. Spreading the Gospel is the responsibility of every believer. Most laymen want to be a part of reaching the world for Christ but they don't know what they can do. Faith Promise giving allows everyone to participate in the missionary endeavour of the church.

Faith Promise giving emphasizes not what you have to give, but what you can believe God to supply. If you feel that your faith is weak, you have every right to ask God to increase it. Of course, committing to God what we already have in our possession prepares us to believe Him for additional resources.

One of the exciting things about Faith Promise giving is that it enriches the life of the giver. His faith stretches past its former boundaries into areas he hasn't claimed before. The excitement of having God supply the funds to

pay the Faith Promise encourages the giver to believe for spiritual as well as material needs.

Faith Promise giving can revitalize a church. Testimonies from congregation after congregation reveal that they have received both financial and spiritual blessings because of the excitement and faith generated in their midst by the church uniting in Faith Promise giving. This faith has enabled many churches to be of greater service in their own communities than they would have dared to believe possible before they experienced the adventure of Faith Promise giving.

Our founder, Dr. Oswald J. Smith, who led The Peoples Church to become one of the greatest mission-giving churches in the world, introduced the Faith Promise plan. He said, "If I had waited until I had cash, I would not have given at all. But I gave when I did not have it. I gave when I had to trust God for it".

A Faith Promise is a means of giving to God when we do not have anything to give. How much can you trust your Heavenly Father to channel through you to reach the multitudes that He loves and yearns for?

Fundraising through the Faith Promise Challenge.
The Faith Promise Challenge is the cornerstone of fundraising in the Missionary Conferences.

The call goes out to every individual: young or old; student or millionaire; housewife or corporate employee. Each is challenged to decide on a "faith promise", the amount they believe God will put into their hands to give to missions, apart from their regular Sunday offering. They are urged to trust God to supply the amount, and praise God for the miracle as the funds are supplied each month. No reminders are sent out and miraculously, almost every year, more than the amount promised comes in. Each year, the challenge is to see how much more will be pledged than the previous year's commitment.

No one present in the early days will forget Oswald's often unorthodox gathering of collections. In the shadow of the great banners blazing challenging slogans from wall to wall over the choir loft: *"You can't beat God at giving; give and it shall be given unto you; God is no man's debtor;"* Oswald would raise his arms and call for the ushers to begin again, because he "heard too much silver going into the plates!" Far from appearing to be flim-flam manipulations, however, the needs and objectives were always clearly stated and fulfillment encouraged in an attitude of joyful giving.

Oswald took the "faith promise" concept around the world, challenging congregations wherever he went, with the result that global missions giving hit levels never before dreamt possible.

Raising the excitement level.
During the meetings, pledges are handed to the ushers as they move up and down the aisles. Night after night, banks of volunteers total the amounts on adding machines. Radio listeners and television viewers occasionally call in pledges, and these are handed to the speaker to announce. In the early days, the thermometer was the focal point of the platform. Each night, the red marker inched up, closer to the goal, reflecting the excitement level of the audience. Even with Power Point, by the final night, the suspense becomes almost unbearable until, with a dramatic flourish, the "faith promise" total for the coming year is announced. Not a soul can remain seated as voices unite in the "Hallelujah Chorus" to express their passion for reaching the nations with the Good News.

Excerpts from *The Story of My Life*, by Oswald Smith, 1962.

1937

"Another great Annual Missionary Convention has closed. The offering laid at the Master's feet on Sunday, April 18th, was over $43,000. while 240 young people volunteered for foreign service. Praise the Lord!

"Five great services were held on the closing day. The first was at 11 a.m., when the auditorium was filled. The second was at three in the afternoon. The third service was scheduled to commence at seven, but on account of the great crowd filling the enlarged auditorium to its utmost capacity, with scores standing, it started away before the hour and continued until 8:30, the entire program being broadcast. The fourth service started at 9:30 and continued until 10:30, the auditorium being filled to the top seat in the second gallery. It, too, was broadcast. The closing service of the day commenced at 11 o'clock at night, when the grand total of over $30,616. was announced, after which the choir and orchestra sang and played the 'Hallelujah Chorus,' Eldon B. Lehman leading."

1939

"Almost forty thousand dollars! Such was the amount announced on Sunday, April 30th, the closing day of the Annual Missionary Convention.

"To describe the interest, enthusiasm and excitement would be impossible. It increased as the hours passed by, until, at night, people were sitting in the aisles, on the floor, and standing up around the walls on every side.

"The last service commenced at 9.30 p.m. and closed at 10.30, and the crowd was larger than ever. Everyone waited to hear the verdict, which came about three minutes before going off the air. There was a breathless interest as Dr. Smith finally made the announcement. At first the people cheered and applauded.

Hundreds of exclamations of praise to God ascended from all parts of the vast audience, and then the Doxology was sung as it has seldom been sung even in The Peoples Church."

1944

"The largest missionary offering ever received in The Peoples Church and, so far as we know, in the whole of Canada, was announced by Dr. Oswald J. Smith on Sunday night, April 30th, to a congregation that packed the church to its utmost capacity.

"The offering last year was $77,000. The amount that actually came in was over $78,000. But this year broke all records, the offering being over $117,000.

"It would be impossible to describe the enthusiasm of the people. The great auditorium was filled again and again throughout the day, scores upon scores being compelled to stand. Choruses were sung and many an 'Amen' and 'Praise the Lord' was heard as Dr. Smith called out the amounts. Rev. Peter Deyneka assisted. His enthusiasm was contagious. Again and again the people broke out in applause. There were many tear-stained eyes as the offering mounted higher and higher.

"When the offering got up to approximately $90,000 and the people were so excited that they could hardly contain themselves, suddenly Dr. Harold Strathearn was called upon by Dr. Smith to say a word, and no one who was present will ever forget what he said.

"Dr. Smith thought he was going to make an announcement about Mr. LeTourneau's magazine, but instead he told the people that Mr. LeTourneau had decided, after having been present at the morning service, to make a donation of $10,000. to the missionary fund. To describe the scene that followed his announcement, would be impossible. The great congregation rose and sang the Doxology. It was so unexpected that the enthusiasm of those present knew no bounds."

1945

In May, 1945, the Smitty Girls Quintette sang for the first time at the Missionary Convention. This was a group that had ministered with the Jackie Burris Evangelistic organization for a number of years and for those days were extremely "far out". They sang contemporary music, belting it out without any reservations, smiling and moving as they sang. For those days they were very avante-garde. As I look back on them now, I suppose modern young people would consider them rather "square" relative to the music of our times but they were a shock in many ways to the evangelical community of 1945. This group returned to the Convention for a great many years and all of them were dearly loved and will always be remembered by our people.

In 1945 the Faith Promise offering amounted to $114,854. with an average of $56.00 per person. The money during those years was used for much the same purposes as it is today. We supported one hundred and seventy-eight Canadian foreign missionaries, one hundred and fifty-four students and national evangelists; foreign literature was published but no specific amount was given for physical needs such as we now give for World Relief. However, it should be remembered that most of our missionaries were involved in helping people physically. Many of them were nurses, teachers and doctors and although we never said a great deal about it, the evangelical churches of the world have always been deeply involved in the physical needs of the people they serve. The only reason we didn't talk about it was that we felt that spiritual needs were a great deal more important and it should be taken for granted that missionaries and all Christian workers would also be "Good Samaritans" on the human level. I refuse to buy the concept that evangelicals have not been interested in humanitarian efforts. It is just that we have said very little about it. On the other hand, liberal churches and missionaries have little else to talk about and therefore they stress their humanitarian projects.

– from *The Story of My Life*, by Oswald Smith, Marshall, Morgan and Scott, London, 1962.

The Smitty Girls Quintette.

Our Twenty-Fifth Missionary Convention

While the first annual Conference of Faith Missions wasn't held until 1934, Oswald Smith had held regular Missionary Conventions, beginning in 1923, in the Christie Street Tabernacle.

APRIL 4th to 18th
1948
THE PEOPLES CHURCH
100 Bloor East, Toronto, Canada

Another Annual Missionary Convention will be held in The Peoples Church from April 4th to 18th inclusive. A large number of delegates will come; many from distant lands. Gifted speakers have been invited.

We are now contributing approximately $10,000.00 per month toward the personal support of 240 missionaries on 24 fields under 31 Faith Missionary Societies. We are not responsible for service support. The amount we contribute is the amount originally set by the Missionary Societies themselves. In the majority of cases, it is $600.00 per year for each missionary.

Last year — 1947, we contributed $157,000 for Missions and spent $33,000 on ourselves at home. If we are to carry our Budget through 1948 and 1949, we will require at least $160,000.00 for our Foreign Missionary programme.

We look forward to the day when we will be able to meet the personal support of at least 500 missionaries.

What we are going to do, we will have to do quickly. The clouds are gathering; the shadows of the great tribulation are already discernible; God's clock in Palestine is striking loudly. If Russia marches, it will mean the End-time of this present dispensation.

We would urge our people to give as never before, and to pray most earnestly for the success of our Twenty-fifth Annual Missionary Convention.

THE MINNEAPOLIS GIRLS' QUINTET
They will sing at all sessions of the Convention.

1949

"It was ten-thirty Sunday night. The Peoples Church was packed for its fourth service of the day. All around the sides people were standing, unable to get seats, and they had been standing since 6.45 p.m., over three and a half hours. Away up in the elevation the aisles were crowded, while numbers stood everywhere in the gallery. The triumphant strains of the Hallelujah Chorus had just died away and the atmosphere was electric.

"A few minutes earlier the pastor, Dr. Oswald J. Smith, amid breathless silence, had announced the grand total – $181,000. It was a momentous occasion. Thousands had prayed and God had sent in the largest offering ever given in the history of The Peoples Church. The present missionaries – over 200, could now be supported for another year, and thirty-eight new ones, already accepted, sent out."

The Peoples Magazine, 1949.

1951

"An immense crowd thronged every inch of space. Enthusiasm was running high. It was the fourth service of the day. Some 9,000 people had attended. Hundreds were standing. As Dr. Smith mounted the platform, the audience awaited in breathless silence the announcement of the grand total – $216,443. A crescendo of joyful praise gripped the vast assembly, as the people united with the splendid choir in singing the Hallelujah Chorus.

"Over 50,000 had attended during the three weeks of the Convention. This was the first time in history that a missionary convention had been held for such a long period. There had been no begging for funds. No solicitors had ever been sent from door to door. It was God's people getting God's vision and carrying out God's program. It was giving to evangelize the world and brine back the King. It was a red-letter day in my experience."

Dr. Fred D. Jarvis of Japan.

1952

By 1952 the church was partially supporting 296 missionaries, with a total missions budget of $258,000.

The objective this year was a quarter of a million dollars. The amount received was $228,960. It was the longest convention in the world's history – three weeks, four Sundays and one day. A total of 54,000 people attended – 8,000 each Sunday. The Peoples Church now has over 30 missionaries. Never in our wildest imaginations did we ever expect to see a quarter of a million dollars raised for missions. "This is the Lord's doing, and it is marvelous in our eyes."

The Peoples Magazine, 1952.

1954

The Convention lasted for four weeks and five Sundays. It was the longest ever held. There were three meetings each day and four on Sundays. On the last Sunday there were more than 8,000 at the four services. Hundreds had to stand and many were turned away. Rev. Paul B. Smith assisted in the Convention. As soon as the Thermometer was broken, the Choir sang the Hallelujah Chorus. For the first time the afternoon service saw the total reach a quarter-of-a-million dollars and, for the first time, the Thermometer was broken during the 7 o'clock service. On Saturday 250 people met for an emergency prayer meeting. The objective was $265,000.0, but God answered and sent in $280,423.

The Peoples Magazine, 1954.

1955

To describe the scene at 10:30 p.m., when Dr. Smith announced the grand total of $283,406. would be impossible. It was $25,000. above the goal. The service started at 6:25 p.m., so great was the crowd, and the people stood until 10.30 – 452 by actual count – after nearly 2,000 had been seated. It was the largest offering for Missions ever received.

The Peoples Magazine, 1955.

World - Vision Crusade

The Thirty-first Annual Missionary Convention

OF

THE PEOPLES CHURCH, TORONTO

100 BLOOR STREET EAST, - WA.1-9000

MARCH 28th to APRIL 25th

Dr. Oswald J. Smith and Rev. Paul B. Smith, Pastors

1954 PROGRAM

SUNDAY - MARCH 28th

11:00 a.m. — Rev. E. V. Thompson of the West Indies Mission

3:00 p.m. — Dr. Clarence Jones of Radio Station HCJB, South America.
— "In the Footsteps of the Witch-doctor" — Sound Film showing how Science and Salvation combat Superstition and Satan in Africa.

7:00 p.m. — Dr. Clarence Jones
— Rev. E. V. Thompson

9:00 p.m. — "The Life Story of William Carey" — Sound Film depicting the heartaches and victories of one of the world's pioneer missionaries.

MONDAY - MARCH 29th

3:00 p.m. — Dr. Clarence Jones
— Mr. Peter Letchford, M.A. (Oxon), B.Mus., of the South Africa General Mission with Colored Pictures.

7:45 p.m. — Rev. E. V. Thompson
— "Vision and Victory" — Sound Film of the Land of Intrigue South of the Border.

TUESDAY - MARCH 30th

3:00 p.m. — Rev. E. V. Thompson
— Rev. Raymond W. Frame of the China Inland Mission with Colored Pictures.

7:45 p.m. — Dr. Clarence Jones and his Trombone.
— "Power on Earth" — Sound Film in beautiful color depicting the power of print in South East Asia.

WEDNESDAY - MARCH 31st

3:00 p.m. — Dr Clarence Jones
— Rev. Raymond W. Frame with Colored Pictures

7:45 p.m. — Rev. E. V. Thompson
— "Hope for China" — Colored Sound Film of the Land behind the "Bamboo Curtain."

THURSDAY - APRIL 1st

3:00 p.m. — Mr. Peter Letchford
— Sudan United Mission with Colored Pictures.

7:45 p.m. — Rev. Raymond W. Frame
"Flower of Tibet" — Sound Film in Natural Color brought back by popular demand.

CLAUS INDIAN FAMILY

R. G. LeTourneau

Dr. Clyde W. Taylor

FRIDAY - APRIL 2nd

3:00 p.m. — Rev. Raymond W. Frame
— Sudan United Mission with Colored Pictures.

7:45 p.m. — Rev. Peter Letchford
— "Tibet-Land of Mystery" — Colored Sound Film of the Gospel beyond the backyard of civilization.

SUNDAY - APRIL 4th

11:00 p.m. — Don Hillis of The Evangelical Alliance Mission in India

3:00 p.m. — Don Hillis
"Beyond Our Own" — Sound Film with a Missionary Challenge you will never forget.

7:00 p.m. — Rev. M. A. Darroch, Th.D., of The Sudan Interior Mission

9:00 p.m. — "Korea" — Sound Film of the most-talked about nation in the world.

MONDAY - APRIL 5th

3:00 p.m. — Mr. Derwood McIntosh of The Bolivian Indian Mission.
Rev. Peter Letchford with Colored Pictures.

7:45 p.m. — Don Hillis
— "Japan Shall Hear" — Sound Film of "The Land of the Rising Sun."

TUESDAY - APRIL 6th

3:00 p.m. — Mrs. W. H. W. Paget of the Ceylon and India General Mission.
— Mr. Derwood McIntosh with Colored Pictures.

7:45 p.m. — Dr. M. A. Darroch
"Miracles in Inca Land" — "Dynamite" sets off a "chain reaction" in India.

WEDNESDAY - APRIL 7th

3:00 p.m. — Mr. Derwood McIntosh
— Mrs. Paget with Colored Pictures.

7:45 p.m. — Dr. M. A. Darroch
— "The Great Light," (Part 1) — Sound Film of Communism and Christ in Germany.

THURSDAY - APRIL 8th

3:00 p.m. — Rev. Dale W. Kietzman of The Wycliffe Bible Translators
— Mrs. Paget with Colored Pictures.

7:45 p.m. — Dr. Theodore H. Epp of The Back-to-the-Bible Broadcast, Lincoln, Nebraska.
"The Great Light," (Part II)

FRIDAY - APRIL 9th

3:00 p.m. — Rev. Leslie Millin of The Scripture Gift Mission.
Rev. Dale W. Kietzman with Colored Pictures.

7:45 p.m. — Dr. Theodore H. Epp
— "That They May Hear" — Sound Film with a potent portrayal of "The Great Commission."

SUNDAY - APRIL 11th

11:00 a.m. — Dr. Theodore H. Epp

3:00 p.m. — Dr. Francis R. Steele of the North Africa Mission.
— "Call of the Navajo," (Part 1) — Colored Sound Film: see a coyote attacking a flock of sheep and the Gospel enlightening a tribe of Indians.

7:45 p.m. — Dr. Theodore H. Epp

9:00 p.m. — "Call of the Navajo," (Part II).

Neil and Pat Macaulay

The Faith-Promise Plan

By Rev. Wesley Paul Steelberg (Abridged.)

The Peoples Church of Toronto, Canada, has the largest missionary giving of any single church in the world. Its missionary giving for the year 1959 was over $300,000.00

Part of the reason for this tremendous accomplishment (and I say part of the reason, because it is a foregone conclusion that the Spirit of God must move in the hearts of men for such a vision) is the "Faith-Promise Offering" plan.

Describing such a plan is rather difficult on paper, but perhaps you can at least catch a glimpse of some of the methods that Dr. Smith has found workable. It must be understood that the details of this plan have been worked out and modified through the years and that they now produce tremendous results when employed prayerfully and carefully. Every detail is important.

Dr. Smith has a yearly Missionary Convention, and it is at this time that the Faith-Promise Offering is received. The Peoples Church is exposed to the ministry of a good many missionaries, but the Sunday that the Faith-Promise Offering is taken, it is the leader, Dr. Oswald J. Smith himself, who ministers and receives the Faith-Promise Offering.

Careful plans are laid so that the actual occasion of the Faith-Promise Offering is without disturbance or confusion. Everyone knows what is expected, and what to do, ahead of time.

Dr. Smith, for instance, gathers together the ushers who are to be a part of the Faith-Promise Offering plan and instructs them carefully. He assigns to them a position on the given aisle in the church. He instructs them to smile and to be prayerful throughout the entire offering, and to be enthusiastic in their whole approach to the matter. He instructs them that when the Faith-Promise Offering envelopes have been filled out they are to pick up single envelopes as soon as folks have them ready. He instructs them

never to take more than two or three envelopes to the front at a time, and then to return to their station and pick up others. The purpose of this is that the motion and commotion of many people moving from their assigned stations in the aisles, to the front, with these Faith-Promise envelopes filled out, often encourages others to make Faith-Promises when they see that so many are taking part in it.

Dr. Smith brings a message concerning the great need in the world and of the responsibility of Christians to take this Gospel out and to send substitutes around the world by Faith-Promise offerings. At the close of his message he goes immediately into the Faith-Promise Offering by asking ushers to take their stations in the aisles. Other personnel, who help in the offering, take their positions at this time as well. Dr. Smith has two or three who sit at a table beneath the platform who receive the envelopes from the ushers and multiply the monthly amounts by twelve. This is the Faith-Promise figure for the year. It is written in blue ink on the outside of the envelope. Then a co-ordinator, takes the envelopes from the table below to Dr. Smith. He reads the amount of the Faith-

Wesley Steelberg

Promise aloud, giving no mention of the name of the giver, but only the amount of the Faith-Promise as tallied for the year. These amounts are read in rapid succession and the envelopes passed back to the co-ordinator who takes them over to a table on the platform where they are tabulated by adding machine. From time to time during the reading of the Faith-Promises, there is a pause when Dr. Smith asks for a current total, and this total is in turn announced, and the person at the thermometer is asked to run the thermometer up to this amount.

The following words appear on the envelope: "In dependence upon God I will endeavour to give toward the support of the missionary programme of my church . . . payable monthly for one year, the amount checked." And then there are designations of $2.00 to $100.00 with appropriate spaces to be checked.

At this point Dr. Smith explains the difference between a pledge and a Faith-Promise. A Faith-Promise is a contract you make with God for a specified amount monthly. The difference between a Faith-Promise and a pledge, says Dr. Smith, is that a pledge denotes a contract between an individual and some other individual or organization. You may be dunned for this pledge. A Faith-Promise is a contract made with God, in faith. Dr. Smith encourages folks to believe God for an amount given regularly that they do not yet have, but they believe God will enable them to give monthly for a year.

When this explanation has been given Dr. Smith then asks them to ask God what He would have them to do, and they are instructed to quietly and quickly fill out their Faith-Promise Offering Envelope, and pass it to the nearest aisle, and then the tabulation begins.

Amazing things result from this plan.

The Peoples Magazine — Second Quarter, 1964

I Saw It Happen

By Rev. John Russell,
U.S. Secretary, Sudan United Mission
(Abridged.)

"I see you are back again", remarked a fellow missionary traveller one night as he saw me standing at the SUM booth in The Peoples Church, Toronto. "We all need the inspiration this convention brings to us," he continued. "What a lift it is!"

The truth expressed had implications not generally known to the Christians who give so generously to keep The Peoples Church missionary program alive. The main objective of the convention is to raise more than $300,000 annually. This is always accomplished, and the final day of the convention as the faith promises are totalled, is a thrilling one. But it does more, much more than help raise the personal support for some 350 missionaries.

Missionaries from around the world meet each other there and a spiritual rapport is established that lasts a lifetime.

There is still another significant reason for the unparalleled blessing experienced in this type of conference, it is the encouragement each missionary and deputationist receives.

The Peoples Church has been the cause, under God, of reviving the sometimes sagging spirits of many a tired worker and giving him the financial support that has been the means of rescuing him for many years of extra service.

The extra years of service through Peoples Church's support of Sudan United Mission alone would make a thrilling story. Who could begin to evaluate the 135 years of missionary service completed by Ella Hildebrand, Lydie Roberts and Rev. and Mrs. Veary? How could they have done it without the help of Peoples Church?

Why do I personally like to get back for the convention? I'll tell you, I too need the lift.

When a letter from Dr. Oswald J. Smith arrives inviting me to participate in The Peoples Church Annual Convention, I feel grateful. The memories of the last convention and the one before that crowd in upon my thinking. I take a fresh look at things and determine by God's grace to be worthy of the trust.

Then I prepare myself for the missionary event of the year, that of watching Dr. Smith with God's help raise the $300,000 and more, needed for the ensuing 12 months. The month of meetings hasten to conclusion. Then I brace myself for that final service.

I watch his tall spare figure, topped by an abundance of lustrous white hair, grow taller on that last thrilling Sunday. I listen to that resonant voice as he loses himself in the task that has been uniquely his since 1934.

The thermometer has already reached $225,000. I feel that everyone who has even the slightest interest has sacrificed to the limit. Then his call comes to "repent". "If you have already signed a faith promise envelope and would like to add to the promised amount, repent! and send up a second one, even a third or a fourth, there is no limit to your repentance. The task of world missions must be effective. It calls for sacrifice. What can you do without this year to accomplish the task?"

Second and third faith promise envelopes start to roll in. The thermometer once again begins to climb, closer, ever so slowly, to the $300,000. You can hear the rustle of the choir preparing in faith to rise soon to crown the final meeting with their famous

John Russell

interpretation of the Hallelujah Chorus . . . but not just yet . . . $40,000 more are needed. How can Dr. Smith ever get that $40,000?

Miraculously the thermometer reaches $280,000, then to the delight of even Dr. Smith, to $290,000. But the goal hasn't been reached yet. The choir settles back for a few minutes. The congregation is expectant. The moment of climax is approaching! We can feel it! We know it will come!

Dr. Smith pleads and cajoles in a voice still vibrant and strong. The tape on the thermometer crawls upward painfully slowly as the last promises are read off. $298,000 . . . then a pause . . . a chorus is sung. The missionaries are all bowed in prayer. The support of their colleagues is at stake and maybe their own. Will Peoples Church make it? Will God give them another victory?

Suddenly an usher runs down the aisle. He holds aloft another envelope. the final one. You just feel this is it. It must be . . . it has to be. The suspense can't last. Dr. Smith accepts it. reads it to himself, hesitates for an instant and then triumphantly announces $300,000. AMEN! The choir jumps to its feet, more than 2,000 people are standing with them. Joy is overflowing and the Hallelujah Chorus rings through the rafters. And 350 missionaries around the world are sure of another year's supply.

There is just no place in the world like Peoples Church, Toronto, on the final service of a month of missionary meetings.

The same thrilling blessing is felt in Park St. Boston when at the end of their conference Dr. Ockenga announces $274,000 this year for Missions. This program was also started by Dr. Smith many years ago. And Dr. George Linhart of Grace Chapel, Havertown. Pa., states that $115,000 has been promised for another year for missions. This is another of the many conventions launched by Dr. Smith.

Songs of thankfulness are heard in remote villages in Thailand and in the jungles of Brazil.

The Peoples Magazine — Fourth Quarter, 1966

Our Missionary Policy

1. Each year we hold a Missionary Convention, at which time Faith-Promises are made for the next twelve months. Only those Societies under which Missionaries are supported are invited and, since it is for Foreign Missions, no home works are represented.

2. Speakers are invited upon the understanding that they will not solicit names or send appeals to our contributors. Should any gifts be received as a result of the Convention, they should be turned over to the Church Office and a cheque obtained to cover them.

3. Missionaries are accepted for support with the definite understanding that they will not solicit or accept funds from the adherents of The Peoples Church for their extra needs. These must be secured elsewhere.

4. Our policy is to support missionaries under the Societies accredited by the Inter-Denominational Foreign Mission Association of North America, in order to safeguard the funds with which we are entrusted.

5. Missionaries assigned to us by the various Boards are gladly accepted for support, even though we have never seen them, in addition to those from our own church, as God provides the funds.

6. Our Convention Offering of over a quarter-of-a-million dollars a year is used exclusively for work on the Foreign Field and the overhead is borne by the Church. Every dollar designated for missionary work goes to the field.

7. We do not administer the work on any of the Fields. Our policy is to deal directly with the Board and then leave the Board to deal with the missionary.

8. We contribute $1,200.00 a year toward the personal support of each couple and this encourages them to go out and raise the balance. If we are to support our 350 workers regularly, we cannot provide for extras such as outfits, transportation and special field needs.

9. It is our conviction that the supreme task of the Church is the evangelization of the world. Therefore, we work with the Societies that concentrate on reaching the two thousand un-evangelized tribes of earth. Why should anyone hear the Gospel twice before everyone has heard it once?

10. We differentiate between physical and spiritual needs. Material appeals are not emphasized, since even the unsaved will respond to physical needs, whereas only those who have a vision of a lost world will give to spiritual needs.

11. Our promise holds good for 12 months, provided God sends in the funds, and it is then renewed on the basis of our Convention Offering.

12. We continue payment of the allowance for a period of one year after the missionary comes home on regular furlough and then, if he is not going to return, our responsibility ceases.

13. Our policy is to support Canadians only and we are willing to accept all those sent out as God meets the need. Allowances commence with the first quarter after the missionary has gone and are then forwarded regularly.

14. We contribute large sums to Foreign Literature, believing that "the gospel must first be *published* among all nations"

• •

MOTTO

"I had rather wear out than rust out."—*George Whitfield*.

• •

and that "house to house" evangelism is God's method for reaching "every creature".

15. We work with the so-called Faith Missions because they are free from Modernism and they are true to the Word. Their vision is to evangelize the unreached millions of earth and bring back the King. They do not major on institutional, educational and medical work. They base their allowances on needs, not worth or ability.

16. We do not give out of sympathy. Our policy is to hasten the return of the Lord by following His programme for this Age, which is to "preach the gospel in all the world for a witness to all nations" and "to take out of them a people for His name".

17. If we are to meet the regular allowances of our missionaries throughout the year, we cannot take up special offerings for those who visit us from time to time between Conventions.

18. We are always glad to pass on special contributions, but we would much rather have our people loyally support the missionaries listed in our Magazine, for whom we are responsible. To give to Societies direct does not help us to meet our own heavy obligations and makes it impossible for us to continue the regular support of our missionaries. All gifts should go through The Peoples Church.

19. We believe in Home Missions, but we feel that those of us who have the vision, and know God's programme, should concentrate on the Regions Beyond, leaving it to others to contribute to the many worthy movements at home.

20. We seek to work with societies whose overhead is low, and where most of the money given gets to the field.

UNTOLD MILLIONS STILL UNTOLD!

HARVEST IS PAST AND WE ARE NOT SAVED!

Norma Cooper and her Missionary Dramas

Norma Cooper, from South Africa, arranged and directed the dramas and the pageant (1964).
Hope Evangeline Smith Lowry produced the artwork and helped in many other ways.

Into all the World

The conversion of the Philippian jailer.

Chris Lachona and Lloyd Knight as Paul and Silas
singing in the jail to the prisoners at Philippi.

More than a Conqueror

The story of the Apostle Paul, a full-scale missionary opera, written in three acts by David E. Williams, with the libretto by Hope Smith Lowry – presented to overflow crowds on two successive Sundays during the 1965 Missionary Conference.

Chris Lachona (from California)
as Paul.

Gordon Hamilton (the lame man),
Lloyd Knight and Timothy Prihodko as Peter and John.

Country Church Gives $46,000 to Missions

by Rev. Homer Kandel

I am a country Pastor. My church is a country Church. It is known as Farmerstown Mennonite Church and it is located at Baltic, Ohio. We only have 80 members.

Taking the news of Salvation to a lost and dying world has always challenged me but I did not know how to do it. I was always told that we must take care of the problems at the Home Base before doing anything in the Foreign Field but the longer we waited to clean up things here at home, the worse they got. I knew that a Missionary Diet is the best medicine for a sick church.

Before I became Pastor of the Farmerstown Church, I applied to the Mission Board to be sent out as a missionary but each time I was turned down. To this day I do not know why I was rejected.

My wife, Dorothy, and I, decided to support a missionary on our own. This we did and I felt that we were obedient to the Great Commission.

However there was no programme in our Church for Missions and I was greatly burdened about it. I wondered how God could use a little country Church to send the Gospel to the ends of the earth.

Sunday after Sunday I preached on Missions and to my utter amazement and delight, I found that the Holy Spirit was speaking to the members of my Church. Soon they, too, had a burden for Missions. Finally in 1962, we held our First Missionary Conference. I had never attended a Missionary Convention but I did the best I could. The Conference lasted for a week. However no missionaries were sent out and no money was provided for the support of missionaries.

Then I started hearing and reading about Dr. Oswald J. Smith. I got hold of his books. There was one book that I could not get away from. It was called "The Passion for Souls". We had heard about the Faith Promise Offering and I began searching for all the information I could get about it but we were afraid to launch such a programme. We heard of other churches that had been greatly blessed, yet, we hesitated.

Finally, I discovered that Oswald J. Smith was still living and that he was active in Missionary Work. The Holy Spirit seemed to tell me to go and see him. Toronto was nearly 400 miles away. I wondered if it would be a waste of time and money.

Finally one day, I drove to Toronto to see Dr. Smith. On the way, I wondered if anything could happen in our little country Church. However I was excited at the possibility.

As I drove into the parking lot of The Peoples Church, I saw Dr. Smith through the window sitting in his office. To say that I was scared is putting it mildly. However in a few minutes, a friendly young lady introduced me to Dr. Smith.

Never will I forget the warmth, the friendliness, the concern for Missions that this man had. I was a stranger and he took me in. After talking for some time about a Missionary Conference, he introduced me to Dr. Robert Watt. Dr. Watt spent an hour or more with me discussing a Missionary Convention.

I could hardly wait to get home and report to the congregation how God had led. The news was received with great joy and we anticipated wonderful blessing.

Our little Church of 80 members met and set a goal of $8,000 for our First Faith Promise Offering. This was in the year, 1966.

To our utter amazement, the offering came to $16,000. There were tears of joy.

A year later, we had our next Convention. Dr. Watt had led us in our First. Now we asked him to conduct our Second. The Faith Promise Offering this time was $25,000.

Dr. Watt came once again for the Third Convention and we had other missionaries sharing in the programme. The Faith Promise Offering rose to $35,000.

Our Fourth Convention was conducted by Dr. Oswald J. Smith, himself. He spoke each night from Thursday night until Sunday night and also on Sunday morning. The Holy Spirit again worked. Dr. Smith took up the offering on Sunday morning and to our astonishment, in spite of what God had already done, we received $46,000.

That is an average of $575.00 for each member for the year. In addition, we took up an offering of $1200.00 for Dr. Smith's Foreign Literature work.

At our 1969 Conference, a little girl, 5 years of age, made out a Faith Promise Offering of 10c a month. The very first month after, she was playing outside when she found a dime. The second month her uncle gave her 10c to buy a bottle of pop. She came running to her mother and said she would use it to pay her Missionary Offering. One day, a little later, she found a dollar bill frozen in the ice. She and her mother dug it out. This made $1.20, the exact amount she had promised for Missions.

We have had many such testimonies from our people. God has opened the windows of Heaven and poured out a blessing upon us. We have discovered that it pays for a church to hold a Missionary Convention and take up a Faith Promise Offering. We now have a Missionary Programme for which our people pray daily. I would recommend Faith Promise giving to any Pastor and to any Church for without faith, it is impossible to please God.

The Peoples Magazine — First Quarter, 1971

When asked for his opinion of Christianity, the British wit, George Bernard Shaw, replied, "I don't know. I have never seen it practiced!"

In 1973, H.P. Collins noted that Mr. Shaw had obviously never attended a Missionary Conference at The Peoples Church and experienced the joy of missionary giving – based on faith.

He went on to say that less than three thousand people at The Peoples Church had been astounding both Christians and non-Christians, like Shaw, ever since the Church donated its first missionary offering more than 40 years before. Oswald Smith's dream continued to put foreign missions first – and to draw the largest crowds to Sunday School and Sunday evening services in Canada, while still retaining only 23 percent for home support.

The 1973 Missionary Conference was no exception; excitement pervaded the Church from the very moment it began. Laying the time-tested foundation for missionary giving, 300 prayer warriors met on Friday night in the Founder's Hall, in great anticipation of what would follow.

Dr. Paul Smith introduced the various speakers for the days ahead and the Conference was on. People all over the world wondered whether enough faith and money could be raised to share substantially in the support of 400 missionaries.

1973 Missionary Convention

Throughout the week, fair weather or foul, the crowds came. Kenn Opperman strengthened their faith again and again. Anders Eriksson, who was besieged to sing repeatedly, "The King is Coming", elevated Gospel singing and preaching to new heights.

At last the final Sunday of the Conference arrived. The 1000 plate Youth Inter-Action banquet was over; the speakers had done their best. The Sunday morning tally read $447,534!

Speaker Paul Kauffman joined in the jubilation of The Peoples Church that Sunday night when the victory words rang out in song. The Peoples Church had reached a total of $728,725! The Sunday School alone had promised $363,076!

What must have been in the mind of Dr. Oswald J. Smith that night in 1973? Sixty years before, he had written in his diary:

> "Sick and discouraged. My life seems so useless, so worthless. My dreams of service have never yet come true. I am doing so little, oh, so little."

The crowds heard from singer and speaker alike that more and more missionaries were needed. They learned of areas where doors were closing, but also where many doors were opening. They were reminded of the unique position The Peoples Church has in World Missions — a reminder that strengthened the resolve of the people to live up to its name.

"The Peoples Church is known all over Sweden."

Anders Eriksson

Shadrack Maloka, former leader of a rebellious African gang, touched every heart as he revealed his sincere concern for his people and his deep appreciation for The Peoples Church. He told his story of being rejected by his parents and well-meaning associations, and warmed hearts with his passionate preaching and living proof that Christ is ever with the believer. Later on during the Convention, he wept openly, unable to contain his tears, so great was his love for Africa and the giving people of The Peoples Church.

ACCORDING TO YOUR FAITH

1973 Final Sunday night: $728,725!

By the third Sunday morning: $447,534.

By the second Sunday night: more than $300,000. No one in The Peoples Church felt they could not meet the Missionary challenge.

By the second Sunday morning: $237,795. Oswald Smith was praying for $300,000. by the end of the day.

By the first Missionary Sunday night: $92,742.

First Missionary Sunday morning, the thermometer read: $47,000.
– A LONG WAY FROM THE $500,000 needed to support the 400 missionaries.

Returning for their third visit to The Peoples Church, the 25 members of *The Living Sound* preached and sang as only 25 dedicated Christians of such caliber can.

"Without missions and faith-promises, we'd have an empty church."
OJS

"I can't image the Mission Field without the conferences of The Peoples Church."

Kenn Opperman

Kenn W. Opperman, the dynamic preacher (formerly of Toronto's Avenue Road Church).

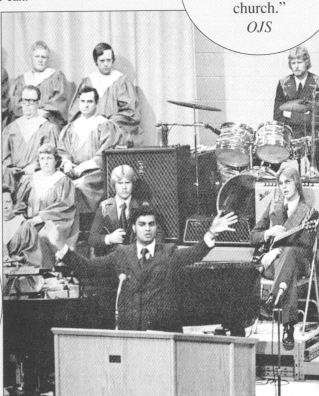

Ravi Zacharias, powerful defender of the Christian faith.

Mission Conferences

Into all the world

WORLD MISSIONS

Oswald J. Smith
Founder
April 28-April 29

Paul B. Smith
Minister

Donald B. Patterson
April 19-April 22

Paul Finkenbinder
April 23-April 27

TELEVISION SPECIAL—SUNDAY, APRIL 27
9:00 a.m. to 1:00 p.m.

PAUL B. SMITH
in
THAILAND

Metropolitan Toronto Callers 368-6711
Outside Toronto Area Callers 1-800-268-6330

APRIL 19

MISSIONARY EXHIBITS
IN THE GYMNASIUM
APRIL 27 TO MAY 4

The Antone Indian Family
April 19 to 27

The Stone Brothers
April 27 to 29

The Sharretts
April 30 to May 4

Jerry Ballard
April 27

Paul Kauffman
April 30-May 4

Sundays—11:00 a.m. and 7:00 p.m.

$1,285,011.00 RAISED

7:45 p.m.

7:00 p.m.

• **Donald B. Patterson**
• The Antone Indian Family

Live Telecast

HEAR

Donald B. Patterson
The Antone Indian Family

Donald B. Patterson and The Antone Indian Family
—Fellowship Hour—

Donald B. Patterson
The Antone Indian Family
—Fellowship Hour—

Sunday, April 27	**Monday, April 28**	**Tuesday, April 29**	**Wednesday, April 30**
9:00 a.m. to 1:00 p.m.	7:45 p.m.	12:00 to 1:15 p.m.	12:00 to 1:15 p.m.
Live TV Special		*Don Lonie*	*Don Lonie*
7:00 p.m.	*Oswald J. Smith*	—7:45 p.m.—	—2:00 p.m.—
Paul Finkenbinder		*Oswald J. Smith*	*Ladies Prayer Meeting*
THE ANTONE INDIAN FAMILY	The Stone Brothers		—7:45 p.m.—
THE STONE BROTHERS	The Mizo Choir	The Stone Brothers	*Paul Kauffman*
—Fellowship Hour—	—Fellowship Hour—	The Mizo Choir	The Mizo Choir / The Sharretts
		—Fellowship Hour—	—Fellowship Hour—

CONFERENCE '80

TO MAY 4

NOON HOUR SPECIALS—APRIL 29 to MAY 2

WITH DON LONIE

- The Stone Brothers
- The Sharretts
- The Mizo Choir

12 NOON to 1:15 p.m.

Don Lonie

The Mizo Choir from India
April 30 to May 4

NATIONAL LEADERS
WILL TAKE PART
IN EVERY SERVICE

Augustus Marwieh
Liberia

Cecil Siriwardene
Sri Lanka

Chris Marantika
Indonesia

Simon Sircar
Bangladesh

Badu Bediako
Ghana

Sudhir Wesley
India

Mission
Conferences

FOR WORLD MISSIONS!!

Wednesday, April 23	Thursday, April 24	Friday, April 25
1:45 p.m.	7:45 p.m.	7:45 p.m.
Ladies Prayer Meeting	*Jim Wilson*	Paul Finkenbinder
—7:45 p.m.—		
Jim Wilson		
The Antone Indian Family	The Antone Indian Family	The Antone Indian Family
—Fellowship Hour—	—Fellowship Hour—	—Fellowship Hour—

Thursday, May 1	Friday, May 2	Saturday, May 3	Sunday, May 4
12:00 to 1:15 p.m.	12:00 to 1:15 p.m.	7:30 p.m.	11:00 a.m.
Don Lonie	*Don Lonie*	**IN CONCERT**	*Live Telecast*
—7:45 p.m.—	—7:45 p.m.—		7:00 p.m.
Paul Kauffman		The Antone Indian Family	*Paul Kauffman*
Mizo Choir	same as Thursday	The Mizo Choir	The Antone Indian Family
The Sharretts	and	The Sharretts	The Mizo Choir
		and	and
		The Set Free Singers	The Sharretts
—Fellowship Hour—	—Fellowship Hour—	—Fellowship Hour—	—Fellowship Hour—

Into all the World

The gates of hell have not prevailed! World Missions is a massive assault on the fortress of hell. It is the offensive of the Church "and the gates of hell shall not prevail."

Richard Wurmbrand
staggered from Communist captivity in 1964. He carried on his body the scars of cruel torture – 18 holes burned in his torso and many broken bones, including four vertebrae. Richard and Sabina Wurmbrand are Jews who lost most of their families to the Nazis and then suffered imprisonment, separation and cruelty for fourteen years at the hands of the Communists in Romania. Pastor Wurmbrand is a Lutheran minister and educator.

Marvin Rosenthal
may be the most exciting prophetic preacher to minister among us. Rosenthal is a Jew with an unbelievable grasp of his peoples' history and an ability to communicate to a large audience in a manner that we seldom see.

Arthur Gee
tells of the incredible reports of a church in China that is not only alive, but vibrant and purified. Gee has interviewed hundreds of Chinese who are moving in and out of China daily through Hong Kong.

Hal Lindsey
is the most widely read prophetic author in the world – a frequent speaker at The Peoples Church.

Stuart Briscoe
author of a dozen books including, *What Works when Life Doesn't*, returns to our church for two days.

World Missions '82

"Now, over a million dollars for World Relief."

"Tortured for Christ."

"A funny thing happened."

"A billion is my parish."

"Don't forget Mexico."

"England and Nairobi."

"Don't just drink. Buy a record."

"Standing room only."

Merv Rosell
joined our World Missions Conference Staff in 1981. Rosell is one of our world's most effective evangelists and missionary statesmen.

Donald Botsford
will be in charge of the four noon-hour sessions with the Academy students. Botsford is pastor of the rapidly growing Church of the Canyons in California.

Enrique Cepeda

reports on Latin America which has been reeling from insurrection, rebellion, guerrilla attacks and other forms of violence and atrocities.

Anand Choudhari

trained to follow in his father's footsteps as a Brahman priest. What would make him forget his caste and touch "the untouchables"? Find out.

Paul Kauffman

spent the first 17 years of his life in China and Korea. He returned to Asia to birth a Third World missionary organization, *Asian Outreach,* which is now carried on under strong national leadership. Based in Hong Kong, *Asian Outreach* has centers in six principle cities of Asia and penetrates twelve countries and also the Peoples Republic of China. Kauffman has been an intrinsic part of our conference ever since 1968.

Augustus Marweih

will describe the joys and heartaches of serving God in the steamy land of Liberia – that little-known African country hanging on the bottom of the continent's "bulge". The story of Gus Marweih is that of illiterate jungle boy to national educator in one short lifetime. The Peoples Church has been deeply involved in his work in Liberia for many years.

The Samuelson Brothers

The Samuelson Brothers, from Sweden, have been one of our favourite singing groups over the years. They return this year after a fairly long absence from our conference, and will be heard at every service during the second week. It goes without saying that they will be featured at the noon hour services with the Paul B. Smith Academy students.

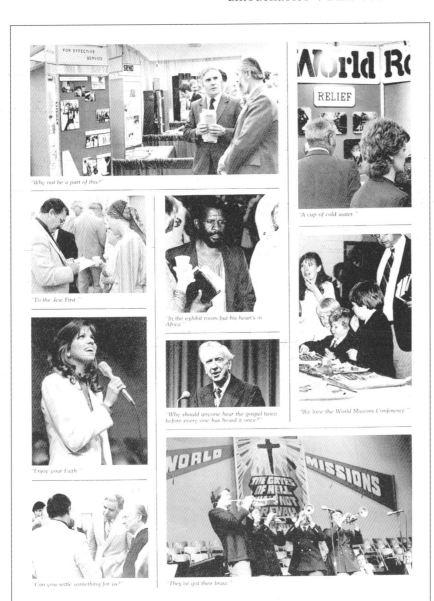

"Why not be a part of this?"

"A cup of cold water."

"To the Jew First."

"In the exhibit room but his heart's in Africa."

"Why should anyone hear the gospel twice before every one has heard it once?"

"We love the World Missions Conference."

"Enjoy your Faith."

"Can you settle something for us?"

"They've got their brass."

Chuck Ohman And The Ohman Brass

– Chuck Ohman is in a class by himself – a flawless performer without a peer in his field – a tremendously effective communicator of the Gospel through music.

Tami Cheré

A little lady with big horizons! Tami combines the exciting sounds of the young with her mature grasp of the Gospel – a musical talent that has to be heard to be believed.

Mission Conferences

1984.

Amero Bire, a New Guinea warrior decked out in his traditional warrior garb of grass, feathers, beads and ivory, whooped through the auditorium doors, brandishing his spear. Running down the aisle, feathers bobbing and grass flying, his brown skin glistened as he bolted up onto the platform. In perfect English, he delivered greetings from the church in Papua, New Guinea, to the startled Peoples Church audience.

Don Jost and 94 year-old Oswald Smith.

When it was time to announce the "faith promise" offering, Paul Smith announced the remarkable total of $1,330,062.00 for World Missions. Just over $1.2 million was raised in 1983.

Paul then slipped out to a telephone, and asked those sitting with 94-year-old Oswald to, "Tell father his people have done it again!"

Peter Deyneka, Jr., gave a stirring account of the tremendous move of the Holy Spirit in Russia. David Wang thrilled the people with the miraculous account of the Gospel reaching Inner Mongolia. Missionaries from the Phillipines stirred hearts with stories of the lives of lost children. Christian leaders from Thailand and Liberia gave radiant testimonies.

Susan Pons brought revelations of the plight of the Chinese church and its immense sufferings amid beatings, torture and imprisonments; yet inspired everyone with the news of how the church had multiplied fifty-fold.

In the final meeting, Franklin Graham asked,
  "Who will go? Who will give their life to
    the cause of World Missions?"
The stage had been set for a great response, but when between six and eight hundred young people poured into the aisles in a tidal wave of response, no one was prepared: it was overwhelming.

Susan Pons.

David Wang.

Franklin Graham.

Into all the World

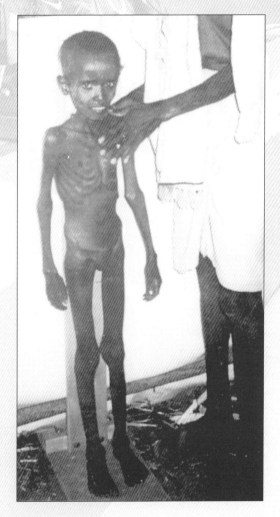

1985

In the face of such suffering, what can one say? In 1985, so desperate was the situation in Ethiopia, that a spontaneous, one-hour telethon for the famine was held. The result was the highest missions giving so far: $1,740,447.00.

The Pag-Asa Singers

1988 Jubilee Missionary Conference

The Mizo Choir

Goal: $2,000,000.00!

Ravi Zacharias

1928 Jubilee '88 1988
PEOPLES

Allen Finley

Hal Lindsey

Richard Wurmbrand

Sombat Sapkasetrin

Charles Stanley

Augustus Marwieh

Stuart Briscoe

Bill Boerop

Sam Kansonso

Ed Lyman

Ester Nasrani

Galo Vasquez

Paul Finkenbinder

John Dekker

George Chen

Melvin Floyd

Jill Briscoe

Greg Tingson

Gaetano Sotille Family

David Anderson

Marvin Rosenthal

Paul Chang

Wuninip Weya

Anthony Campolo

David Wang

Final Tally — Over the Top!!!!
$2,041,998.00!
First time ever over two milion dollars!

Jubilee '88
The past
with gratitude
r s
the future
with confidence.

The Antone Indian Family Singers. " No missionary service at The Peoples Church is complete without the Antone Indian Family," Dr. Jost always said. "When (Oswald Smith) heard them sing, he loved it so much he'd say, 'One more time around the Throne, Antones!'" The Antones sang at Dr. Smith's memorial service in 1986.

Into all the World

Pearls
~ never to be lost ~
from the Missionary Jubilee

Get up, get out, and get on with it! Now!

David Wang

The message that Jesus saves is free, but the delivery is so very, very costly.

David Wang

The closer we are to the end of the race, the harder we must run.

Paul Finkenbinder

We have an assignment: to bring into this sad world the smile of heaven.

Richard Wurmbrand

The harvest is not completed until the crops are safely in the barn.

Paul Kauffman

My mission field is any piece of geography between my two feet, at any given time.

Jill Briscoe

Every golden era in human history proceeds from one individual who knows their God and knows where God is going.

Ravi Zacharias

"We are embarking upon the most important season on our church calendar - our global mission conference!"

John D. Hull
SENIOR PASTOR

- 1998/99 Faith Promise Giving Goal: **$1.45 Million**

- The Peoples Church supports 413 missionaries (332 serve outside Canada), 165 nationals, representing 57 agencies

- 53.4 % of our missionaries outside North America are in the "10/40 Window"

- 58.5 % of overseas missions dollars go to ministry within the "10/40 Window"

- Short-term mission trips in summer, 1998 include trips to Spain and Costa Rica

SUNDAY SERVICES
11:00 am & 6:30 pm

WEEK NIGHT SERVICES
7:30pm

TICKETS REQUIRED FOR:

MEN'S POWER BREAKFAST
May 2nd, $7.00 each

CHURCH-WIDE DINNER
May 6th, $6.00 each

WOMEN'S BRUNCH
May 9th, $10.00 each

1998

Sunday	Monday	Tuesday	Wednesday	Thursday	Friday	Saturday
	CONFERENCE PARTICIPANTS				**APRIL 17th** 7:30 PM — Prayer Meeting	**APRIL 18th** 8:00 AM - 4:00 PM — Equip Seminar — John Maxwell
APRIL 19th SERVICE 11:00 AM — SERVICE 6:30 PM — John Maxwell	John Maxwell	Margaret Nikol				**APRIL 25th** MARKET 5:00 PM — CONCERT 8:00 PM — Global Youth Market '98 — Rebecca St. James
APRIL 26th SERVICE 11:00 AM — SERVICE 6:30 PM — Margaret Nikol	George Sweeting	Tony Campolo				**MAY 2nd** BREAKFAST 9:00 AM — Men's Power Breakfast — Arnell Motz — International Church Addis Abba, Ethiopia
MAY 3rd SERVICE 11:00 AM — SERVICE 6:30 PM — George Sweeting	Rebecca St. James	Arnell Motz	**MAY 6th** DINNER 5:30 PM — SERVICE 7:30 PM — Janis Smith	**MAY 7th** SERVICE 7:30 PM — Prime Time — John D. Hull	**MAY 8th** DINNER 5:30 AM — Short-Term Missions Dinner — Mark Middleton	**MAY 9th** BRUNCH 10:00 AM — Women's Brunch — Libby Little
MAY 10th SERVICE 11:00 AM — SERVICE 6:30 PM — Tony Campolo	Janis Smits	Mark Middleton				
	Libby Little	You				231

For nearly 20 centuries the followers of Jesus Christ have sought to fulfill the great commission of Matthew 28:19-20: "Go ye therefore, and teach all nations, baptizing them in the name of the Father, and of the Son, and of the Holy Ghost: teaching them to observe all things whatsoever I have commanded you…"

In the days of the Apostles the gospel spread quickly after Pentecost, aided by the stress of persecution. In Acts 8:4-5, Luke writes, "they that were scattered abroad went everywhere preaching the Word. Then Philip went down to the city of Samaria and preached Christ unto them."

In Mark 16:15 we read that Jesus said, "Go ye into all the world and preach the gospel to every creature." Clearly the emphasis was placed on preaching the Word, preaching Christ and preaching the gospel. Each phrase is virtually synonymous with the other. Throughout history the Holy Spirit has prompted believers to preach the Word of God to faithfully present Christ and the gospel.

The vital part of Church history and missions is not the struggles between powerful church leaders and worldly kings, but how the gospel spread to new nations by preaching the Word of God to the people in their own language. This often involved, as it still does today, reducing unwritten languages to a written script so that people could be taught to read the Bible for themselves.

How the Word of God spread
God has blessed the spread of his Word in an amazing way among many language groups of the world. At the start, most of the Old Testament was written in Hebrew or Aramaic and the New Testament was written in Greek—the language of the eastern Mediterranean. The Old Testament also became available in Greek in 200 BC in the version called the Septuagint.

In the second century the area around Antioch and Syria had their own Syriac version. A Coptic version was probably available by 200 AD for Egypt on the African continent. At some point early in the 3rd century the Scriptures began to be translated into Latin—the language of the Romans and the western Mediterranean.

The Armenian nation was the first kingdom to officially convert to the Christian faith. This took place in the late 3rd century, just before the Roman Empire declared itself for Christ under Constantine (d.337). But it was not until the 5th century that an Armenian alphabet was created so that they could have the Scriptures in their own tongue.

The gospel in early Britain
The gospel appears among the early Britons, perhaps coming with Roman soldiers or traders in the 2nd century. Patrick (c.390-c.460) came from Roman-occupied Britain, but took the gospel to Ireland. His writings are consistent with the Scriptures and he certainly did not believe the mediaeval superstitions prevalent in the Dark Ages.

From the Irish church planted by Patrick, Columba (c.521-597) took the gospel to Iona, a small island off the coast of Scotland and from there he evangelized much of Scotland. Around the same time Augustine of Canterbury brought the gospel to the Anglo-Saxon kingdom of Kent in southern England in AD 597. Later, Aidan (d.651), a monk from Iona, took the gospel to the northern English kingdom of Northumbria and established a monastery on

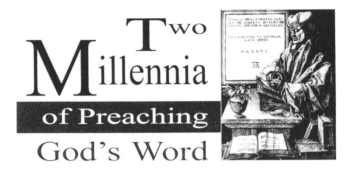

Two Millennia of Preaching God's Word

Pausing to look back – regaining perspective – seeking clear direction from God – for carrying the Gospel into the new century.

Charles A. Tipp

the island of Lindisfarne. From thence these Irish monks evangelized much of northern England. The Lindisfarne Gospels are evidence that the Scriptures were considered most important in evangelizing the people of this kingdom. Later the scholar Bede (c.673-735) translated the Gospel of John into Anglo-Saxon in the 8th century.

Light in the Dark Ages
The famous Jerome (c.342-420), working in Bethlehem, had translated the Bible into Latin, called the Vulgate because it was in the language of the people. After Jerome died his translation became the official version of the mediaeval Roman Catholic Church. But as the years passed, fewer people understood Latin and by the 13th century the Roman Catholic Church forbade the Scriptures to the laity.

In these Dark Ages, which lasted roughly from the fall of the Western Roman Empire in 476 until 1000, only a relatively few people could read or write or had access to the Word of God in their own language. Yet in every age God had servants who understood the importance of his Word.

By the 9th century the Arabs had the Scriptures but the majority of them were turning to Islam. In the same century, good King Alfred (849-899) of Wessex in southern England requested more of the Scripture, especially the Psalms, to be translated into the Anglo-Saxon language for his people.

Also around this time, two remarkable missionary brothers from Greek-speaking Constantinople—Cyril (826-869) and Methodius (c.815-885)—preached the gospel of Christ to the Slavic people of Moravia. They, like many missionaries through the years, had to reduce the Slavic language to writing, and they used Greek letters to do so. Because of this, the languages of most Slavic peoples use Greek letters to this day.

The later Middle Ages and Scripture translation
After AD 1000, more Scripture was translated into European languages. A wealthy Frenchman by the name of Peter Valdes (d. c.1210) used his wealth to have the Bible translated into several of the emerging languages of Europe like Provençal in Southern France, early Italian and Spanish. Valdes also sent his followers out two-by-two to preach Christ. Waldensian churches still exist in Europe today.

Another evangelical voice in this period was John Wycliffe (c.1330-1384), one of God's choice servants, who furthered the understanding of God's Word in England by translating the Bible into the emerging English language of the 14th century. He also organized his followers, called Lollards, into teams in order to preach Christ throughout England. Jan Hus (c.1372-1415) and his Bohemian followers preached similarly in central Europe. All these faithful followers of Christ simply preached the written Word of God according to the missionary mandate.

The Reformation: a revival of God's Word
The Great Reformation was basically a revival of trust in the Word of God. It came because more people were hearing the Word of God in their own language and the Spirit of God brought them understanding of the gospel of salvation through faith in Christ alone. It is true that some kings made decisions severing links with the papacy and the Church of Rome but the real Reformation occurred in the hearts of people who responded to the preaching of the gospel.

Scriptures available	Century	Important events
OT in Hebrew, Aramaic, Greek, NT written in Greek for eastern Mediterranean	1st	Church established
Syriac version for Antioch and Syria	2nd	Gospel introduced to Britain
Coptic version for Egypt, Latin for Romans and western Mediterranean	3rd	Armenia and Roman Empire declared Christian
Latin-Vulgate version by Jerome	5th	Patrick brings gospel to Ireland
	6th	Gospel reaches Scotland and England
Anglo-Saxon translation of Gospel of John	8th	Rise of Islam
Scriptures available to Arabs, more scripture in Anglo-Saxon, Slavic	9th	Gospel reaches Moravia
European languages: Norman French, Provencal, Italian, Spanish	12th	Era of Peter Valdes
Wyciffe's English translation	14th	
	15th	Jan Hus in central Europe, Gutenburg invents printing press
German NT by Martin Luther, English NT by William Tyndale, French translation by Pierre Robert Olivetan	16th	Protestant Reformation, works published by Jean Calvin, John Knox in Scotland, Menno Simons leads Anabaptists in Netherlands
1611 King James Version in England, 1663 John Eliot translates Bible into Algonquin	17th	John Bunyan writes *Pilgrim's Progress*
	18th	Great Revival in Britain, Whitefield and Wesley brothers in England, 1793 William Carey goes to India
Modern French translation by Louis Segond, Scriptures translated into many languages	19th	British and Foreign Bible Society formed, era of Charles Spurgeon, D.L. Moody, David Livingston, Hudson Taylor
Translation of Scriptures continues	20th	Great expansion of missionary effort

By the grace of God, printing was invented just before the time of the Reformation. As millions of people learned to read they were able to search the Scriptures for themselves. Martin Luther (1483-1546), for instance, completed a German New Testament in 1522 that soon became a bestseller in that language. Other translations worthy of note are those of William Tyndale (c.1494-1536), who finished his version of the English New Testament in 1525, and Pierre Robert Olivetan (c.1506-1538), a cousin of John Calvin (1509-1564) who translated the Scriptures into French.

With the Scriptures more available, some great leaders came on the scene to lead God's people. In England, Thomas Crammer (1489-1556), the Archbishop of Canterbury, compiled the Book of Common Prayer and helped draw up the Thirty-Nine Articles, the theological foundation of Anglicanism. In France and Switzerland, Jean Calvin wrote his theological classic, *The Institutes of the Christian Religion* and John Knox (c.1513-1572) helped to establish the Word of God in Scotland. Meanwhile, Menno Simons (1496-1561) in the Netherlands became the leader of a significant group of Anabaptists later known as the Mennonites.

The King James Version of the Scriptures was published in 1611, destined to become a major influence throughout the English-speaking world. To illustrate biblical truth, John Bunyan (1628-1688) wrote *The Pilgrim's Progress* in 1678, which over the years has helped bring multitudes to salvation in Christ. In America, John Eliot (1604-1690) preached Christ to the Indians. He translated the New Testament into the Algonguin language in 1661 and the whole Bible two years later. Unfortunately there is not a single person alive today who can read Eliot's translation, this Native American tribe having become extinct shortly after Eliot's death.

The modern missionary movement

When things began to decline spiritually in the late 16th century and early 17th century, God raised up the Pietists in Germany and George Whitefield (1714-1770) and John (1703-1791) and Charles Wesley (1707-1788) in England. In the revival and awakening that resulted in the mid-18th century, thousands heard the Word of God preached in the open air and were converted. Sunday schools were formed to teach children the Scriptures and literacy.

By 1793, William Carey (1761-1834) set out to preach the gospel in India and thus began the modern missionary movement. In Britain, the Baptist Missionary Society was started, followed by many others. Another significant development in the spread of the gospel worldwide was the formation of the British and Foreign Bible Society in 1804. Over the last two centuries millions of Scriptures have been printed and translated into many new languages by this and many other similar societies.

In their day, Charles Spurgeon (1834-1892) and D. L. Moody (1837-1899) exemplified the preaching of the gospel. David Livingstone (1813-1873) in Africa and Hudson Taylor (1832-1905) in China accelerated the expansion of missionary outreach. Thousands of young people went into evangelical ministries at home and overseas due to the example of such men of God.

20th century trends

In the 20th century, despite increased liberalism, secularism and resurgent Catholicism since Vatican II (1962-1965), God has blessed the preaching of his Word in many parts of the world. Thousands of missionaries from the third world have now joined missionaries from western countries on the mission field.

In spite of atheistic communism in the Soviet republics and China, there are now millions of Christians in these countries. Recent figures indicate nearly 100 million Christians in China. And although most of the world's 6 billion people do have the Bible in their own language there are still hundreds of smaller tribes and peoples with no Scripture at all. The challenge, though, is to encourage people to read God's Word.

During the last 50 years, millions of people have heard the message of salvation by faith in Christ—in evangelistic crusades or through radio and television. The video *Jesus* has enabled many millions (who may not be able to read) to hear the gospel in their own language.

As the year 2000 approaches, many churches and missions are trying to do their part to reach the whole world. In this age of relativism and religious confusion, we need to keep the gospel clear. We believe that the evangelical faith based on the Word of God is the true apostolic faith according to the Scriptures.

We have not done all that we should in obedience to Christ's command but we are determined to press on like Paul and to be faithful to the Great Commission of our Lord, "to preach the gospel to every creature."

Charles A. Tipp, M.A., M.Th., was the first Secretary of the FEBInternational Board. He was professor at Central Baptist Seminary and Ontario Bible College for 27 years and served on the Mission Commission of the World Evangelical Fellowship from 1980 to 1989. He was also Associate Director of InterServe Mission. He and his wife, Olive, are members at Willowdale Baptist Church in Toronto.

This was taken from The Evangelical Baptist Magazine, Nov./Dec. 98

Guest Speakers

Ravi Zacharias

Kim Phuc

Gordon MacDonald

Paul Borthwick

Tony Campolo

Jim Cantelon

Continuing The Vision

2003 WORLD MISSIONS CONFERENCE

234

The Peoples Church Supports:

361	Missionaries
157	Nationals
72	Agencies
65	Countries
3	Short-term mission trips in 2003
34	Missionaries from The Peoples Church & Peoples Christian Academy

Missions Committee:

Reg Andrews
David Barker
Ginny Bridle, *Missions Assistant*
Bernd Gerber
Martha Kenney
Lorna Lawrence
Mee-Sha Lim
Connie Mycroft
Charles Price
David Williams, *Chair*

WMC Director of Operations:

Terry Bridle

The Peoples Church is an evangelical community committed to strategic global evangelization, the value and potential of people and integrity in all its ministries.

"A Community of Believers Putting Missions First!"

Peoples CHURCH TORONTO

374 Sheppard Avenue East
Toronto, Ontario
M2N 3B6
Phone 416-222-3341
Fax   416-222-3344

Into all the World

2003
MISSIONS CONFERENCE

Charles Price with some of the staff and participants of the 2003 Missions Conference.

Into all the World

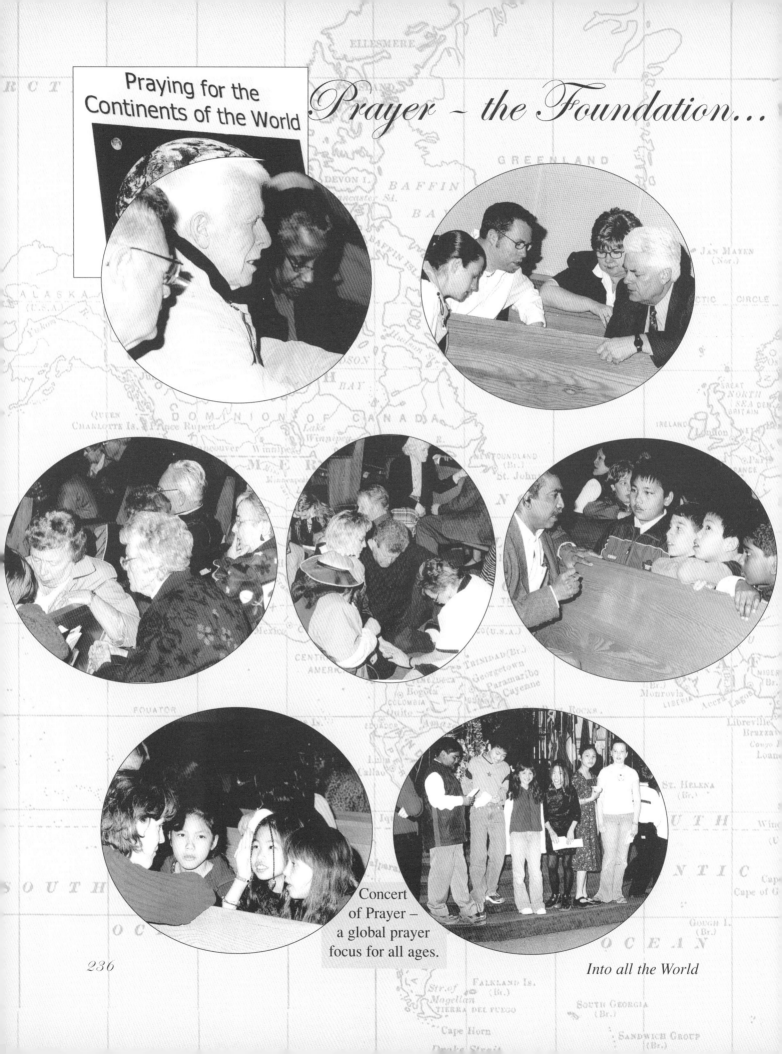

Praying for the Continents of the World

Prayer ~ the Foundation...

Concert of Prayer – a global prayer focus for all ages.

Speakers – to Communicate the Need...

Ravi Zacharias, world-renowned defender of the Christian faith.

Charles and Hilary Price with Kim Phuc, "the girl in the picture", who escaped from the Vietnam war. O.J. Smith in portrait.

Tony Campolo – Professor Emeritus of Sociology at Eastern College, PA; world-renowned Christian conference speaker.

Jim Cantelon, Founder and President of Visionledd, an agency devoted to addressing the AIDS crisis in Africa's Sub-Sahara. Well-known Canadian author and television host.

Paul Borthwick – Senior Consultant with Development Associates Int'l, a group dedicated to church leadership development in the under-resourced world.

Dr. Chris Marantika from Indonesia spoke at the Men's Breakfast.

Tom and Dr. Jean Froese (Chamberlain), reporting on their close encounter with tragedy in the slaying of three medical missionary personnel in Yemen.

Gordon MacDonald, Chairman of the Board of World Relief.

Stephen Saint, Mincaye and Charles Price. Stephen is the son of missionary pilot Nate Saint, who was killed by Auca Indians in the jungles of Ecuador. Mincaye was one of the killers.

Into all the World

Great Music...

The Visionaires from Indonesia.

Jeorge Zambrano & Michio Ozaki.

Sweet strains.

Sonia Reid.

The Peoples Church's own.

Major Youth Focus...

Soularize
Youth Band.

Into all the World

A Church with a World View...

Charles Price teaching a Missions seminar.

Great Stuff for Kids...

Into all the World

Mission Displays...

Willing Workers,
Good Food and Fellowship.

Into all the World

"I've had a
change of heart.
I'm convinced that we can
reach a city as well as a world
at the same time."
OJS

Eight

The Life and Ministry
of
The Peoples Church
in Toronto

The Life and Ministry of the Church in Toronto.

The church at home.

The Peoples Church has become known as, *"The family church that puts World Missions first."*

Initially, the emphasis on Missions and evangelism at The Peoples Church far outweighed the family aspect. During the latter part of 1951 and the first half of 1952 alone, there were no less than nine special series of meetings that ran every night except Saturday and often included three services on Sunday – 11:00 a.m., 3:00 p.m. and 7:00 p.m. Some even had a fourth service on the final Sunday at 9:00 p.m. The amazing thing is that they all attracted enormous crowds.

However; with the tremendous changes in social structure, international mobility and the nature of the needs of the church members; growth meant changing with the times – not in terms of changing the message – just the delivery.

With the move to Sheppard Avenue, The Peoples Church increasingly became more of a nurturing body, strengthening its families and growing deep roots from which to reach out to the world. The departmental work of the church developed more with Paul Smith's ministry than it ever had under Oswald's leadership. Concentration on building the Sunday School, the Youth Ministry, the Christian School, the Musical Organizations, and other kinds of events – while still maintaining the missionary fervour – built The Peoples Church into what it is today.

In the early days, reaching out to the community was all about evangelism; while today's church focusses both on connecting man to God *and* to the church community. Oswald was tremendously interested in supporting such work as ex-Rabbi Bregman's outreach to the Jews in Toronto, Jimmie Johnson's ministry to ex-convicts, the Toronto Medical Institute, outreach to the children in the slum areas, and in developing a summer program in the Muskokas where people could vacation affordably in a Christian environment.

Through all the changes, the church family supported one another individually and as a body. It is impossible for a human group to remain static. Sometimes looking back can mean a bittersweet nostalgia, a longing for the "good old days," but a solid foundation affords even more hope for the future than blessing in looking back.

Family scrapbook

Family scrapbooks detail snippets of family history through the years: memories shared; loss of loved ones; recital programmes and milestones. That's the stuff of this chapter – the church family at home.

TORONTO GOSPEL

TABERNACLE

42 Gerrard Street E., near Yonge.   Rev. Oswald J. Smith, Pastor

THE WATCHMAN

The official organ of the Toronto Gospel Tabernacle, 42 Gerrard Street East.

Office: 22 Kendal Avenue, Toronto, Canada.

Telephone: Midway 5859.

Editor - - - - Oswald J. Smith

Managing Editor and Treasurer L. Watson.

The Watchman is distributed, free of charge, to everyone attending Communion in the Tabernacle on the first Sunday of each month, and is mailed to all contributors outside the city.

"I have made thee a watchman: therefore hear the Word at my mouth ,and give warning" (Ezek. 3:17).

"Watchman, what of the night? Watchman, what of the night? The watchman said, The morning cometh, and also the night" (Isa. 21:11-12).

The Toronto Gospel Tabernacle is an independent, evangelistic, missionary work, co-operating with all evangelical organizations, but connected with none. It stands four square for the great fundamentals of the Faith.

*   *   *

Associate Pastors

Rev. E. Ralph Hooper, B.A., M.D.
Rev. H. W. Jackson   Rev. A. Sims
Rev. R. Cecil Palmer, M.A. (Cantab.)

Elders

John Souster, Edward Day, R. H. Johnston, Sid. Perkins, H. H. Phinnemore, Chas. Wayman, J. A. Garratt, Chas. Brothers, Thos. Ward, Eldon B. Lehman, S. Hawthorne, L. W. Wood, R. J. Hall, R. C. Dunn, G. W. Scott, E. Wenzel, J. Pike, Henry Bregman, George Angus, H. P. Wanless, J. C. Bradley, Fred Turney, L. Watson, L. F. Shields, F. W. Stockhausen, Dr. A. O. Derbyshire.

*   *   *

SUNDAY

1. **Senior Sunday School**—10 a.m., Chas. P. Wayman, Supt.
2. **Adult Bible Class**—10 a.m., Rev. R. Cecil Palmer, M.A. (Cantab.), Teacher.
3. **Elders' Prayer Meeting**—10.15 a.m., H. P. Wanless, Leader.
4. **Junior Sunday School**—11 a.m., Chas. P. Wayman, Supt.
5. **Preaching Service**—11 a.m., Rev. Oswald J. Smith.
6. **Men's Bible Class**—3 p.m., Samuel Hawthorne, Teacher.
7. **Meeting for Prayer**—6 p.m., Cecil Young, Leader.
8. **Preaching Service**—7 p.m., Rev. Oswald J. Smith.

MONDAY

9. **Christian Boys' Association**—7.30 p.m., Wm. Cundy, Leader.
10. **Junior Girls**—8 p.m., Mrs. H. Howard, Leader.
11. **Young Men**—8 p.m., S. Hawthorne. Leader; L. Watson, Teacher.
12. **Young Women**—8 p.m., Margaret McKee, Leader; Mrs. O. J. Smith, Teacher.

WEDNESDAY

13. **Women's Prayer Meeting**—2.30 p.m., Mrs. G. W. Scott, Leader.
14. **Preaching Service**—7.45 p.m., Rev. Oswald J. Smith.

FRIDAY

15. **Children's Service**—at 8 p.m., Fred. Turney, Leader.
16. **Prayer Meeting**—8 p.m., A. Porter, Leader.

NOTE

Mr. Smith preaches Sundays at 11 a.m. and 7 p.m. Wednesdays at 7.45 p.m.

Full Choir at all three Preaching Services, Eldon B. Lehman, Song Leader and Choir Director.

The Sunday Evening Service is broadcast from 7 to 8.30 over Radio Station CKCL.

The Lord's Supper is observed on the First Sunday of each month at the Morning Service, Edward Day, Director.

Personal Workers' Class meets on the First Sunday of each month at 4.30 p.m. Mr. L. Watson, Miss Alice Porter and Miss Blanche Creiger in charge.

Christian Volunteers meet on the first Tuesday of each month at 7.45 p.m. Mrs. Maud Howe and Miss Reba Fleming, Leaders.

A Half Night of Prayer is held on the last Friday of each month.

Office: 22 Kendal Ave.   Phone MIdway 5859
Miss Alice Porter - Office Secretary
Treasurer - - - Mr. L. Watson
Secretary - - Mr. W. C. Willis
Janitor - Chas. Edwards, Waverley 7058
Head Ushers: R. H. Johnston, H. H. Phinnemore, John Souster.

*   *   *

Foreign Missions

The Toronto Gospel Tabernacle is represented in the Foreign Field by three soul-winning Missionary Societies:

The Russian Border Mission, where our missionaries are preaching the Gospel on the Soviet Border of Russia. Pastor John Kurcit, Superintendent.

The Russian Refugee Mission, where our missionaries are evangelizing the thousands of Russians in France. Judge George Urban, Director.

The Spanish Gospel Mission, where we are training young men in our Bible School, and sending them as flaming Evangelists into Central Spain. Rev. F. David Sholin, Dean.

All this in addition to our work in Ethiopia, Northern Ontario, and among the Jews in Toronto.

Remittances are forwarded to the various fields on the first day of each month.

Send all gifts for the support of this great work to the Toronto Gospel Tabernacle, 22 Kendal Ave., Toronto, Canada.

Facts About the Peoples Church

The work of The Peoples Church has been most encouraging. Every department reports progress. It is a veritable beehive of activities.

Campaigns

Various speakers have occupied the pulpit from time to time.

Ralph Underwood, a converted atheist, formerly Associate Editor of "The Godless World", delivered four addresses to splendid audiences, Feb. 13th to 16th.

Mrs. Charles M. Alexander Dixon, who founded the Pocket Testament League, spoke on "Days of Heaven on Earth" to a capacity audience Sunday morning, February 18th.

Rev. Thos. M. Chalmers, D.D., head of the New York Jewish Mission, delivered four addresses, Feb. 20th to 23rd. Dr. Chalmers recently returned from a visit to the Holy Land.

Mr. Wm. R. Newell, noted Bible Teacher, will speak in The Peoples Church, each night, March 13th to 16th inclusive.

Engagements

Rev. Oswald J. Smith went to Detroit to hold special meetings, Feb. 27th to March 2nd.

From March 6th to 9th Mr. Smith is speaking in the Alliance Tabernacle, Ottawa, Ont.

He then goes to Carnegie Hall to speak at the Alliance Convention, Pittsburgh, March 13th to 16th.

From March 20th to 23rd, Mr. Smith goes to Chicago to hold special meetings.

He is booked for Toledo to speak at the Alliance Convention, April 3rd to 6th.

May 11th to 13th Mr. Smith will be delivering addresses at the Missionary Convention in the Moody Church, Chicago.

Mr. Smith conducts Revival Services in the Tabernacle at Birmingham, Alabama, May 24th to June 3rd, following the Annual Council of the Christian and Missionary Alliance.

From June 23rd to July 1st Mr. Smith speaks each day at the American Keswick, New Jersey, under the auspices of The Sunday School Times.

Young People's Work

Miss Hilda L. Aldridge, Leader of the Young Women, writes as follows: "This is the fourth year of our Young Women's work in The Peoples Church. We have an average attendance of 75 each Monday night when we meet to study God's Word and enjoy Christian fellowship. Miss Blanche Creiger has been leading us in a study of the Old Testament and its spiritual teaching. Each month we correspond with Mrs. Sholin, our missionary in Spain, and her letters in response are always a great inspiration as well as a prayer challenge. We had the joy of providing six families with Christmas baskets, in conjunction with the young men, last year. On two occasions all the young people have met in a joint meeting. Rev. Silas Fox of India was the speaker the first time and the Evangelistic Band of the Toronto Bible College took charge on the second night."

Young Men's Work

Mr. Herb Whaely, Leader of the Young Men's group, writes as follows: "Mr. L. Watson is the teacher for the Young Men, and he has been speaking on the parables. Real interest has been manifested each Monday night and many of our young men are attending and enjoying the fellowship."

Sunday School

Mr. J. Pike, Secretary of the Sunday School, sends in the following report: "Our Sunday School has three departments. The Primary, under the leadership of Miss Peterman, meets from eleven to twelve, and has an average attendance of 54, and a Cradle Roll of 35. The Juniors meet at the same hour and have an average attendance of 74. The Senior School, with the Adult Bible Class, meets at ten with an average of 88 attendance. The School has been supporting a missionary in the foreign field and providing partial support for another. The aim of the Superintendent, Mr. C. P.

Dr. P.W. Philpott (left), with the noted tenor soloist, Arthur W. McKee (right), held a great evangelistic Campaign in November of 1934. Dr. Philpott was known world-wide as the Pastor of the famous Moody Church in Chicago.

1936 – Thirty-seven of the forty-six Elders of The Peoples Church.

Wayman, and his staff of workers, is to lead the scholars to Christ and then to send them out to tell others. Many definite decisions have been made.

Women's Prayer Meeting

Mrs. G. W. Scott, Leader of the Women's Prayer Meeting group, writes as follows: "Under the direction of the pastor we opened the first Women's Weekly Prayer Meeting in The Peoples Church in May 1931 with eleven present. The interest has deepened and the attendance has increased until now we have an average of well over 60. Our meetings from the beginning have been honored with the presence of the Holy Spirit. As we have taken on our hearts in prayer all the activities of the Church, including Foreign work and outside requests, our vision has been enlarged so that we girdle the Globe with our prayers. Many women who were timid in prayer have developed into strong prayer-warriors, and we rejoice in the answers received."

Junior Girls

Mrs. H. Howard, Leader of the group of 'teen age girls, sends in the following report: "Our Junior group was started in the fall of 1931 for girls from eleven to sixteen years of age. The membership then was six. It has increased to 40 with an average attendance of 28. We have a splendid leader in the person of Miss Lillian Pepper. She has been most faithful with Miss Vivian St. Clair as pianist and Miss Evelyn Landon as secretary. During the summer several girls took part in open air services. Others were active as personal workers. Last year the Million Testament League supplied us with Testaments for distribution among High School and Collegiate students. Over 400 were given out on the condition that at least one chapter be read every day."

Junior Boys

Mr. Gordon Whaely, Leader of the Boys, reports as follows: "In these days of doubt it is a great privilege to present the Gospel to 'teen age boys. We have now an average attendance of nine and every one is a professing Christian. These boys are being taught God's Word and led into Christian service. They are eager to see others brought to Jesus Christ. We meet each Monday night and would appreciate the prayers of those interested.

Choir and Orchestra

It is impossible to express our appreciation and the appreciation of countless thousands in Radio Land for the work of the Choir and Orchestra, under the able leadership of Eldon B. Lehman. Every Wednesday night, every Sunday morning, and through the long hours Sunday night, these faithful singers stand by us in getting out the Message. In spite of the fact that many of them have to get up as usual and go to work Monday morning, they are with us until eleven o'clock Sunday night. There are

more than 100 altogether connected with these two organizations. We thank God for an evangelistic choir and orchestra, for singers willing to sing simple Gospel messages and thus reach the hearts of thousands who are unable to appreciate classical music. Mr. Lehman has the one outstanding qualification, next to spirituality, which is absolutely indispensable in a Song Leader. God has given him the gift which has been denied many great and highly trained musicians. We praise Him for such a leader and for every voice in our choir, for singers consecrated, and for the blessing that our songs have been to vast multitudes everywhere.

Elders and Ushers

Our Elders faithfully serve the Communion on the first Sunday of each month and regularly visit the sick. At every service our Ushers are busy taking care of the crowds. The Personal Workers are always ready when the invitation is given. God alone knows what we owe to the Prayer Warriors who intercede on behalf of souls.

Converts

It was a great joy to hear testimonies from converts of the past four years at a special meeting held in February. Groups won during 1930, 1931, 1932, 1933 and even 1934 joyfully told of how they had been converted. There may be some who come to the altar who are not saved, but there are certainly a large number as was evidenced by the testimonies, who have had a real experience of salvation and have stood true for months and even years. May God more and more make The Peoples Church the birthplace of hundreds of souls.

$25,000

For many, many months, on account of the large crowds, we have been requested to build a great central auditorium, and from time to time we have suggested that someone might have $25,000 available for such a purpose. We have suggested such a sum as a "fleece", that we might know positively the mind of the Lord. We do not believe in church mortgages, nor in debt. Hence we feel that we must have sufficient before we commence. It would be very easy for us to build a large evangelistic centre and put a mortgage on it for some future generation to pay, and upon which there would be heavy interest for many years, as other churches do. But we feel so strongly about this that we would rather continue in our present building, which seats 1,500, and have it overcrowded, than to involve our people, especially in these days of depression. It is our conviction that God has a man or a woman somewhere who has plenty of money, more than will ever be needed in this life, who will be led to make such an investment. We have had a gift of $500.00 for this purpose, but we are still praying and

waiting to see God work. There is nothing too hard for Jesus.

Large Crowds

The Peoples Church does not commence to accommodate the crowds attending. We do not advertise in the newspapers at all and yet on Sunday nights scores have to stand, sometimes more than 100, around the walls, throughout the entire service, and large numbers are turned away. This does not apply to special occasions. It is a weekly affair, just in our ordinary work. We regret exceedingly the limited capacity of our building for the multitudes are still hungry for the Gospel and are eager to attend where it is preached. We seat 1,500, but we often have more present, especially on Sunday nights. Thank God the days of revival have not yet passed.

Radio

For three hours every Sunday night we are on the Air. We broadcast over CKCL. Multiplied thousands listen in. Letters received tell of untold blessing and many have been saved. We have had wonderful testimonies from some who heard the Message over the Air and were definitely converted. We consider our Radio ministry our most valuable work aside from what we are doing in the foreign field. We go off the Air the last Sunday in April and will not be heard again in Radio Land until the first Sunday of October.

Foreign Fields

The Peoples Church is carrying on work in five different foreign fields, namely, on the Soviet Border of Russia, among the Russian Refugees of France, Spain, the Isle of Bali, and Peru. Full allowances have been paid throughout the year. We received more than $23,000 for our foreign work alone during 1933. Advances have been made and many souls definitely won to Christ.

The Watchman

Our magazine, "The Watchman", is published monthly. It contains prophetic articles and reports direct from the Fields. We send it free to all those living outside the city of Toronto, who contribute a dollar or more toward our missionary work. Those living in Toronto get it on Communion Sunday in The Peoples Church. It is published from October until May, inclusive, each year.

Books

Orders are being received from all over the world for our books. We now have six on Prophecy at 25c each, paper bound, and five on the Deeper Life at 75c, cloth bound. Many letters have been received telling of unique blessing. Our Salvation booklets are now going into the prisons and jails of Ontario through the instrumentality of "Benny" Wilson, the Street Preacher. We would covet the prayers of God's people for His blessing upon the prisoners.

TESTIMONIES

"Let the Redeemed of

"I thank God for leading me to The Peoples Church Oct. 2, 1931, when I was restored back to my loving Saviour and am enjoying a born-again experience. Praise the Lord."—*Mrs. E. P.*

* * * * *

"On Nov. 4th, 1934, I found the Lord Jesus as my personal Saviour, and am serving and praising Him."—*Mr. W. Y.*

* * * * *

"Our sinful past has been forgiven, our present is hid with Christ in God, our future is in the hands of Him who saved us. For Jesus Christ became our Saviour on Sept. 13th, 1931, in The Peoples Church."—*Mr. and Mrs. G. S. W.*

* * * * *

"On Nov. 4th, 1934, I found the Lord Jesus as my own personal Saviour, and since then, 'My hope is built on nothing less than Jesus' blood and righteousness. I dare not trust the sweetest frame, but wholly lean on Jesus' name'."—*Mrs. W. Y.*

* * * * *

"On April 8th, 1934, I was born again, washed in the Blood, cleansed of sin, and am now a new creature in Christ. Praise God, He saves, He keeps, He satisfies."—*Mary E. F.*

* * * * *

"I praise God for saving my soul, April 8th, 1934, from the doom which I was headed for. I would not exchange salvation for the world and all its wealth."—*A. J. F.*

* * * * *

me in His love. I will be thirteen years old in June."—*Jack G.*

* * * * *

"Seeking salvation from sin and happiness in life, I found both in Jesus, God's Son. What a privilege it is to know the love of Christ!"—*W. E.*

* * * * *

"I was restored to fellowship with Christ in The Peoples Church. This has been the happiest year of my life. 'There is joy in serving Jesus'."—*L. N.*

* * * * *

"I am glad to be able to testify to the saving grace and keeping power of the Lord Jesus Christ. I accepted Him on the fourteenth of January, 1932, and will never cease praising Him for all He has done. My song shall ever be 'Jesus! Jesus only!' "—*F. B.*

* * * * *

"In the month of September, 1933, at The Peoples Church, I was restored from backsliding. I have found in Jesus a Saviour who is mighty to save and to keep."—*E. N.*

* * * * *

"On Sept. 16th, last year, at The Peoples Church, I was restored from a backslidden condition, and since then I have found that God hears and answers prayer."—*R. L.*

* * * * *

"While Mr. Smith was holding revival services at Victoria Presbyterian Church, the Lord spoke very definitely to me on the text John 1:5-12, and I saw myself a lost sinner although a church member, and then and there, May 17, 1933, I accepted the Lord Jesus Christ as my own personal Saviour, and oh, the joy and peace that has been mine since that happy night."—*H. E. H.*

* * * * *

"I am glad to testify to the saving and keeping power of the Lord Jesus Christ. In the early summer of 1931 I accepted Him as my own personal Saviour."—*Mrs. H. C. P.*

* * * * *

"I was converted Sept. 23, 1934. I am so glad to have found the Lord Jesus. 'Therefore being justified by faith we have peace with God through our Lord Jesus Christ'."—*Mrs. M. A.*

In the early years, The Peoples Church enjoyed a perennial revival. Every week great crowds gathered and souls were saved. In 1934, over 400 responded to the invitation to accept Christ. In 1935, the number rose to nearly 500. Sunday after Sunday, hundreds of people stood in the aisles and vestibules, and walked down the aisles to accept Jesus Christ. The Peoples Church became known as Toronto's great evangelistic center for revival work.

OF CONVERTS

the Lord Say So"

"Accepted Jesus Christ on December 10th, 1933, in The Peoples Church. John 3:16 is my assurance. Now permanently employed bringing other souls into His Kingdom."—*H. L.*

* * * * *

"I was saved Nov. 1931, through listening to the services broadcasted from The Peoples Church. 'He that heareth my Word and believeth on Him that sent Me, hath everlasting life'."—*Mrs. E. B.*

* * * * *

"At my Radio, Oct. 15th, 1933, I was gloriously saved by God's wonderful grace and mercy. How truly I can say, ' *I have been born again'*. I'll praise His name forever."—*W. T.*

* * * * *

"In 1930 I came to know Jesus Christ as my own personal Saviour at a service conducted by Rev. O. J. Smith. I rejoice in having been called out of darkness into His blessed light."—*Miss G. R.*

* * * * *

"On Jan. 3rd, 1935, at 1.30, in the office of The Peoples Church, Mr. Smith led me to Jesus. If you want to know why I'm happy, read Romans 8:38, 39." —*Wm. R. J. W.*

* * * * *

"I was saved in May, 1933, over the Air, and can truthfully say, 'O happy day that fixed my choice'. To the sinner I say, 'O taste and see'."—*Mrs. W. L.*

* * * * *

"I had been in turn an Anglican, a Roman Catholic and Baptist. On April 15, 1934, I was 'born again', brought into fellowship with God through Jesus Christ, my sin-bearer."—*Miss J. L.*

* * * * *

"Two years ago at The Peoples Church a self-righteous, religious sinner asked Jesus to save her. And He did. I praise God for the joy, gladness and peace that have been mine ever since—a peace that the world cannot give and cannot take away."—*Miss L. B.*

* * * * *

"I was wonderfully saved on Jan. 17th, 1934, at The Peoples Church, and I have rejoiced in life since I accepted Jesus Christ as my personal Saviour."—*Mrs. A. E.*

"I have given my heart to Jesus. I have peace within my soul. He has set the joy-bells ringing. And He has made me whole. Hallelujah!"—*Mrs. E. B.*

* * * * *

"I was saved in Jesus Christ Jan. 6, 1935, and can honestly say I have never before known such peace. I am glad to acknowledge Jesus as my Redeemer."—*M. G.*

* * * * *

"I am glad Jesus saved my husband and myself Easter Sunday, 1933. We are now happy in Him and we know that we are His and He is ours."—*Mr. and Mrs. L.*

* * * * *

"I was saved in The Peoples Church last October. I had read the Bible but never before did I clearly understand it. Now, since being 'born again', the more I read it the more I know what the peace that passeth all understanding is."—*Mae B.*

* * * * *

"For nearly two years my Saviour and I have travelled life's pathway side by side, and to me this world's pleasures have grown strangely dim since my pleasures are now found in Him. I was born again Jan. 25, 1933.—*Miss D. S.*

* * * * *

"Saved June 11th, 1931. I had never been in any church for eleven years. I shall ever praise God that when I did go it was to The Peoples Church where I found Him."—*Miss C. C.*

* * * * *

"Saved 1934. Jesus said: 'I am the door: by Me if any man enter in he shall be saved' (John 10:9). I thank God I have found that door through Jesus Christ."—*Mrs. H. M.*

* * * * *

"I was saved May 8th, 1933. The world lured me back, but did not satisfy. I came back to Jesus April 15th, 1934, in The Peoples Church, and have found complete satisfaction in Him."—*H. S.*

* * * * *

"I was saved in The Peoples Church Jan. 28th, 1934, and I have found joy and peace in serving Jesus, and I know God answers prayer. Praise His name!" —*Mrs. R. W.*

Ex-Rabbi Bregman, Founder of "The House of Seekers after Truth", a Faith Mission to the Jewish people.

Ministry to the Jews.

In the early days, The Toronto Gospel Tabernacle (later The Peoples Church) was very supportive of ex-Rabbi H. Bregman's work among the Jewish people of Toronto. Oswald Smith felt his work to be of great importance in the city.

Bregman had a deep compassion for the Jewish people, not only because of their suffering under the hands of Hitler and the Nazis, but because there was a great deal of confusion among them with regard to Christianity. Most Jews thought all Germans were Christians. This lack of distinction between "Gentile" and "Christian" had become an enormous stumbling block in preaching the Gospel to them. He held Bible classes and great open-air meetings in Toronto where Jews gathered around him by the hundreds and received tracts as he preached to them in their own language. The Peoples Church worked alongside him supportively, often holding joint services in reaching out to the Toronto Jews.

1934 – Ex-Rabbi H. Bregman preaching to an audience of Jews on Spadina Avenue.

House of Seekers After Truth, 312 Borden Street, Toronto.

Missionary Medical Institute.

The Missionary Medical Institute was the realization of one of Oswald Smith's dreams. For years, he had seen missionaries in remote areas trying to cope with medical problems for which they had little or no training. He shared his burden with Miss Louise Kirby, a Toronto teaching nurse. Together they formed the Medical Institute under the umbrella of The Peoples Church, using the church's facilities at 100 Bloor Street East.

From 1936 to 1944, the church conducted the Institute at 14 Park Road, Toronto, under the leadership of Louise Kirby. Prospective missionaries were given a year's instruction in medicine and tropical diseases by 12 Toronto physicians, surgeons and dentists who volunteered their teaching services. Several Toronto hospitals granted the Institute hospital privileges to hold clinics.

By 1941 the Institute had outgrown its church facilities and the congregation purchased the adjoining property at l4 Park Road to house the growing medical facility. By 1943, 145 missionaries had graduated from the one-year course with a diploma in tropical, infectious and children's diseases and other related subjects.

The institute, now called "Missionary Health Institute", exists as a consortium of doctors' offices near North York General Hospital. As specialists in tropical diseases, the medics who practice there serve missionaries and other travelers with shots and advice.

In recommending the work of the Missionary Medical Institute of The Peoples Church, the biographer of the great pioneer missionary, James Gilmour of Mongolia, quoted him as saying:

> "I am told that professional men are suspicious of giving a little medical knowledge to young men going out as missionaries. I sided with them till I came here, but here the case is different. At home it is all very well to stand before the fire in your own room, within sight of the brass plate on the doctor's door on the opposite side of the street, and talk about the danger of a little knowledge; but when you are two weeks' journey from any assistance, and see your fellow traveller sitting silent and swollen with violent toothache for days together, you fervently wish you had a pair of forceps and the dangerous amount of knowledge."

Students of the Missionary Medical Institute of The Peoples Church, Toronto. Miss Kirby, Superintendent, far right. In 1937, there were 25 students in the Institute.

FINANCIAL STATEMENT OF

For the Year Ended, December 31st, 1939

CHURCH ACCOUNT

RECEIPTS		DISBURSEMENTS	
Cash Balance in Bank, January 1, 1939 ...... $ 466.21		Allowances, proportion	$ 2,033.20
Offerings and Radio Gifts for year 22,323.12		Pastor's Stipend	4,800.00
		Superannuation Fund	587.50
	$22,789.33	Campaigns and Pulpit Supply	2,499.22
Bank Overdraft, December 31, 1939	836.02	Radio Broadcasting	3,801.75
		Pipe Organ (total cost)	3,500.00
		Equipment and Supplies	1,615.68
		Maintenance and Repairs	395.62
		Light, Fuel, Gas and Water	1,058.09
		Telephone and Telegraph	163.57
		Stationery, proportion	148.20
		Sundry Office Expenses, etc.	506.37
		Bank Exchange	15.14
		Advertising	196.57
		Postage, Proportion	310.97
		Magazine Expense (less advertising receipts) proportion	1,220.99
		Relief	386.51
		Music Supplies	249.35
		Sunday School Supplies	136.62
		Total Disbursements for year	$23,625.35
	$23,625.35		$23,625.35

Telephone ELgin 1453   **Gunn, Roberts & Co.**   Cable Address "Gunroco"

Edmund Gunn
Frank E. Roberts
Fred'k C. Hurst
Guy W. Smith

Chartered Accountants
36 Toronto Street
Toronto 2, Canada

London Agents
Derbyshire & Co.,
Chartered Accountants
4 Southampton Row, W.C.1

February 15, 1940

Rev. Oswald J. Smith, D.D., President
The Peoples Church
100 Bloor Street East
Toronto, Ontario

Dear Sir,

We enclose herewith five signed copies of our report in connection with the audit of the accounts of the treasurer. We understand that it is your intention to publish these Statements of Receipts and Disbursements, together with our certificate, in The Peoples Monthly, published by you.

We take this opportunity of expressing our appreciation of the assistance afforded us by Mr. Lehman, and would like to congratulate him on the efficient way in which he keeps his books of record.

If we can give you any further assistance we shall be pleased to hear from you.

Yours very truly,
GUNN, ROBERTS & CO.

BUILDING ACCOUNT

RECEIPTS		DISBURSEMENTS	
Cash Balance in Bank, January 1, 1939 ...... $ 183.26		Mortgage, on account of Principal	$5,000.00
Pledge Percentage transferred from Missions $6,992.48		Mortgage Interest (1 year to April 30, 1939)	1,000.00
Sundry Receipts 100.00		Taxes (1939)	446.82
Bank Interest 26.86		Legal Fees and Charges	204.10
		Total Disbursements for year	$6,650.92
Total Receipts for year	7,119.34	Cash Balance in Bank, December 31, 1939	651.68
	$7,302.60		$7,302.60

Note—Original cost of land and building in 1937 ...... $65,000.00
Paid on account to Dec. 31, 1939 ...... 50,000.00

Balance owing as at Dec. 31, 1939 ...... $15,000.00

REPORT OF AUDITORS

We have examined the Church, Missions, Building and Books Accounts of The Peoples Church, Toronto, for the year ended December 31st, 1939, and report that the attached Statements of Receipts and Disbursements are in accord therewith.

Vouchers covering disbursements have been presented to us, and the receipts have been verified in so far as to determine that they are in agreement with amounts shown in the books.

The bank balances have been reconciled with a certificate received by us from the bank.

GUNN, ROBERTS & CO.,
Chartered Accountants

Toronto, February 14, 1940.

THE PEOPLES CHURCH

Eldon B. Lehman, General Treasurer

MISSIONS ACCOUNT

RECEIPTS		
Cash Balance in Bank, January 1, 1939		$ 6,996.87
Contributions	$39,414.76	
Specified Gifts	6,661.40	
	$46,076.16	
Less Pledge percentage transferred to Building Account	6,992.48	
Total Receipts for year		39,083.68

Total Income from all sources .. $77,904.09

DISBURSEMENTS		
Russian Refugee Mission	$8,014.04	
Russian Border Mission	5,110.31	
Spanish Gospel Mission	843.21	
West Indies Mission	3,853.20	
		$17,820.76
Christian and Missionary Alliance—		
French West Africa	900.00	
French Indo-China	900.00	
Dutch East Indies	1,933.63	
		3,733.63
Evangelical Union of S. America	1,440.00	
South African General Mission	1,310.00	
Unevangelized Fields Mission	1,285.00	
China Inland Mission	600.00	
Sudan United Mission	1,391.00	
The India Mission	906.26	
Colombia, South America	921.69	
Indo-Burma Pioneer Mission	1,323.50	
South Sea Evangelical Mission	319.32	
Greek Amer. Missionary Society	237.00	
Bethel Mission—China	1,311.84	
United Aborigines Mission of Australia	259.07	
Mr. Silas Fox, India	283.23	
European Evangelistic Fellowship	250.84	
Other Fields	450.21	
		12,288.96
Total to Foreign Missions		33,843.35
Home Missions		4,101.07
Total to all Missions		$37,944.42
Magazine Expense and Postage, proportion		1,100.00
Convention Expenses		469.81
Allowances, proportion		1,500.00
Stationery, etc., proportion		316.28
Bank Exchange		16.15
Total Disbursements for year		$41,346.66
Cash Balance in Bank, December 31, 1939		4,733.89

$46,080.55 $46,080.55

BOOKS ACCOUNT

RECEIPTS	
Cash Balance in Bank, January 1, 1939	$ 928.01
Sales for year	5,758.86

DISBURSEMENTS	
Publications and Purchases	$3,570.65
Commissions	628.25
Allowances, proportion	1,000.00
Magazine Expense, proportion	200.00
Advertising	319.96
Postage	154.49
Supplies and Stationery, proportion	103.71
Bank Exchange	4.01
Total Disbursements for year	$5,981.07
Cash Balance in Bank, December 31, 1939	705.80

$6,686.87 $6,686.87

Our Work in Toronto's Worst Slum District

By Rev. John Addison, Supt. The Peoples Mission, a work recently taken over by The Peoples Church

COULD I, with my pen, paint an accurate picture of slum conditions it would be hard for the reader to believe that such conditions actually existed in the city known as "Toronto the good, the city of churches". Ex-Lieut.-Governor Bruce some time ago stated that the district of the Don was Toronto's worst slum. It is of this district I wish to speak.

For three years I have laboured for the Lord in this district, and have seen the hand of the Lord work in a mysterious way, both in the work of the mission and also in the lives of the people.

Our district lies in the south middle-east of the city, from Parliament Street to River Street. This district runs south to the lake, where large oil refineries and coal docks help to create dreadful odours and lay a smoke screen over the entire district. There are many factories, and under the shadows of these large, noisy places of industry hundreds of small homes shelter.

One of the first things that strikes the stranger to the district is the hundreds of little streets, or as we call them, Places —little alleys running off alleys, rows of houses built in the backyards of what was at one time a respectable home. Many of these Places will have as many as thirty-eight homes with approximately two hundred and fifty people living in them. I once entered a home that had forty people living in it; there were thirteen living in two rooms, or rather, in a dining room and parlour. The mother had to turn the table upside down and make a bed in it for the baby in order to find enough room. There are other smaller rooms, with far too many sleeping and eating in them.

Not only are the homes crowded, but also the backyards are very small, and to look down from above at them they look more like the little pens at a country fair used to keep pigs in a huddle. These backyards force the boys and girls to play on the street, and their little lives are hazarded by the heavy traffic that must pass through the streets to the factories. Another peril to these little lives who must play on the dirty streets is the terrible blaspheming and cursing, foul language and behaviour of drunken men and women. I have many a time looked out from my study window and have seen thirteen or more men and women lying or sitting on the street curb drunk, and all too many times we see women, mothers of large families.

As one considers these circumstances they can readily see why we say that many of the children of this district have very little idea of what home life is, or the love of a mother and father. From babyhood up they hear nothing but swearing and cursing from a drunken mother or father. Not only is drink a curse but so many of the women of the district, because of poverty, have become prostitutes, and little girls and boys see this evil practiced right before their eyes. Lust has such a grip on these poor, benighted souls that often a brother has no thought for his sister, or father for

Rev. John Addison

his own daughter, and often children are born into the family because of this indecent behaviour. I know of one case that is worthy of mention.

A certain young girl who is now saved and is desiring to be baptized, tells the sad story—facts that have ruined, to a certain extent, her whole life. At the age of fourteen or fifteen she gave birth to a child, the child lived only a few months, but the girl testified that her own father was the father of her child. Had this young girl come to know Christ as she knows Him now this terrible thing would not have happened to her. This girl is only one; there are many more who need our help, who need Christ.

Speaking of sin, I would like to mention a remarkable conversion of a young girl of nineteen. One night I was speaking on John 3:16. As I gave the invitation, along with several others, this young lady raised her hand signifying her desire to accept Christ as Saviour. While being dealt with, tears ran down her cheeks. giving expression to agony of soul; she told us how she had travelled the underworld, she had associated with Chinamen, and had come to the place where she intended committing suicide in the Don River, which flows nearby the mission. After she had told of her sinfulness she asked, Can Christ save such a sinner as I? Can He give me a new life and a new start in life?

The worker's reply came as dew from heaven. Yes, Christ can do all that and more. for the Word of God promises that He will restore the years that the locust has eaten. This young lady there and then accepted the Lord Jesus Christ as her personal Saviour, and took her cigarettes out of her purse and put a New Testament in. A life saved from a watery grave. a life saved from hell, a life saved for time and eternity because she met Christ in our mission.

Send all gifts for The Peoples Mission to The Peoples Church, 100 Bloor East. Toronto.

Young People – 1941.

In the forties, the Young Peoples group met on Monday evenings at 8:00 p.m., and 80 of them participated in a choir on Wednesday evenings. Led by Fred Swallow, the purpose was to conserve and develop spiritual talents in young men and women through a variety of activities and to equip them to serve the Lord at home and on the foreign field.

Two trained groups of young people were ready to take meetings, and received practical experience in preaching, taking charge of meetings, personal work and the development of musical talent. They conducted open-air work on the streets of Toronto and in neighbouring towns. This type of work proved to be one of the most fruitful mediums through which souls might be won to Christ, and at the same time, the young people, themselves, be built up in the faith. By this means, in 1940, 80 souls made decisions for Christ and over fifteen thousand tracts were distributed on the street corners of Toronto. The young people were challenged to get into what was claimed to be one of the most important fields of Christian work – Children's work.

Sunday School, 1941.

From the time the Sunday School was first organized in the early thirties, with seven children, it increased to approximately 700 by 1941, with well-organized 9:30 a.m. classes for all ages.

The first duty of the teachers was to lead the boys and girls and men and women, to a personal surrender of their lives to the Lord Jesus Christ. Memory work was allotted each Sunday, giving an opportunity to hide God's Word in their hearts.

The importance of foreign missions and their support by systematic giving was a vital part of the education of all Sunday School pupils. This was evidenced by the fact that $1,300 per annum was given to Missions through all departments and classes. Mostly self-supporting for supplies, Sunday School papers, etc., the Sunday School took great pride in the fact that a number of its young men and women were already serving in foreign fields

Children's Evangelistic Campaign.
In response to a startling report form the Chief Constable of Toronto, stating that the number of juvenile crimes had risen from 383 in 1933 to 693 in 1935, The Peoples Church sent invitations to 42 Sunday School Superintendents of various denominations to confer in arranging a city-wide Children's Evangelistic Campaign. With active response from seven churches, great campaigns were held, resulting in 250 decisions for Christ.

Long before the campaigns actually began, the children of The Peoples Church held their own prayer meetings. When the time came, they went into action, canvassing the district and bringing in many children. The chalk-talks of Rev. Millaard Cairns of Los Angeles will live long in the memories of those who heard him. Prizes were given for bringing friends, Scripture memorization and the writing of essays. To any child who would promise to read the Gospel of John, a New Testament was given.

1935-The Highlands. In July and August 1935, Dr. Smith sponsored a Summer Bible Conference in Muskoka in a hotel called "The Highlands". There were 443 guests (400 of whom were young people) who paid between $12.00 and $20.00 per week, including rooms, meals and meetings.

The purpose was to provide an affordable center wholly given over to young people's work, where they could engage in all kinds of activities, both on land and water. The food, lodging and beach were excellent; the meetings were well attended and many lives were transformed.

HIGHLANDS SUMMER CONFERENCE

THE HIGHLANDS, on Lake Joseph, near Footes Bay, has one of the most beautiful situations in all Muskoka, with a wonderful vista of lake, islands and green hills. It is on a point surrounded on three sides by water, with a number of exquisite little bays. It has a number of fine tree-clad ridges, and plenty of cleared, level fields for games.

Nearly 200 acres, and its groves of trees, give ample room for hikes, while the deeply indented bays and the open lake provide every facility for boating, sailing or canoeing. It has one of the finest white-sand beaches in the district, gently sloping, and safe for the smallest children; while for those who want diving and deep water, there is plenty of scope at the dock, with its excellent spring-board.

HOW TO REACH THE HIGHLANDS

By Motor—134 miles north of Toronto by King's Highway No. 11, to Gravenhurst; turn left at Post Office on to Bala Road, a fine Provincial Gravel Highway, thence through Bala to The Highlands. Well marked; look for "The Highlands" sign. Arrangements are being made for De Luxe Coach Service on Saturdays at a special rate of $5.00 return.

By Train—Canadian National Railways from Toronto to Lake Joseph Station, and steamer to The Highlands dock, arriving in early afternoon. An alternative trip is by C.N.R. to Muskoka Wharf, or C.P.R. to Bala, and steamer through Lakes Muskoka, Rosseau and Joseph to The Highlands dock, arriving about 7 p.m. A wonderful scenic trip. Buy tickets and check baggage direct to The Highlands.

RECREATION—will be in charge of a competent Sports Director and a good time is assured to all. Baseball, tennis, boating, bathing, swimming and diving, aquatic sports; there is always something doing for those who wish to play. Boats or canoes may be rented by day or week.

ACCOMMODATION—Comfort without luxury. The Highlands is primarily a Young People's Conference. But for those who desire it, there are single and double rooms in the Hotel building at a little higher price. Beds are restful, meals ample and varied, with the very best in foods, well cooked and temptingly served; water, pure by Government test, milk pasteurized; meats, fish and vegetables fresh and wholesome. Cakes and pies baked in our own kitchens. You will be satisfied at The Highlands.

TUCK SHOP—We will have for sale souvenirs, candy, ice-cream, books, Kodak films, and many other small articles.

POST OFFICE—We have our own post office at which mails arrive and depart twice each day. Postal address is "Hamills Point, Lake Joseph, Muskoka". **Highlands operates on Toronto Time.**

PROGRAM—A spiritual program has been arranged for each day, with meetings at 11 a.m. and 8 p.m. Prominent Christian leaders will be present throughout the entire season. A folder announcing their dates will be printed and mailed later. They will speak twice daily. The services will be bright, brief and evangelistic in character.

RATES—Standard: $12.00 per week. $2.25 per day. (Four to six in a room). There are also a number of rooms in the hotel for those who desire more expensive accommodation. Rates: Two in a room $16.00 per week. $3.00 per day. Single rooms $20.00 per week. $3.50 per day. Children under twelve, half price. Due on arrival. The fee for registration is $1.00, payable with application,

Mel Trotter, formerly a drunkard, whom God saved and mightily used. His first appearance in Toronto was in 1906 in Massey Hall in the Torrey-Alexander meetings.

Mary Agnes Wagner, known as "The Girl Preacher". Her voice was deep and her descriptive portrayal of Old Testament characters unique.

Anthony Zeoli, shown above left as an ex-convict; right in 1937. A dynamic evangelist, he spoke with spiritual fervor and a great sense of humour, holding the rapt attention of his audience from start to finish. Billed as "The Walking Bible", he quoted Scripture, giving chapter and verse without a moment's hesitation. A converted Roman Catholic, former gangster and dope-fiend once headed for the electric-chair, he preached Jesus from a heart overflowing with the joy of the Lord.

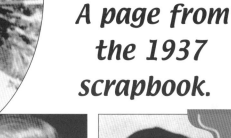

Chief White Feather, a great opera singer, who sang for the King and Queen. A mighty preacher of the Gospel, he held a great campaign in The Peoples Church.

A page from the 1937 scrapbook.

Chas. F. Weigle preached for two and a half months in the fall of 1937.

Evangelist Henry Grube, a favourite.

The gifted Swedish tenor soloist, Einar Waermo, a devoted Christian and a winner of souls, who ministered with Rev. Talbot.

Evangelist Jimmie Johnson was a frequent guest at The Peoples Church, and was particularly well-loved by the youth.

Benny Wilson's Mission on Parliament Street, Toronto.

Benny Wilson's Mission.

Benny Wilson's Mission in Toronto was taken on as The Peoples Church main home mission in 1938. It was a home for released prisoners and other unfortunates at 205 Parliament Street. Meetings were held every night. The Peoples Church set a regular monthly allowance aside for the Mission. They considered Benny's Mission as their home work and did whatever they could to support it in a systematic way. A consensus of the opinion of the church body confirmed the belief that such a Mission could do more for men than all the jails and penitentiaries combined, the Gospel being "the power of God unto Salvation." From Benny Wilson's Mission were born many trophies of God's grace.

The Russian Bible Institute.

Opening in January, 1943 with 50 students, the Russian Bible Institute was formed to train Russian students to take the Gospel to their own people in North and South America, Alaska and Europe, following the War. It offered a three-year theological course, with all classes being conducted in the Russian language. The only institute of its kind in Canada, it drew many Russians from Western Canada, others mainly from Ontario.

Formed under the auspices of the Russian Gospel Association, in conjunction with The Peoples Church, it

was housed in a building just behind the Bloor Street Church. Rev. Henry Janzen of Kitchener, Ontario, served as the Principal. The entire work was supported by free-will offerings. No fees were charged.

The Russian Bible Institute and first class of Russian students, 14 Park Road, Toronto.

1942 – Burning the Mortgage on Bloor Street

On the last Sunday of October the mortgage on The Peoples Church was officially burned. The total cost of the Church and the two houses, including the entire property on Park Road – from Bloor Street to Asquith Avenue – was $75,000.00. $20,638.00 was paid for repairs, equipment and interest, making a grand total of $95,638.00.

During all the years, the Missionary Work never suffered as the huge amount was paid off, year by year. As a matter of fact, the givings to Missions increased every year. In addition, the Missionary Medical Institute and The Peoples Mission were launched. It was a thrilling sight when the mortgage was burned by the Pastor in a large urn on the platform. The entire property was finally owned and controlled exclusively by the Members.

Into all the World

"All Because of One Man"

By Evangelist J. L. BURRIS, Field Director of The Peoples Missionary Society

A LITTLE phrase has been going through my mind the last few days, and I want to pass it on to you. "All Because of One Man." The world is plunged into the bloodiest war that the human race has ever known. With bombs breaking overhead, massive shells screaming across international borders, poison gas drifting through the air, and ships of the sea being blown to atoms by lurking submarines, we are facing international suicide, "All Because of One Man".

The allied nations say, "We have taken up the sword in desperation, but we shall fight on until this man and his principles are driven from civilization." Oh, the heroism of the hour, against the man of the hour, but the man of this hour is only a festering carbuncle; when and if he is eliminated, other carbuncles will form.

The word of God teaches us that we are headed for a period of "Great Tribulation" such as the world has never known; that during that period there is to be regimentation of the human race and centralization of power in the hands of "One Man". Everyone will do his will or be liquidated. Without the "Mark of the Beast" no man will be able to buy or sell.

This mark will be the "Brand of Hell" and will involve a blasphemous denial of God, and Revelation the 14th chapter, verses 9 to 11 says, "If any man worship the Beast and his image, and receive his mark in his hand or his forehead, the same shall drink of the wine of the wrath of God, and he shall be tormented with fire and brimstone. And the smoke of their torment ascendeth up forever and ever: and they have no rest day nor night, and whosoever receiveth the mark of his name".

This man, in Bible terms, is called the Anti-christ. We are living in the day of swift and certain fulfillment of the prophecies of the Word of God. The dictatorships of today are only leading up to the final world dictatorship of the Anti-christ.

The nations do not seem to understand that after all the centuries of fighting against evil men and ruthless aggression, evil still continues in the world and "All Because of One Man". We must therefore have another Man—a man who can deal with the situation in its entirety, a man who deals not with "carbuncles" but with "causes". The sin, corruption, and suffering to be found in all nations is "All Because of One Man". In Romans the 5th chapter, verses 12 to 21, it is made clear that by one man sin entered into the world, and that by One Man salvation is now offered as the Gift of God to all that believe in Him.

There are only two families comprising the human race, namely, the Adam family and God's family. We all came into the Adam family by physical birth. There is only one way to get into God's family and that is by a spiritual birth, through personal faith in the Lord Jesus Christ. He who bore your sins in His own body on the cross, saves you by His grace, the minute you forsake your sin and receive Him as your personal Saviour.

But, thank God, there is another Man from heaven. "The Man Christ Jesus." "For as by one man's disobedience all were made sinners; even so, by the obedience of One Man all who believe in Him are made righteous." We commit sins because we are sinners by nature; this nature we have received through "One Man" Adam. But God offers a new nature, and when we have received it we will have to say "He has made me what I am, by His own grace". We do not achieve salvation by good works, religious ceremonies, baptisms, or church attendance; neither are we saved just because we decide to live a better life and turn over a new leaf. But through simple faith in the Gospel message that One Man, the Man Christ Jesus, took our place and died in our place as a substitute.

You could read your Bible or prayer book faithfully all your life, and pray from now until doomsday for forgiveness, and still die a lost soul. God does not forgive sin in the sense of just overlooking it, but He forgives the sinner of his sin for Jesus' sake. Jesus Christ has paid for sin, and God justifies the person who believes in Him.

If I owed a thousand dollars at the bank, and another man paid it for me, I would be free from the debt—not because the bank had forgiven it—but because the bank had legally accepted the payment of my debt from another man. When we walk the streets of glory, and dwell in the mansions of splendor in the land where there is no more war, sorrow, heartaches or sin, we will shout with a glad heart, until heaven rings, that we have been saved, kept and delivered "All Because of One Man"—the Man Christ Jesus.

It seems incredible to think that "Because of one man" the whole world is again plunged into a world conflict—when no nation wants war—but we all know that he *has* done it; and wars will never permanently cease until "Another Man" causes all swords to be beaten into plowshares and spears into pruning hooks. This Man, of course, is the Lord Jesus Christ, who at His second coming, as the Prince of Peace, will establish His own kingdom of righteousness. Until that time we will continue to have wars and rumours of wars.

We will hear a lot of uninformed people talking about world peace to be brought about by education, religion, or peace treaties. But this is not in keeping with the teaching of the Bible or even of good sense. We entered the last world war to end all wars, and to make the world safe for democracy, but we are farther from that today than we were then. As long as men are at war with God they will be at war with one another.

War begins in the human heart, not at the Maginot or the Siegfried lines.

REV. J. L. BURRIS

The Church at Home

Charles Jeffries, for many years guardian of The Peoples Church.

Keith Whittaker, a wonderful organizer; particularly appreciated in recruiting, motivating and mobilizing volunteers.

Well-loved Gus Webber, who ministered to the children of The Peoples Church for nearly 50 years.

Snapshots of a few special workers.

The Peoples Church has been blessed with exceptional ministers, executives and helpers throughout its history. Because of time and space constraints as well as variations in availability of photographs, it is impossible in such a volume as this, to give adequate representation of the many wonderful people all down through the years who have made The Peoples Church what it is today – people like Mrs. Ralph Chadwick, leader of the Girls' Club; Tom Webb, active in personal work; Dr. Bruce Dunn, the first Sunday School pupil; James McConaghy, a missionary whose son later became the Chair of the Board; Bernard Aldridge, the first song leader on Gerrard Street; and Vern Matts, who kept the high-energy Youth in line with his "Matts patrols"! All these and more should be profiled, were this a thoroughly comprehensive history of The Peoples Church.

Oswald Smith with Clara Caddell, who read poetry on "The Peoples Hour" radio broadcast for 16 years, and was interim editor of *The Peoples Magazine* during 1995 and 1996. Clara's husband, Wilbur Caddell, was the official church photographer for many years.

Walt Huntley, a close friend of Oswald Smith. Walt owned a radio station in Toronto and donated all of the sound equipment and later upgrades when the Church moved to Sheppard Avenue.

Charlie Jeffries, faithful Custodian of The Peoples Church for 50 years, 1937 – 1987. Charlie helped with 1,117 weddings.

Harold Botsford, the first Minister of Stewardship. Elder and Sunday School Superintendent for many years.

John E.T. Dade, longtime Chairman of the Board and Sunday School Superintendent.

Irene Kenyon, who looked after the office and The Peoples Magazine when Oswald Smith was travelling.

Hilda and Herbert Whealey, first missionaries sent out from The Peoples Church (1936). They served in Cuba, Haiti and Mexico; then translated Scriptures with the Wycliffe Bible Translators.

A few of many special workers.

Snapshot – 1945

There were four Assistant Pastors in 1945: Rev. C. L. Whitman, Evangelist Ben Spicer, Evangelist George Stenton, and Dr. J. Edwin Orr. None of them were actually on the staff of the church; with the exception of Dr. Orr.

Edwin Orr and family, Associate Pastor-evangelist of The Peoples Church, commenced his association with Dr. Smith in January 1939.

Tom McCormick, President of Dominion Stores and for many years a church Elder.

Stan Anderson, Head Usher with The Peoples Church 1953 – 1995. After retiring, he offered his services to the Church, helping in a myriad of ways. He was a friend to everyone.

"The Modern Moody" – Filling the pulpit with special guests.

Oswald Smith believed he was called of God to preach in pulpits around the world as an extension of his work through The Peoples Church. Billed as the "Modern Moody", he greatly enjoyed his evangelistic travels and, despite suffering deep loneliness, he went around the world teaching congregations to become "missions first" churches.

During his absences, Oswald made sure that his home congregation was treated to some of the finest speakers and guest musicians in the world; people like John R. Rice, Vance Havner, Dr. Walter l. Wilson, Gypsy Smith, Harry Ironside (pastor of the great Moody Church in Chicago) and Jackie Burris. Desiring only the best for his people, he was delighted when the messages surpassed his own.

Billy Graham.

One of the particularly special guests came to Oswald's attention in 1944. It was a young evangelist who had been invited to speak to the young people's group. Oswald was pleased to meet up with the young fellow once again on a train as they both travelled to a Youth For Christ conference in Switzerland. The young man was known as "Billy" Graham, and was by this time an evangelist with YFC. As they journeyed, Billy plied Oswald with questions about many aspects of evangelism and Oswald, now in his mid-fifties, was glad to share many valuable lessons learned thorough the course of his ministry.

The following year, in 1945, Oswald was thrilled with news of meetings in Hollywood, California, where the power of God, quite unexpectedly, fell on the audience and hundreds streamed from their seats to the altar to accept Christ. The evangelist was his young friend, Billy. With Hurst's order to his newspaper empire to "Pump Graham", it wasn't long before the whole world began to hear about what God was doing through this young man. Oswald flew to California to rejoice with Billy in the great wave of blessing. It was the first of many Billy Graham Crusades he visited to encourage Billy and pray with him. The two developed a warm bond which grew steadily through the years.

Oswald and Paul Smith with Billy Graham.

Lee Childs, Shakespearean actress, was saved in one of Oswald's meetings in the home of Stuart Hamblin.

One-time Black Panther leader Eldridge Cleaver.

Paul Smith leading the Melody Hour.

Continual series of special meetings at home.

Even while home, Dr. Smith continued his policy of conducting a continual series of special meetings in the church – sometimes end to end as can be seen by the summer schedule of 1945:

Rev. Henry Grube, July 8-18
Rev. John Linton, July 25-August 3
Rev. John Gamble, August 5-26
Rev. Bruce Dunn, August 27-September 2

These represent four series of meetings within one summer and the amazing part of it was that they all drew relatively good crowds even on the weeknights. The Sunday night services were usually packed to capacity. Sometimes the doors had to be closed and people were turned away. During that period, the Sunday morning services were never extremely large. There was usually a relatively good crowd but the building was rarely packed and there was always room for more. This stands in contrast to the present in which the reverse is generally true.

As the years went on, the church enjoyed a parade of musicians, preachers and celebrities; from Dale Evans, Lee Childs and Malcolm Muggeridge; to astronaut Jim Irwin and one-time Black Panther leader, Eldridge Cleaver.

1946 – Melody Hour.

Although Paul Smith was not yet on the staff of the church, he conducted an after-church Singspiration called "The Melody Hour," which was held from nine until ten each Sunday night. The attendances averaged from 1,400 to 2,000. Young people from churches all over Toronto flocked to the Melody Hour for unforgettable evenings of singing.

Paul B. Smith with actress, Dale Evans Rogers.

Paul Smith with astronaut James Irwin who spoke not only of space, but of the Lord of space.

Into all the World

HIS MINISTRY HAS RAISED $3,562,000 IN 25 YEARS

By Elizabeth Cuddy, Telegram Staff Reporter

The minister whose church raises more money for missions than any in the world will celebrate his 25th anniversary in the pulpit of The Peoples Church, Bloor St. E., on Sunday.

Rev. Oswald J. Smith, D.D., LL.D., Litt.D., took over the ministry of The Peoples Church the last Sunday in March, 1930, and during the past quarter century collections have amounted to $3,562,000.

Of this total, $2,754,000 has gone to support missionaries.

"The big thing we exist for is missions," declared the white-haired pastor who still considers himself a Presbyterian minister, although practically all his ministry has been of a non-denominational nature.

The Peoples Church supports 380 missionaries on 40 mission fields.

CROWDS AMAZING

But equally amazing as the amount of money he raises are the crowds he attracts to services. In an era when many churches have only a handful at the evening service, there is standing room only at The Peoples Church which seats 1,800.

Morning services "merely" draw a capacity congregation.

"We have no special attraction," claims Dr. Smith, "just a simple bright service with cheerful singing. We don't have much ceremony or form but it must be dignified, because being ordained a Presbyterian minister, I can never get away from that."

Dr. Smith now spends six months of each year carrying on missions in foreign countries and has preached in 45. He will add another one to the list in the autumn when he and Mrs.

Smith go to South Africa for three months.

BOOKS AND HYMNS

Another important fact of his ministry is writing books. He has 25 to his credit, which have been translated into 20 foreign languages and have reached over 1,000,000 copies. He has also written 600 hymns, many of them cowboy songs.

Prolific as he is in book, hymn and poem writing, Dr. Smith never writes a sermon. At least he never writes one before he delivers it, although he often writes it afterwards to include in a book.

He freely admits that he repeats sermons. If one has been particularly popular at The Peoples Church he will repeat it to movie stars when he is preaching in Hollywood or on a missionary tour.

Although a wizard at raising money, he is inclined to be niggardly at spending it, except for his beloved missions. Last year, givings amounted to $338,230 but only $39,000 was spent for the upkeep of the church and

salaries. He refused to accept more than $4,800 as a stipend.

Dr. Smith explained that besides this he gets honorariums and royalties from books sold in Great Britain and the United States. Royalties from all other sales go into the mission fund.

TURNED DOWN

His great interest in missions stems from the fact that his first church work was as a student at the Toronto Bible College when he spent a summer on an Indian Reserve near the Alaskan boundary. Later he asked the Presbyterian Church to send him to India as a missionary but he was not accepted.

"It has been better this way, as I have been able to send so many missionaries out. God knew what he was doing and it was very wise of the Presbyterian Church to turn me down."

BIRTH AND EDUCATION

Born in Odessa, he grew up in Embro where his father, B. J. Smith of Pickering, was then the station agent.

After taking a course at the

Mr. Proctor and Mr. Dade, presenting a silver tea set to Dr. and Mrs. Smith.

Toronto Bible College, he attended Manitoba College, Winnipeg; McCormick Theological Seminary, Chicago; and did a year's post-graduate work at Knox College.

He was ordained as a Presbyterian Church minister and his first charge was as assistant to the late Rev. J. D. Morrow at Dale Presbyterian Church. When Dr. Morrow went overseas during World War I he took charge. In 1921 he was called to Parkdale Tabernacle and later built the Alliance Tabernacle on Christie St., where he remained until going to The Peoples Church.

Hope and Don; Anita and Paul; Mrs. Smith, Dr. Smith and Chrissie.

Veteran Pastor to be Honored by Congregation

By Miss Jane Scott in the Toronto Globe and Mail
March 26th, 1955.

The minister who coined the slogan: Why should any one hear the Gospel twice before everyone has heard it once—will be feted tomorrow by one of the most enthusiastic and loyal congregations in Canada. That minister is Dr. Oswald J. Smith, founder and organizer of The People's Church at 100 Bloor St. E.

The tall, slender, greying pastor who has packed his church every Sunday for 25 years, and raised $3,563,000 in the same period, $2,754,000 of which was spent on world-wide missionary work will preach at both services.

During the past quarter century Dr. Smith has emphasized evangelism and missions. Many of the best known evangelists of this century have preached from his pulpit. Last year 3,000 adherents of the church contributed $280,423 to cover the personal support of 365 full-time missionaries in 40 countries.

In addition to his pastoral duties Dr. Smith has carried on an aggressive evangelistic ministry around the world; he has written a score of books and over 600 poems and hymns, many of which have been circulated in a dozen different languages. The Peoples Church has been broadcasting regularly for 25 years and is now heard over a network of 38 stations from coast to coast and throughout the world.

$225,000

Dr. Oswald J. Smith has been in the Western States holding Missionary Conventions for various churches. During the three or four weeks he was absent God enabled him to raise a total of $225,000.00 for Missions.

He held Conventions in Portland, Oregon, where the offering was $40,000.00; in Los Angeles, California, where it was $90,000.00; and then in Olympia, Washington; in Lodi, California; in San Jose, California; in Pomona, California; and in Tucson, Arizona.

We praise God for His blessing on these meetings. The various churches he served contributed $2,300.00 toward his literature fund for the publication of his salvation booklets in foreign languages. Aside from the $2,300.00, the balance of the amount of $225,000.00 was raised for the churches he served.

Mrs. Proctor presenting Chrissie Frenc with a birthstone ring in appreciation for her years of helping the Smith family and contributing to the ministry of The Peoples Church.

1956 – Rev. George W. Stenton.

Rev. George W. Stenton was listed as the Assistant Pastor and that year had made 201 visits, dealt with 180 prayer requests, wrote 360 comfort and encouragement letters and distributed 40,000 Gospel tracts and books. He made his living reading hydro meters and was not a paid staff member. In 1956 our deacons were W. H. Black, Charles Jackson, W. F. Wright. T. C. Lutey, Harold Irving, D. W. Buchanan, W. L. Small, George Trumble, H. E. Turner, Frank Kerr and L. Y. King. Frank Kerr was the Chairman of the Deacons' Board.

Evangelist George Stenton.

A few of the guest preachers in 1956.

Guest preachers included six of the Open Air Campaigners from Australia and New Zealand. They stayed six weeks from the middle of July to the middle of September – Jim Duffecy, Frank McInnes, Bryce Hartin, Neil Gough, James Wardlaw, and Muri Thompson. Rev. John M. Moore brought a team from Scotland and Rev. E. Buckhurst Pinch came from England for a Prophetic Conference.

1958 – Dr. Oswald J. Smith resigned.

Dr. Oswald J. Smith resigned as Senior Minister at the end of 1958.

1957 – The 50th Anniversary of Oswald's ministry. A great celebration in Varsity Arena boasted a choir of 600. The Church presented the Smiths with a new car.

Visitation focus.

On February 16, 1959, a major visitation program was begun. The first supper meeting drew a group of 120 visitors. Gradually, the numbers rose to a high of 220. Oswald Smith trained the workers and organized the program personally. In 1958 there had been 173 decisions for Christ made publicly, but after starting the visitation work, there were 350 decisions in the first 11 months.

Guests in 1959 included: Wycliffe Booth, Commissioner for Canada of the Salvation Army; Nicholas Bhengu of South Africa; Don Brandeis, young Jewish evangelist who packed the church during every visit; Chuck Ohman, from the Calvary Baptist Church in Detroit; Jimmie McDonald, from Philadelphia; the remarkable Pent Family, who specialized in quoting the Bible in unison; the Open Air Campaigners; Buckhurst Pinch, for a prophetic conference; Jimmie Johnson and Ed Lyman, for Ed's first visit to The Peoples Church; and Bill McGarrahan, for a Kids Crusade.

Winter Bible Conference.

In January of 1959, a Winter Bible Conference was inaugurated with Wilbur M. Smith from the Fuller Theological Seminary and David Allen from the Calvary Baptist Church in Detroit.

The amazing Pent family: Dr. Arnold Pent and his wife Persis and children.

The Peoples Ranch 1962 – 1980.

Bruce Chapman, Director of The Peoples Ranch.

The Peoples Ranch.
From 1962 to 1980, The Peoples Church operated The Peoples Ranch. When it was sold to Bruce Chapman, the name was changed to Rocky Ridge Ranch; it remains a Christian ranch.

Golden Wedding Anniversary.
On September 12, 1966, the Church celebrated the Golden Wedding Anniversary of Dr. Oswald and Daisy Smith. It was a great celebration with 2,200 in attendance. Even at this event, there were 18 decisions for Christ, a great thrill for Oswald and Daisy.

Diamond (60th) Jubilee celebration.
In 1968, Billy Graham was the guest speaker at the Diamond (60th) Jubilee celebration of the ministry of Oswald J. Smith. The crowd, estimated at 4,000, began gathering in the early afternoon for the 7:00 p.m. service. When he entered the pulpit, Dr. Graham listed 10 reasons why Dr. Smith's ministry had been so successful during the full 60 years.

Of all the many honours Oswald received throughout his life, he claimed that the greatest came when Billy arrived in Toronto to personally help celebrate Oswald's 60th anniversary in ministry. In summarizing Oswald's life, Billy said:

> "No other man that I know has the drive, determination, or the singleness of mind to serve God. Oswald Smith has been a legend in his time. He stands tall in Canada and the nations of the earth. My whole life and my ministry have been touched and directed by Oswald J. Smith. I want to do the same as he has done as long as I have breath."

Line-up to hear Billy Graham speak at Oswald Smith's Jubilee.

Billy Graham speaking at The Peoples Church.

Two hearts as one.

Into all the World

PEOPLES CHURCH SUNDAY SCHOOL TEACHERS AND OFFICERS - January 1959

Front Row: Mrs. E.L. Klemm; E.L. Klemm, Former Supt.; Mrs. O.J. Smith; Dr. Paul B. Smith, Pastor; H.N. Botsford, Supt.; Mrs. Paul B. Smith; Dr. O.J. Smith, Pastor Emeritus; Mrs. H.N. Botsford; J.E.T. Dade, Former Supt.; Second Row: C. Bradley; H. Lowry; A. Pauls; C. Caddell; A. Manthorpe; B. Jones; B. Graham; D. Nelson; G. Sutherland; M. Phibbs; Third Row: A. Orr; D. McLeod; G. Caddell; S. Watt; G. Arkell; R. Geary; K. Hurley; I. Anger; D. Palmer; A. Elford; E. Brown; S. Dunlop; E. Hamilton; Fourth Row: Rev. R. Watt; F. Trenchard; J. Scott; B. Fogerty; C. Pauls; C. Ralston; D. Freeman; K. Elford; J. McLeod; K. McDonald; G. Webber; D. Graham; J. Turner; W. Caddell at Camera

1961 Sunday School staff.

The Peoples Church Sunday School on the birthday of Dr. Oswald J. Smith,
November 8, 1970. 2096 present.

Into all the World

In 1971, The Peoples Church established an educational ministry known as The Peoples Christian Schools. In 1982, Ethel Wright wrote this article in *The Peoples Magazine*, chronicling the school's history to that point.

The Peoples Christian Schools

by Ethel E.K. Wright

Paul Smith welcomes students on the first day of classes in 1971.

Vision! A Christian School you say! But the money! Teachers! A principal! Supplies? Courses of study? Red tape! An endless list - mind boggling, in fact!

Unaffected by such lists and spurred on by dozens of supporters, Dr. Paul B. Smith, our dedicated pastor, clearly saw the vision, prayed fervently, and began setting the affair in motion. By his side, working tirelessly, was Dr. Daniel E. Edmundson, Minister of Christian Education at The Peoples Church. Working equally tirelessly along with Dr. Edmundson was Mrs. Ruby Taylor, an amazing Christian worker, who gave years of her abilities to our school. Nothing was too much for Ruby.

But then--why bother? It's too much work - money - etc. - and besides, we'll only be producing "HOTHOUSE" circumstances in which to raise our young people! Wasn't the public system adequate? It was good enough for our parents and grandparents. Many a Prime Minister was raised in the little red schoolhouse. "The HOTHOUSE is a good place to get little plants started before thrusting them into the garden" countered our pastor. Let's be realistic. Times have changed. We're not talking about the little red schoolhouse of the past - but school in a very changing society - our children need a Christian school!

Finally the day arrived. After months of planning - discussing with the Department of Education, much publicity, and a successful search for qualified, Christian teachers and a principal - it was September 1971. The sun shone brightly, Dr. Paul, Dr. Dan, staff of the school and numerous parents and friends, gathered to mark the stirring event. A spirit of prayer and blessing filled all of us. And, happiness filled the air at The Peoples Christian School!

Needs arose! Prayer was raised! Needs were met! The first Principal, William Vimont, was experienced in starting Christian schools. Excellent basic principles of curriculum and discipline were laid down by this Christian gentleman, who has since been promoted to Glory. At the conclusion of his one year contract, Vimont went elsewhere to begin yet another Christian school. The Lord immediately provided the dedicated and experienced leadership of Norman Asplund, who, along with his talented wife, Marilyn, provided seven years of excellent service, which earned them the love and respect of teachers, parents and students. Kindness and fair play were overflowing! Academics, choir, orchestra, art - all flourished under the principalship of Mr. Asplund, who once wrote: "We work towards a continuous spiritual growth in a student's life, and to produce a student who is academically equal or better than the student emerging from the public school system".

In The Peoples Magazine - first quarter 1973 - a small insert read: "The Peoples Christian School trains the mind, spirit and body of its 300 pupils". On the same page there was a picture of a gym class crowded into the Founder's Hall. Almost double the original enrollment, rooms full, no real gym - you guessed it! Time for expansion. Time to start thinking of a new building to house the senior students. Three years later that dream became reality. September 1976, after many meetings of many minds - a beautiful new highschool building (complete with a large - double size gym, a lab and many classrooms) opened its doors to our senior level students - and, along with the new school came a new Principal for the Academy - Jeremy Sinnott, who had previously taught in the school and won the hearts of his students.

Now, with a gym, our students were spurred on to do great things in competitive sports, both intra mural and extra mural. Also, although the school has no swimming pool, there has been a strong swim team which has honoured the school on several occasions with cups brought back victoriously from swim competitions.

Exciting opportunities for short-term missionary service, have been given to the school orchestra on four occasions. What tremendous excitement there was as the students and chaperones, gathered with sleeping bags, suitcases, instruments, etc. ready to catch the plane for Mexico, Jamaica, Eleuthra and California. One of the students writes following one of the trips: "Looking back I see the need the world has for the Gospel of Jesus. I see the impoverished areas, the hands reaching out, the

people stopping everywhere to read our tracts. I was overflowing with joy as I led one person to the Lord. This trip renewed my Christian faith and I will someday return to this land or some other country like it".

And so the years roll on. On Sunday evening, June 20, 1976, the first graduates, capped and gowned, walked in a processional line to the platform to receive their diplomas. Those little shining-faced angels who entered the brand new school that sunny morning in September 1971 - now grown up; young adults - on the doorstep of leadership. Unbelievable, but true. One of our valedictorians said on a stately graduation night: "The graduates leaving through these doors are hopefully more rounded and better equipped to face the rapidly changing world because of the combined spiritual and academic approach this institution has taken. Behind us lies the clearly defined educational road which we have already travelled, while before us stretch countless paths. Pray that we will select the one that will allow God to use us to the utmost, that we will not limit Him and ourselves by our choice".

How the Lord has blessed. The school opened its doors with an enrollment of 187 students in Kindergarten through Grade 8 with nine teachers. Today, eleven years later, the school has approximately 600 students, and forty-one teachers, divided into two schools - The Oswald J. Smith Elementary School, Junior Kindergarten through Grade 8 with Principal Jeremy A. Sinnott, and The Paul B. Smith Academy, Grades 9 through 13 with Principal Donald F. McNiven.

J. Sinnott and D. McNiven.

Daisy Smith – till we meet again.

In 1972, her 80th year, Daisy Smith was not well. After nine world trips with Oswald, speaking with great blessing to countless women's meetings, and fulfilling her roles within the family with excellence, Daisy was tired. Having to live as a chronic invalid after several falls, she had been absent from the church for a long period.

It was no wonder Paul was startled when, on the platform leading the 44th Missionary Conference, he saw his mother being assisted into the church. The entire church applauded. Having missed her familiar presence, they appreciated her determination not to miss the conference.

On November 1, 1972, Oswald knelt and prayed beside Daisy, who was by that time unconscious; kissed her gently on the forehead and went to bed. That night, in her sleep, Daisy slipped away into the presence of the Lord.

Large church family.

By the mid-seventies, the five-acre parking lot was regularly jammed and it was necessary to run regular shuttle buses back and forth to their cars parked in a nearby plaza. More cars lined the streets for five or six blocks. According to Oswald, Daisy's support was an enormously important factor in the growth of the work.

"No one will ever know how lonely she was as she held the ropes that I might go. I could never have accomplished what I have, had it not been for her."

OJS

at the end of his ministry.

FOCUS ON CANADIAN CHURCHES
Sixth in a series on significant Canadian churches.
by Douglas Percy *(Abridged)*

(Copied from "Communicate," June, 1980, used by permission)

PEOPLES CHURCH, TORONTO

The "Smith's" with David Mainse.

"Through its many spheres of service, The Peoples Church has contributed to the moral and spiritual welfare of our nation; and through its mission projects it has become one of the best-known churches in the world."

Greetings from Bill Davis, Premier of Ontario at the 50th Anniversary of The Peoples Church, September, 1978.

The Sunday services are well planned. They consist of attractive music (including a 45-piece orchestra and a 90-voice adult choir) and a simple but forceful presentation of Jesus Christ as Savior. Services are aired over both radio and television with 150,000 viewing the eleven a.m. service each week.

Since taking over as senior pastor, son Paul has sought to develop a solid ministry to the total family. Presently, the Sunday School enjoys an average attendance of 1,600, ranging from babies to senior citizens. Every Tuesday evening, June through August, oustanding Bible teachers and Christian personalities fill the pulpit to share in the Summer Bible Conference. The Paul B. Smith Academy, an elementary school and high school with some 650 students and an efficient and dedicated faculty of about 32, opened in 1971.

The younger Smith envisions a family-oriented church and makes much of this concept. He has also added a weekly television program that covers much of Ontario and is also shown in parts of the United States.

But of all its activities, The Peoples Church is alive with missions. Even as this is being written, the 1980 Missions Conference has drawn to a close with a pledge offering of $1,285,011.

This brings total missionary offerings over 52 years to well over $15 million. This means a share in the support of over 500 missionaries serving in 70 different countries under 40 mission boards (all interdenominational) and helps support many "home" agencies as well, including Ontario Bible College.

Since its founding, the church has always put world missions first. This is evidenced by the constant exposure of missions in the total program of the church. World mission conferences now last two full weeks, beginning with a kick-off prayer meeting which is "vitally important," according to Dr. Smith. Each conference features dozens of missionaries, Christian national leaders, and missionary communicators, who, together with outstanding musical talent, produce evenings of information and inspiration.

To function adequately, the church tasks are parcelled out to ten ministers (including one woman), a Board of Managers and nearly 250 elders. Organized and orderly; spiritual and biblical; dynamic and dedicated—these are but a few of the adjectives used to describe Peoples Church, Toronto.

Whenever public issues regarding ethics, morals, church dialog or theological discussions arise, Dr. Paul is invariably called upon to be the spokesman for the evangelical community.

But the pastor does not equate publicity or size or money as the dynamic of the church. Rather, he emphasizes its strong biblical position and the emphasis on faithful prayer ministry as the reasons for its success story. Indeed he would emphasize that "except the Lord build the house, they labour in vain that build."

Here then is a building of the Lord, used for His praise and glory and for the extension of His kingdom. Little wonder that around the world there are men and women, boys and girls who can rise up and call the peoples Church and the Smiths "blessed" for all they mean and all they do for the church worldwide. May their tribe increase!

Dr. Percy is Professor of Missions and Director of Public Relations at Ontario Bible College.

Jesus is Lord and God

The Peoples Magazine, November/December 1980

The Church at Home

"Is this Revival?"

It was a question asked not only by Paul Smith, but by many who sensed a tremendous move of the Holy Spirit following the World Missions Conference of 1982. Response to the ministry was remarkable. In the first three months of 1983, almost three times as many people registered public decisions for Christ as at any time in the history of the church. Dr. Paul pointed to his associates in ministry at the time, as eight of the obvious reasons for the blessing of God on the church.

Dr. George D'Sena was a unique Bible teacher and pastor. While serving as an army doctor, God called him to teach pathology in a missionary medical college, where he was filled with the Holy Spirit. From there, God led him to leave medicine and teach His Word. Many years before he left India, Dr. D'Sena spent time praying with Dr. Paul Smith in the tower of an old church in Calcutta. Following nine years of teaching in the Calcutta Bible College, he joined the staff of The Peoples Church.

Richard Robb took over his duties as Minister of Christian Education in August, 1882. More than once, Dr Paul made appreciative reference to him as one of the hardest workers on the ministerial staff. Richard's leadership in the Evangelism Explosion ministry made a powerful impact on that area of the work. Almost every Tuesday night when the Evangelism Explosion teams visited neighbourhood homes, people were led to Christ.

Mel Svendsen began as the Minister of Youth in June, 1982. Young, a great athlete and friendly with everyone, he was just the person the church had been needing for some time. Mel led a spiritual program that tremendously energized the youth groups. His Tuesday and Wednesday night Bible Studies both exceeded a hundred in attendance every week. While tremendously capable in all aspects of youth ministry, Mel's forté was Bible Study and prayer.

Jim Johnston Having been the President of an Insurance firm, Jim took an early retirement and joined The Peoples Church in the capacity of Director of Stewardship in December, 1983. He had been Superintendent of the Sunday School for a number of years. A very successful business man, Jim ministered spiritually to the Peoples Church family in matters of stewardship. Jim's son, Keith, and his family served as missionaries of Trans World Radio.

Rev. Norma Cooper arrived at The Peoples Church from South Africa, where her parents founded and pastored one of that country's major evangelical churches in the city of Durban. She had a personal charisma and ability to work that turned everything she organized into a spiritual success. Ordained to the ministry shortly after graduation from an American Bible College, she was well-known to the television audience as, "the beautiful lady who prays". Norma led the Pioneer Girls, was the Minister of Christian Education for four years and helped raise the finances for the high school building. As the Minister of Outreach, one of her major focuses was the Seniors, many of whom were unable to get out to church.

Don Jost became the Associate Minister of the Peoples Church in June, 1981. Having previously served in the Metropolitan Bible Church in Ottawa and as the platform director for Canadian evangelist, Barry Moore, Don was given full charge of the Christian Education program. He led most of the major services and supervised such platform ministries as outreach, counselling and youth. Dr. Paul referred to him as "one of the most remarkable men I have ever met". A superb chairman, Don mixed with people in a warm-hearted manner and with rare devotion. He spent a great deal of time in personal and marriage counselling, and performed most of the marriages.

David E. Williams, while a brilliant musician, derived his greatest pleasure from organizing opportunities for people to serve God with their musical and drama talents. His choirs, orchestra and other groups numbered nearly four hundred people. The revival fires that began to burn in 1983 were no doubt partly an answer to David's prayers and his years of faithful service in the church. Though only eight years old when he was saved, he knew he had become a new creature in Christ. "That night as I walked home, it seemed as if my feet were hardly touching the ground. How my heart sang. Now for over 40 years, that song has been in my heart..."

Wilfred J. Wright devoted his exceptional managerial and business qualifications to the administration of The Peoples Church. He joined the staff as General Manager of Operations in June, 1980. His job description included business administration, acting as Superintendent of the two schools (then 600 students) and exercising jurisdiction over all ministries except those pertaining to the platform. Prior to joining the staff, Wilf was active in the church as General Superintendent of the Sunday School and First Vice-President of the Board, as well as many other areas.

Into all the World

The Church at Home

277

Graduation to Glory

On January 25, 1986, Oswald J. Smith graduated to Glory at the age of 96, after almost 80 years in the service of his Lord and Saviour, Jesus Christ.

Memorial Service

Thursday, January 30, 1986.

Organ — Frank Trenchard
Call to Worship – Ruth 2:12 (Favourite scripture)
Invocation and Committal – Dr. D. Jost
Hymns — The Song of the Soul Set Free
He Rose Triumphantly
Comfort from Scripture – Dr. Henry Hildebrand
Prayer — Dr. Paul Finkenbinder
Choir and Orchestra – Dr. David E. Williams
Oswald J. Smith Medley
The Hallelujah Chorus
Tributes — T.W. Wilson
Dr. Jack McAllister
Dr. Paul E. Kauffman
Special Music – The Antone Indian Family
George Beverly Shea
Message — Dr. Billy Graham

"Someday you will hear that Oswald Smith is dead. Don't you believe it At that moment I will be more alive than ever, for I have an indestructible life!"

OJS
(50 years prior to his homegoing.)

"The name, Oswald J. Smith, symbolizes worldwide evangelization. Some men of God are called to minister the Gospel to a city, others to a nation; and a few in each century to the whole world. Oswald J. Smith was a prophet to the nations of the world. He will go down in history as the greatest combination pastor, hymn writer, missionary statesman and evangelist of our time. He was the most remarkable man I have ever met.

"I've lost a dear friend, the man who had more impact on my life than any other – a man who stands equal with Dwight L. Moody and Reuben A. Torrey."

Billy Graham.

Dr. Billy Graham.

George Beverley Shea.

Jack Van Impe.

George Beverly Shea,
beloved Gospel singer.

Ted Smith, pianist for Billy
Graham Crusades.

Jerry Johnston, dynamic
youth evangelist.

Dave Boyer.

Warren Wiersbe.

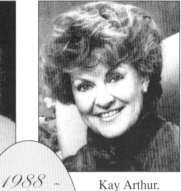

Kay Arthur.

Bruce W. Dunn, Pastor of
Grace Presbyterian Church.

*1988 –
A few who
helped us
celebrate...*

1928 **Jubilee '88** 1988
PEOPLES
Missions First

Barry Moore.

Rick Stanley, brother of
Elvis Presley.

"At times when other churches are reconciling themselves to smaller congregations, The Peoples Church is a religious phenomenon. With 2,600 worshippers on Sunday morning, plus another 180,000 watching by television, almost certainly this is Canada's largest congregation. It has probably given more money to world missions, for both preaching and relief ministries, than any other congregation in the world.

"'*A great church built on the priority of missions,*' says The Billy Graham Association which places The Peoples Church first in its list of the world's great congregations."

Reader's Digest, April, 1979.

Wally Williams on
Prophecy.

Ed Lyman.

Into all the World

"Home Bible studies are the timber we use to build the church! Prayer, love, hospitality, gift sharing, teaching, service, worship and growth are all wrapped into this 'care' package."
– Donald J. Jost, Associate Minister.

Mary Anita (Lawson) Smith, First Lady of The Peoples Church from 1959 to 1993.

Home Bible Study groups.

In 1985, impressed with the tremendous impact of small cell groups on the growth of Dr. Yonggi Cho's church in Korea, and Dr. Stuart Briscoe's exploding congregation in Milwaukee, The Peoples Church began planting cell groups of 10-12 people per group throughout the city.

A time for gifts.

In 1985, the AOB organ, custom-built for The Peoples Church and given by John E.T. Dade, was dedicated. Another wonderful gift, a golden communion service, (shown below) was donated to The Peoples Church by Wilson and Cora Morris.

1990 – Dr. Paul's Jubilee.

In October of 1990, after 50 years of ministry and preaching over 9,020 sermons since his first in 1940, Dr. Paul Smith celebrated his Jubilee year of ministry. Greetings arrived from all around the world.

Anita Smith – First Lady from 1959 to 1993.

Having suffered for a long time with cancer, Anita Smith went to be with the Lord on May 22, 1993. Because of her request that no sadness should be perpetuated by her death, a "Promotion to Glory Celebration" was held.

"For years I've made it a priority to be a part of a home Bible group." – Richard P. Robb, Minister to Children.

"Home Bible studies provide an effective arena for a more involved and intimate level of personal fellowship, prayer, Bible study and encouragement – structure not present in many churches."
Gregg S. Bryce, Minister of Youth.

L – R: Jimmie Johnston, Michael Sherbino, Paul Smith, Donald Jost, Wilson Morris and Wilfred Wright.

Frank Trenchard, at the Dade organ, was the official organist for 50 years.

The Living Christmas Tree — an annual musical extravaganza for many years.

Dr. Paul Brainerd Smith.
1921 – 1995

Dr. Paul Smith – 'Till we meet again.

Dr. Paul, who had not been well for a couple of months, had a heart attack on Sunday, April 30, 1995, the opening day of the 1995 Missions Conference, and God called him home.

Dr. Paul had resigned as Senior Pastor in May of 1994, handing the reins to Dr. John Hull. He had travelled to over 100 countries and raised millions of dollars for Missions.

The memorial service was held on the final Friday night of the Missions Conference. The family had invited Dr. Ravi Zacharias to be the guest preacher. His address will be long remembered.

Memorial Celebration

Opening Remarks	– John D. Hull
Prayer	– George J. Hay
Hymn # 13	– The Congregation
Solo (taped)	– J. Jann Smith
Scripture	– I Corinthians 13
	– Daniel M. Murdoch
Eulogy	– David E. Williams
Solo	– Diane Susek
Tributes	– Bishop Marwieh
	– Charles Templeton
Choir and Orchestra	– D. Daniels
Solo	– Diane Susek
Message	– Ravi Zacharias
Closing Prayer	– Hal Warren
Doxology	
Ethel Wright	– piano
Bill Carter	– organ

"Dr. Paul's skin was white, but he had a multi-coloured heart.
"Great men achieve much because they sacrifice much.
Dr. Paul was a great man.
"He had the abiity to take complex truths and make them simple.... Many times I would team up with him in preaching events. How focused he was. How intense he was. Yet how profound were the implications of what he said."

Ravi Zacharias

The "New Generation," under the direction of Jeremy Sinnott and Donna Wood.

Stephen Bempong, Allan Northcott and Glen Roadknight.

Matthew Beerman.

The Peoples Christian Academy.
In 1995 the two schools, the Oswald J. Smith Elementary School and The Paul B. Smith Academy were integrated under the title of "The Peoples Christian Academy". Now, with over 800 students, it is the largest independent Christian school in Ontario.

With an academic education from the Christian world-view, the high school program is university-preparatory, with students graduating to the institutions of their choice across North America. Grades 9-12 are inspected and accredited by the Ontario Ministry of Education and Training for the purpose of issuing the Ontario Secondary School Diploma.

The elementary division of PCA schools 450 children at the west side of The Peoples Church complex, and contains classrooms, a gymnasium and a computer laboratory. At the east side is the 360 student high school wing, with a large gymnasium, classrooms, a music room, science laboratory, art room, and two modern computer laboratories.

"King's Kids," under the direction of Donna Wood.

W. F. White, Chairman, Board of Directors and Managers.

The Peoples Church Annual Report

for the year ending August 31, 1999

A word from the Chairman, William F. White

...growth has resulted in a broader financial base, enhancing stability and potential...

Your Board of Directors and Managers for 2000 consists of John Hull (Senior Pastor), Brian Dawkins (Business Manager), Don McNiven (Headmaster), Bill White (President), George Gooderham (Vice-President), Gary Patriquin (Treasurer), Tommy So (Secretary), and David Williams. A special thanks goes to George Gooderham and Gary Patriquin for their 11 years of faithful service as members of this Board and their agreement to serve as Officers and Directors for a further year. We finished our Annual Meeting with the singing of "Praise God From Whom all Blessings Flow". Our goal is to be diligent in prayer, seeking to obey the will of GOD. Our plans are born out of a desire to please GOD and to accomplish His purposes.

I give thanks with a grateful heart to almighty God - for His continued trust in us, our dedicated ministry team, teachers, missionaries, elders, choir, orchestra, organizational staff who labour behind the scenes, our faithful Church Advisory Council, Peoples Christian Academy Governance Council, Business Services Governance Council, the 20 committees and more than 150 volunteers who serve faithfully, in order to see souls come to faith in Christ from among the nations.

As my first duty as Chairman of the Board and President of The Peoples Church, Toronto it was a privilege and an honour to welcome, in January, 2000 Dale McConaghy, Jeff Petch and David Welsh to the Church Advisory Council.

These individuals have served the Lord faithfully for many years.

As we start the New Year 2000, we continue to focus our devotions on prayer and hearing from God. I believe GOD is saying to us "I tell you, if you do learn to seek my face as a group, and hear my voice, that will be a very significant contribution to my church in your culture; it will make a significant impact on the church": God wants us to be dependent on HIM and trust HIM and He will tell us what to do tomorrow or next week or next month. GOD is teaching the Board of Administration of Peoples a number of things. How He speaks is one of them and how He works is another.

Church

If asked to pick a phrase to describe our present church situation, I would select "well-positioned". That phrase expresses exactly where we are as we look out over the vistas of year 2000 and beyond.

Geographically - Sheppard Avenue is becoming a "showcase" boulevard in one of the world's great cities. Our location is easily accessible for new growth.

Statistically - In 1999, Peoples expanded to 4 week-end services and experienced 25% growth. This growth has resulted in a broader financial base, enhancing stability and potential.

Philosophically - We are rooted to our core values of Biblical inerrancy, the Lordship of Christ, and the evangelization of our city, nation and world. These have been foundational since our birth 72 years ago!

The Peoples Magazine

Average Sunday Attendance

Sunday Totals — 2500, 2000, 1500, 1000

Year — 93, 94, 95, 96, 97, 98, 99

On the eve of the new century...

Spiritually - Our leadership is convinced our efforts will be powerless unless we're committed to prayer and the fullness of the Holy Spirit. It's good to be well-positioned and experiencing the Father's blessings. Join me in celebrating His goodness.

World Missions

Missions emphasis continues to be a strong part of our success in ministry.

The World Missions Conference produced a Faith Promise Offering of $1,750,000, an increase of $150,000 above our goal! This enabled us to continue to increase our missionary force in the field through 60 plus agencies. Our commitments to direct support of the missionary enterprise increased to $1.2 million in this fiscal year, which is the highest amount in more than a decade. I also believe that it may be among the highest levels in the history of The Peoples Church. To God be the glory!

We continue to see members of our church body respond to the Lord's call to the mission field and a strong team of adults spent part of July working on a short-term project in Finland. We also continue to work with inner city missions to extend the hand to Christ to the disadvantaged in our own city.

Television

This fiscal year has been a challenge for our television outreach. The Christian television market is experiencing rapid change and competition is greater. Revenues increased a modest 3.4% from the previous year but our costs increased largely as a result of our decision to purchase air time on Crossroads Television System. The resulting economic loss is a concern and is being addressed. We continue to see lives changed by the transforming power of the Gospel through this important ministry.

A number of new initiatives are underway to improve our financial performance but competition in the market place is accelerating. Our new Call Centre is adding a personal touch to our audience and the positive feedback reassures us of the value of the work we do in this area of ministry. Please pray that the Lord will give us clear direction as we chart the course for the future.

Academy

The past year at Peoples Christian Academy has been one of significant growth and substantial change. Demand for our school has increased and we have worked hard to meet the demand. In the fall of 1998 we opened yet another portable and in the fall of 1999 it was integrated into the Wilfrid Annex. From our success in attracting top quality staff to the impact of all our teachers on the lives of the young people God has placed in our charge, we see the evidence of God's hand at work.

The 1998 - 99 school year saw our enrollment expand to 405 students in the elementary school and 208 students in the high school. We continued the major task of reviewing and updating our curricula from Kindergarten to 12/OAC as well as building our student computer resources. Our financial results were positive and much work was done to improve our facility. Eighty percent of our 1999 graduating class were Ontario Scholars, again demonstrating the academic excellence that prepares them to continue on to institutions of higher education for further development.

We are grateful to God for the quality of our Board, staff and parent volunteers who work so well together to accomplish our mission of delivering quality education in the context of a Christian day school with emphasis on preparing the next generation for the Lord's service.

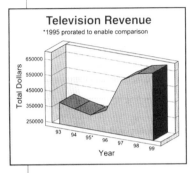

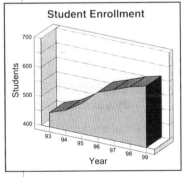

The Church at Home

John W. Rush leads Evangelism Explosion at The Peoples Church.

MAIN FEATURE

A Global Legacy

By John W. Rush

"On September 9, 1928, Oswald J. Smith stepped onto the platform of Massey Hall, and The Peoples Church was born. At that time it was actually called 'The Cosmopolitan Tabernacle'."

You must go or send a substitute....

So writes Lois Neely in the official biography of Oswald J. Smith entitled, "Fire In His Bones".

What O. J. Smith had in his heart was to create a centre for evangelism and missions that would impact the whole world with the Gospel of Jesus Christ. Rejected by mission boards because of his own frail health, he built a ministry around the concept: "You must go or send a substitute!"

Evangelism Explosion in The Peoples Church is a cosmopolitan ministry made up of people from a wide cross-section of languages and cultures found in Toronto. What Dr. O. J. was unable to do personally he has accomplished corporately, for God has brought the mission fields to our very doorstep!

Every Tuesday evening people from twenty-one nations with twelve different mother tongues meet with a common purpose and a sense of family. We are there to learn the EE material in English, and to equip each other in the ministry of evangelism for a multi-cultural city. Our long-term objective is to stock materials in many languages and to have evangelism teams equipped and ready to reach out to the various cultures present in the greater Toronto area.

The Evangelism Explosion training course is designed to fit into a thirteen-week semester. Each unit builds on the material of the the previous one in a process know as "incremental learning".

Each unit requires the trainee to read assigned lesson materials, memorize a portion of the outline and to make contact with his or her two prayer partners. They are expected to pray with those prayer partners each week for a minimum of fifteen minutes. Nothing in the ministry of evangelism can be accomplished without the power of God's Holy Spirit, and He has instructed us to pray for the harvest!

The most important element in our training does not take place in the classroom, but in the living room! "On-the-job-training", or "OJT", as we like to call it, is the opportunity for the trainer to model the methods of EE for the trainee until the trainee feels comfortable sharing the Gospel presentation alone. Evangelism is better "caught" than taught!

In 1999 our teams visited 669 homes, most of which came to us through the "Friendship and Communication Cards" which are distributed every Sunday in our services. These visits resulted in 349 presentations of the Gospel being made and 96 people making a personal commitment to Jesus Christ for the first time. Twenty-nine others also recommitted their hearts to Christ and received the assurance of their salvation.

Each person who makes a profession of faith during one of these visits receives a follow-up call a week later, to confirm their faith and understanding of the Gospel. At that time they are encouraged to begin attending church

The Peoples Magazine

regularly and to develop a personal discipline of Bible study and prayer.

This semester we will be launching a new discipleship ministry for new converts leading them through eight lessons in small groups. The groups will be meeting in homes within a four kilometer radius of the church, and will be led by two facilitators who have been trained in Evangelism Explosion. A small group will be meeting somewhere every night of the week, allowing our new Christians to choose the one most convenient to them.

Upon completion of the eight week discipleship training the new believer can then continue for a few more weeks of extended study material, or transfer to a cell group meeting in their particular neighbourhood. In this way they will become acquainted with older Christians and feel more inclined to become a regular part of our congregation on Sundays.

Jesus told His disciples that the fields were "white already to harvest" (Jn. 4:35). In over thirty years of using Evangelism Explosion in my ministry I have never seen the harvest fields as ripe as they are right now! There are literally millions of people in our country who are desperate to hear of Jesus Christ and His redeeming love! They have come to Canada to start a new life, and on the surface they appear to be from Eastern religions, or from orthodox denominations, but they are willing to listen to what we have to offer from the Gospel of Jesus Christ. If they discover that what we have found in Him is superior to their old ways, they are prepared to lay aside those traditions and embrace the Saviour!

Among those who recently have come to Christ are Moslems, Hindus, Buddhists, Sikhs, and many from former communist countries in Eastern Europe, who have had no faith at all!

Evangelism Explosion is also being blessed nationally, as interest is strong in Quebec, Ontario, Manitoba, and British Columbia. New interest is being expressed in the Maritimes, with churches in New Brunswick and Nova Scotia actively engaged in this work. A desire has been strongly expressed for EE to be launched in Newfoundland, but a church has yet to be identified there which will embrace this exciting equipping ministry.

The ministry of EE International has also seen the powerful hand of God at work. For the first time since Jesus gave the Church its Great Commission it can be said that the Gospel is being preached and discipleship is taking place in EVERY COUNTRY OF THE WORLD! Dr. D. James Kennedy challenged his international vice-presidents with the vision of planting an EE ministry in every nation of the world by the end of 1995. The task seemed totally beyond reason at first, but by the grace of God it was accomplished with a ministry being founded in North Korea by December, 1995! It could then be said that EE was actively ministering in all 211 nations of the world! Since that time one of the nations split into two, and EE was able to increase our number of nations without adding any personnel, because we were situated in both halves of the nation that divided! We are now serving the cause of Christ in 212 nations! Praise the Lord!

I have never seen the harvest fields as ripe as they are now.

The Peoples Magazine

The 21st Century Peoples Church

Something

for everyone...

International Student Ministries Canada

Who?
All international students.
What? Fellowship and reflections on the sermon.
Where? The Peoples Church.
When? Each Sunday 12:45 p.m.
Why? International Student Fellowship is a ministry designed to help students visiting Toronto from around the globe meet, make friends, enjoy refreshments and develop English skills. For further information, contact International Student Ministries, Canada (ISMC) 416-492-6983.

The Haven.
The Haven is a weekly Bible class for women of all ages and stages, run by Hilary Price and held every Thursday evening from 7:00 – 9:00 p.m. Biblical teaching with opportunity for discussion and interaction. The Haven is a placeof:
Hope
Acceptance
Vulnerability
Encouragement
Nurturing.

World Missions

Our mandate is to go, to send, to give and to pray.
The Missions Coordinator can be reached at
41 6-222-3341 ext 138.

Doulos Fellowship

Singles and "Single Again," ages 35 to 50. A light meal is served at 6:30 p.m. followed by worship at 7:15 p.m. Interesting studies on relevant topics.

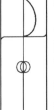

Young & Married's Fellowship
A ministry designed for couples married less than 10 years.
We aim to deepen our relationship with God, our families and other families.
Ministry in three areas:

1. The Main Group Meeting
The first and third Friday of each month at 7:30 p.m. – worship, fellowship and teaching. Childcare is provided.

2. Women of Couples
The second Saturday morning of each month at 9:00 a.m. Bible Study, fellowship and prayer in the home of one of the group members. Ladies only. Childcare not available.

3. Men of Prayer
8 a.m. each Saturday of the month (except for the second Saturday when the ladies meet)
For more information, please e-mail yams@look.ca

Alpha

Friendship Class
Ages 15 and up. A morning church alternative for the developmentally challenged, designed to communicate the Gospel of Jesus Christ at a level of understanding appropriate for each student. It is our desire that each student will come to know the Lord and grow in their understanding of who he/ she is in Christ.

North of Forty
Singles and Singles Again.
We seek to be a sharing, loving fellowship. God is calling Singles and Singles Again in the Greater Toronto Area to grow spiritually, to esteem one another in love, and to use their gifts to encourage each other.

Evangelism Explosion
Tuesday evenings. Teams of three meet from 6:30 to 10:30 p.m. for training. The teaching format includes lectures, on-the-job training and reporting sessions. Just thirteen short weeks until you can give the Gospel on your own.

Music and Worship Arts
Music, drama and other worship arts.

Peoples Prayer Ministries

Oasis – The flagship prayer meeting at The Peoples Church. A powerful time of prayer and a special time of teaching. Wednesdays @ 7:30 p.m.
Prayz – Passionate prayer with the Prayz Prayer Team and modern praise featuring the Soularize Band. Third Saturday of each month @ 7:30 p.m.
Men's PrayerMeeting – A small group prayer meeting for men. Saturdays @ 8:00 a.m.
Young and Married's Mens' PrayerMeeting – A small group prayer meeting for men with an emphasis on listening to God. Saturdays @ 8:00 a.m.
Ladies' Prayer Meeting – Focus on both missionaries and the local ministry of the church. Wednesdays @ 1:00 p.m.
Elders' Prayer Meeting – For the Sunday ministry at The Peoples Church. Sundays @ 8:30 a.m. & 10:00 a.m.
North of 4O PrayerMeeting – North of 40 group: 416-222-3341

PSALM Fellowship

Drop In Center
A Great Place to Meet Friends
Tuesdays 10:00 a.m. - 2:00 p.m.
Celebration 10:30 a.m. every 3rd Saturday – fellowship followed by a hot meal.

timothy@peoplesministries.org

Sundays
9:15 & 11:15 a.m.
Nursery Ministry: Birth to 23 months, Sunday School: 2 years to 12 years
Sundays 6:30 p.m.
Birth to 7 years.
Camp Highlife – summer day-camp: July and August.

Soularize

Jr. High through College & Career. Every Sunday at 11:15 a.m., we gather together to celebrate life with laughter, friendship, music, and encouragement from God's Word.
Jr. High (Grades 7-8)
Bi-weekly gatherings – usually crazy fun!
High School Small group interaction, surprise events and activities – Wednesdays at 7:27 p.m.
College & Career Weekly discussion groups and monthly activities.

Young Adults Christian Fellowship
A dynamic fellowship designed especially for single adults between the ages of 26(ish) to 40(ish). Small Group Bible Study – Thursdays at 7:30 p.m.

Ministry to the Deaf
This ministry will target an often forgotten minority group. Signing will be provided by professional interpreters during the 11:15 a.m. service. Let's pray for this ministry and do all we can to see that those involved feel welcomed into the life of the church.

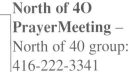

 E.S.L.
English as a Second Language meets every Tuesday 7:00 – 9:00 p.m.

1973 – Celestial City Musical, directed by David Williams.

1985 Passion Play, directed by David Williams.

1976 Living Christmas Tree, directed by David Williams.

Nine

Music in
The Peoples Church

Worship has always been a vital part of The Peoples Church. Music, drama and other worship arts are important components of the worship experience as we seek to bring worshippers into a fresh and exciting encounter with the living God.

SAVES.

THE GIFT OF GOD IS ETERNAL LIFE.

Music in The Peoples Church

Musical Leadership

Eldon Lehman.

When the Cosmopolitan Tabernacle congregation (later named The Peoples Church) moved from Massey Hall to the St. James Square Presbyterian Church building on Gerrard Street, a young Director of Music by the name of Eldon B. Lehman was already established there. It soon became apparent that he was the most valuable asset The Peoples Church had inheirited from the Presbyterians. At that time Eldon was also a businessman working with National Grocers. It was he who shaped the sort of musical ministry that The Peoples Church would enjoy for the next sixty years – including a choir, orchestra and radio broadcast on CFRB.

It was not until the early 1930's that Eldon left the business world and went into the work on a full-time basis. He filled three roles – Musical Director and Business Manager for the church, and Canadian Director of the Rodeheaver Music Company. The Rodeheaver Company paid one third of his salary, which in those days amounted to $225.00 a month, with no additional benefits. Eldon Lehman was the only paid associate Oswald Smith ever worked with until Oswald's son, Paul joined the staff in 1952.

Directors of Music.

Eldon Lehman was the Director of Music from 1930 to 1941. Then followed George Gay (1941 – 42), Norman Barrington (1943 – 47), William McCaul (1947 – 52), Donald Newman (1952 – 59, also the Church Business Manager during that time), David Williams (1961 – 91), Rick Manafo (1991 – 93), Danny Daniels (1993 – 1998), Don McNiven (1999 – 2002) and Jared Erhardt (2002 –). Frank Trenchard directed the choir between the time Don Newman resigned

Eldon B. Lehman.

George Gay.

William McCaul.

Donald Billings – first pianist.

Frank Trenchard – organ.

Donald Newman.

David Williams

Rick Manafo.

Danny Daniels.

Don McNiven.

Jared Erhardt.

(December 1959) and Dave Williams came (October 1961). George Gay, Norman Barrington and William McCaul were not actually on the staff, but supported themselves in the business world and worked for the church on a volunteer basis.

Always innovative.
The music of The Peoples Church has always been innovative. From the early days of Oswald Smith's lively original hymns to David Williams' musical extravaganzas, music has been a top priority.

David Williams.
David Williams, the longest serving Director of Music will always be remembered for his outstanding contribution to the Church. A hard-driving, yet jovial Director, he was gifted not only with musical brilliance, but with relationship skills that endeared him to the hears of all with whom he worked. Unfailingly courteous to the other musicians involved, he often got more from the orchestra and choir than they knew they could give.

David Williams wrote a great deal of music for the children's and youth choirs, as well as for spectaculars like the "Living Christmas Tree." He says, "God wants our best – whether it's contemporary songs, or Gregorian chants, John R. Peterson or Johann Sebastian Bach – we do a broad spectrum of music."

A place for everyone.
Where the music groups for the different ages once operated under the umbrella of the music department, other than the orchestra and choir, they now operate within the associated ministries. Despite the changing times, there is still recognition of the tremendous benefit – both to the congregation and to the musicians – in being involved in a group such as the church choir.

> **Music Ministries
> – a place for everyone.**
> • The Peoples Church Worship Choir
> • The Peoples Church Worship Orchestra.
> • Vocal and/ or Instrumental Ensembles.
> • Worship arts: acting, dance, set design, scriptwriting and directing.
> • Technical ministries: staging, sound, video, lighting, projections.
> • Conservatory lessons: available in voice and many instruments.

Mr. Music – Dr. David E. Williams.

No history of The Peoples Church would be complete without a special tribute to the man who made the music of The Peoples Church legendary. From "The Rainbow Singers" children's choir, to "The Salt Company" youth choir, David took great pleasure in providing opportunities for everyone, who so desired, to serve God through music. He trained groups professionally and tailored productions with both musicians and audience in mind. For special occasions, he wrote, scored, arranged and conducted magnificent musicals. His "Living Christmas Tree" became an annual 'must see' for thousands of people.

Dr. David E. Williams.

Building The Living Christmas Tree, 1970.

The Soul Survivors – photo from album cover.

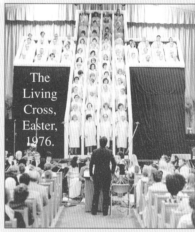

The Living Cross, Easter, 1976.

ThePeoples Church choir, Sheppard Avenue.

The Peoples Church choir and orchestra – Bloor Street.

Rehearsing.

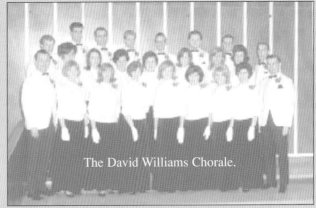

The David Williams Chorale.

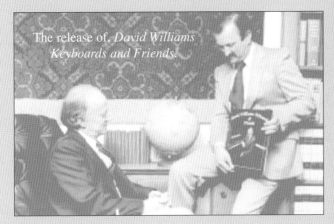

The release of, *David Williams Keyboards and Friends*.

The Praise Ringers Bell Choir.

The Set Free Singers, 1979.

Lloyd Knight.
The most consistently popular tenor soloist ever to grace The Peoples Church, Lloyd Knight has been active in many facets of Christian work; from conducting crusades throughout North America to church Business Administration, Youth for Christ work, choir directing, Sunday school teaching, song-leading and speaking. When he sings, "The King is Coming", a favourite with Lloyd Knight fans, he transports the audience to a special place of praise.

Lloyd Knight.

Into all the World

Guest musicians from the four corners of the earth have thrilled The Peoples Church congregation with their singing and playing ever since the early days, when Oswald would engage the top musicians of the day – both to draw crowds and to minister to people through the variety of music ministries.

Musical Guests

The Cleveland Male Quintet visited the Christie Street Church in 1923. So successful was their appearance that the services continued every night for three months. Crowds packed the barn-like tabernacle and great throngs of people sought and found Jesus Christ as Saviour and Lord.

Music – as important as preaching.

"I believe music is as important as preaching in the service. As much of the Word of God gets out through singing as through the sermon. It's a part of the preaching – not just the preliminary part of the service."

Dr. Paul Smith

The Jubilee Singers sang twice daily for three weeks in 1933. Singing from from the heart, they gave their personal testimonies, emphasizing the fact that they had been born again and were trusting only in the Blood of Christ. Each Sunday night for three weeks in succession, the service was held in the great Massey Hall, which seated approximately 3,000. Large numbers had to be turned away. Many found salvation.

The British Evangelistic Team – 1946.

The Minneapolis Girls' Quintet – 1948.

The Blind Quartet – from Charleston, West Virginia. They sang in Pat Winthrow's campaign in The Peoples Church, 1937.

Ethel Waters, 1967.

The Claus Indian Family – 1951.

Hiram Joseph 2002.

Janz Bros. 1954.

The Watoto Children's Choir 2002.

1988 Back to the Bible Quartet.

1988 – Diane Susek.

1990 Randy Stonehill.

The Mizo Choir 2002.

1988 Johnny Hall.

1988 Willa Dorsey.

Redd Harper 1953.

The Amigos 1981.

The Samuelsons from Sweden, 1967.

Music

299

The Writing of My Hymns

by Oswald Smith

(Abridged)

In *The Story of My Life*, Dr. Oswald Smith recounted some of the circumstances surrounding the writing of his hymns.

Hymns, like people, have to be well married to really live. To B. D. Ackley I owe a debt of gratitude that I will never be able to repay, for he had such a gift of melody that the music fits the words as though the two had been born together. We collaborated for 28 years. He died on September 3rd, 1958.

Then too, much credit must be given to The Rodeheaver Co. for the popularization of these hymns, for were it not for them, many of them would never have become known. But they have put them in their books and thus introduced them to multiplied thousands. Many of them are on victrola records, and a number have been translated. Rodeheaver paid me $50.00 for the words of each hymn, and Ascap over $3,000 a year for their use.

Poets, they say, are born, not made. Well, perhaps so. Be that as it may, the gift, I know, has to be developed. When I was in my early twenties I purchased volumes of poetry. Such works as Milton's *Paradise Lost* and Dante's *Inferno* I read line by line, aloud. Tennyson, Browning, Byron, Bryant, Longfellow, Hood, Whittier, Shakespeare, and a whole shelf of others, I literally devoured.

Never will I forget the thrill that was mine when I saw the first printed copies of two of my hymns. It was in 1914 when I was twenty-four. The music was by Dr. D. B. Towner. The ecstasy of that moment will never be erased. But in those early years only a few of my hymns ever really saw the light of day. I wrote scores, but for years it was a struggle with many discouraging experiences.

I have never written in a mechanical way just for the sake of writing. As a rule I wait until I am passing through some great crisis, and then I cannot help writing. And because they have been born out of personal experiences, they appeal to others. They sound the deepest depths and the highest heights of my inner life. Writing has been my greatest source of comfort and relief. When writing them I have been drawn unusually close to God. Moments of ecstasy and exaltation of spirit indescribable have been mine.

My early work was with Dr D. B. Towner, of the Moody Bible Institute, and after his death, George C. Stebbins. Then, one day, in the Churchill Tabernacle, Buffalo, in 1930, when I was 40, I met the world's greatest living composer of gospel music – B. D. Ackley. Again I began to write. Hymn after hymn I sent to him and the music that he wrote so fitted the words that they were in immediate demand. They were brought out by The Rodeheaver Co., and they have now published more than 200 of my hymns and gospel songs. Almost immediately America's leading soloists began singing them both on the air and to audiences all over the country.

"Dr. Smith has played upon a harp of many strings, touching the varied experiences of men in a winsome and appealing way. His hymns bring joy and comfort to God's children on their homeward way."

George C. Stebbins, world famous composer in D. L. Moody's day, and personal friend of O.J. Smith.

"Oswald Smith's 1,200 hymns, poems and Gospel songs have made him Canada's best known and most prolific hymn writer. Not only so, but his hymns have more spiritual depth than most contemporary productions, and they excel in quality of word and music the popular songs of the Nineteenth Century."

J. Edwin Orr, Th.D., D.Phil.

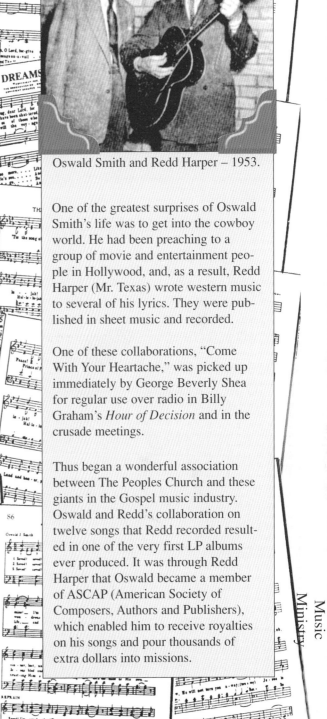

Oswald Smith and Redd Harper – 1953.

One of the greatest surprises of Oswald Smith's life was to get into the cowboy world. He had been preaching to a group of movie and entertainment people in Hollywood, and, as a result, Redd Harper (Mr. Texas) wrote western music to several of his lyrics. They were published in sheet music and recorded.

One of these collaborations, "Come With Your Heartache," was picked up immediately by George Beverly Shea for regular use over radio in Billy Graham's *Hour of Decision* and in the crusade meetings.

Thus began a wonderful association between The Peoples Church and these giants in the Gospel music industry. Oswald and Redd's collaboration on twelve songs that Redd recorded resulted in one of the very first LP albums ever produced. It was through Redd Harper that Oswald became a member of ASCAP (American Society of Composers, Authors and Publishers), which enabled him to receive royalties on his songs and pour thousands of extra dollars into missions.

Oswald Smith and B.D. Ackley.

In 1934, The Peoples Church radio broadcasts offered "Oswald Smith's Gospel Songs" to those who would write in. It was a book containing thirty of his most beautiful compositions. This wide exposure led to greatly increased familiarity and use of the hymns. The music was by B. D. Ackley, Geo. C. Stebbins, D. B. Towner, Robert Harkness, and other well-known writers. It featured solos, duets, choir pieces, congregational hymns, and several special radio favorites.

STAND fast therefore in the liberty
wherewith Chrīst hath made us
free, and be n̲̲̲̲
with the yoke o̲̲̲

2 Behold, I Pa̲̲̲
if ye be circum̲̲̲
profit you nothi̲̲̲

3 For I testify
that is circumcis̲̲̲
or to do the who̲̲̲

4 Chrīst is beco̲̲̲
you, whosoever
by the law; ye a̲̲̲

5 For we thro̲̲̲
for the hope o̲̲̲
faith.

6 For in Jē′su̲̲̲
cumcision availe̲̲̲
circumcision; bu̲̲̲
eth by love.

7 Ye did run w̲̲̲
you that ye sh̲̲̲
truth?

8 This persuasi̲̲̲
that calleth you.

9 A little leaven
lump.

10 I have confi̲̲̲
the Lord, that y̲̲̲
wise minded: b̲̲̲
you shall bear
soever he be.

11 And I, breth̲̲̲
circumcision, w̲̲̲
persecution? th̲̲̲
the cross ceased̲̲̲

12 I would the̲̲̲
which trouble yo̲̲̲

13 For, breth̲̲̲
called unto lib̲̲̲
liberty for an o̲̲̲
but by love serv̲̲̲

14 For all the l̲̲̲
word, *even* in t̲̲̲
thy neighbour a̲̲̲

15 But if ye bit̲̲̲ and devour one
another, take heed that ye be not
consumed one of another.

16 *This* I say then, Walk in the
Spirit, and ye shall not fulfil the lust

to the other: so that ye cannot do
the things that ye would.

18 But if ye be led of the Spirit, ye
̲̲̲ w.

̲̲̲ of the flesh are
̲̲̲ *these;* Adultery,
̲̲̲ ness, lascivious-

̲̲̲ raft, hatred, vari-
̲̲̲ rath, strife, sedi-

̲̲̲ rders, drunken-
̲̲̲ d such like: of
̲̲̲ before, as I have
̲̲̲ e past, that they
̲̲̲ gs shall not in-
̲̲̲ f God.

̲̲̲ of the Spirit is
̲̲̲ ngsuffering, gen-
̲̲̲ aith,
̲̲̲ perance: against
̲̲̲ .

̲̲̲ are Chrīst's have
̲̲̲ ith the affections

̲̲̲ Spirit, let us also

̲̲̲ desirous of vain
̲̲̲ e another, envy-

̲̲̲ ER 6
̲̲̲ *Harvests*

̲̲̲ man be over-
̲̲̲ lt, ye which are
̲̲̲ ch an one in the
̲̲̲ considering thy-
̲̲̲ be tempted.

̲̲̲ other's burdens,
̲̲̲ of Chrīst.

̲̲̲ nk himself to be
̲̲̲ e is nothing, he

̲̲̲ n prove his own
̲̲̲ l he have rejoic-
̲̲̲ , and not in an-
other.

5 For every man shall bear his own
burden.

6 Let him that is taught in the word
communicate unto him that teacheth

"I believe the only way we can evangelize the world in our generation is with the printed page. The Christian workers are in place, but they are saying, 'Give us the tools and we will finish the job.' We can never send out sufficient missionaries, but we can complete the task of getting the Gospel of Jesus Christ to the whole world by means of the printed page. 'Faith comes by hearing, and hearing by the Word of God,' whether it is the spoken Word or the written Word."

OJS

302

Ten

Communicating with the World

Print
Radio
Internet
Television

Communicating with the World

Print, Radio, Internet and Television

Books by Oswald Smith.
Oswald J. Smith wrote 35 books which were translated into 128 languages, including four in Braille, with a distribution of six million copies. His sermons were distributed as booklets or single-fold tracts. By 1960, the tract, *Only One Way,* had a

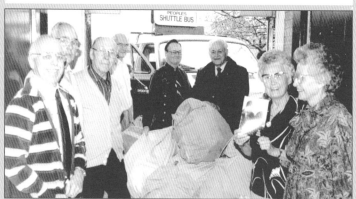

Getting books out to missionaries.

circulation of one million. All profits on Oswald Smith's English books went to The Peoples Church, to be poured into missions.

He gave thousands of his books to pastors in Third World countries, (even paying the postage) and encouraged them to sell them to help fund their ministries.

In 1957 the church sent 7,000 cloth bound books to missionaries all over the world as Christmas gifts. Equipping missionaries with printing presses to enable them to distribute portions of Scripture and hymn books was one of Oswald's top priorities.

"It will go on speaking for me long after I am gone."
O.J.S. on the power of the printed page.

Dr. Oswald Smith's books were translated into 128 languages.

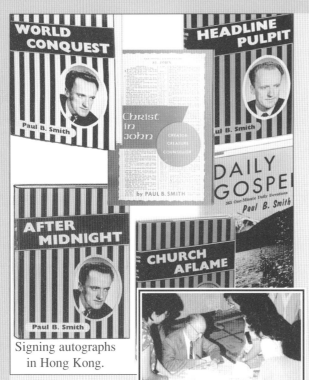

Signing autographs
in Hong Kong.

Books by Dr. Paul B. Smith.

A prolific author, Dr. Paul wrote a total of twenty books, including *Church Aflame*, *Naked Truth*, *World Conquest*, and *The Church on the Brink*. In later years, he wrote a series of books on the Gospels: *Jesus, by John; Jesus, by Mark; Jesus, by Matthew*; and *Jesus, by Luke*. He published an eschatalogical book on Revelation and a devotional book entitled, *I Have Walked Alone With Jesus*.

In 1983, Dr. Paul filmed *The Promise* series, four 16mm motion pictures on world missions and faith promise offerings. These thirty-minute preaching films were distributed by World Thrust, Inc. (Atlanta, Georgia.)

Books by Charles Price.

Charles Price has written six books:
• *Christ for Real* (15 English language editions have been published since 1985. In Britain the title is, *Stop Trying To Live For Jesus*.)
• *Alive in Christ* (10 English language editions. Published in Britain as *Christ In You*.)
The above two books have been translated into various languages including German, French, Spanish, Dutch, Italian and Russian.
• *Discovering Joshua* (Also available in Hindi.)
• *Paul: Moulded by His Message*
• *A Commentary on The Gospel of Matthew*
• *Transforming Keswick* (A history of the famous Keswick Convention in England and the worldwide Keswick Movement. Jointly written with Ian Randall.)
Charles Price has also contributed sections to a number of other books including *Shaping Tomorrow, Starting Today – The Church's Strategy for the Future* (Christian Focus Publications, UK) and *Lessons in Leadership* (Kregel Publications, USA), as well as various compendiums of sermons preached at the Keswick Convention in England.

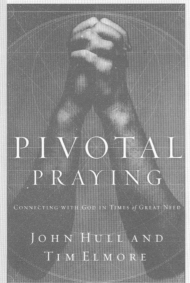

Pivotal Praying by Dr. John Hull
and Tim Elmore.

Communications

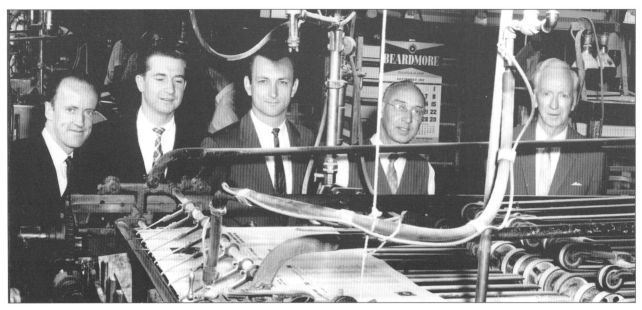

Watching the printing of *The Peoples Magazine* at Livingstone Press: (l-r) Paul Smith, Daniel Edmundson, David Williams, Robert Watt, Oswald Smith.

The Peoples Magazine.

The Peoples Magazine has been published and has circled the globe since 1921. Throughout his ministry, Oswald Smith edited

The Peoples Magazine himself, each month gathering or writing the articles and doing the layout. Paul Smith and John Hull took the baton in turn as it was passed to them, maintaining the magazine as a highly functional and inspirational communication tool.

When Charles Price arrived on the scene, he re-evaluated the advisability of continuing the magazine in its traditional format, in light of twenty-first century technology. The result was the birth of *Peoples Progress*, an updated, bi-monthly internet version of *The Peoples Magazine,* featuring all of the news and inspiration of the church – now accessible not only in the church, but throughout the world at www.thepeopleschurch.ca – without the enormous print and postage costs.

The Peoples Hour crew.

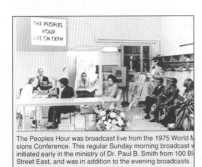

The Peoples Hour was broadcast live from the 1975 World Missions Conference. This regular Sunday morning broadcast was initiated early in the ministry of Dr. Paul B. Smith from 100 Bloor Street East, and was in addition to the evening broadcasts.

Broadcasting live on CKFH from the Missions Conference.

Using the airwaves around the world. In 1945, a program was broadcast over HCJB in Quito, Ecuador each Monday at 9:45 Eastern War time.

Preparing The Peoples Hour broadcast.

Radio

In 1930, with the move to St. James Square Presbyterian Church, the congregation (then known as "The Toronto Gospel Tabernacle") began to broadcast over CFRB and CKNC radio stations, featuring music with Eldon B. Lehman, the choir leader, and Oswald's messages. The first broadcasts were heard at 5:00 p.m. on Sunday afternoons. Soon CKCL requested the morning services.

While few churches wanted anything to do with its new "tool of the devil", Oswald recognized the enormous opportunity to reach thousands and thousands of people he could not otherwise reach. "The Back Home Hour" evolved as 45 minutes of music with a 15-minute message by Oswald. The station manager heralded it as, "the best variety show on radio!" Before long, it seemed that every home in Toronto was tuned in to The Peoples Church broadcasts. The church became even more jammed, with people scurrying off the streetcars, running to be in time to get a seat!

Stay home!

One of the first uses of the media was to ask people not to come to church. On November 16, 1936, the publisher of Toronto's Globe and Mail gave $20,000 towards the purchase of the Bloor Street Church. The whole city was moved, and the purchase of the church became a common topic of discussion. The crowds overflowed the capacity. On radio broadcasts, Oswald would beg listeners:"The fire marshall has warned that we're dangerously over-crowded, *so please stay home!*"

Long-time member, Bruce Fogarty, recalls, "Then he'd announce the evening service, and it sounded so exciting you just couldn't stay away!" Even though all newspaper advertising was stopped for several years, still the Church could not accommodate the crowds.

With Mr. Lehman's great volunteer choir of 135 voices and an orchestra of 40, the entire evening service went out to multiplied thousands. For a time, The Peoples Church was on the "air" for three hours each Sunday night – the entire Sunday Evening Service was broadcast from 7:00 to 8:30 p.m., and then the Back Home Hour came on from 9:30 to 11:00. Years later, Walt Huntley built a radio studio right in the Church. From 1953 to 1955, the Church broadcast over 42 stations across Canada and throughout the world.

Scores were saved.

The whole emphasis was evangelism. Every Sunday an invitation was given and scores were saved in radioland.

Into all the World

LETTERS OF APPRECIATION
From Our Large Radio Audience

Dear Mr. Lehman:

This is just a brief letter to thank God for the most beautiful singing I have ever heard. I have listened to many choirs, but I must say that the choir of The Peoples Church is the best in Toronto.

The singing is not for vain glory but is in the Spirit, for the glory of God and the edifying of the congregation. I have felt lifted and inspired while listening to the beautiful strains of the good old Gospel hymns.

I realize that a great deal of the success lies in your expert handling of both choir and orchestra.

Yours in the High Calling of our Lord,

H. E. N.

Dear Mr. Smith:

I listened to the Back Home Hour last night and enjoyed it very much. You spoke so plain and clear. It made me see things a lot different than I had before. You seemed to speak right to me.

Your friend,

M. T.

Dear Mr. Lehman:

Words fail to convey the joy I derive listening to the singing of your choir. You lead from the heart and in the Spirit, and it is a foretaste of that great day when we shall join the choir in heaven.

One Sunday I sat beside a lady from Florida who told me that she came as often as possible to The Peoples Church when in Toronto because there was nothing like it in the United States.

You and your choir have the great privilege of singing the Gospel message into the hearts of the people.

J. G. B.

Dear Sir:

I want to tell you how eagerly we await the Back Home Hour. We enjoy it so much. It is a treat in these days to listen to such a Gospel Service. It comes over very clear.

Yours in Him,

E. J. C.

Dear Brother:

I enjoy anything that Mr. Lehman has to say and also much appreciate the good, sound, snappy, Scriptural talks of Mr. Smith. I would appreciate more good plain Gospel singing of the old familiar songs. They are the most effective.

Yours in His service,

H. L. H.

Dear Sir:

It is a comfort for one to hear the grand old hymns. I have been an invalid in bed for the past four years.

Yours truly,

L. W.

Dear Sir:

When 9.30 strikes it finds our family gathered around the Radio to listen to your hour. We certainly receive a great blessing.

Yours in Christ,

D. S.

Dear Sir:

Last Sunday evening, for the first time, my husband and I were in your church, and oh, what a blessing we received! We rather expected something sensational to draw such crowds, but soon found that there was nothing of the sort, but just the simple Gospel preached to the "masses" not to "classes". Praise God for that!

I have been a soloist in a church for years but was not saved until about two years ago, which goes to prove that one may sing the praises of the Lord but not know Him as a Saviour. .

From that day I have sung nothing but the Gospel. My friends, the choir leader, and others have been urging me to sing more oratorios and classical music, but God tells me I must not.

Yours sincerely,

G. G. H.

Hundreds wrote in for copies of favorite hymns written by Oswald. The members of the Choir and Orchestra sacrificed to the limit, remaining right up until eleven o'clock at night, while hundreds gave of their means, thus making it possible to stay on the Air.

Peoples Church Radio Network

1954 100 BLOCR STREET EAST, TORONTO

CITY	STATION	DIAL		TIME
Barrie, Ont.	C.K.B.B.	1230	· · ·	Sun. 1.45 p.m.
Brockville, Ont.	C.F.J.R.	1450	· · ·	Sun. 2.45 p.m.
Chatham, Ont.	C.F.C.O.	630	· · ·	Sun. 11.15 p.m.
Chilliwack, B.C.	C.H.W.K.	1270	· · ·	Sun. 10.15 p.m.
Cornwall, Ont.	C.K.S.F.	1230	· · ·	Sun. 2.30 p.m.
Dauphin, Man.	C.K.D.M.	1230	· · ·	Sun. 8.15 a.m.
Dawson Creek, B.C.	C.J.D.C.	1350	· · ·	Sun. 9.30 a.m.
Fort Frances, Ont.	C.K.F.I.	800	· · ·	Sun. 2.00 p.m.
Hamilton, Ont.	C.H.M.L.	900	· · ·	Sun. 9.30 a.m.
Kamloops, B.C.	C.F.J.C.	910	· · ·	Sun. 2.15 p.m.
Kenora, Ont.	C.J.R.L.	1220	· · ·	Sun. 10.45 p.m.
Kirkland Lake, Ont.	C.J.K.L.	560	· · ·	Sun. 8.15 a.m.
Kitchener, Ont.	C.K.C.R.	1490	· · ·	Sun. 3.30 p.m.
Nelson, B.C.	C.K.L.N.	1240	· · ·	Sun. 3.30 p.m.
Niagara Falls, Ont.	C.H.V.C.	1600	· · ·	Sun. 10.45 p.m.
North Bay, Ont.	C.F.C.H.	600	· · ·	Sat. 10.30 a.m.
Orillia, Ont.	C.F.O.R.	1570	· · ·	Sun. 4.00 p.m.
Oshawa, Ont.	C.K.L.B.	1240	· · ·	Sun. 9.45 a.m.
Owen Sound, Ont.	C.F.O.S.	1470	· · ·	Sun. 10.45 p.m.
Pembroke, Ont.	C.H.O.V.	1350	· · ·	Sat. 4.00 p.m.
Port Arthur, Ont.	C.F.P.A.	1230	· · ·	Sun. 10.00 p.m.
Prince George, B.C.	C.K.P.G.	550	· · ·	Sun. 9.15 a.m.
Quebec West, Que.	C.J.Q.C.	1340	· · ·	Sun. 9.05 a.m.
Quito, Ecuador	H.C.J.B.	15.1 Meg.	· · ·	Sat. 4.15 p.m.
Sault Ste. Marie, Ont.	C.J.I.C.	1490	· · ·	Sun. 2.45 p.m.
Sherbrooke, Que.	C.K.T.S.	1240	· · ·	Sun. 11.15 p.m.
St. Catharines, Ont.	C.K.T.B.	620	· · ·	Sun. 8.15 a.m.
St. John's, Nfld.	V.O.C.M.	590	· · ·	Sun. 9.00 a.m.
St. Thomas, Ont.	C.H.L.O.	680	· · ·	Sun. 1.45 p.m.
Stratford, Ont.	C.J.C.S.	1240	· · ·	Sun. 1.30 p.m.
Sudbury, Ont.	C.K.S.O.	790	· · ·	Sun. 10.30 p.m.
Sydney, N.S.	C.J.C.B.	1270	· · ·	Sun. 8.30 a.m.
Timmins, Ont.	C.K.G.B.	680	· · ·	Sun. 2.00 p.m.
Toronto, Ont.	C.H.U.M.	1050	· · ·	Sun. 11.00 a.m.
Vancouver, B.C.	C.K.M.O.	1410	· · ·	Sun. 9.45 p.m.

Walter Huntley, Manager — Don Lowry, Assistant.

Into all the World

Communications

Telephone Church.

On March 14, 1959, Dr. Paul became Toronto's Telephone Pastor. Using the personal column of *The Toronto Star*, he advertised, "If you need spiritual help, call your Telephone Pastor. Simply dial Walnut 3-9122 and listen for one minute."

Just before noon, the edition of the newspaper carrying the advertisement hit the streets, and the first caller buzzed into the electronic machine, receiving the first recorded Gospel message.

After the first 24 hours, thousands of calls had jammed the entire "Walnut" exchange. The telephone company had to disconnect the Church phones. The next day, *The Toronto Star* read, "An entire metropolitan telephone exchange was hopelessly jammed Wednesday by citizens seeking spiritual comfort from a recorded announcement that played for those dialing the number."

After the bugs were ironed out, the Church continued with six lines which rang almost constantly. On November 14, *The Toronto Telegram* reported the news in a six column article headed, "His Church reaches 12,000 a Day." By the end of the year, Dr. Paul had prepared 365 one-minute Gospel messages which became the basis for his book of daily readings – *Daily Gospel*.

Television.

On January 7, 1973, The Peoples Church started telecasting the morning service. Scores of lives were touched by the Spirit of God each week as a direct result of the program. Besides extending the visual ministry to those who don't go to church for a variety of reasons, the television ministry extended the fundraising base for missions.

Peoples Worship Hour.

For almost 30 years, 52 Sundays a year, homes across Canada were blessed with dynamic speakers, a talented orchestra, and gifted musical artists – all necessary ingredients of an engaging Sunday worship experience.

Telethon.

Telephone Pastor.

Jack McAlister and Dr. O.J. Smith on Television in Hollywood. Because The World Literature Crusade undertook to translate a number of Oswald's books for use around the world, Oswald spent a good amount of time with its founder, Jack McAllister, and became a great advocate of his "Every Home Crusades".

Into every home.

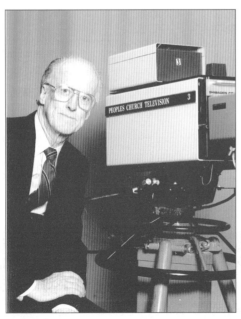

GOLDEN JUBILEE

WORLD MISSIONS CONFERENCE

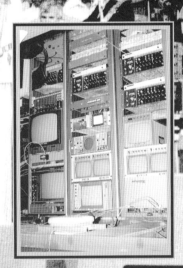

Into all the World

The Peoples Worship Hour reaches into the homes and hearts of over half a million viewers each week. Literally thousands of lives have been transformed as the Gospel message is heard in livingrooms • retirement and nursing homes • hospital rooms • prison cells • and hotel rooms across the country. People of all ages are impacted weekly.

We are encouraged by the thousands of letters received each month from viewers who have given their lives to Christ, or have made a turn, and rededicated themselves to the Christian walk, or request prayer for sick or unsaved loved ones.

Behind the scenes.

In a 2001 article in *The Peoples Magazine*, Bob Wells, head of The Peoples Church television programming, gave interesting insight into what it takes to keep the production going week after week.

Bob's team of 14 is made up almost exclusively of volunteers. Beginning at 8:00 a.m. on Sunday morning, the technical equipment in the control room is fired up and tested. In the sanctuary, cameras are cabled, microphones are positioned and last minute pre-production details are finalized with the pastoral staff. Bob and the crew meet for final debriefing and prayer just before the service begins. Then its time to go "live to tape", meaning that the service is recorded in its entirety as it happens. The service tapes are then edited to fit the program time allocation and sent to the respective television networks.

Not just entertainment.

Bob says, "Even after 25 years in the television industry in both Christian and secular arenas, I still count prayer a key pre-production component of every program. I believe in this way every spoken word and musical note that goes to air will be blessed of God. This is what separates it from being strictly entertainment, and it becomes true ministry.

Bob Wells, Producer/ Director, Peoples Worship Hour.

Bob Wells and a member of the production crew at work.

2003 – Sunday Broadcasting Schedule

Living Truth

Greater Toronto Area
CTS, 9:00 a.m.

Across Ontario
CTV, 10:30 a.m.
(CFTO Toronto)

Across Canada
Vision TV, 1:00 p.m. EST

Fraser Valley/
Greater Vancouver Area
NOWTV, 4:00 p.m. PT

Presenting HISTORICAL BIBLICAL TRUTH with 21st Century Relevance

A Ministry of
THE PEOPLES CHURCH
Toronto

ABOUT US
PROGRAMS
ONLINE STORE
FAQs
CONTACT US
MAKE DONATION

Living Truth Online offers access to program listings, online resources and dynamic ministry updates.

Living Truth

Today, in addition to ministering to the three thousand people who regularly attend the church, The Peoples Church broadcasts nationwide across Canada the weekly, hour-long Television program "Living Truth", (formerly "The Peoples Worship Hour").

The Peoples Church has become known as, *"The family church that puts World Missions first."* When Charles Price took on the mantle of Senior Pastor, he had no intention of migrating from this principle. Indeed, missions is and will continue to be an integral component, not only of The Peoples Church, but of its weekly television program.

Although the message has not changed, the new name is significant. Truth is unchanging – but when truth is coupled with life, which is dynamic and changing, the results are powerful. Each week, Charles Price delivers a powerful message, presenting the eternal truths of Scripture as totally relevant to the changing lives and experience of people in the twenty-first century.

Reaching the World via the World Wide Web.
www.thepeopleschurch.ca

As a passionate fisher of souls, Oswald Smith would no doubt have heartily embraced the "Net". How thrilled he would have been with the potential of such a tool for connecting people in need with those offering resources – whether spiritual, physical or both.

The ability to interact worldwide with a click of the mouse is a far cry from Oswald's old typewriter. Just the thought of having the opportunity to offer books, audio cassettes, CDs and videos over a globally accessed network would have been mind-boggling to him.

Under the dynamic leadership of Charles Price, The Peoples Church has catapulted the pulpit into the twenty-first century, skillfully employing technology to multiply the fruit of the work ordained by God and planted by O. J. Smith.

Into all the World

Communications

The world on our doorstep…

Eleven

Continuing the Vision

Continuing the Vision

Journeying into the 21st Century...

If Oswald Smith would be amazed now by the rapid development of tools and opportunities for fulfilling his vision of evangelizing the world, imagine how shocked he would be over the next 75 years, should knowledge continue to multiply at such a lightning pace.

Despite the astronomical increase in knowledge and tools, the basic needs of the world remain. While the work of The Peoples Church has resulted in thousands receiving the amazing truth that Jesus died and rose again, so that they would not have to suffer in eternal torment, millions remain lost in ignorance.

And now the focus of Missions is not just "over there". No longer recognized as a "Christian" country by the United Nations, Canada is largely populated by "the new pagans", the sons and daughters of our land, who have had their values "clarified" through the moral relativism of the deceptive religion – Humanism. The "heathen", once equated with naked cannibals in "far-off lands", are the people with whom we live and work – people who fret through their lives, oblivious to the abundant life Jesus came to bring.

The future of the church in Canada is one of multiculturalism.
While we welcome the reality that the future of the church in Canada is one of multiculturalism, Canada's pluralistic approach has placed The Peoples Church squarely in the middle of a divisive mosaic of cultures, rather than in the 'melting pot,' where newcomers traditionally came to enjoy the culture of our great land with its Christian foundations. The mission *home* of The Peoples Church has become a major focus of its mission *field*. For that reason, representatives of diverse nationalities within the church are highly valued as effective workers in their own cultures.

Rekindling the Passion for Souls.
If ever there was a time to rekindle the passion for souls that resulted in Oswald Smith's vision to evangelize the world, it is in the early days of this new century. Now, raising funds for missions is not the only avenue available to the ordinary person, in the congregation, to touch the world for Christ. Now, everyone has the opportunity to evangelize – at home as well as abroad. Every Canadian Christian should consider himself or herself to be on the mission field.

Ginny Bridle, one of over 500 congregation members who filled 10-minute slots of reading the Bible from cover to cover.

"The Journey."

With all these changes in mind, Charles Price led the church to begin its 75th Anniversary year with a bold reminder which echoed from the pulpit of The Peoples Church to the furthest reaches of the world – that the Word of God is the foundation for life. Just after the ringing of the 2003 New Year's bells, the Church began "The Journey", a non-stop reading of the entire Bible out loud. While there was never any expectation that any one person would listen to the Bible for four days straight, this was an affirmation of the commitment of The Peoples Church to the divine inspiration and authority of the Scriptures. (Paul Dunlop, a member of the friendship class, actually did sit through the entire reading, fortified by donuts and coffee!) More than just symbolic, the event was an incredible ministry to everyone: listeners, readers and volunteers alike. Many people sat for hours basking in the Word of God as it was read aloud.

Over five hundred congregation members, celebrities and special guests of all ages and nationalities, filled 10-minute slots – reading the Bible from cover to cover – an 81½ hour journey of faith. A grade school girl read the Ten Commandments in the middle of the night; and a couple, married more than fifty years, read the beautiful love story found in the book of Ruth. Tommy So read the final words of Revelation, which paints a picture of heaven filled with the awesome presence of the Lamb of God, Jesus Christ. Hundreds responded in glorious praise and worship with Handel's, "Hallelujah Chorus", a 'foretaste of heaven'.

Logistically, "The Journey" was a daunting task. Filling the 4:00 a.m. shifts was a challenge, as was organizing teams of six staff members to work six-hour rotations; greeting people; organizing readings; keeping time; monitoring the technical equipment and filling the gaps when a reader failed to arrive. *100 Huntley Street* broadcast, "The Journey" on two mornings, with host David Mainse live on location. Local CBC and CTV affiliates, as well as *The Toronto Star* and *The National Post*, ran favourable stories. When the last word of The Revelation was read, there was a great sense of being firmly positioned to continue the vision of The Peoples Church.

JOURNEY
through the *Bible*
January 1-4, 2003 The Peoples Church

Remembering the original vision.

In 1928, The Peoples Church was born out of the vision to establish a center that would reach unbelievers who in turn would grow in Christ and support missionaries around the world. Under God, the church has stayed true to its original vision through the challenges of tumultuous times – the Great Depression, two World Wars and the cultural revolution.

Today, The Peoples Church regularly supports missionaries and nationals in more than 65 countries. From humanitarian relief, to backyard Bible clubs and door-to-door evangelism, a strong effort is made to stay true to the supreme task of the church – world evangelization.

Keeping pace with the changing times.

Staying true to the vision has occasionally meant having to bite the bullet and make changes in the way things are done. Modes of communication are advancing at breakneck speed, requiring constant updating of equipment and development of familiarity with particular technologies. Keeping up with the times is an ongoing challenge. For a congregation stretched by a changing culture, the greatest comfort comes from the fact that the foundation of the church, which is Jesus Christ and the Word of God, will never change. The message is even more relevant today than it was in the days of Oswald Smith.

Maintaining the fire of passion through the generations.

"The word "vision" is often overused, misunderstood or misapplied in business and even in evangelical ministry circles.

As I study God's Word, I find vision to be a future focus and a trust in God's ability to accomplish His will. Biblical vision allows the believer to go forward with the Lord, all the while understanding that a sacrifice will probably have to be made to get there."

Dr. John Hull

The most tragic scenario one could imagine, with regard to The Peoples Church, would have to involve the cooling of the embers of passion. How sad it would be to read of the tremendous move of God, through the life of Oswald Smith in the establishment of such a great missions church, and then have it fizzle into just another monument to a memory.

One of the most vital factors in maintaining the fire, is ensuring the exposure of young people to the reality of God, as witnessed through the lives around them. Because Oswald Smith fastened himself to God at such a young age, he had many years to affect the world for the Kingdom. The more young people who are set aflame with a passion for souls, the greater Heaven's gain.